Shoulder-a-Coffin Kuro by Satoko Kiyuduk

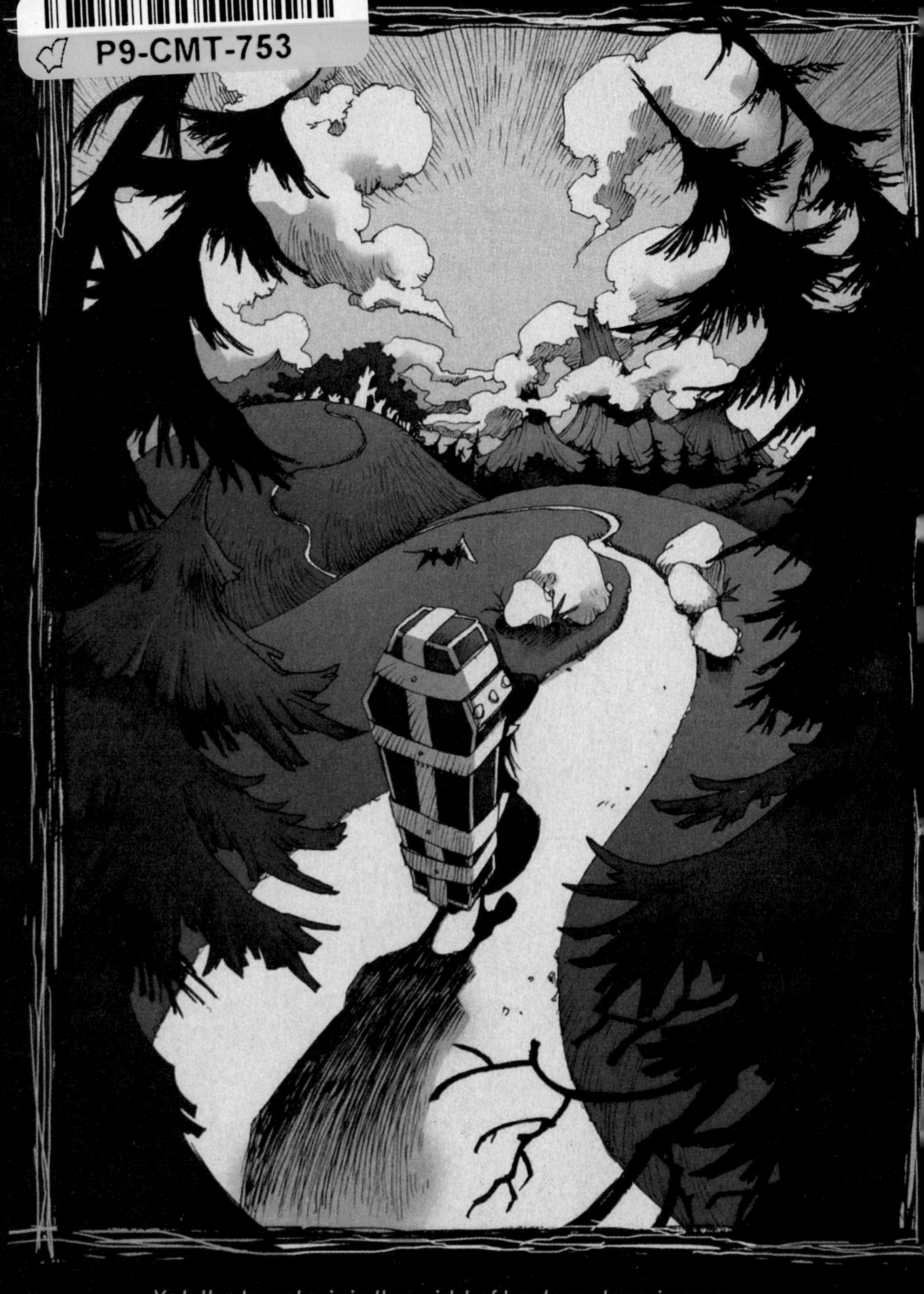

Yet, the traveler is in the midst of her long, long journey...

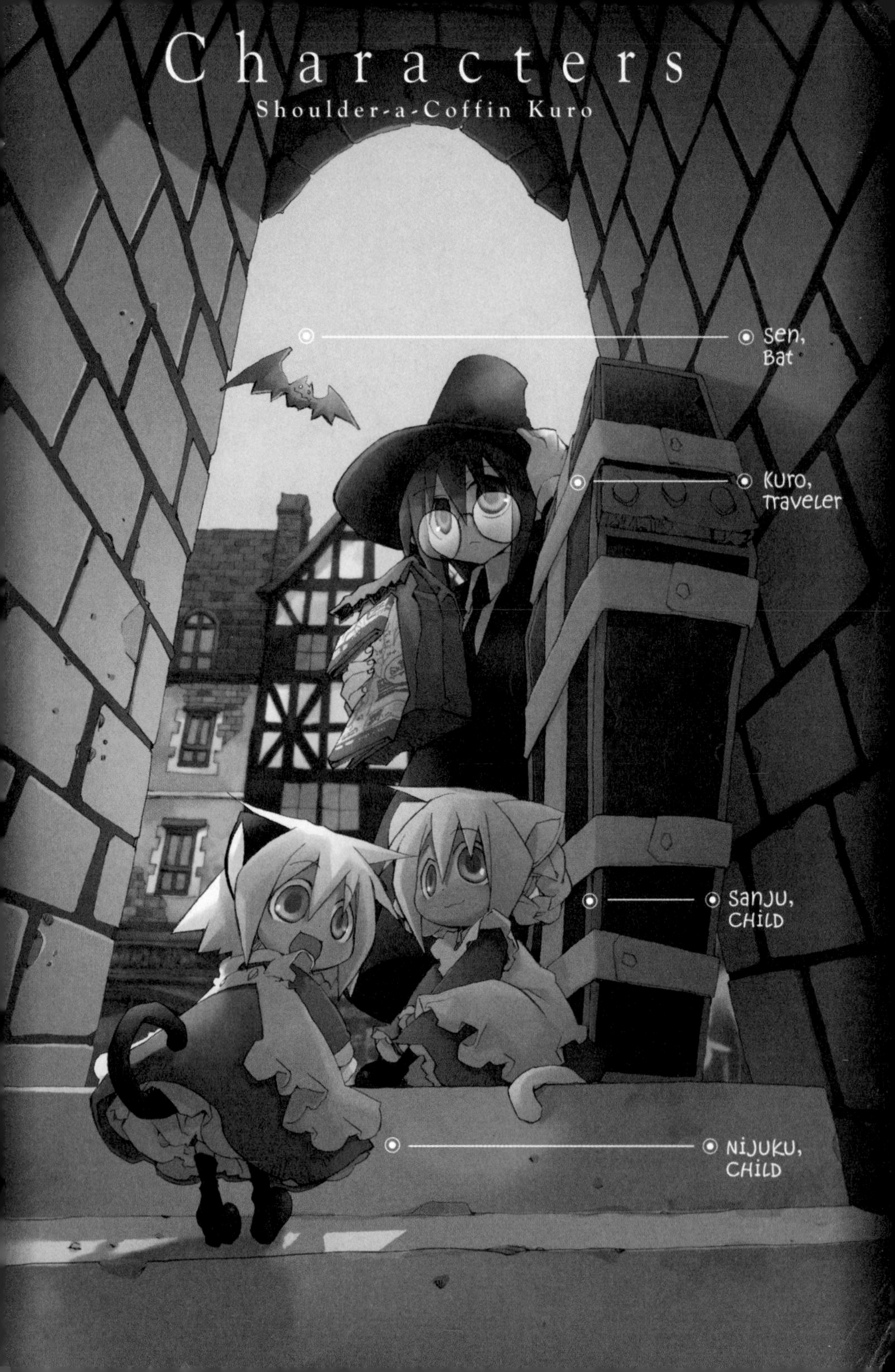
Characters
Shoulder-a-Coffin Kuro
Sen, Bat
Kuro, Traveler
Sanju, Child
Nijuku, Child

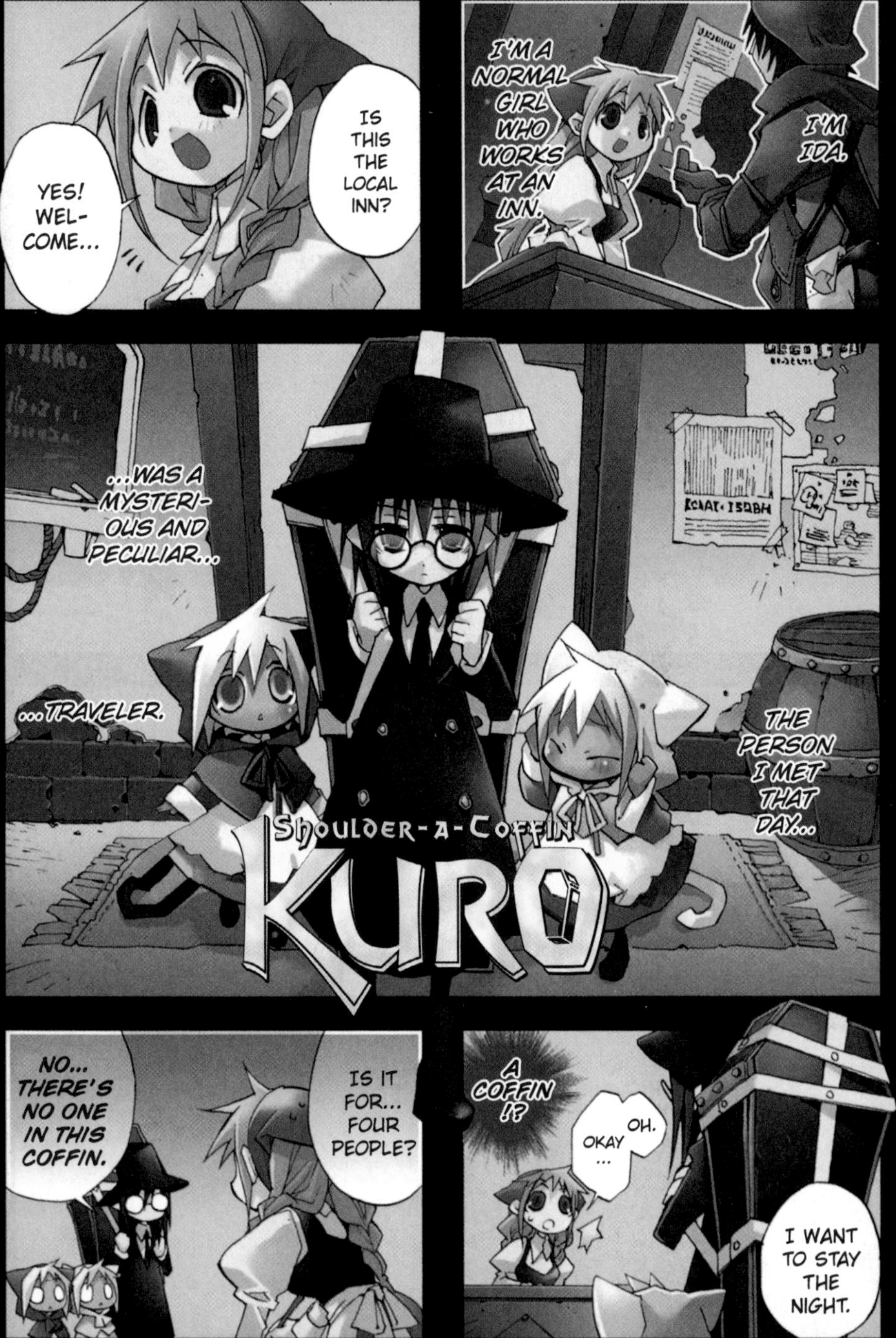
I'M IDA.
I'M A NORMAL GIRL WHO WORKS AT AN INN.
IS THIS THE LOCAL INN?
YES! WEL-COME...
THE PERSON I MET THAT DAY...
...WAS A MYSTERI-OUS AND PECULIAR...
...TRAVELER.
Shoulder-a-Coffin
KURO
I WANT TO STAY THE NIGHT.
OH. OKAY...
A COFFIN!?
IS IT FOR... FOUR PEOPLE?
NO... THERE'S NO ONE IN THIS COFFIN.

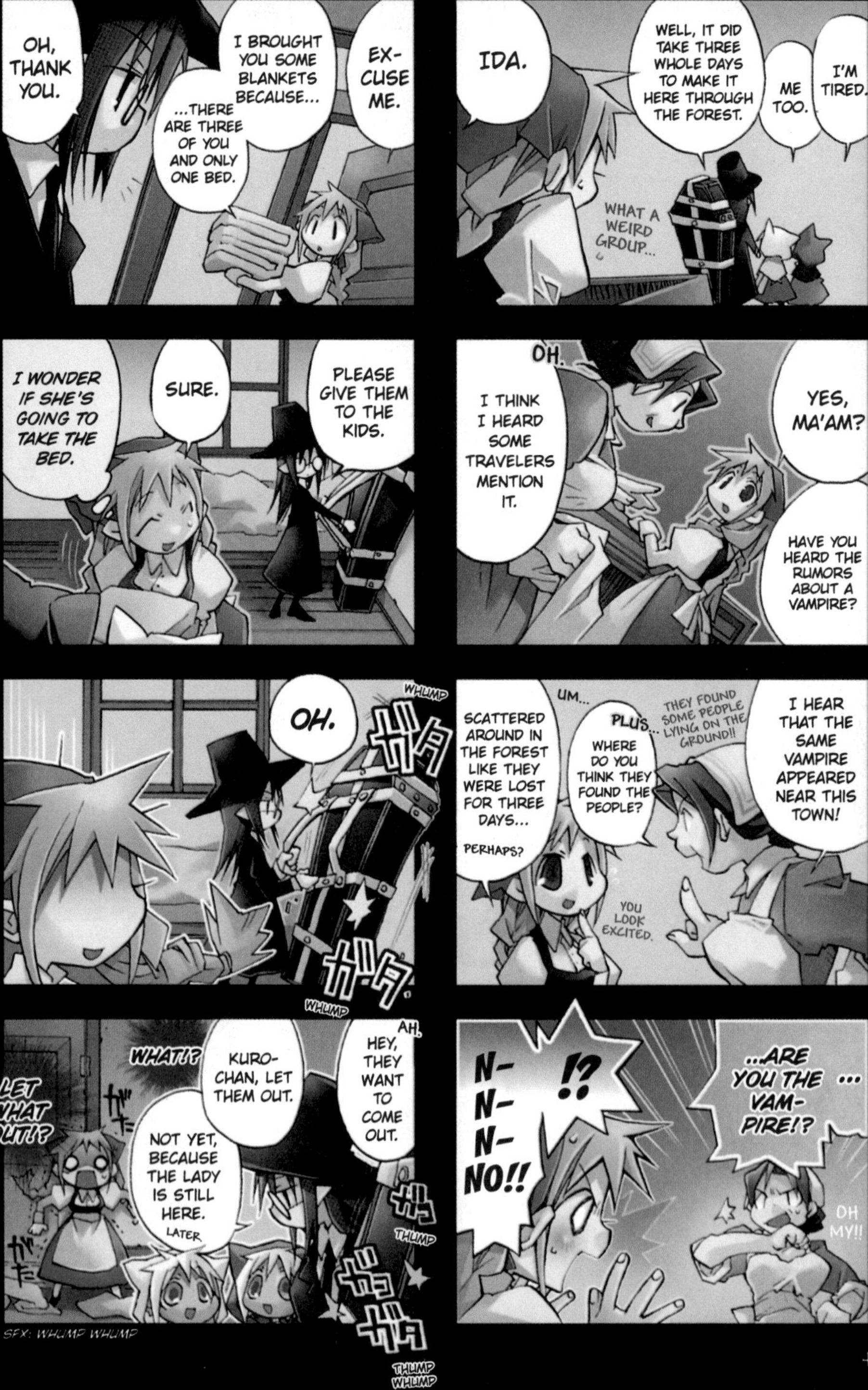
I'M TIRED.
ME TOO.
WELL, IT DID TAKE THREE WHOLE DAYS TO MAKE IT HERE THROUGH THE FOREST.
IDA.
WHAT A WEIRD GROUP...
EX-CUSE ME.
I BROUGHT YOU SOME BLANKETS BECAUSE...
...THERE ARE THREE OF YOU AND ONLY ONE BED.
OH, THANK YOU.
YES, MA'AM?
OH.
I THINK I HEARD SOME TRAVELERS MENTION IT.
HAVE YOU HEARD THE RUMORS ABOUT A VAMPIRE?
PLEASE GIVE THEM TO THE KIDS.
SURE.
I WONDER IF SHE'S GOING TO TAKE THE BED.
I HEAR THAT THE SAME VAMPIRE APPEARED NEAR THIS TOWN!
THEY FOUND SOME PEOPLE LYING ON THE GROUND!!
PLUS...
UM...
WHERE DO YOU THINK THEY FOUND THE PEOPLE?
SCATTERED AROUND IN THE FOREST LIKE THEY WERE LOST FOR THREE DAYS...
PERHAPS?
YOU LOOK EXCITED.
WHUMP
OH.
WHUMP
...ARE YOU THE ... VAM-PIRE!?
!?
N-N-N-NO!!
OH MY!!
AH.
HEY, THEY WANT TO COME OUT.
KURO-CHAN, LET THEM OUT.
WHAT!?
NOT YET, BECAUSE THE LADY IS STILL HERE.
LATER.
LET WHAT OUT!?
THUMP
THUMP WHUMP
SFX: WHUMP WHUMP

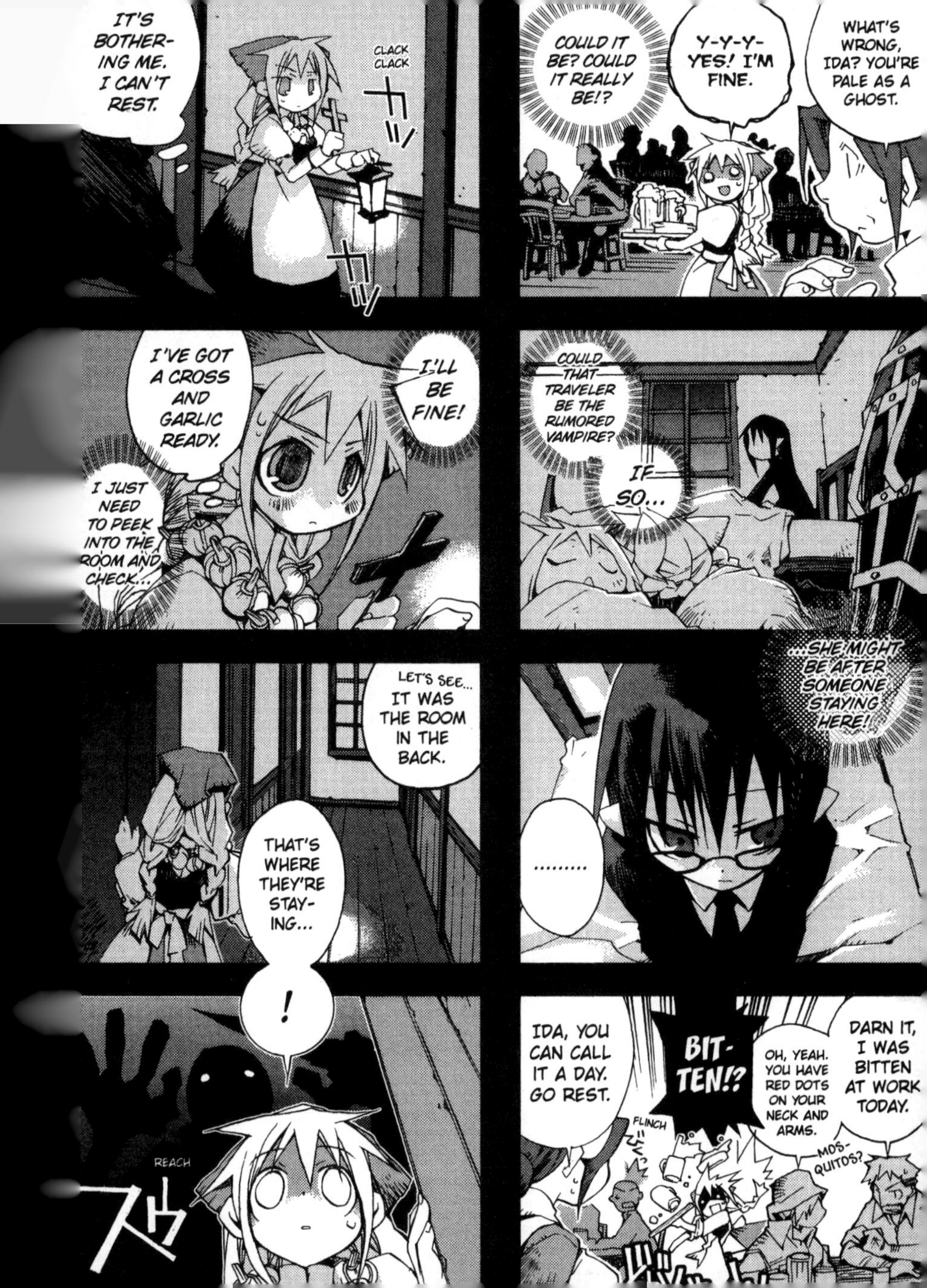
WHAT'S WRONG, IDA? YOU'RE PALE AS A GHOST.
Y-Y-Y-YES! I'M FINE.
COULD IT BE? COULD IT REALLY BE!?
IT'S BOTHERING ME. I CAN'T REST.
CLACK CLACK
COULD THAT TRAVELER BE THE RUMORED VAMPIRE?
IF SO...
I'LL BE FINE!
I'VE GOT A CROSS AND GARLIC READY.
I JUST NEED TO PEEK INTO THE ROOM AND CHECK...
...SHE MIGHT BE AFTER SOMEONE STAYING HERE!
....
LET'S SEE... IT WAS THE ROOM IN THE BACK.
THAT'S WHERE THEY'RE STAYING...
DARN IT, I WAS BITTEN AT WORK TODAY.
OH, YEAH. YOU HAVE RED DOTS ON YOUR NECK AND ARMS.
BIT-TEN!?
IDA, YOU CAN CALL IT A DAY. GO REST.
MOS-QUITOS?
FLINCH
!
REACH

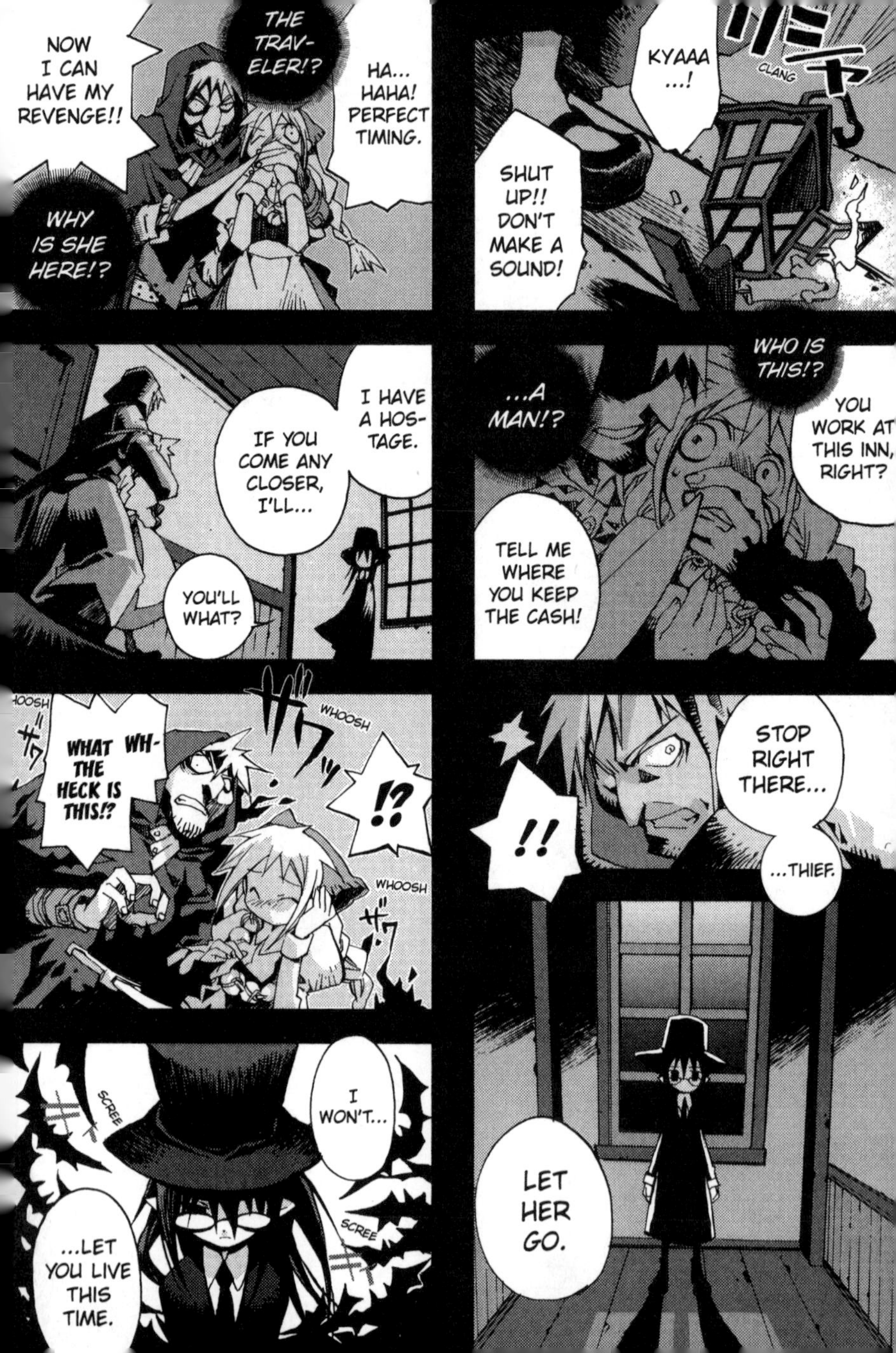
KYAAA ...!
CLANG
SHUT UP!! DON'T MAKE A SOUND!
HA... HAHA! PERFECT TIMING.
THE TRAV-ELER!?
NOW I CAN HAVE MY REVENGE!!
WHY IS SHE HERE!?
WHO IS THIS!?
YOU WORK AT THIS INN, RIGHT?
...A MAN!?
TELL ME WHERE YOU KEEP THE CASH!
I HAVE A HOS-TAGE.
IF YOU COME ANY CLOSER, I'LL...
YOU'LL WHAT?
STOP RIGHT THERE...
!!
...THIEF.
LET HER GO.
WHOOSH
!?
WH- WHAT THE HECK IS THIS!?
HOOSH
WHOOSH
I WON'T...
SCREE
SCREE
...LET YOU LIVE THIS TIME.

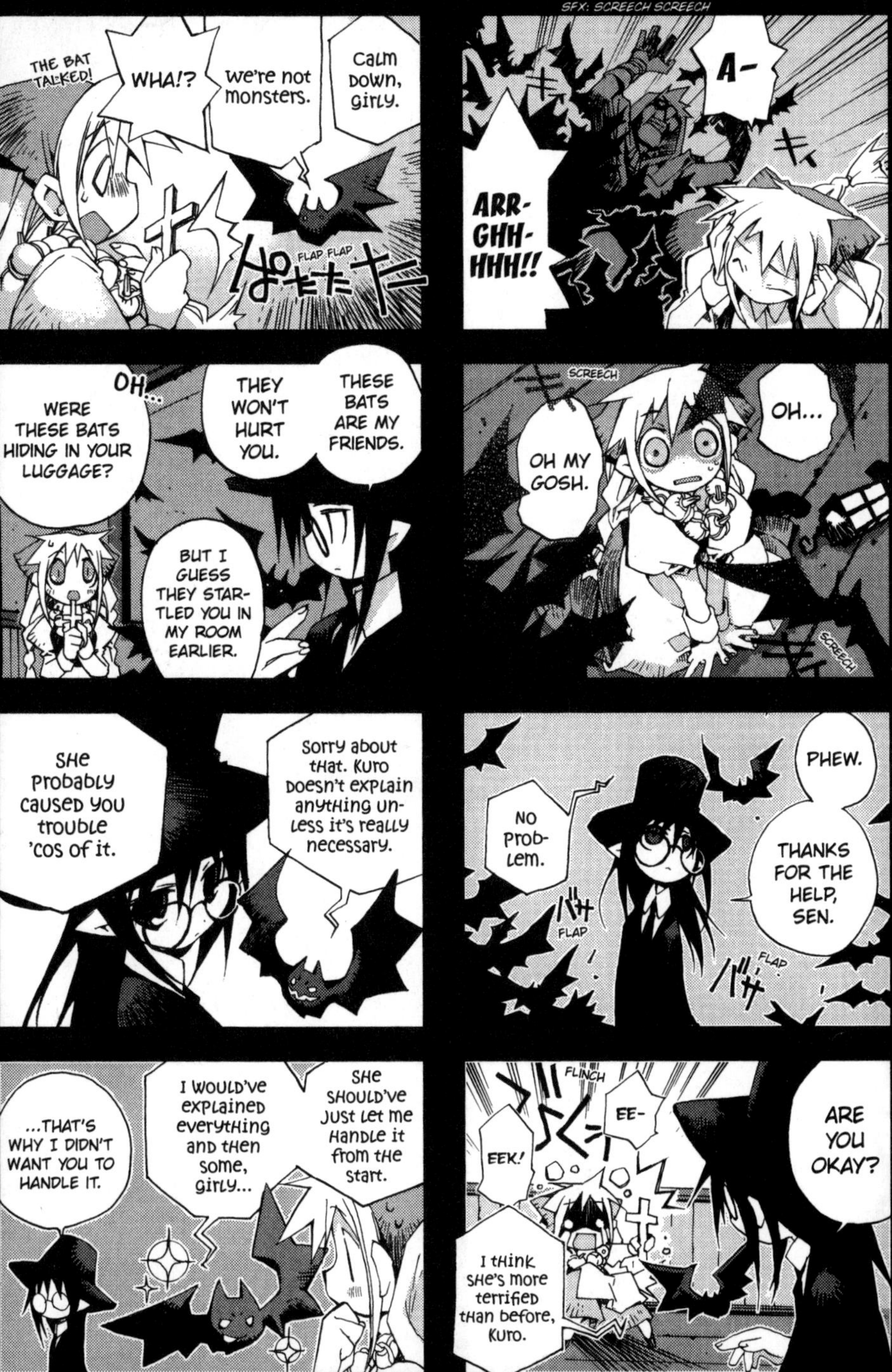
SFX: SCREECH SCREECH
A-
ARR-GHH-HHH!!
Calm down, girly.
We're not monsters.
WHA!?
THE BAT TALKED!
FLAP FLAP
OH...
OH MY GOSH.
SCREECH
SCREECH
THESE BATS ARE MY FRIENDS.
THEY WON'T HURT YOU.
OH...
WERE THESE BATS HIDING IN YOUR LUGGAGE?
BUT I GUESS THEY STAR-TLED YOU IN MY ROOM EARLIER.
PHEW.
THANKS FOR THE HELP, SEN.
NO PROB-LEM.
FLAP
FLAP
Sorry about that. Kuro doesn't explain anything un-less it's really necessary.
SHE probably caused you trouble 'cos of it.
ARE YOU OKAY?
EE-
FLINCH
EEK!
I think she's more terrified than before, Kuro.
SHE SHOULD'VE JUST LET ME HANDLE IT FROM THE START.
I WOULD'VE EXPLAINED EVERYTHING AND THEN SOME, GIRLY...
...THAT'S WHY I DIDN'T WANT YOU TO HANDLE IT.

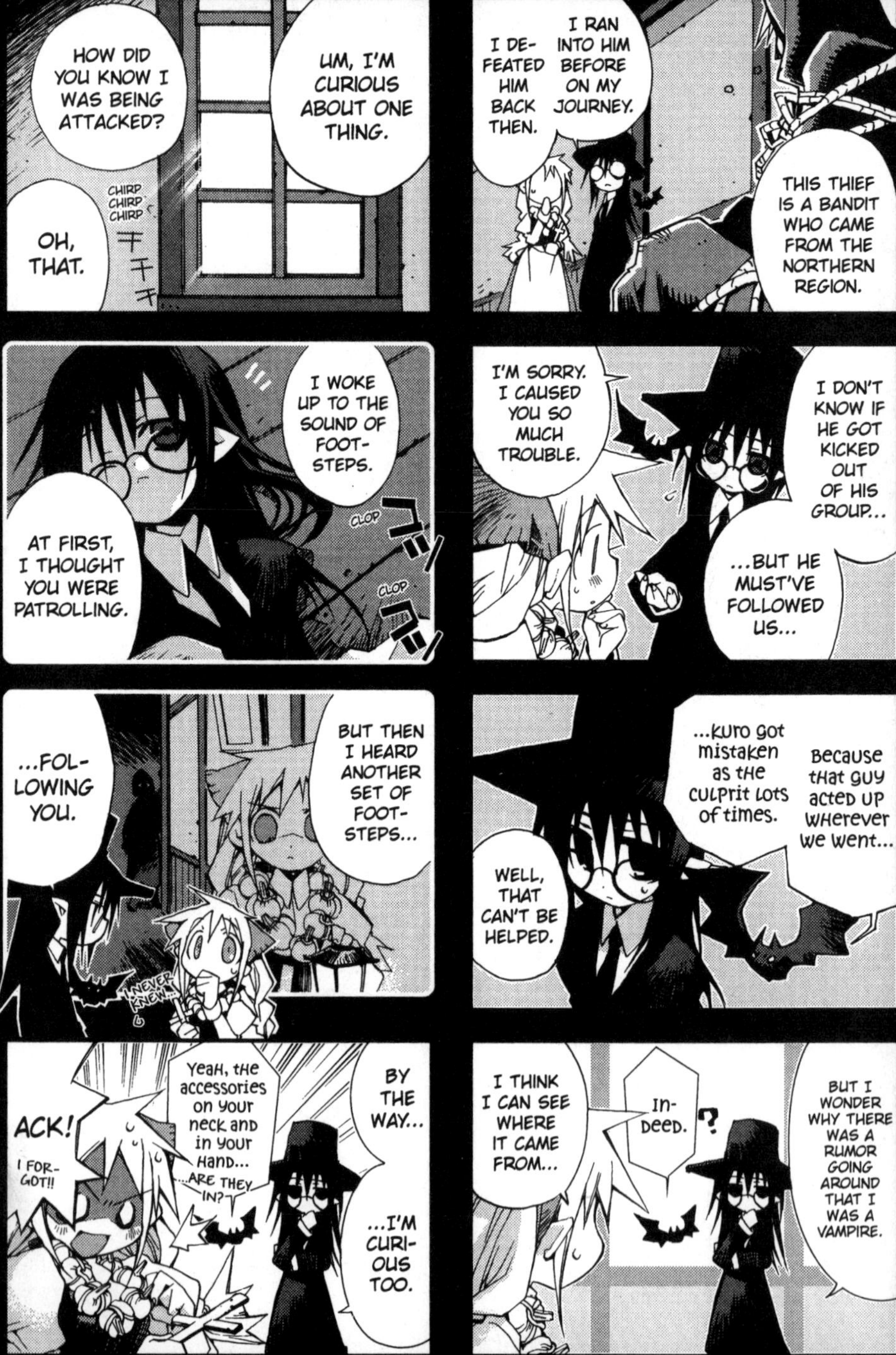
THIS THIEF IS A BANDIT WHO CAME FROM THE NORTHERN REGION.
I RAN INTO HIM BEFORE ON MY JOURNEY.
I DE-FEATED HIM BACK THEN.
I DON'T KNOW IF HE GOT KICKED OUT OF HIS GROUP...
...BUT HE MUST'VE FOLLOWED US...
I'M SORRY. I CAUSED YOU SO MUCH TROUBLE.
Because that guy acted up wherever we went...
...kuro got mistaken as the culprit lots of times.
WELL, THAT CAN'T BE HELPED.
BUT I WONDER WHY THERE WAS A RUMOR GOING AROUND THAT I WAS A VAMPIRE.
?
In-deed.
I THINK I CAN SEE WHERE IT CAME FROM...
UM, I'M CURIOUS ABOUT ONE THING.
HOW DID YOU KNOW I WAS BEING ATTACKED?
CHIRP CHIRP CHIRP
OH, THAT.
I WOKE UP TO THE SOUND OF FOOT-STEPS.
CLOP
CLOP
AT FIRST, I THOUGHT YOU WERE PATROLLING.
BUT THEN I HEARD ANOTHER SET OF FOOT-STEPS...
...FOL-LOWING YOU.
I NEVER KNEW...
BY THE WAY...
...I'M CURI-OUS TOO.
Yeah, the accessories on your neck and in your Hand...
...ARE THEY IN?
ACK!
I FOR-GOT!!

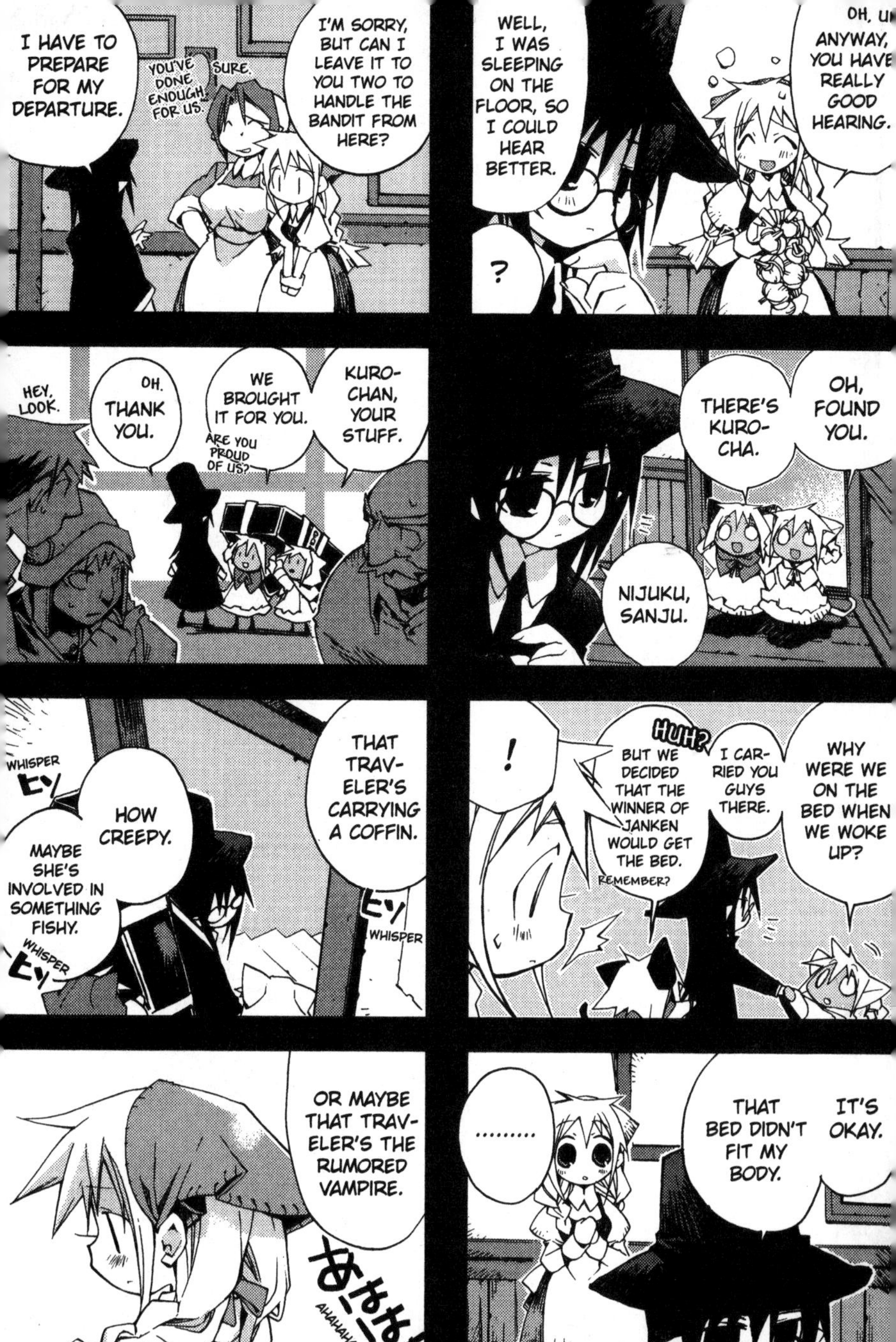
OH, U
ANYWAY, YOU HAVE REALLY GOOD HEARING.
WELL, I WAS SLEEPING ON THE FLOOR, SO I COULD HEAR BETTER.
?
OH, FOUND YOU.
THERE'S KURO-CHA.
NIJUKU, SANJU.
WHY WERE WE ON THE BED WHEN WE WOKE UP?
I CARRIED YOU GUYS THERE.
HUH?
BUT WE DECIDED THAT THE WINNER OF JANKEN WOULD GET THE BED.
REMEMBER?
!
IT'S OKAY.
THAT BED DIDN'T FIT MY BODY.
....
I'M SORRY, BUT CAN I LEAVE IT TO YOU TWO TO HANDLE THE BANDIT FROM HERE?
SURE.
YOU'VE DONE ENOUGH FOR US.
I HAVE TO PREPARE FOR MY DEPARTURE.
KURO-CHAN, YOUR STUFF.
WE BROUGHT IT FOR YOU.
ARE YOU PROUD OF US?
OH. THANK YOU.
HEY, LOOK.
THAT TRAVELER'S CARRYING A COFFIN.
ヒソ WHISPER
HOW CREEPY.
MAYBE SHE'S INVOLVED IN SOMETHING FISHY.
ヒソ WHISPER
ヒソ WHISPER
OR MAYBE THAT TRAVELER'S THE RUMORED VAMPIRE.
あはは
AHAHAHA

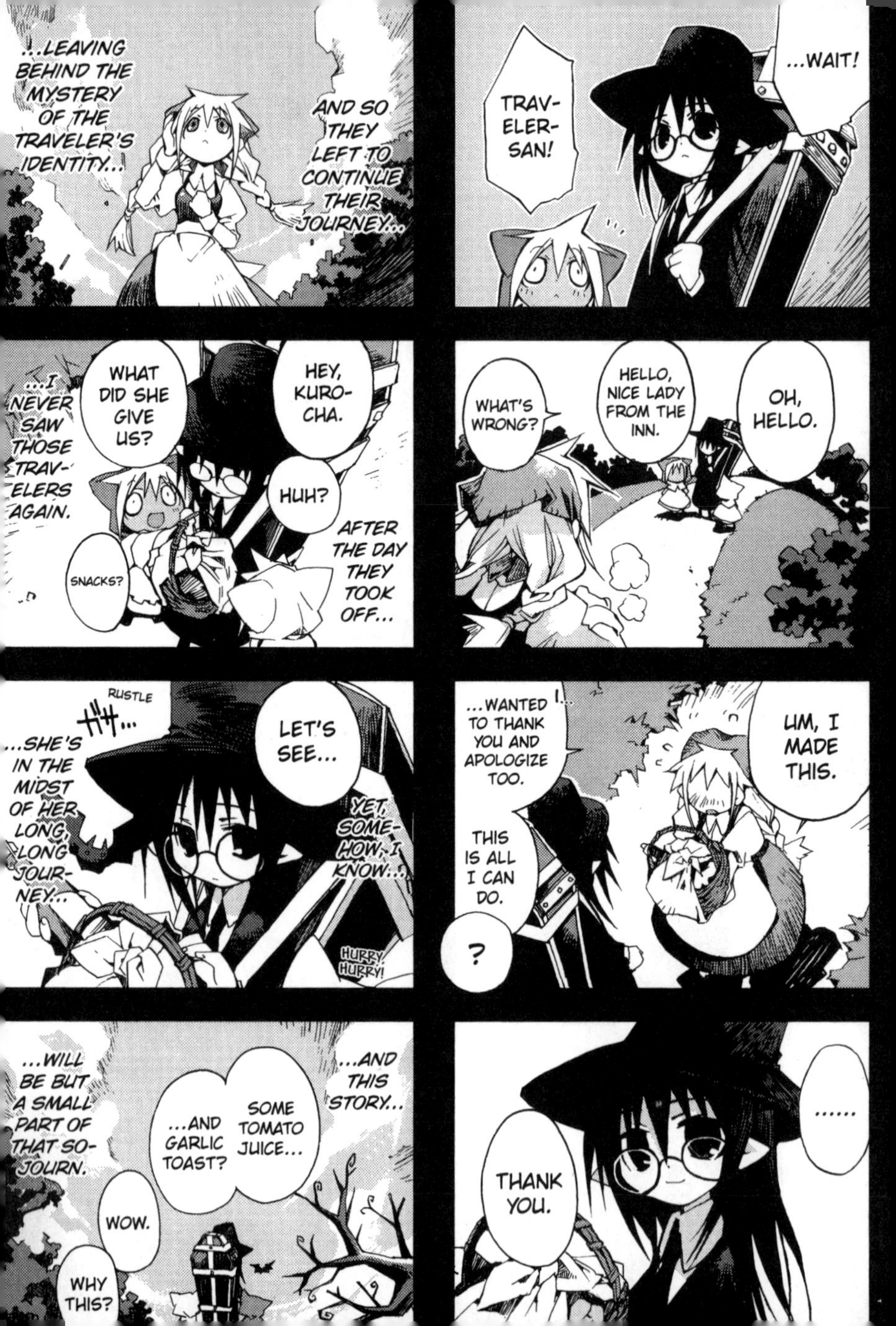
...WAIT!
TRAVELER-SAN!
AND SO THEY LEFT TO CONTINUE THEIR JOURNEY...
...LEAVING BEHIND THE MYSTERY OF THE TRAVELER'S IDENTITY...
OH, HELLO.
HELLO, NICE LADY FROM THE INN.
WHAT'S WRONG?
HEY, KURO-CHA.
HUH?
WHAT DID SHE GIVE US?
...I NEVER SAW THOSE TRAVELERS AGAIN.
AFTER THE DAY THEY TOOK OFF...
SNACKS?
UM, I MADE THIS.
I...
...WANTED TO THANK YOU AND APOLOGIZE TOO.
THIS IS ALL I CAN DO.
?
LET'S SEE...
RUSTLE
ガサ...
YET, SOMEHOW, I KNOW...
...SHE'S IN THE MIDST OF HER LONG, LONG JOURNEY...
HURRY HURRY!
......
THANK YOU.
...AND THIS STORY...
SOME TOMATO JUICE...
...AND GARLIC TOAST?
...WILL BE BUT A SMALL PART OF THAT SOJOURN.
WOW.
WHY THIS?

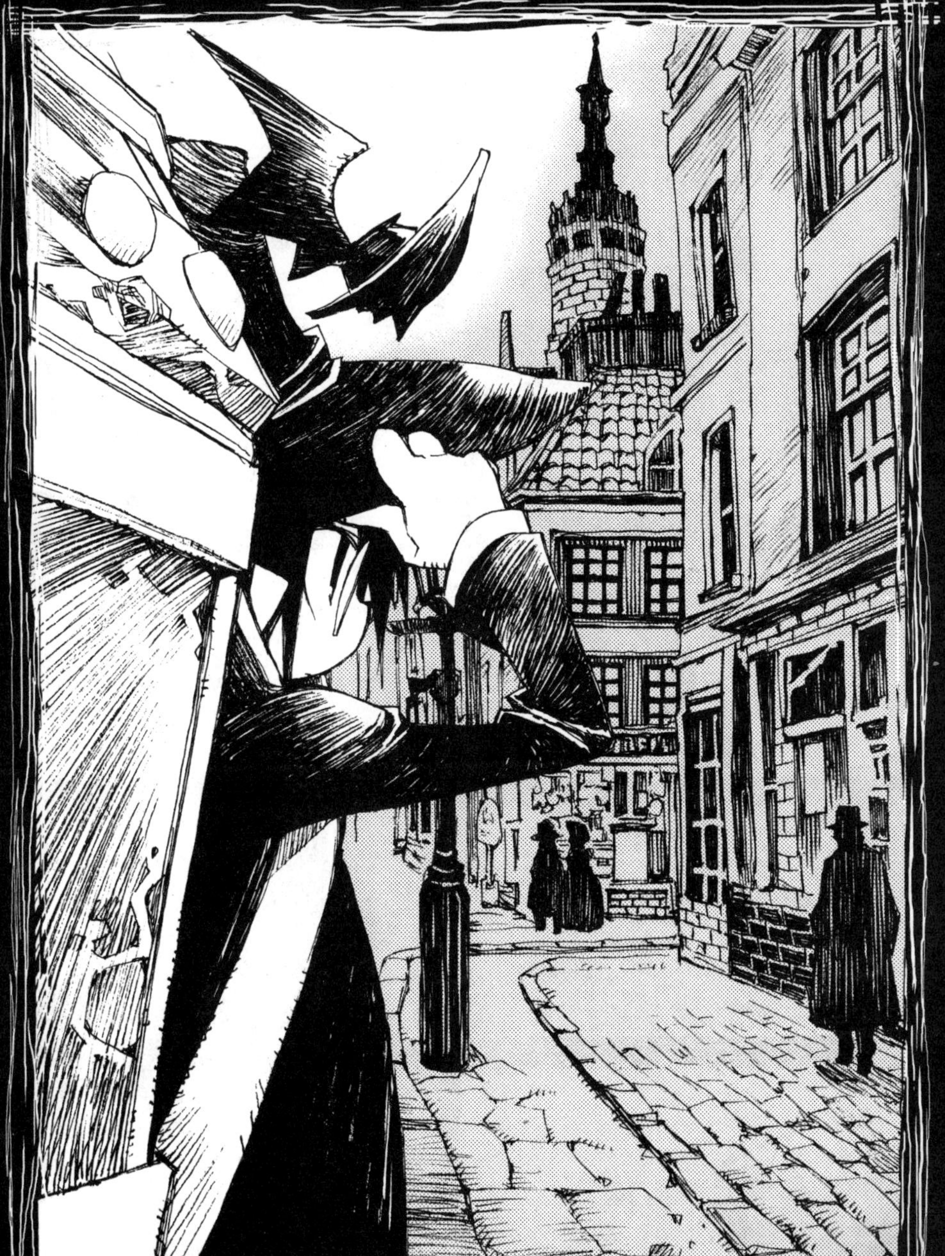

The little girls asked the traveler dressed in black,

"You're all dressed in black, Traveler-san. Who are you?"

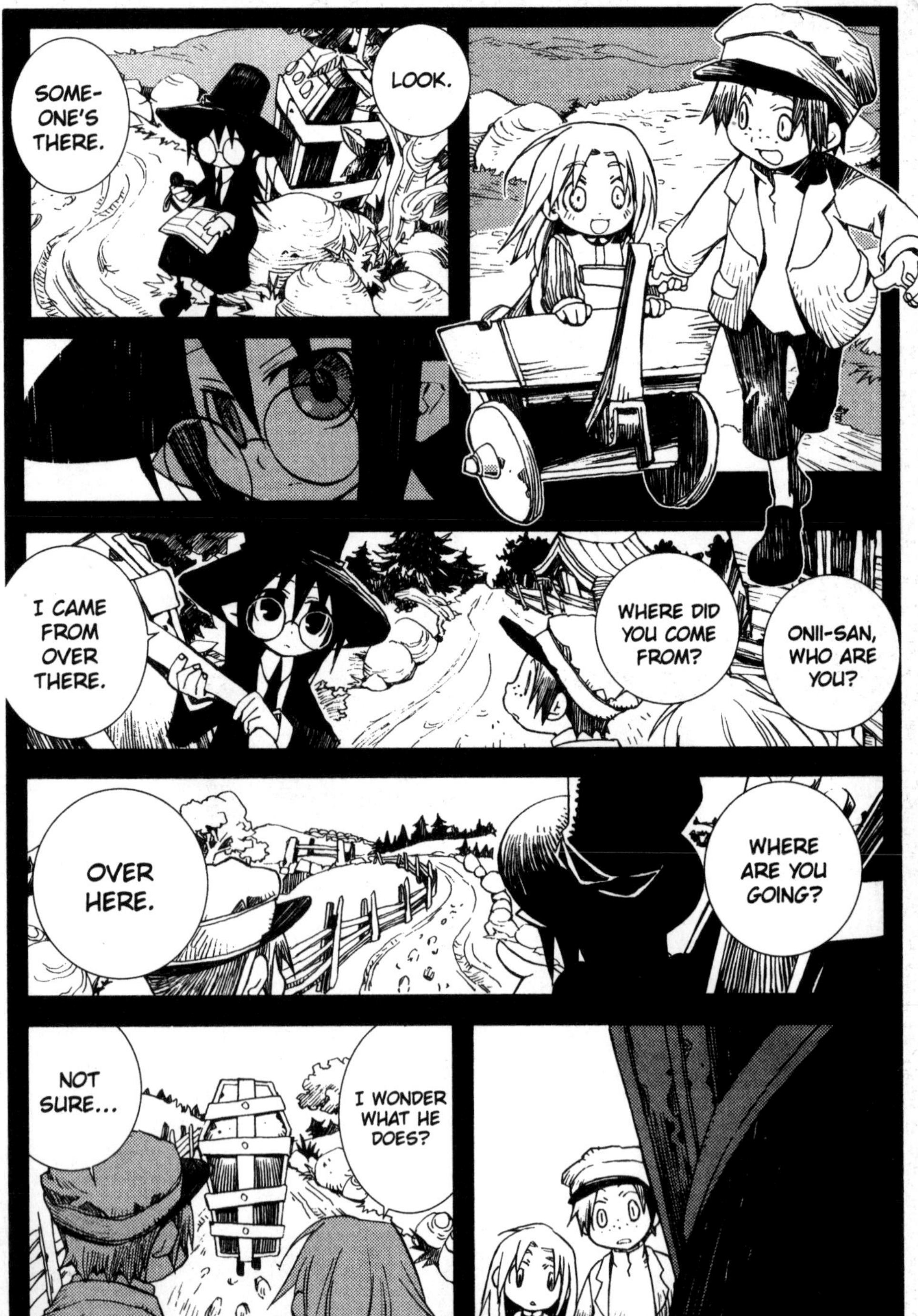
LOOK.
SOME-ONE'S THERE.
ONII-SAN, WHO ARE YOU?
WHERE DID YOU COME FROM?
I CAME FROM OVER THERE.
WHERE ARE YOU GOING?
OVER HERE.
I WONDER WHAT HE DOES?
NOT SURE...

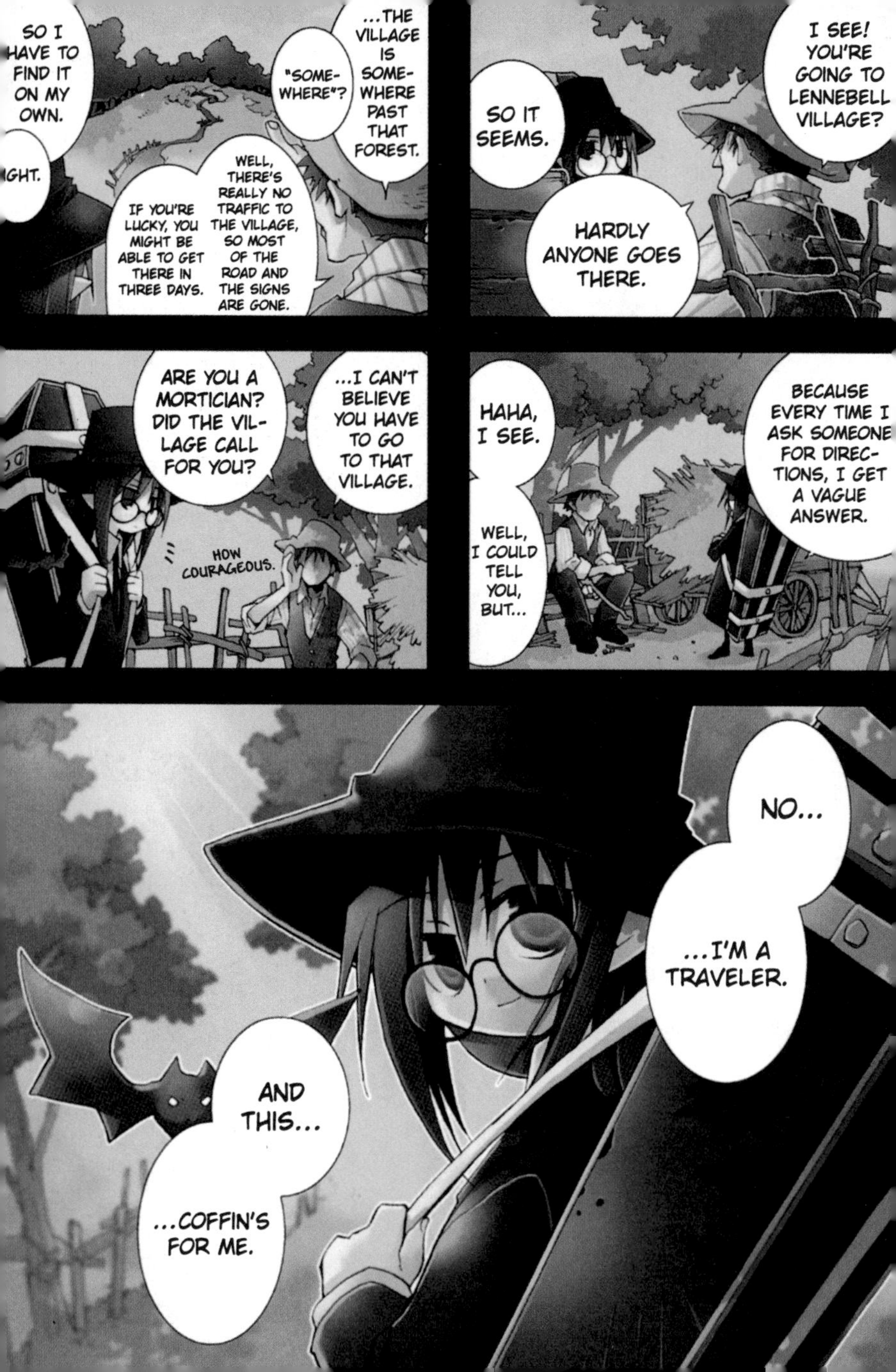
I SEE! YOU'RE GOING TO LENNEBELL VILLAGE?
SO IT SEEMS.
HARDLY ANYONE GOES THERE.
...THE VILLAGE IS SOMEWHERE PAST THAT FOREST.
"SOME-WHERE"?
WELL, THERE'S REALLY NO TRAFFIC TO THE VILLAGE, SO MOST OF THE ROAD AND THE SIGNS ARE GONE.
IF YOU'RE LUCKY, YOU MIGHT BE ABLE TO GET THERE IN THREE DAYS.
SO I HAVE TO FIND IT ON MY OWN.
IGHT.
BECAUSE EVERY TIME I ASK SOMEONE FOR DIREC-TIONS, I GET A VAGUE ANSWER.
HAHA, I SEE.
WELL, I COULD TELL YOU, BUT...
...I CAN'T BELIEVE YOU HAVE TO GO TO THAT VILLAGE.
ARE YOU A MORTICIAN? DID THE VIL-LAGE CALL FOR YOU?
HOW COURAGEOUS.
NO...
...I'M A TRAVELER.
AND THIS...
...COFFIN'S FOR ME.

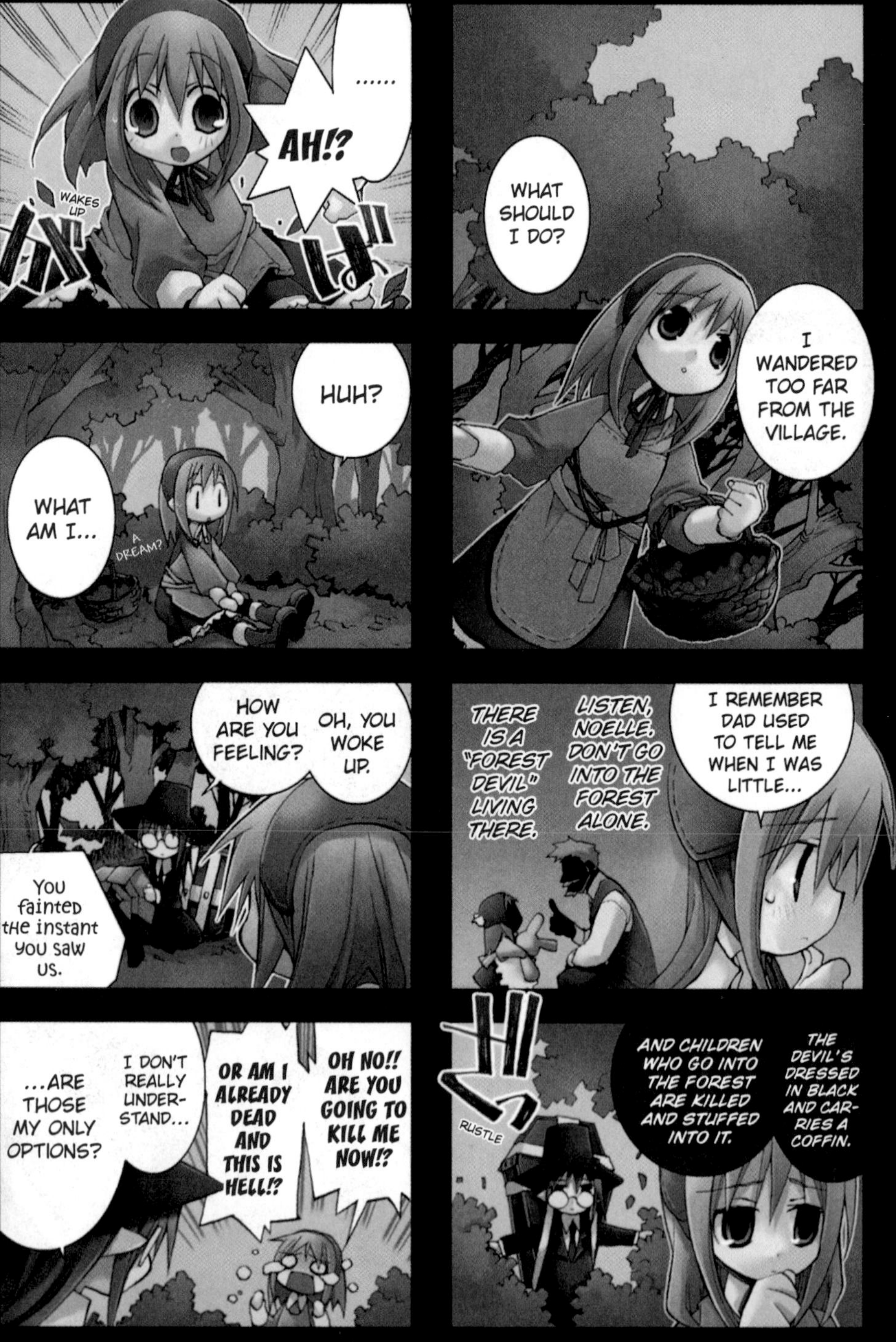
I WANDERED TOO FAR FROM THE VILLAGE.
WHAT SHOULD I DO?
......
AH!?
WAKES UP
HUH?
WHAT AM I...
A DREAM?
I REMEMBER DAD USED TO TELL ME WHEN I WAS LITTLE...
LISTEN, NOELLE. DON'T GO INTO THE FOREST ALONE.
THERE IS A "FOREST DEVIL" LIVING THERE.
OH, YOU WOKE UP.
HOW ARE YOU FEELING?
You fainted the instant you saw us.
THE DEVIL'S DRESSED IN BLACK AND CAR-RIES A COFFIN.
AND CHILDREN WHO GO INTO THE FOREST ARE KILLED AND STUFFED INTO IT.
RUSTLE
OH NO!! ARE YOU GOING TO KILL ME NOW!?
OR AM I ALREADY DEAD AND THIS IS HELL!?
I DON'T REALLY UNDER-STAND...
...ARE THOSE MY ONLY OPTIONS?

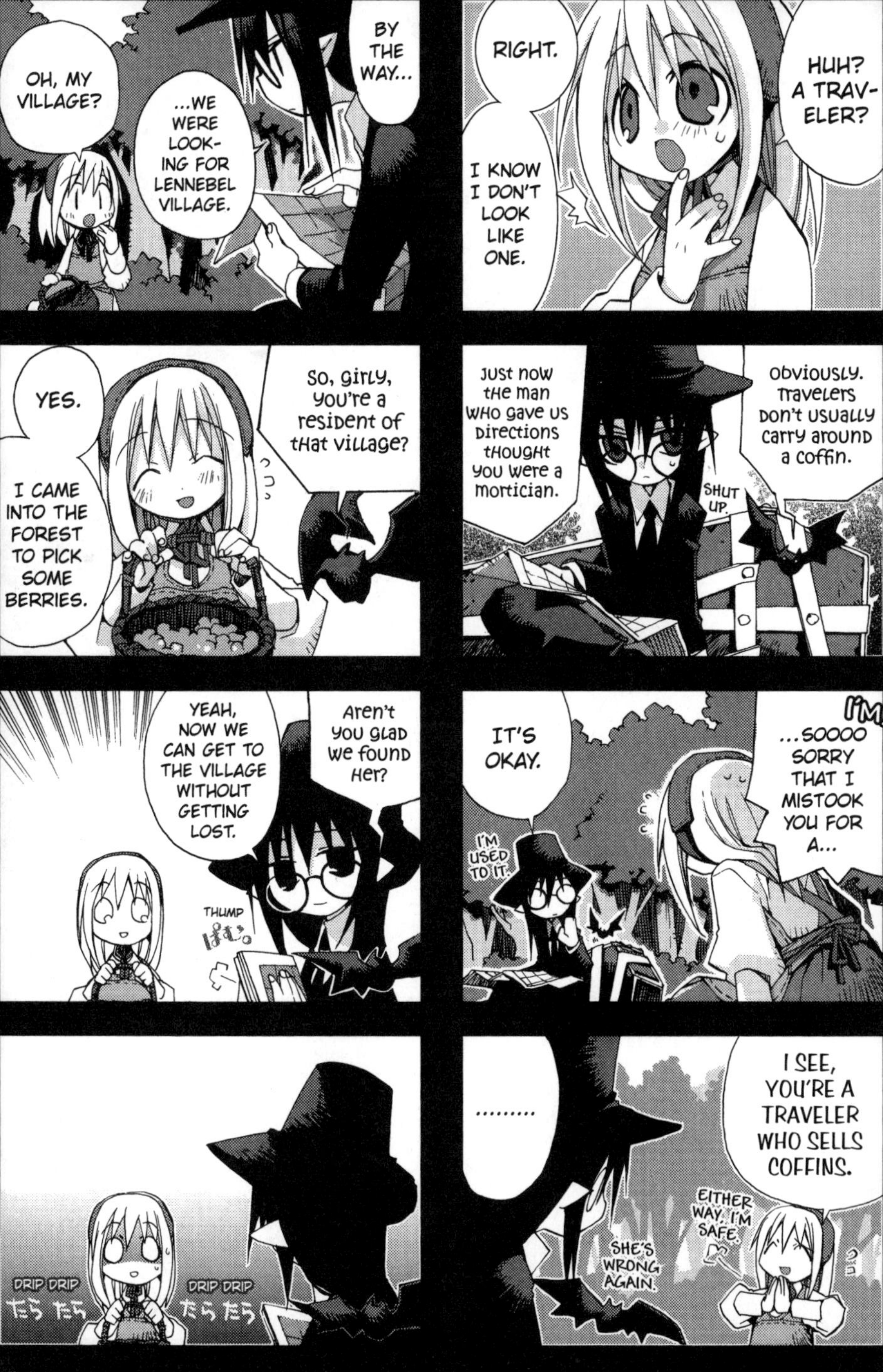
HUH? A TRAVELER?
RIGHT.
I KNOW I DON'T LOOK LIKE ONE.
BY THE WAY...
...WE WERE LOOKING FOR LENNEBEL VILLAGE.
OH, MY VILLAGE?
Obviously. Travelers don't usually carry around a coffin.
Just now the man who gave us directions thought you were a mortician.
SHUT UP.
So, girly, you're a resident of that village?
YES.
I CAME INTO THE FOREST TO PICK SOME BERRIES.
I'M ...SOOOO SORRY THAT I MISTOOK YOU FOR A...
IT'S OKAY.
I'M USED TO IT.
Aren't you glad we found her?
YEAH, NOW WE CAN GET TO THE VILLAGE WITHOUT GETTING LOST.
THUMP
ぱむ。
I SEE, YOU'RE A TRAVELER WHO SELLS COFFINS.
....
EITHER WAY, I'M SAFE.
SHE'S WRONG AGAIN.
DRIP DRIP
たらたら
DRIP DRIP
たらたら

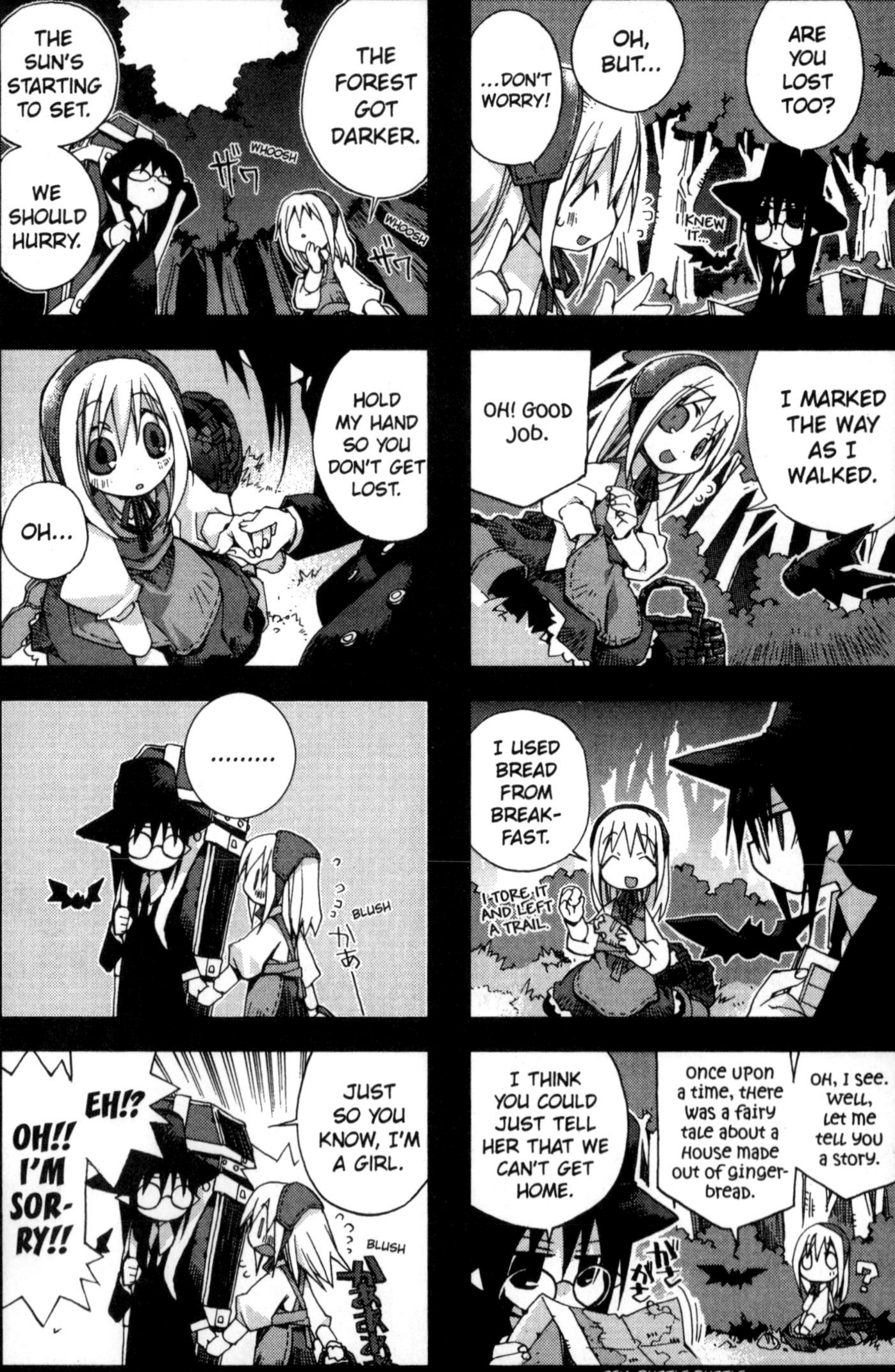
ARE YOU LOST TOO?
OH, BUT...
...DON'T WORRY!
I KNEW IT...
THE FOREST GOT DARKER.
WHOOSH
THE SUN'S STARTING TO SET.
WHOOSH
WE SHOULD HURRY.
I MARKED THE WAY AS I WALKED.
OH! GOOD JOb.
HOLD MY HAND SO YOU DON'T GET LOST.
OH...
I USED BREAD FROM BREAK-FAST.
I TORE IT AND LEFT A TRAIL.
....
BLUSH
かあ
OH, I SEE. WELL, LET ME TELL YOU A STORY.
Once upon a time, there was a fairy tale about a House made out of ginger-bread.
I THINK YOU COULD JUST TELL HER THAT WE CAN'T GET HOME.
?
JUST SO YOU KNOW, I'M A GIRL.
EH!?
OH!! I'M SORRY!!
BLUSH
SFX: RUSTLE RUSTLE

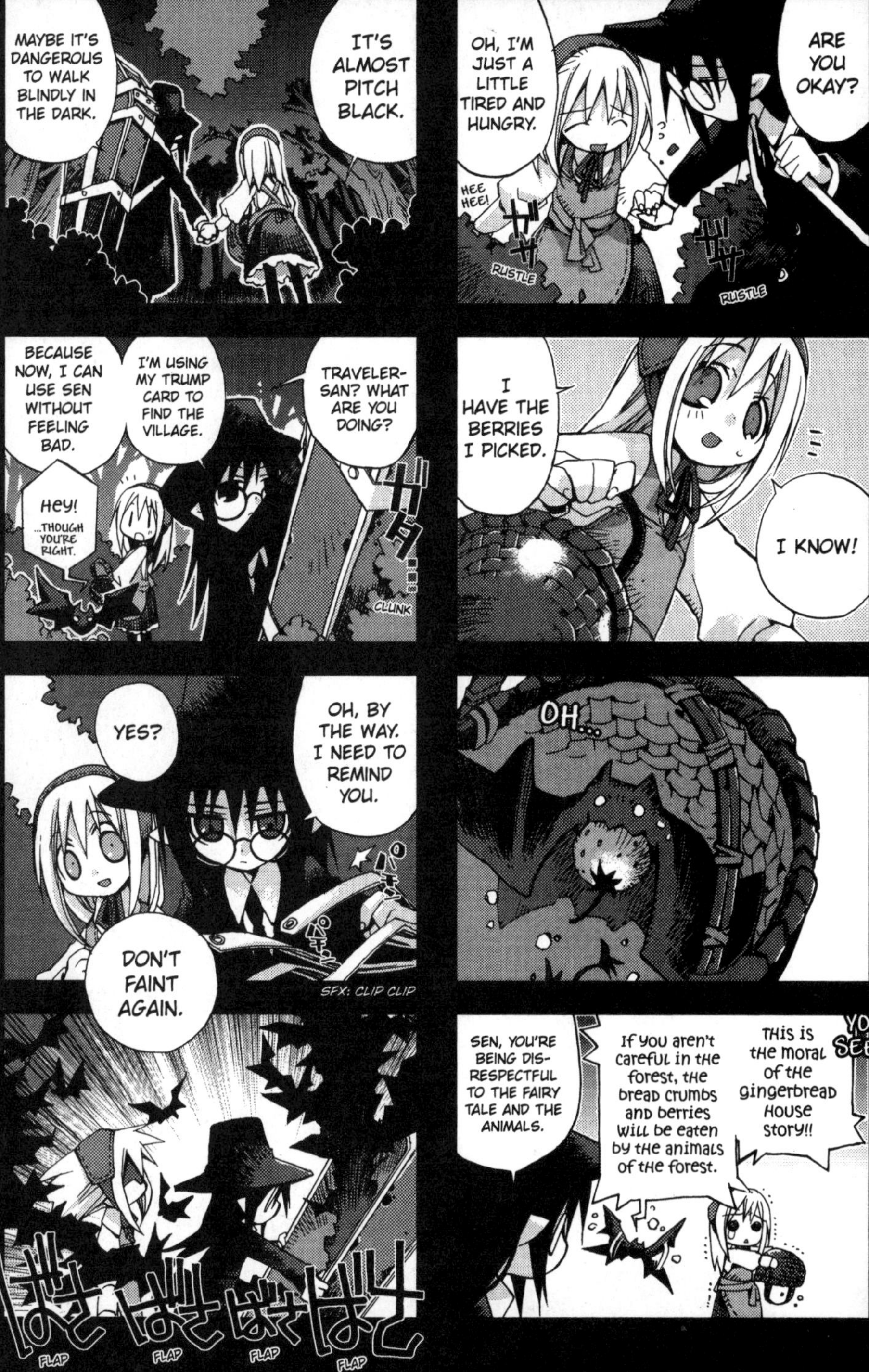
ARE YOU OKAY?
OH, I'M JUST A LITTLE TIRED AND HUNGRY.
HEE HEE!
RUSTLE
RUSTLE
IT'S ALMOST PITCH BLACK.
MAYBE IT'S DANGEROUS TO WALK BLINDLY IN THE DARK.
I HAVE THE BERRIES I PICKED.
I KNOW!
TRAVELER-SAN? WHAT ARE YOU DOING?
I'M USING MY TRUMP CARD TO FIND THE VILLAGE.
BECAUSE NOW, I CAN USE SEN WITHOUT FEELING BAD.
HEY!
...THOUGH YOU'RE RIGHT.
CLUNK
OH...
OH, BY THE WAY. I NEED TO REMIND YOU.
YES?
DON'T FAINT AGAIN.
SFX: CLIP CLIP
THIS is the moral of the gingerbread HOUSE story!!
If you aren't careful in the forest, the bread crumbs and berries will be eaten by the animals of the forest.
SEN, YOU'RE BEING DIS-RESPECTFUL TO THE FAIRY TALE AND THE ANIMALS.
FLAP
FLAP
FLAP
FLAP

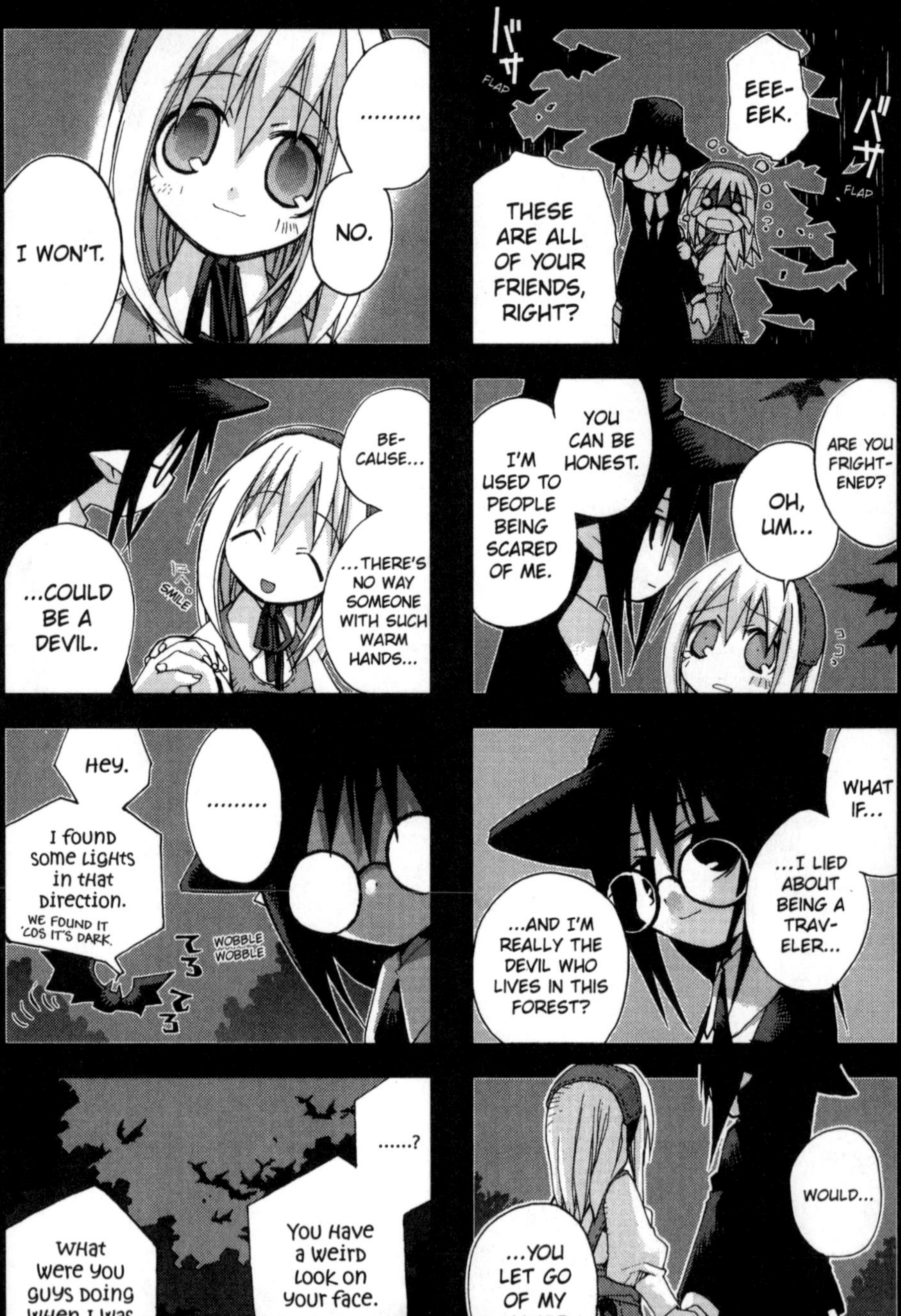
バサ
FLAP
EEE-EEK.
バサ
FLAP
THESE ARE ALL OF YOUR FRIENDS, RIGHT?
....
NO.
I WON'T.
ARE YOU FRIGHT-ENED?
OH, UM...
YOU CAN BE HONEST.
I'M USED TO PEOPLE BEING SCARED OF ME.
BE-CAUSE...
...THERE'S NO WAY SOMEONE WITH SUCH WARM HANDS...
SMILE
...COULD BE A DEVIL.
WHAT IF...
...I LIED ABOUT BEING A TRAV-ELER...
...AND I'M REALLY THE DEVIL WHO LIVES IN THIS FOREST?
....
Hey.
I found some lights in that direction.
WE FOUND IT 'COS IT'S DARK.
WOBBLE WOBBLE
WOULD...
...YOU LET GO OF MY HAND?
......?
You have a weird look on your face.
What were you guys doing when I was gone!?

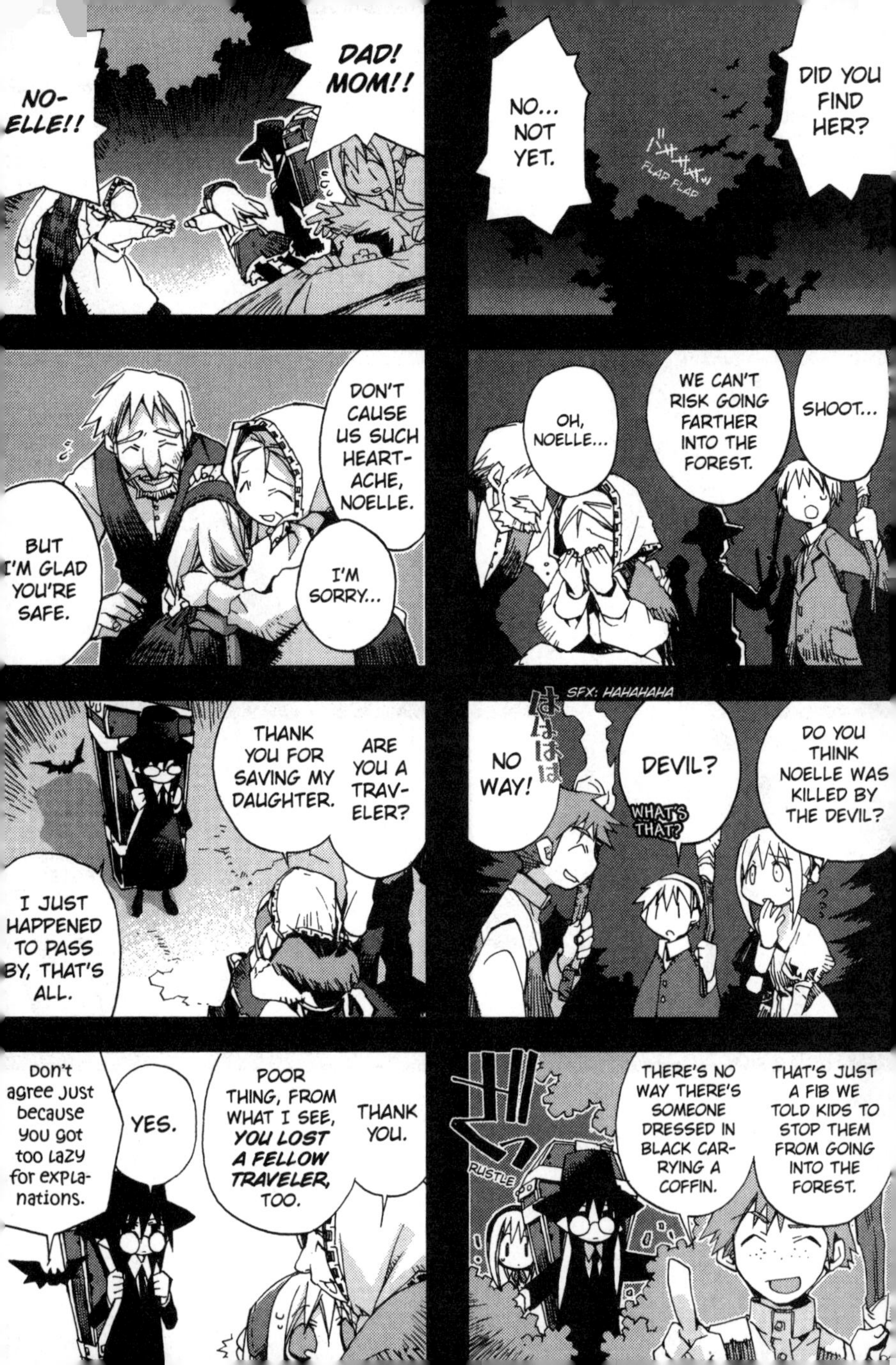

DID YOU FIND HER?
NO... NOT YET.
FLAP FLAP
DAD! MOM!!
NO-ELLE!!
SHOOT...
WE CAN'T RISK GOING FARTHER INTO THE FOREST.
OH, NOELLE...
DON'T CAUSE US SUCH HEART-ACHE, NOELLE.
I'M SORRY...
BUT I'M GLAD YOU'RE SAFE.
SFX: HAHAHAHA
DO YOU THINK NOELLE WAS KILLED BY THE DEVIL?
DEVIL?
WHAT'S THAT?
NO WAY!
ARE YOU A TRAV-ELER?
THANK YOU FOR SAVING MY DAUGHTER.
I JUST HAPPENED TO PASS BY, THAT'S ALL.
THAT'S JUST A FIB WE TOLD KIDS TO STOP THEM FROM GOING INTO THE FOREST.
THERE'S NO WAY THERE'S SOMEONE DRESSED IN BLACK CAR-RYING A COFFIN.
RUSTLE
THANK YOU.
POOR THING, FROM WHAT I SEE, YOU LOST A FELLOW TRAVELER, TOO.
YES.
Don't agree just because you got too lazy for expla-nations.

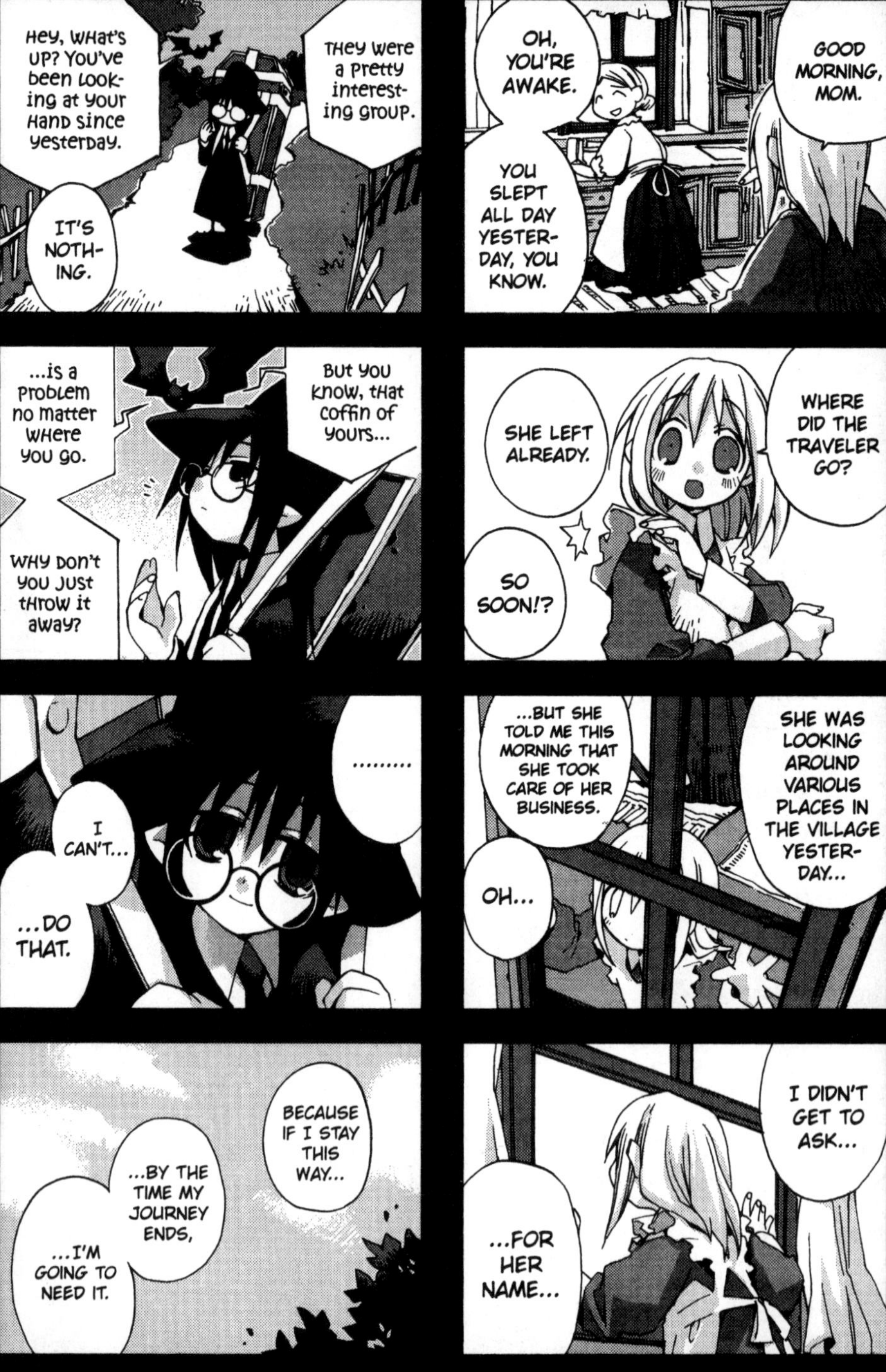
GOOD MORNING, MOM.
OH, YOU'RE AWAKE.
YOU SLEPT ALL DAY YESTERDAY, YOU KNOW.
They were a pretty interesting group.
Hey, what's up? You've been looking at your hand since yesterday.
IT'S NOTHING.
WHERE DID THE TRAVELER GO?
SHE LEFT ALREADY.
SO SOON!?
But you know, that coffin of yours...
...is a problem no matter where you go.
Why don't you just throw it away?
SHE WAS LOOKING AROUND VARIOUS PLACES IN THE VILLAGE YESTERDAY...
...BUT SHE TOLD ME THIS MORNING THAT SHE TOOK CARE OF HER BUSINESS.
OH...
....
I CAN'T...
...DO THAT.
I DIDN'T GET TO ASK...
...FOR HER NAME...
BECAUSE IF I STAY THIS WAY...
...BY THE TIME MY JOURNEY ENDS,
...I'M GOING TO NEED IT.

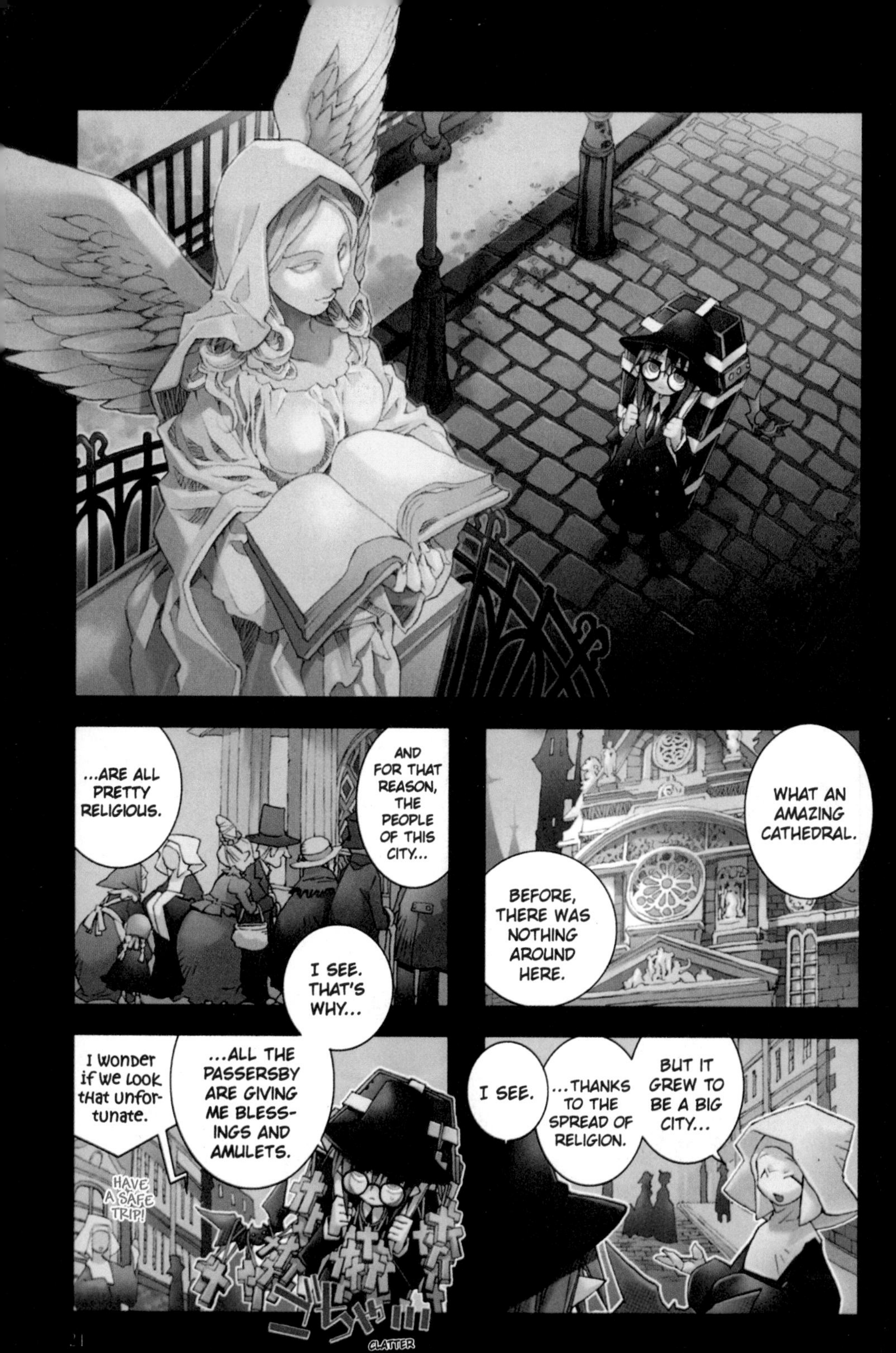
WHAT AN AMAZING CATHEDRAL.
BEFORE, THERE WAS NOTHING AROUND HERE.
AND FOR THAT REASON, THE PEOPLE OF THIS CITY...
...ARE ALL PRETTY RELIGIOUS.
BUT IT GREW TO BE A BIG CITY...
...THANKS TO THE SPREAD OF RELIGION.
I SEE.
I SEE. THAT'S WHY...
...ALL THE PASSERSBY ARE GIVING ME BLESSINGS AND AMULETS.
I wonder if we look that unfortunate.
HAVE A SAFE TRIP!
CLATTER

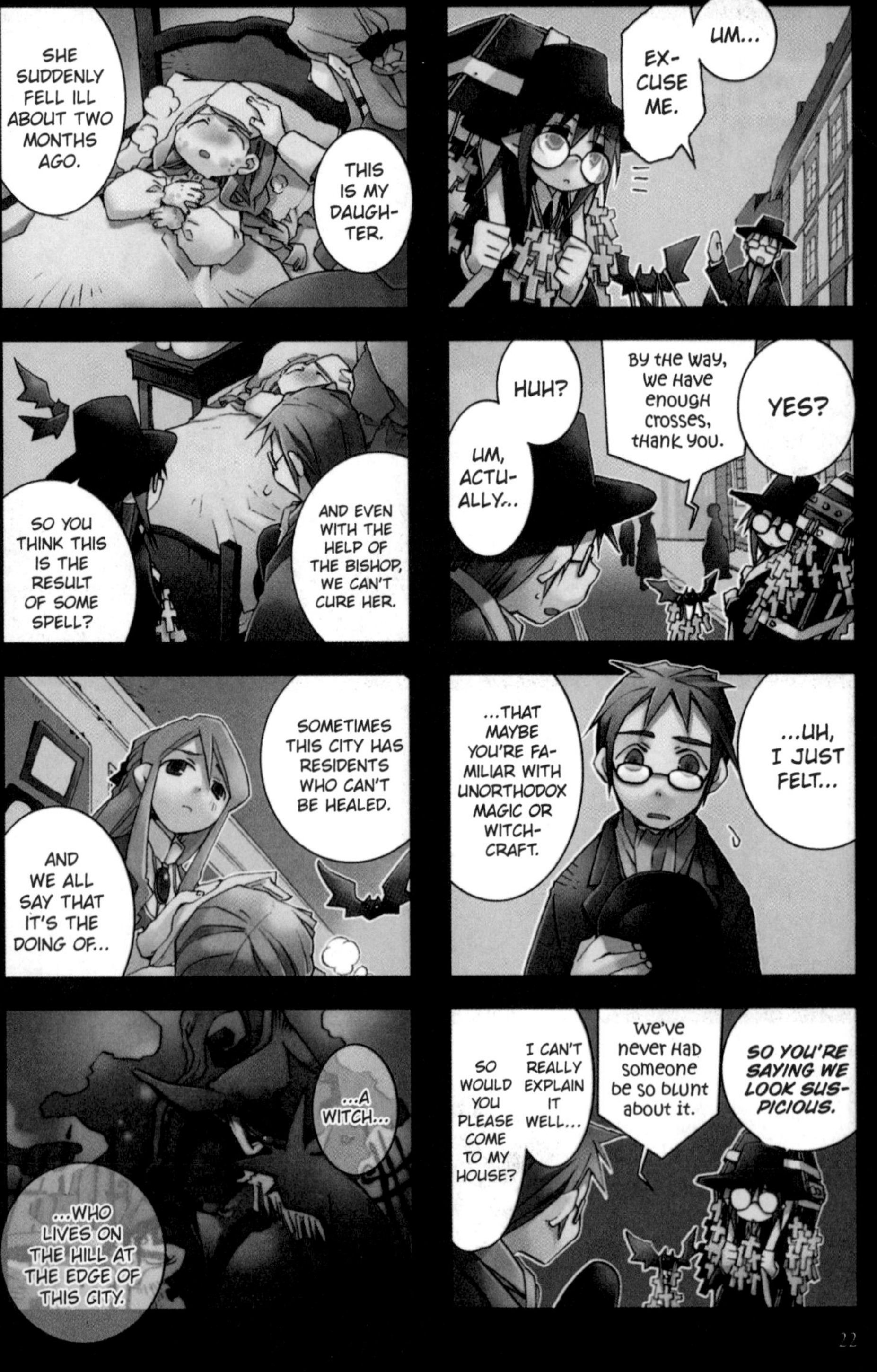
UM...
EX-CUSE ME.
THIS IS MY DAUGH-TER.
SHE SUDDENLY FELL ILL ABOUT TWO MONTHS AGO.
YES?
By the way, we have enough crosses, thank you.
HUH?
UM, ACTU-ALLY...
AND EVEN WITH THE HELP OF THE BISHOP, WE CAN'T CURE HER.
SO YOU THINK THIS IS THE RESULT OF SOME SPELL?
...UH, I JUST FELT...
...THAT MAYBE YOU'RE FA-MILIAR WITH UNORTHODOX MAGIC OR WITCH-CRAFT.
SOMETIMES THIS CITY HAS RESIDENTS WHO CAN'T BE HEALED.
AND WE ALL SAY THAT IT'S THE DOING OF...
SO YOU'RE SAYING WE LOOK SUS-PICIOUS.
We've never had someone be so blunt about it.
I CAN'T REALLY EXPLAIN IT WELL...
SO WOULD YOU PLEASE COME TO MY HOUSE?
...A WITCH...
...WHO LIVES ON THE HILL AT THE EDGE OF THIS CITY.

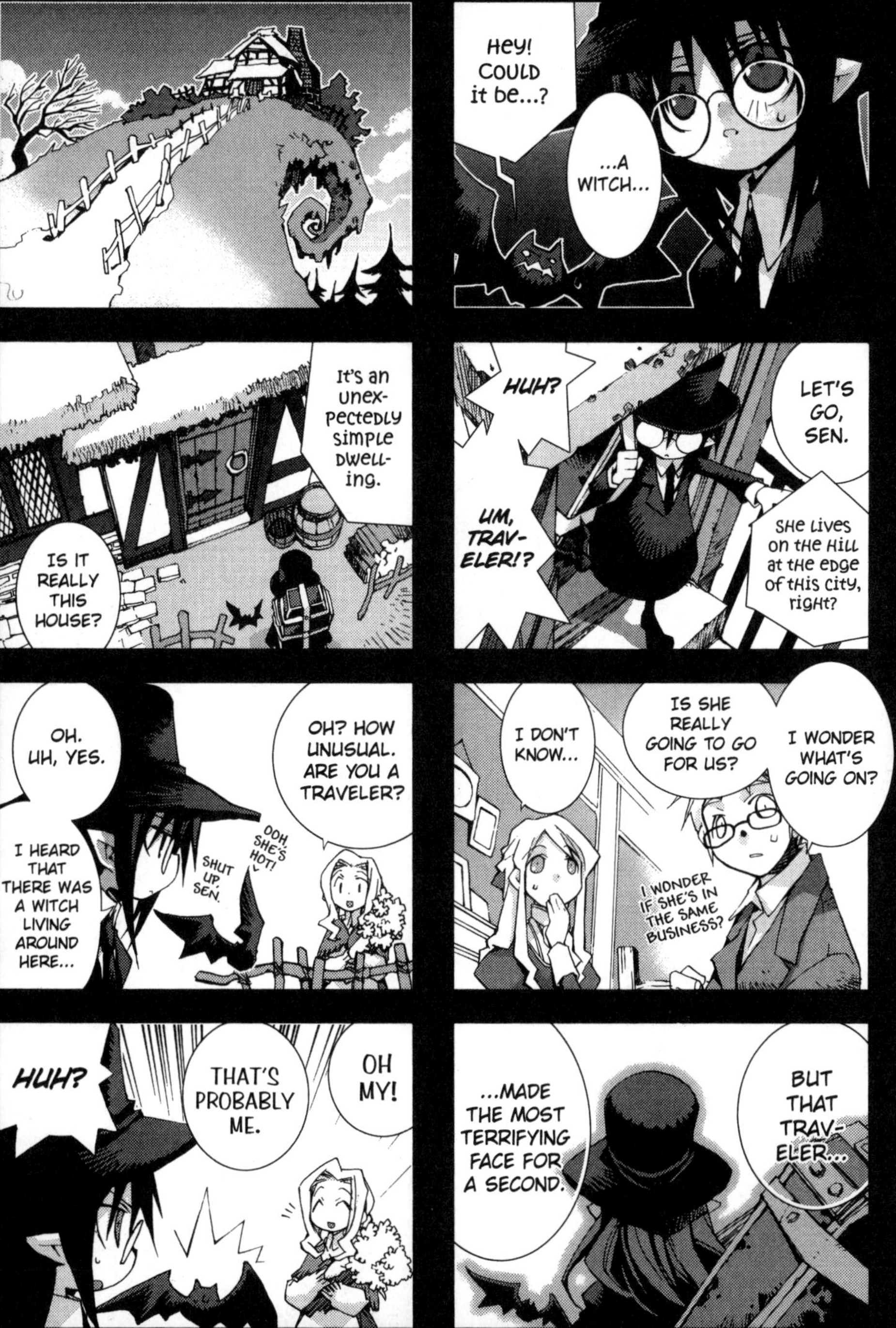
HEY! COULD IT BE...?
...A WITCH...
LET'S GO, SEN.
SHE LIVES ON THE HILL AT THE EDGE OF THIS CITY, RIGHT?
HUH?
UM, TRAVELER!?
IT'S AN UNEXPECTEDLY SIMPLE DWELLING.
IS IT REALLY THIS HOUSE?
I WONDER WHAT'S GOING ON?
IS SHE REALLY GOING TO GO FOR US?
I DON'T KNOW...
I WONDER IF SHE'S IN THE SAME BUSINESS?
OH? HOW UNUSUAL. ARE YOU A TRAVELER?
OH. UH, YES.
OOH, SHE'S HOT!
SHUT UP, SEN.
I HEARD THAT THERE WAS A WITCH LIVING AROUND HERE...
BUT THAT TRAVELER...
...MADE THE MOST TERRIFYING FACE FOR A SECOND.
OH MY!
THAT'S PROBABLY ME.
HUH?

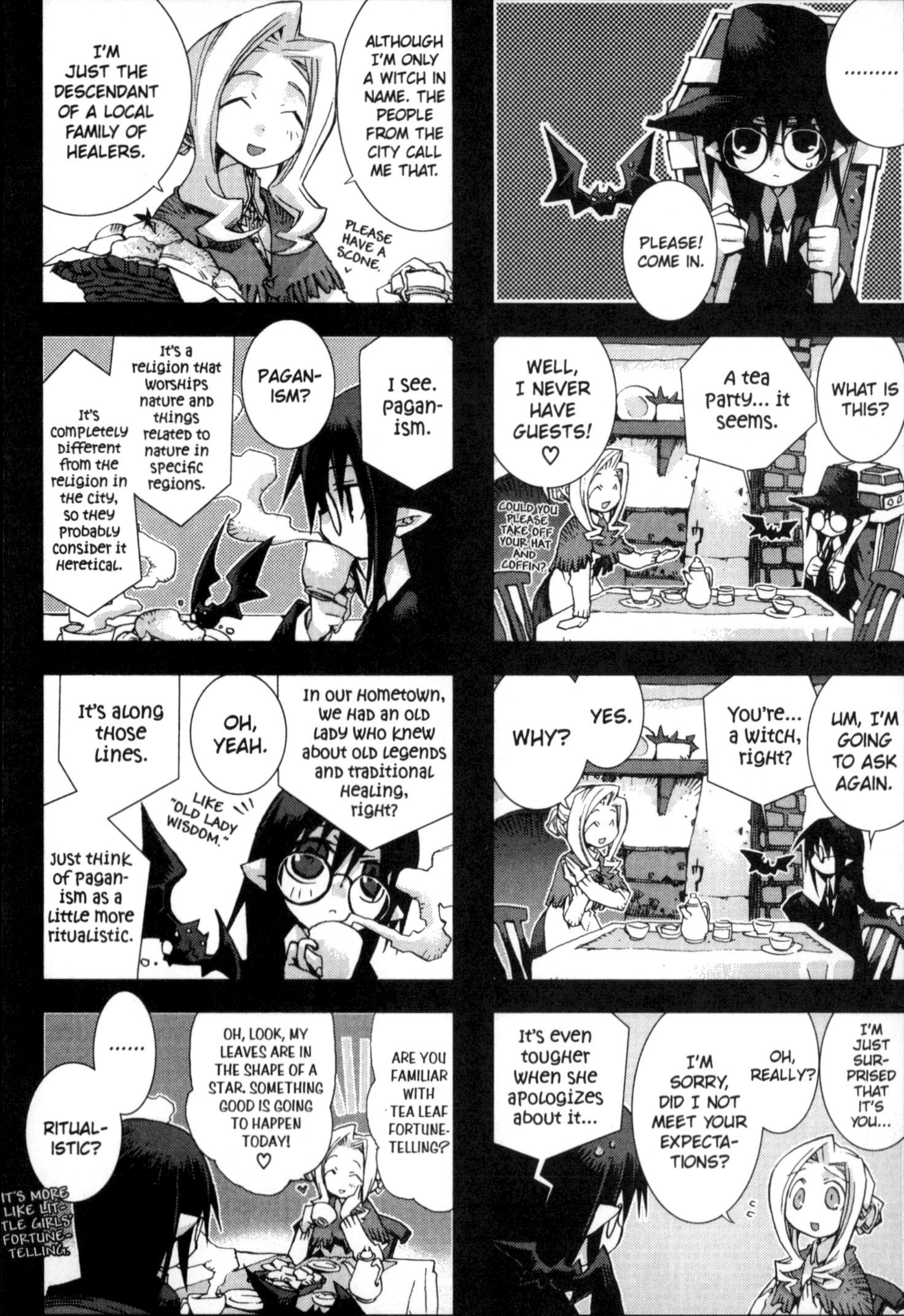

....
PLEASE! COME IN.
WHAT IS THIS?
A tea party... it seems.
WELL, I NEVER HAVE GUESTS! ♡
COULD YOU PLEASE TAKE OFF YOUR HAT AND COFFIN?
UM, I'M GOING TO ASK AGAIN.
You're... a witch, right?
YES.
WHY?
I'M JUST SURPRISED THAT IT'S YOU...
OH, REALLY?
I'M SORRY, DID I NOT MEET YOUR EXPECTATIONS?
It's even tougher when she apologizes about it...
ALTHOUGH I'M ONLY A WITCH IN NAME. THE PEOPLE FROM THE CITY CALL ME THAT.
I'M JUST THE DESCENDANT OF A LOCAL FAMILY OF HEALERS.
PLEASE HAVE A SCONE.
I see. pagan-ism.
PAGAN-ISM?
It's a religion that worships nature and things related to nature in specific regions.
It's completely different from the religion in the city, so they probably consider it heretical.
In our hometown, we had an old lady who knew about old legends and traditional healing, right?
OH, YEAH.
LIKE "OLD LADY WISDOM."
It's along those lines.
Just think of pagan-ism as a little more ritualistic.
ARE YOU FAMILIAR WITH TEA LEAF FORTUNE-TELLING?
OH, LOOK, MY LEAVES ARE IN THE SHAPE OF A STAR. SOMETHING GOOD IS GOING TO HAPPEN TODAY! ♡
......
RITUAL-ISTIC?
IT'S MORE LIKE LIT-TLE GIRLS' FORTUNE-TELLING.

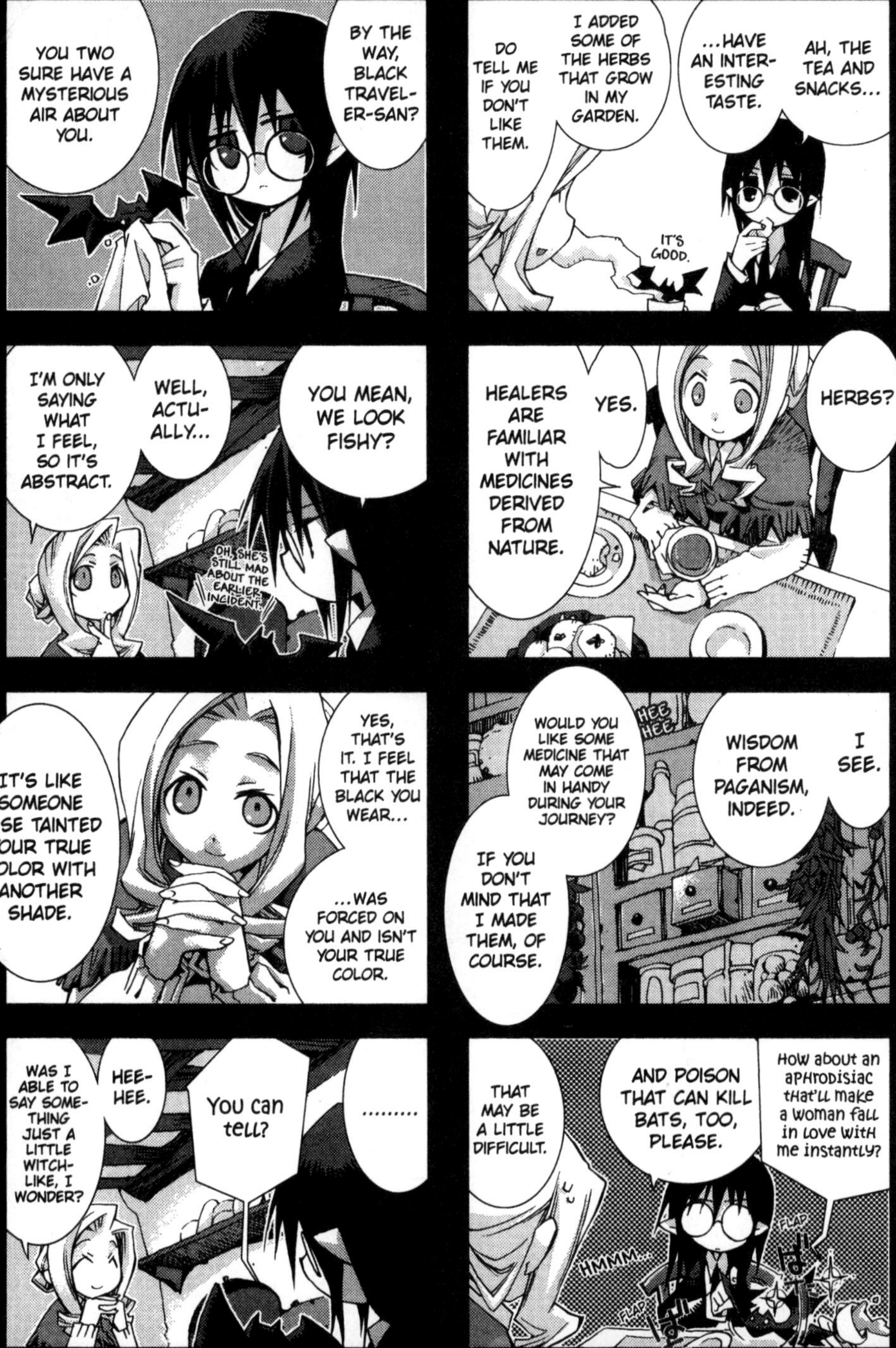
AH, THE TEA AND SNACKS...
...HAVE AN INTERESTING TASTE.
I ADDED SOME OF THE HERBS THAT GROW IN MY GARDEN.
DO TELL ME IF YOU DON'T LIKE THEM.
IT'S GOOD.
BY THE WAY, BLACK TRAVELER-SAN?
YOU TWO SURE HAVE A MYSTERIOUS AIR ABOUT YOU.
HERBS?
YES.
HEALERS ARE FAMILIAR WITH MEDICINES DERIVED FROM NATURE.
YOU MEAN, WE LOOK FISHY?
WELL, ACTUALLY...
I'M ONLY SAYING WHAT I FEEL, SO IT'S ABSTRACT.
OH, SHE'S STILL MAD ABOUT THE EARLIER INCIDENT.
I SEE.
WISDOM FROM PAGANISM, INDEED.
HEE HEE
WOULD YOU LIKE SOME MEDICINE THAT MAY COME IN HANDY DURING YOUR JOURNEY?
IF YOU DON'T MIND THAT I MADE THEM, OF COURSE.
YES, THAT'S IT. I FEEL THAT THE BLACK YOU WEAR...
...WAS FORCED ON YOU AND ISN'T YOUR TRUE COLOR.
IT'S LIKE SOMEONE ELSE TAINTED YOUR TRUE COLOR WITH ANOTHER SHADE.
How about an aphrodisiac that'll make a woman fall in love with me instantly?
AND POISON THAT CAN KILL BATS, TOO, PLEASE.
THAT MAY BE A LITTLE DIFFICULT.
HMMM...
FLAP
FLAP
....
You can tell?
HEE-HEE.
WAS I ABLE TO SAY SOMETHING JUST A LITTLE WITCH-LIKE, I WONDER?

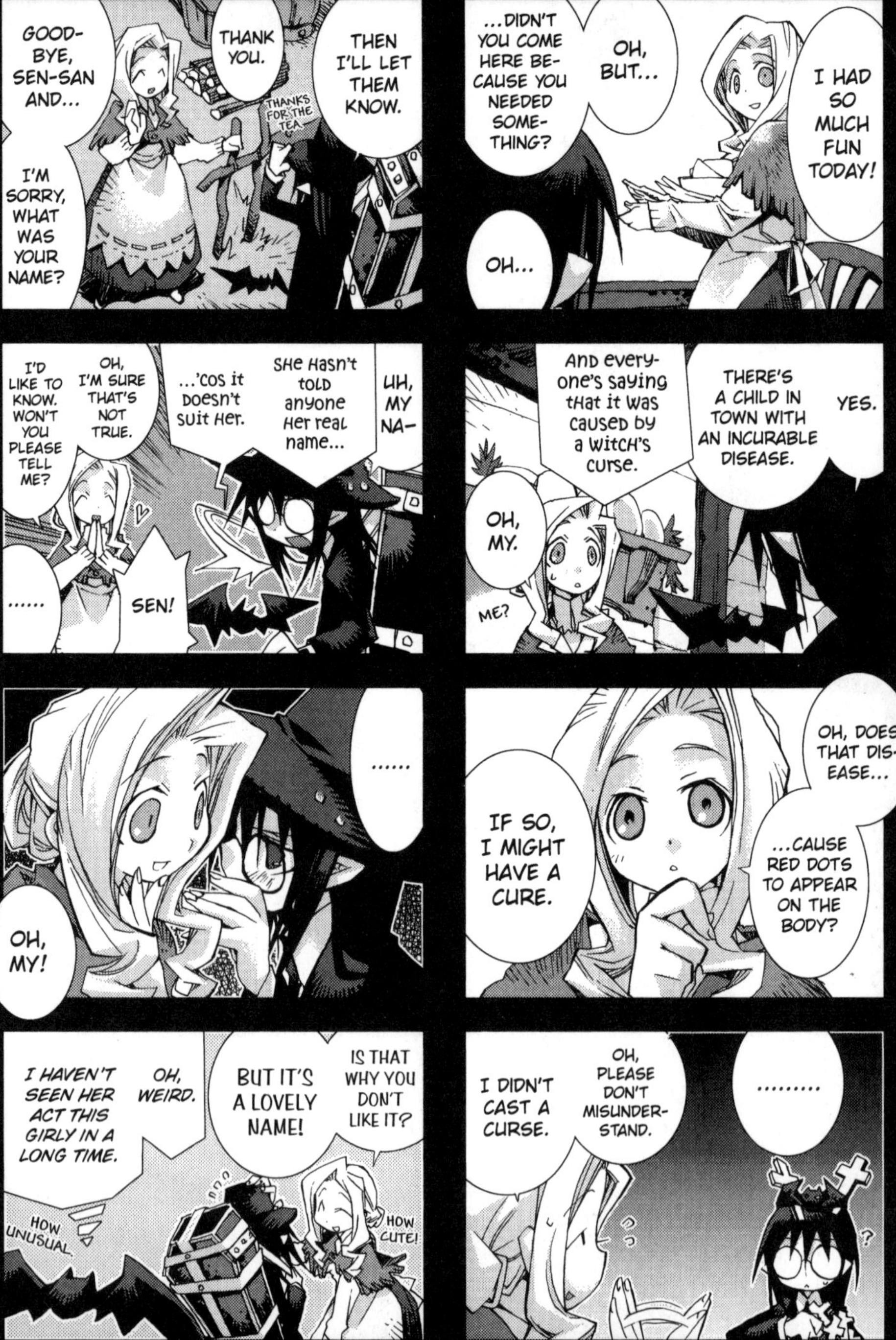
I HAD SO MUCH FUN TODAY!
OH, BUT...
...DIDN'T YOU COME HERE BECAUSE YOU NEEDED SOMETHING?
OH...
THEN I'LL LET THEM KNOW.
THANK YOU.
THANKS FOR THE TEA.
GOOD-BYE, SEN-SAN AND...
I'M SORRY, WHAT WAS YOUR NAME?
YES.
THERE'S A CHILD IN TOWN WITH AN INCURABLE DISEASE.
And everyone's saying that it was caused by a witch's curse.
OH, MY.
ME?
UH, MY NA-
SHE Hasn't told anyone Her real name...
...'cos it doesn't suit Her.
OH, I'M SURE THAT'S NOT TRUE.
I'D LIKE TO KNOW. WON'T YOU PLEASE TELL ME?
SEN!
......
OH, DOES THAT DISEASE...
...CAUSE RED DOTS TO APPEAR ON THE BODY?
IF SO, I MIGHT HAVE A CURE.
......
OH, MY!
....
OH, PLEASE DON'T MISUNDERSTAND.
I DIDN'T CAST A CURSE.
IS THAT WHY YOU DON'T LIKE IT?
BUT IT'S A LOVELY NAME!
OH, WEIRD.
I HAVEN'T SEEN HER ACT THIS GIRLY IN A LONG TIME.
HOW CUTE!
HOW UNUSUAL.

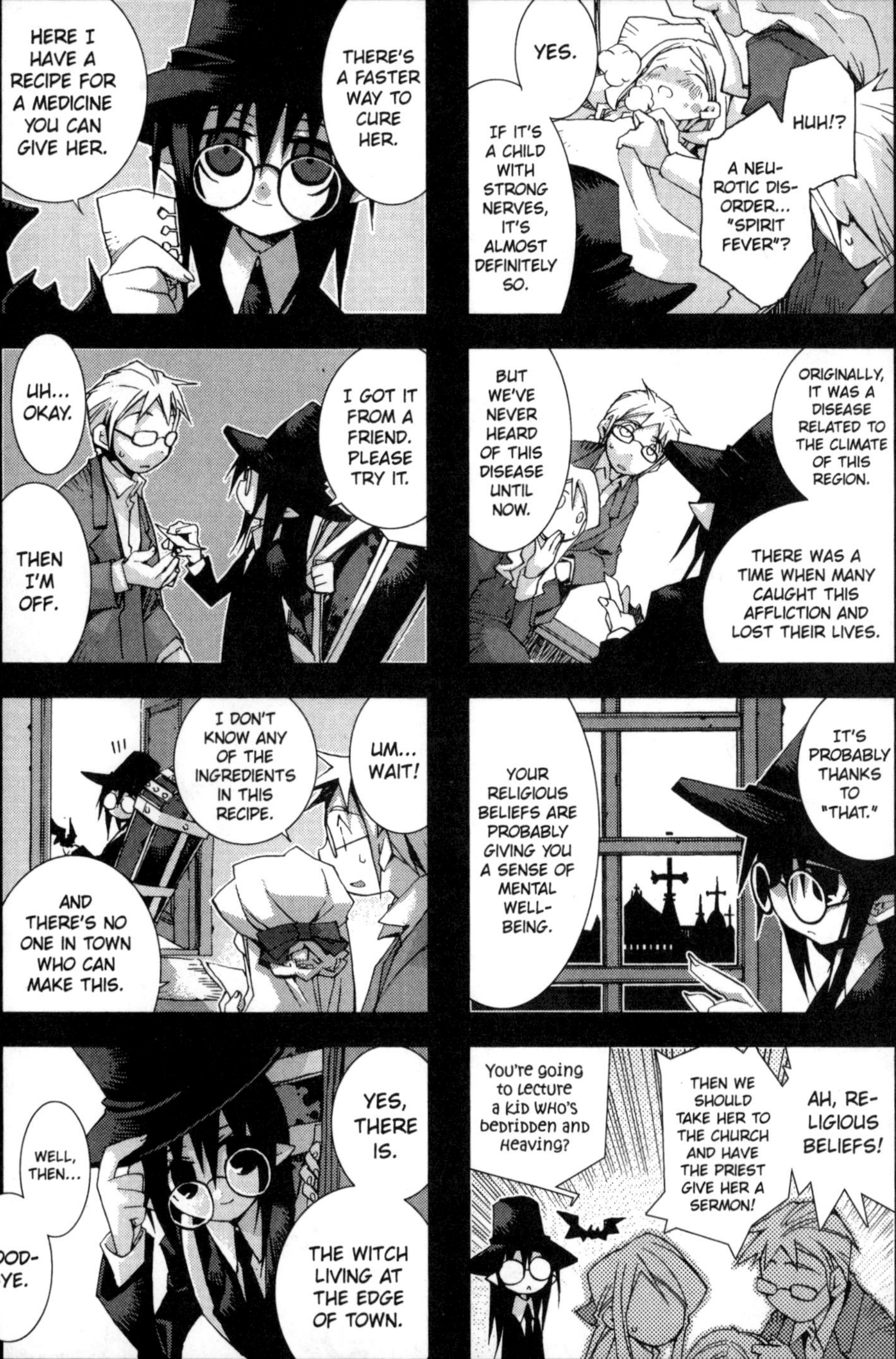
HUH!?
A NEU-ROTIC DIS-ORDER... "SPIRIT FEVER"?
YES.
IF IT'S A CHILD WITH STRONG NERVES, IT'S ALMOST DEFINITELY SO.
BUT WE'VE NEVER HEARD OF THIS DISEASE UNTIL NOW.
ORIGINALLY, IT WAS A DISEASE RELATED TO THE CLIMATE OF THIS REGION.
THERE WAS A TIME WHEN MANY CAUGHT THIS AFFLICTION AND LOST THEIR LIVES.
IT'S PROBABLY THANKS TO "THAT."
YOUR RELIGIOUS BELIEFS ARE PROBABLY GIVING YOU A SENSE OF MENTAL WELL-BEING.
AH, RE-LIGIOUS BELIEFS!
THEN WE SHOULD TAKE HER TO THE CHURCH AND HAVE THE PRIEST GIVE HER A SERMON!
You're going to lecture a kid WHO's bedridden and Heaving?
THERE'S A FASTER WAY TO CURE HER.
HERE I HAVE A RECIPE FOR A MEDICINE YOU CAN GIVE HER.
I GOT IT FROM A FRIEND. PLEASE TRY IT.
UH... OKAY.
THEN I'M OFF.
UM... WAIT!
I DON'T KNOW ANY OF THE INGREDIENTS IN THIS RECIPE.
AND THERE'S NO ONE IN TOWN WHO CAN MAKE THIS.
YES, THERE IS.
THE WITCH LIVING AT THE EDGE OF TOWN.
WELL, THEN...
GOOD-BYE.

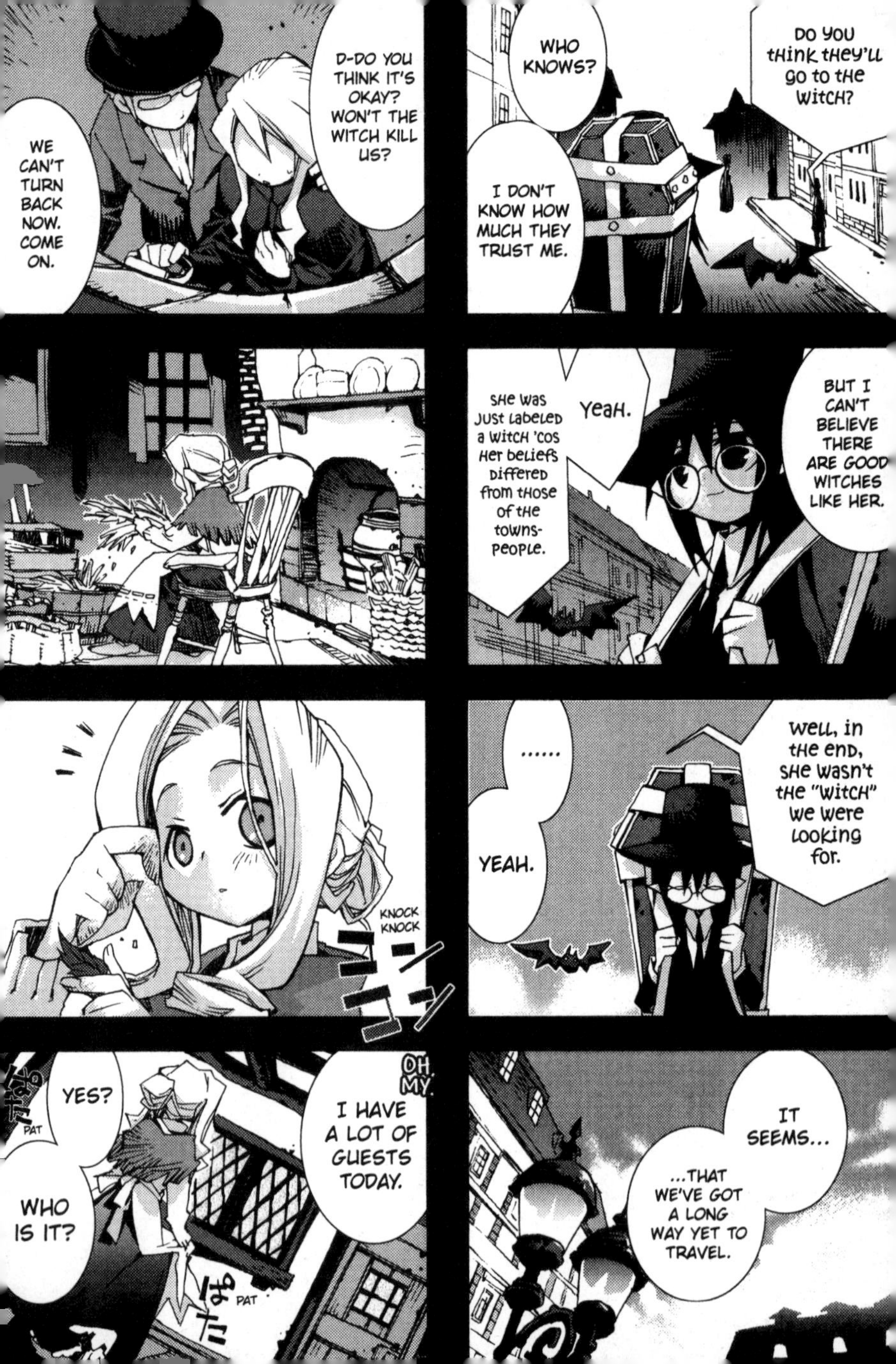
DO YOU THINK THEY'LL GO TO THE WITCH?
WHO KNOWS?
I DON'T KNOW HOW MUCH THEY TRUST ME.
D-DO YOU THINK IT'S OKAY? WON'T THE WITCH KILL US?
WE CAN'T TURN BACK NOW. COME ON.
BUT I CAN'T BELIEVE THERE ARE GOOD WITCHES LIKE HER.
YeaH.
SHE WAS JUST LABELED A WITCH 'COS HER BELIEFS DIFFERED FROM THOSE OF THE TOWNS-PEOPLE.
WELL, IN THE END, SHE WASN'T THE "WITCH" WE WERE LOOKING FOR.
......
YEAH.
KNOCK KNOCK
IT SEEMS...
...THAT WE'VE GOT A LONG WAY YET TO TRAVEL.
OH MY.
I HAVE A LOT OF GUESTS TODAY.
YES?
PAT
WHO IS IT?
PAT

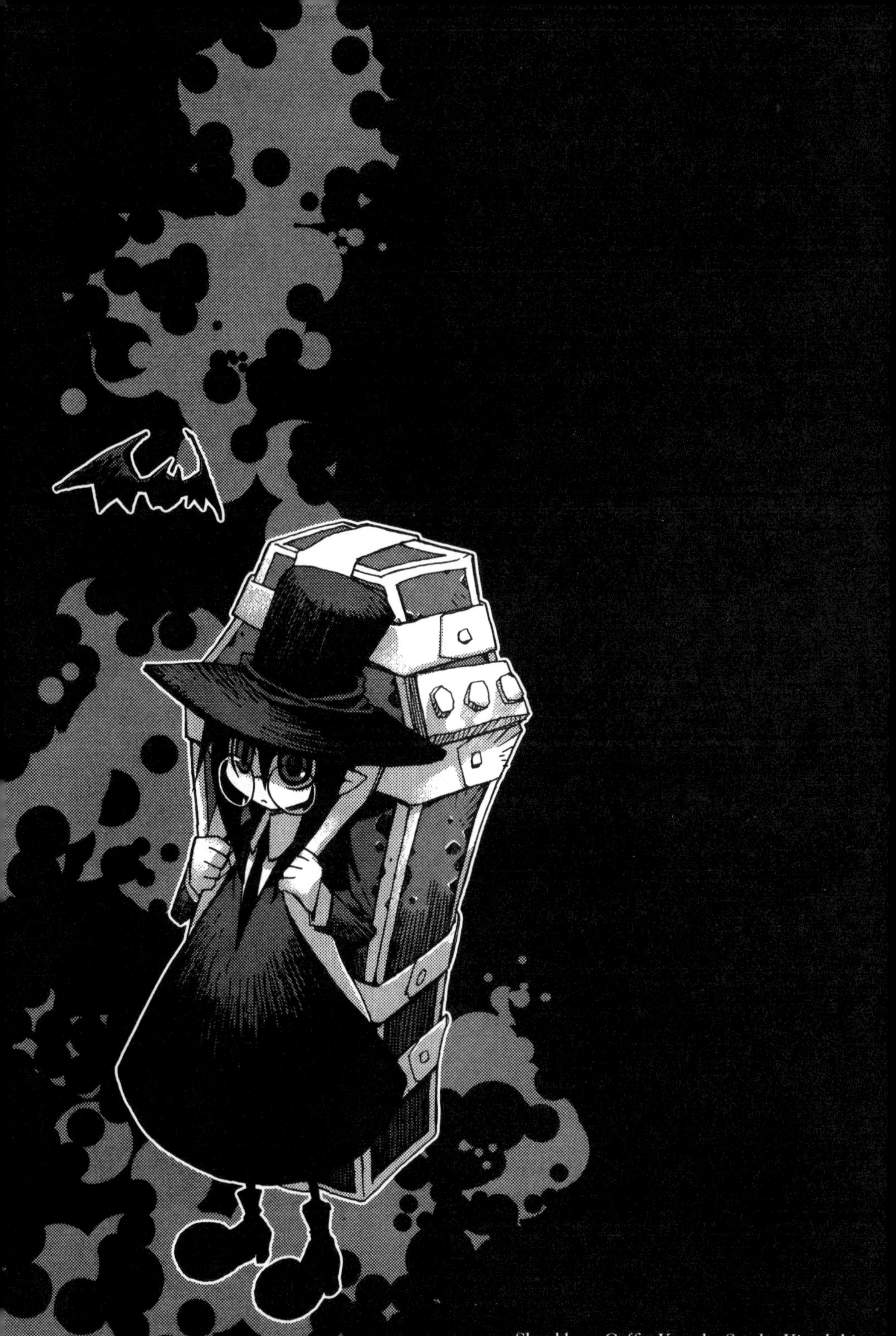

Shoulder-a-Coffin Kuro by Satoko Kiyuduki

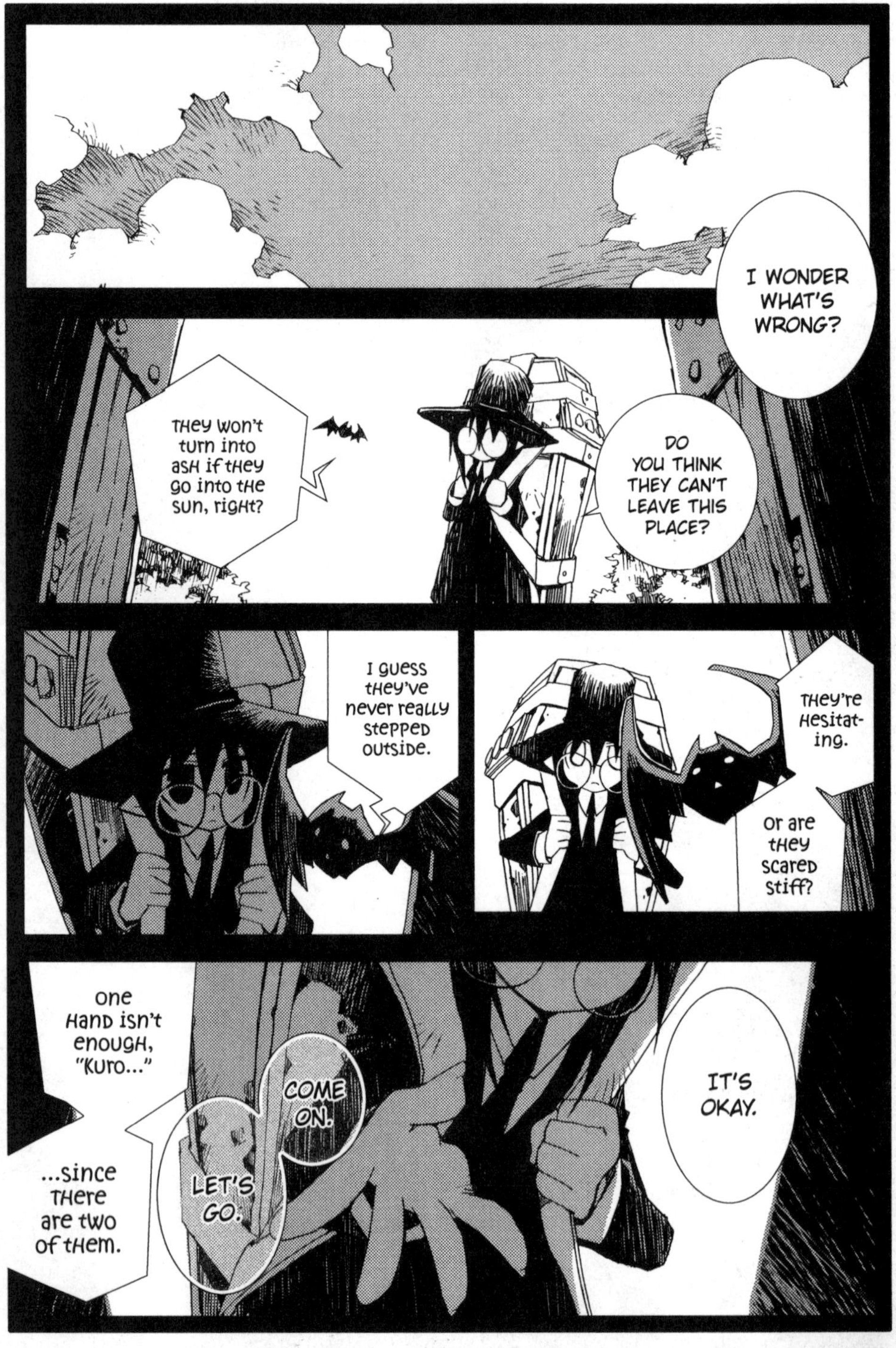
I WONDER WHAT'S WRONG?
DO YOU THINK THEY CAN'T LEAVE THIS PLACE?
THEY WON'T TURN INTO ASH IF THEY GO INTO THE SUN, RIGHT?
THEY'RE HESITAT-ING.
OR ARE THEY SCARED STIFF?
I GUESS THEY'VE NEVER REALLY STEPPED OUTSIDE.
IT'S OKAY.
COME ON.
LET'S GO.
ONE HAND ISN'T ENOUGH, "KURO..."
...SINCE THERE ARE TWO OF THEM.

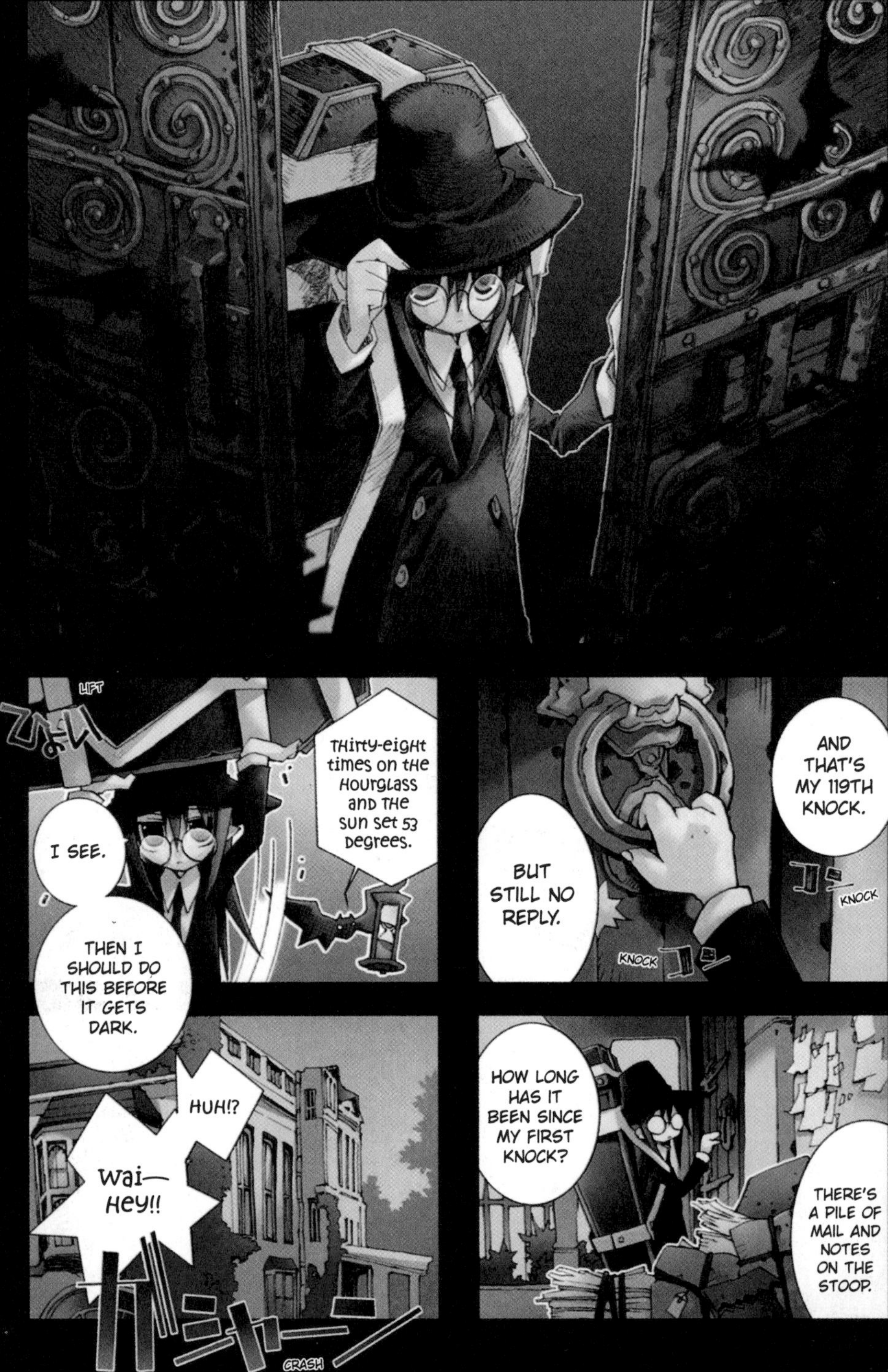
AND THAT'S MY 119TH KNOCK.
KNOCK
BUT STILL NO REPLY.
KNOCK
LIFT
Thirty-eight times on the Hourglass and the sun set 53 degrees.
I SEE.
THEN I SHOULD DO THIS BEFORE IT GETS DARK.
THERE'S A PILE OF MAIL AND NOTES ON THE STOOP.
HOW LONG HAS IT BEEN SINCE MY FIRST KNOCK?
HUH!?
Wai— Hey!!
CRASH

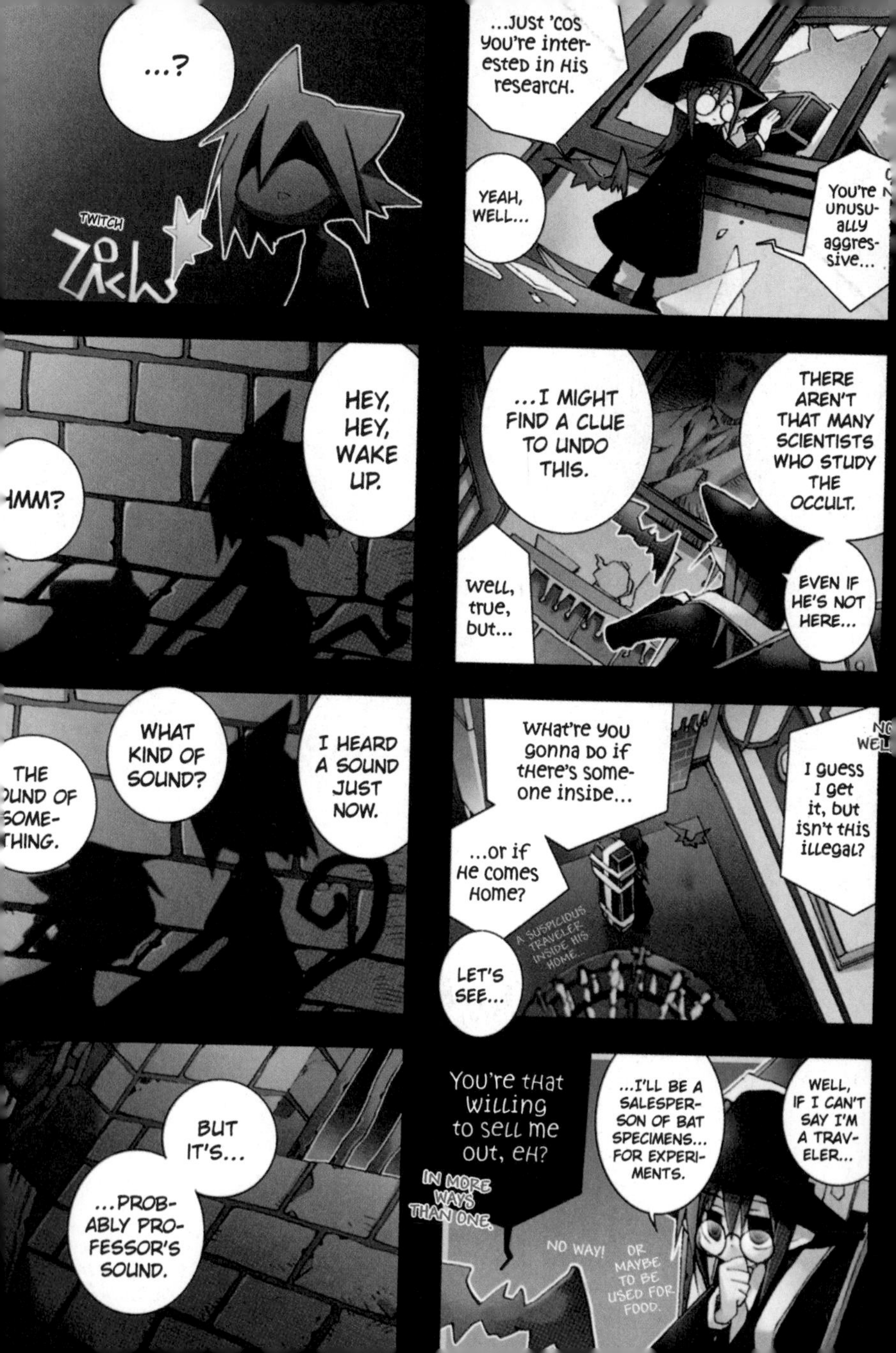
You're n
unusually aggressive...
YEAH, WELL...
...JUST 'COS YOU'RE INTERESTED IN HIS RESEARCH.
...?
TWITCH
THERE AREN'T THAT MANY SCIENTISTS WHO STUDY THE OCCULT.
EVEN IF HE'S NOT HERE...
...I MIGHT FIND A CLUE TO UNDO THIS.
Well, true, but...
HEY, HEY, WAKE UP.
HMM?
NO
WEL
I guess I get it, but isn't this illegal?
What're you gonna do if there's someone inside...
...or if he comes home?
A SUSPICIOUS TRAVELER INSIDE HIS HOME...
LET'S SEE...
I HEARD A SOUND JUST NOW.
WHAT KIND OF SOUND?
THE
UND OF
OME-
THING.
WELL, IF I CAN'T SAY I'M A TRAVELER...
...I'LL BE A SALESPERSON OF BAT SPECIMENS... FOR EXPERIMENTS.
You're that willing to sell me out, eh?
IN MORE WAYS THAN ONE.
NO WAY!
OR MAYBE TO BE USED FOR FOOD.
BUT IT'S...
...PROBABLY PROFESSOR'S SOUND.

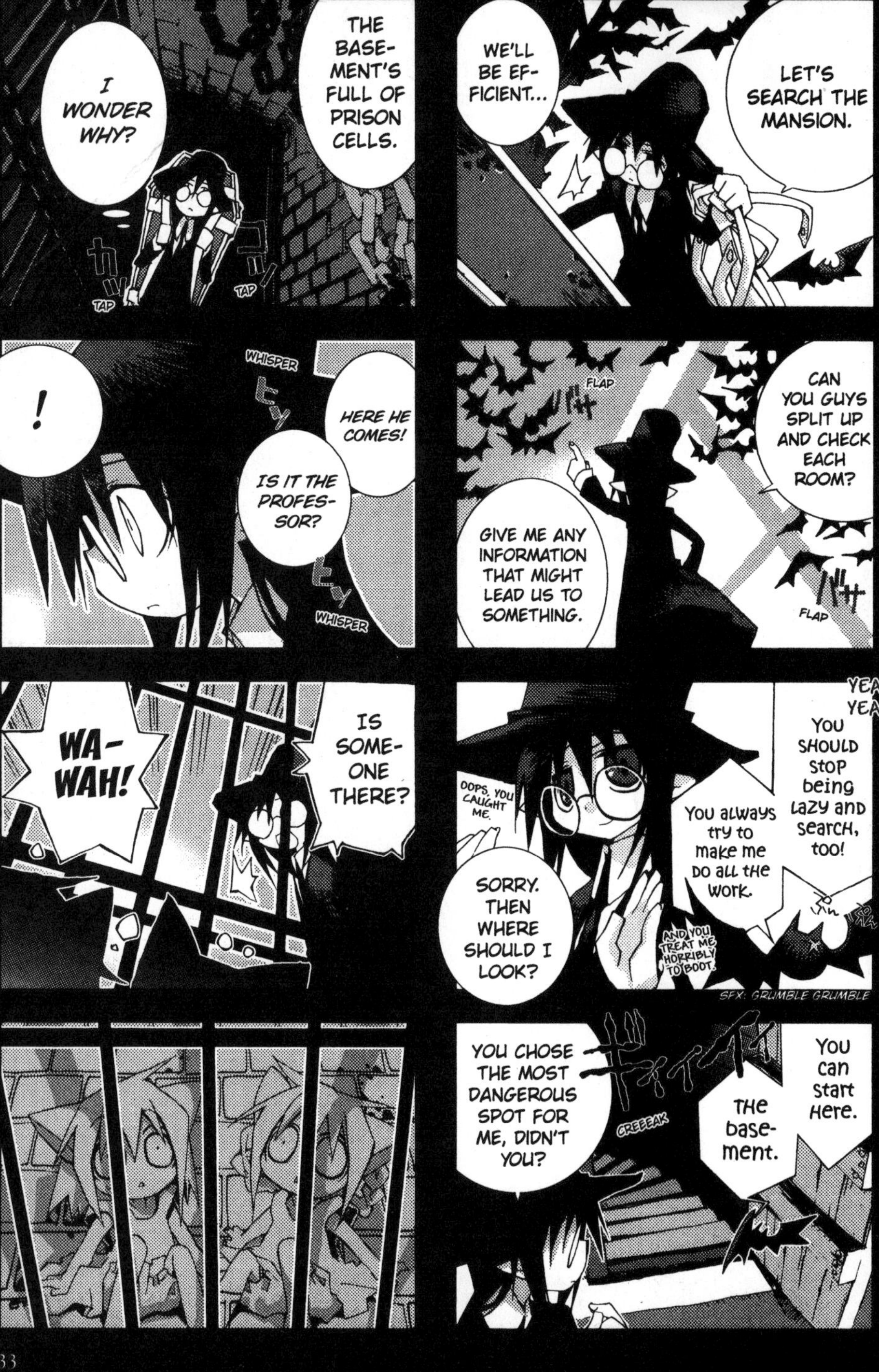
LET'S SEARCH THE MANSION.
WE'LL BE EFFICIENT...
THE BASEMENT'S FULL OF PRISON CELLS.
I WONDER WHY?
TAP
TAP
CAN YOU GUYS SPLIT UP AND CHECK EACH ROOM?
FLAP
GIVE ME ANY INFORMATION THAT MIGHT LEAD US TO SOMETHING.
FLAP
WHISPER
HERE HE COMES!
IS IT THE PROFESSOR?
WHISPER
!
YEAH, YEAH.
You should stop being lazy and search, too!
You always try to make me do all the work.
OOPS, YOU CAUGHT ME.
SORRY. THEN WHERE SHOULD I LOOK?
AND YOU TREAT ME HORRIBLY TO BOOT.
SFX: GRUMBLE GRUMBLE
IS SOMEONE THERE?
WA-WAH!
You can start here.
The basement.
CREEEAK
YOU CHOSE THE MOST DANGEROUS SPOT FOR ME, DIDN'T YOU?

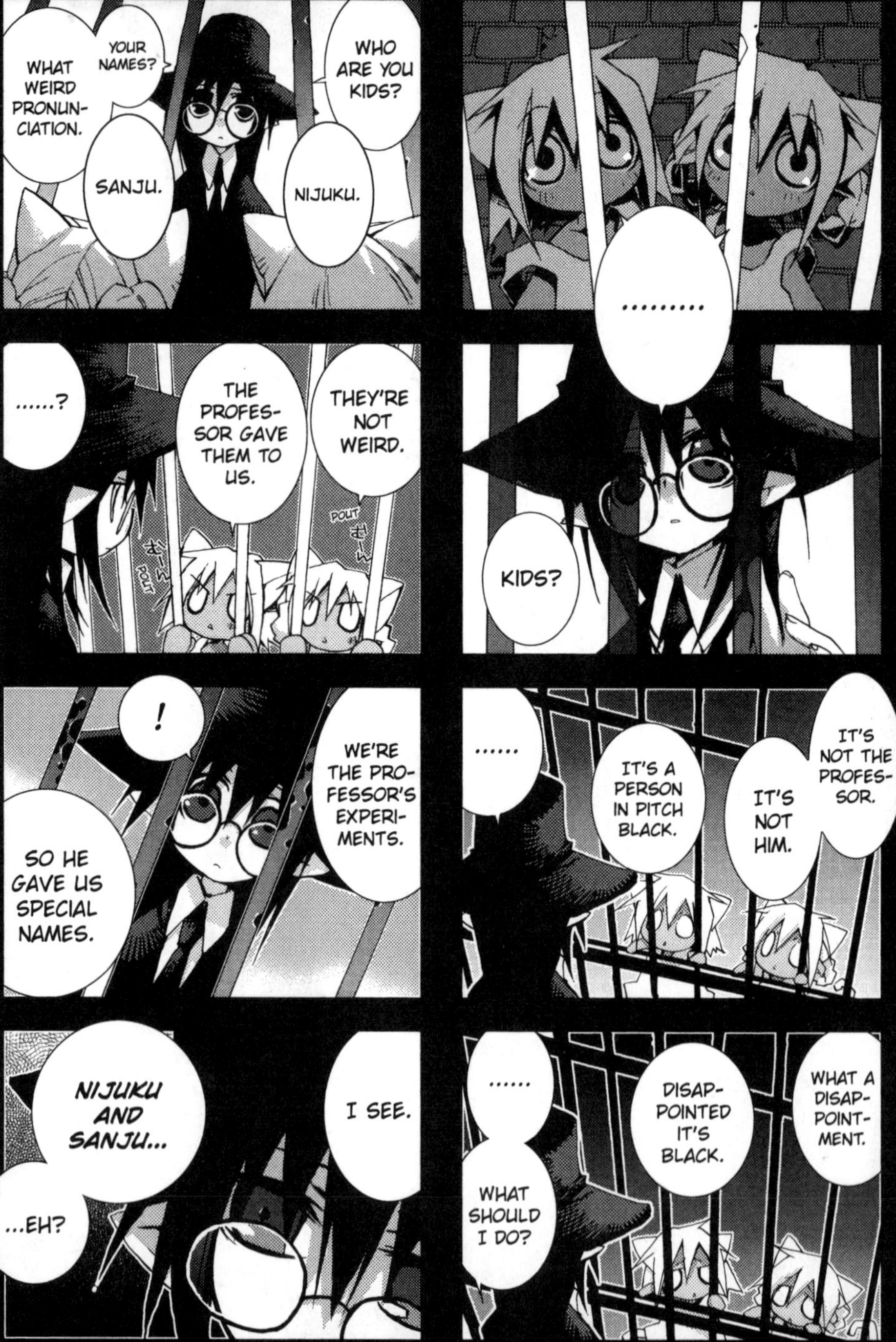
WHO ARE YOU KIDS?
YOUR NAMES?
NIJUKU.
SANJU.
WHAT WEIRD PRONUNCIATION.
....
THEY'RE NOT WEIRD.
THE PROFESSOR GAVE THEM TO US.
POUT むーん
POUT むーん
......?
KIDS?
!
WE'RE THE PROFESSOR'S EXPERIMENTS.
SO HE GAVE US SPECIAL NAMES.
IT'S NOT THE PROFESSOR.
IT'S NOT HIM.
IT'S A PERSON IN PITCH BLACK.
......
I SEE.
NIJUKU AND SANJU...
...EH?
WHAT A DISAPPOINTMENT.
DISAPPOINTED IT'S BLACK.
......
WHAT SHOULD I DO?

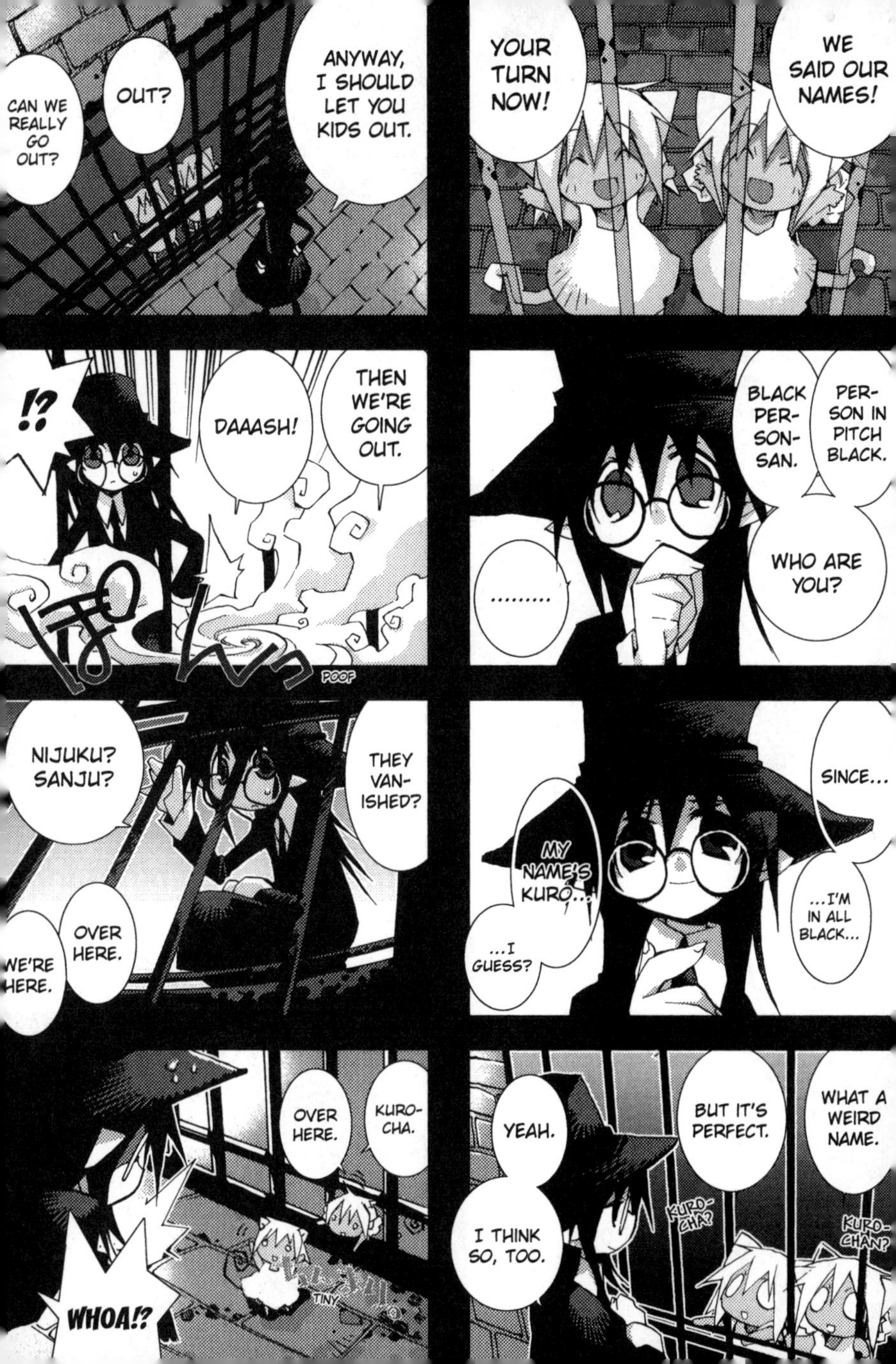
WE SAID OUR NAMES!
YOUR TURN NOW!
ANYWAY, I SHOULD LET YOU KIDS OUT.
OUT?
CAN WE REALLY GO OUT?
PER-SON IN PITCH BLACK.
BLACK PER-SON-SAN.
WHO ARE YOU?
....
THEN WE'RE GOING OUT.
DAAASH!
!?
POOF
SINCE...
...I'M IN ALL BLACK...
MY NAME'S KURO...
...I GUESS?
THEY VAN-ISHED?
NIJUKU? SANJU?
OVER HERE.
WE'RE HERE.
WHAT A WEIRD NAME.
BUT IT'S PERFECT.
YEAH.
I THINK SO, TOO.
KURO-CHAN?
KURO-CHA?
KURO-CHA.
OVER HERE.
WHOA!?
TINY

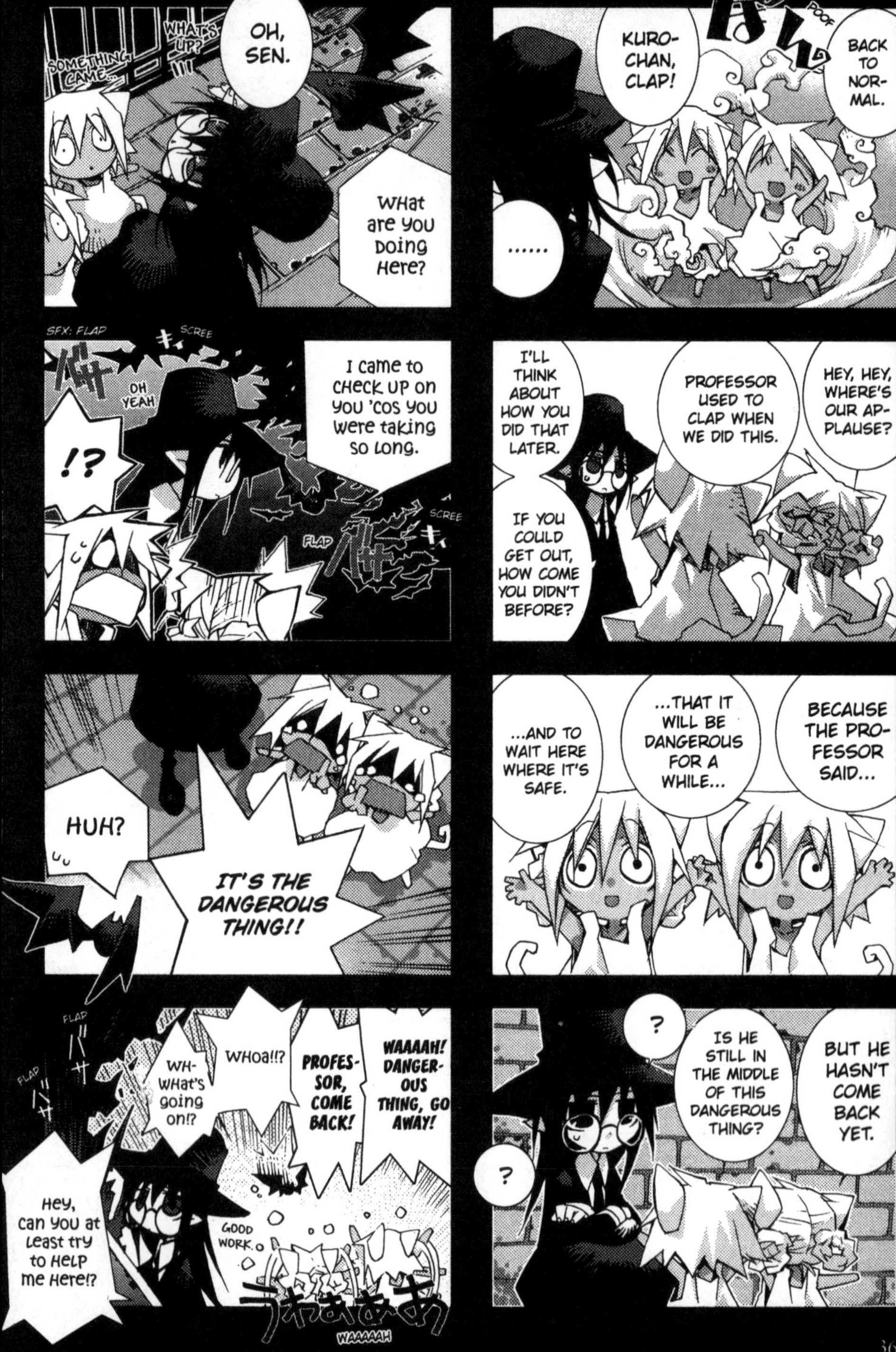
BACK TO NOR-MAL.
POOF
KURO-CHAN, CLAP!
......
OH, SEN.
WHAT'S UP?
SOMETHING CAME...
What are you doing here?
HEY, HEY, WHERE'S OUR AP-PLAUSE?
PROFESSOR USED TO CLAP WHEN WE DID THIS.
I'LL THINK ABOUT HOW YOU DID THAT LATER.
IF YOU COULD GET OUT, HOW COME YOU DIDN'T BEFORE?
I came to check up on you 'cos you were taking so long.
SCREE
SFX: FLAP
OH YEAH
!?
SCREE
FLAP
BECAUSE THE PRO-FESSOR SAID...
...THAT IT WILL BE DANGEROUS FOR A WHILE...
...AND TO WAIT HERE WHERE IT'S SAFE.
IT'S THE DANGEROUS THING!!
HUH?
BUT HE HASN'T COME BACK YET.
IS HE STILL IN THE MIDDLE OF THIS DANGEROUS THING?
?
?
WAAAAH! DANGER-OUS THING, GO AWAY!
PROFES-SOR, COME BACK!
WHoa!!?
WH-WHat's going on!?
FLAP
FLAP
GOOD WORK.
Hey, can you at least try to help me here!?
WAAAAAH

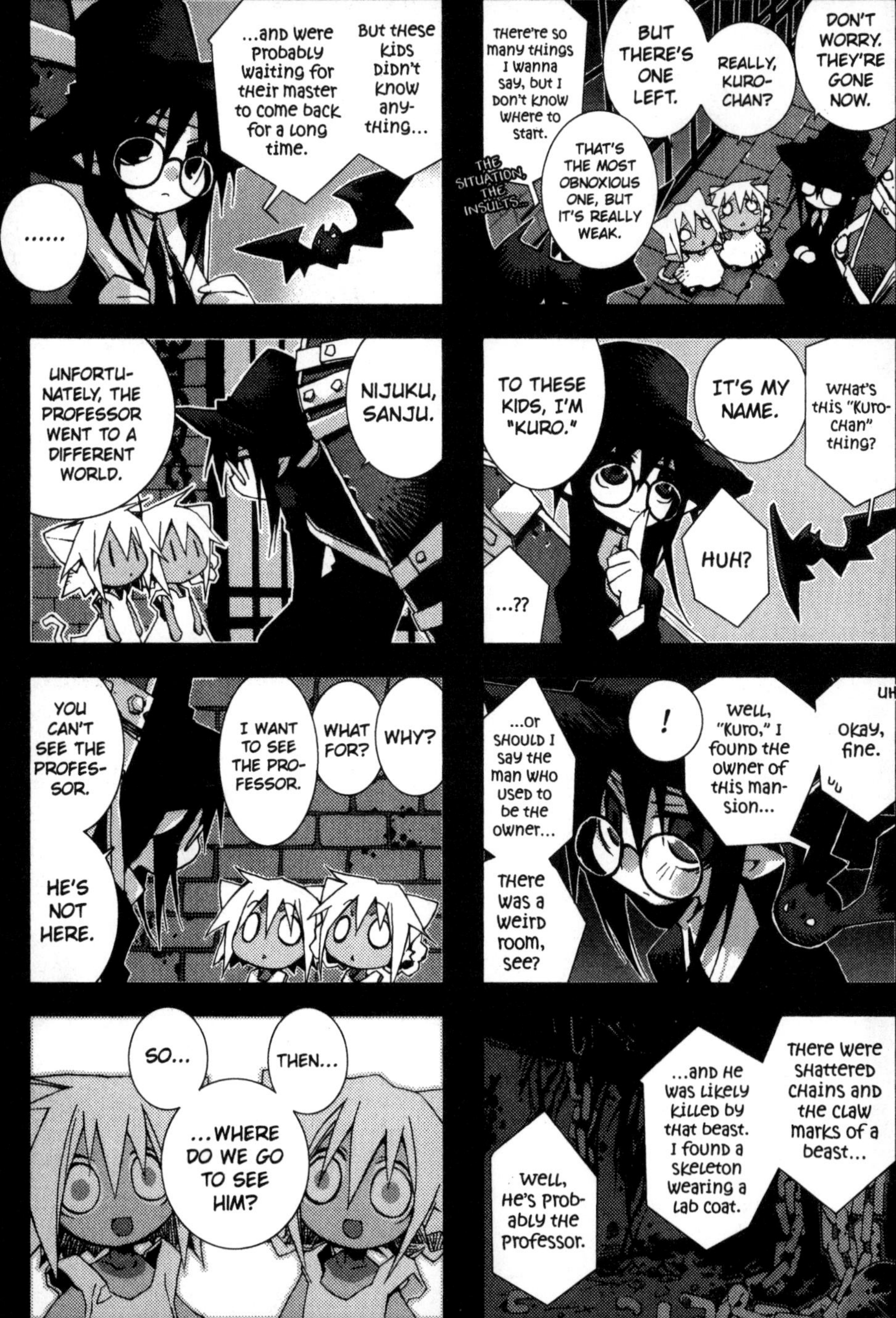
DON'T WORRY. THEY'RE GONE NOW.
REALLY, KURO-CHAN?
BUT THERE'S ONE LEFT.
THAT'S THE MOST OBNOXIOUS ONE, BUT IT'S REALLY WEAK.
There're so many things I wanna say, but I don't know where to start.
THE SITUATION, THE INSULTS...
What's this "Kuro-chan" thing?
IT'S MY NAME.
TO THESE KIDS, I'M "KURO."
HUH?
...??
UH
Okay, fine.
Well, "Kuro," I found the owner of this mansion...
!
...or SHOULD I say the man who used to be the owner...
There was a weird room, see?
There were shattered chains and the claw marks of a beast...
...and he was likely killed by that beast. I found a skeleton wearing a lab coat.
Well, he's probably the professor.
But these kids didn't know anything...
...and were probably waiting for their master to come back for a long time.
......
NIJUKU, SANJU.
UNFORTUNATELY, THE PROFESSOR WENT TO A DIFFERENT WORLD.
WHY?
WHAT FOR?
I WANT TO SEE THE PROFESSOR.
YOU CAN'T SEE THE PROFESSOR.
HE'S NOT HERE.
THEN...
SO...
...WHERE DO WE GO TO SEE HIM?

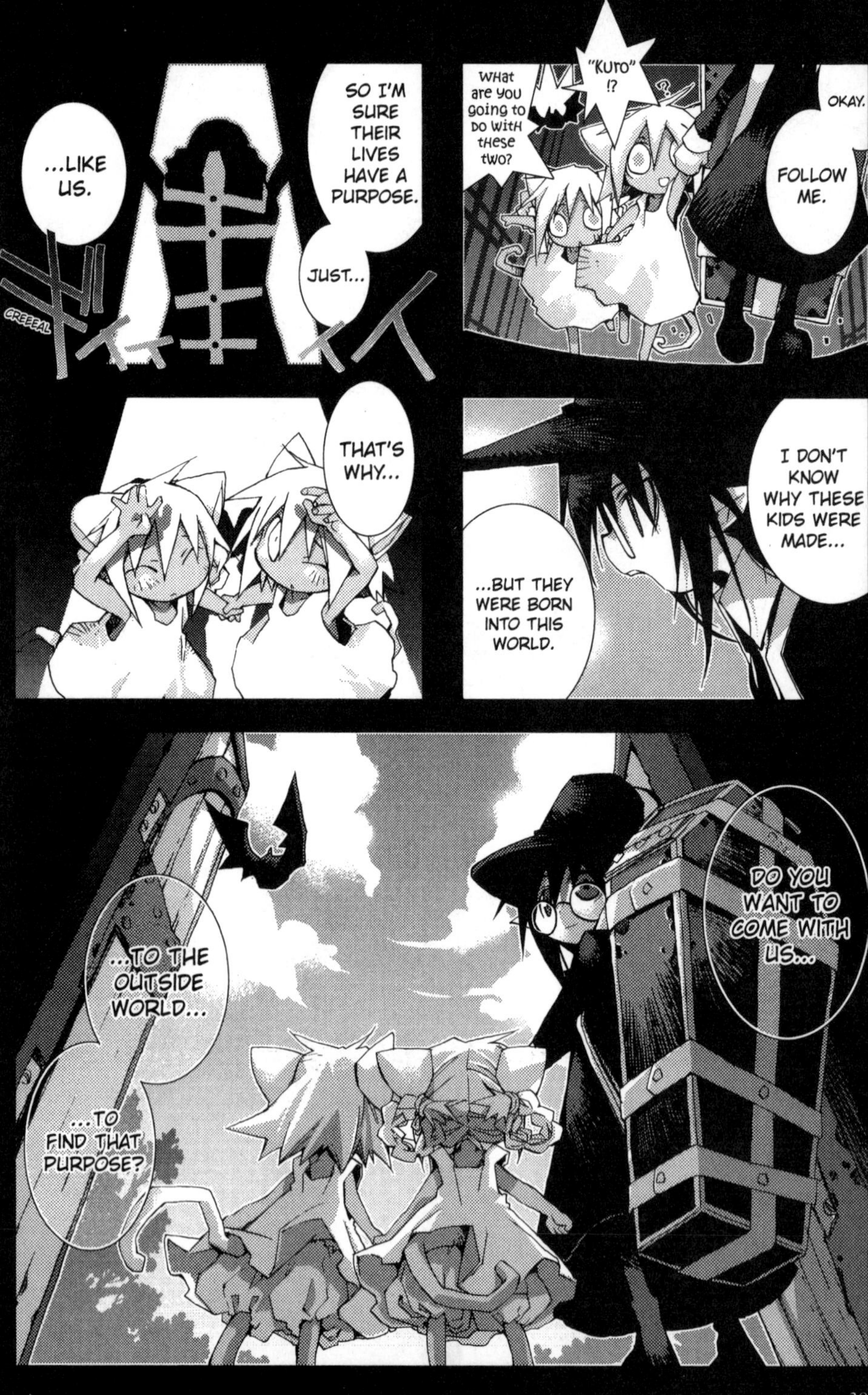
OKAY.
FOLLOW ME.
"KURO" !?
WHAT ARE YOU GOING TO DO WITH THESE TWO?
SO I'M SURE THEIR LIVES HAVE A PURPOSE.
JUST...
...LIKE US.
CREEEAL
I DON'T KNOW WHY THESE KIDS WERE MADE...
...BUT THEY WERE BORN INTO THIS WORLD.
THAT'S WHY...
DO YOU WANT TO COME WITH US...
...TO THE OUTSIDE WORLD...
...TO FIND THAT PURPOSE?

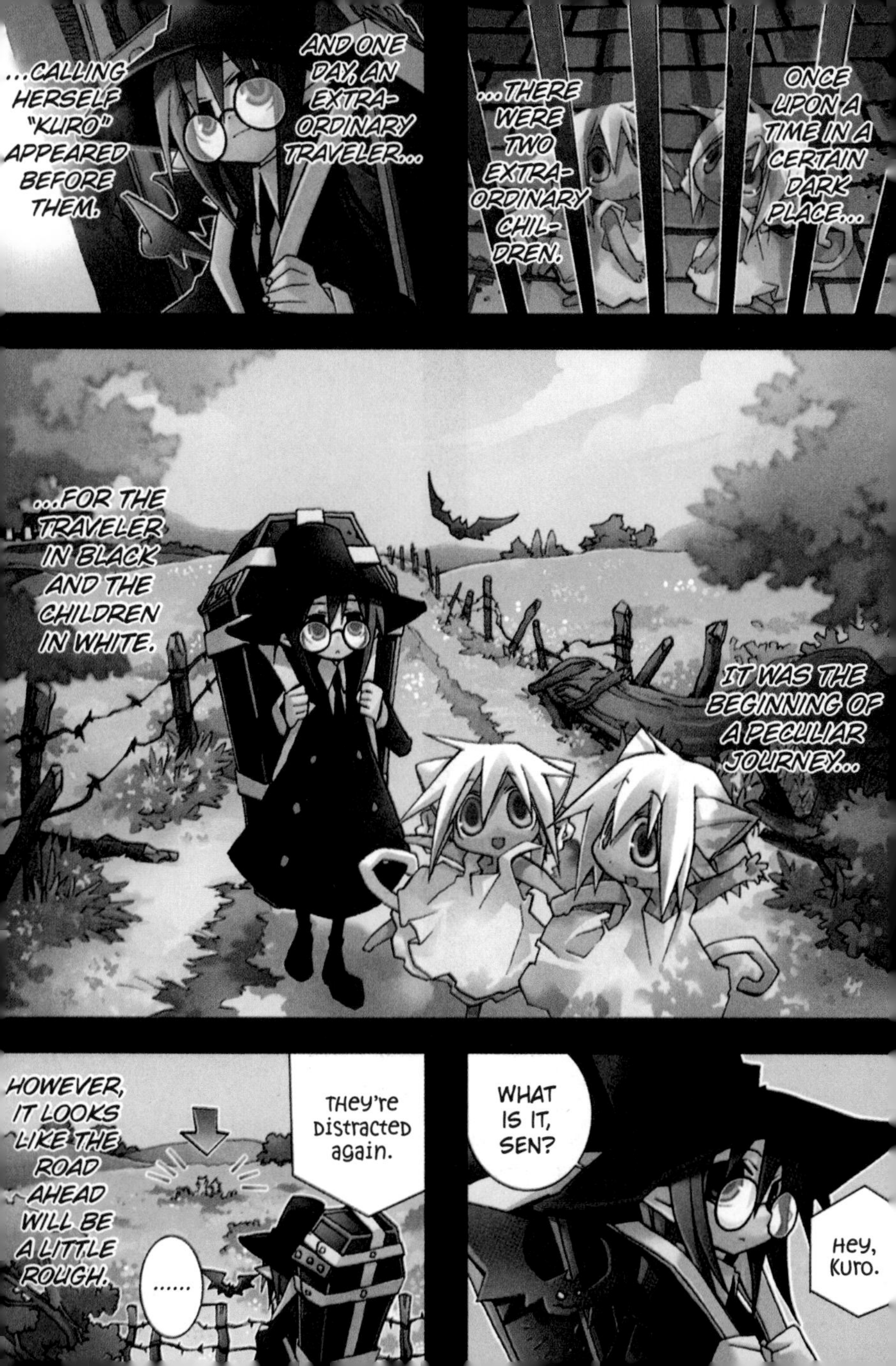
ONCE UPON A TIME IN A CERTAIN DARK PLACE...
...THERE WERE TWO EXTRA-ORDINARY CHIL-DREN.
AND ONE DAY, AN EXTRA-ORDINARY TRAVELER...
...CALLING HERSELF "KURO" APPEARED BEFORE THEM.
IT WAS THE BEGINNING OF A PECULIAR JOURNEY...
...FOR THE TRAVELER IN BLACK AND THE CHILDREN IN WHITE.
Hey, Kuro.
WHAT IS IT, SEN?
They're distracted again.
......
HOWEVER, IT LOOKS LIKE THE ROAD AHEAD WILL BE A LITTLE ROUGH.

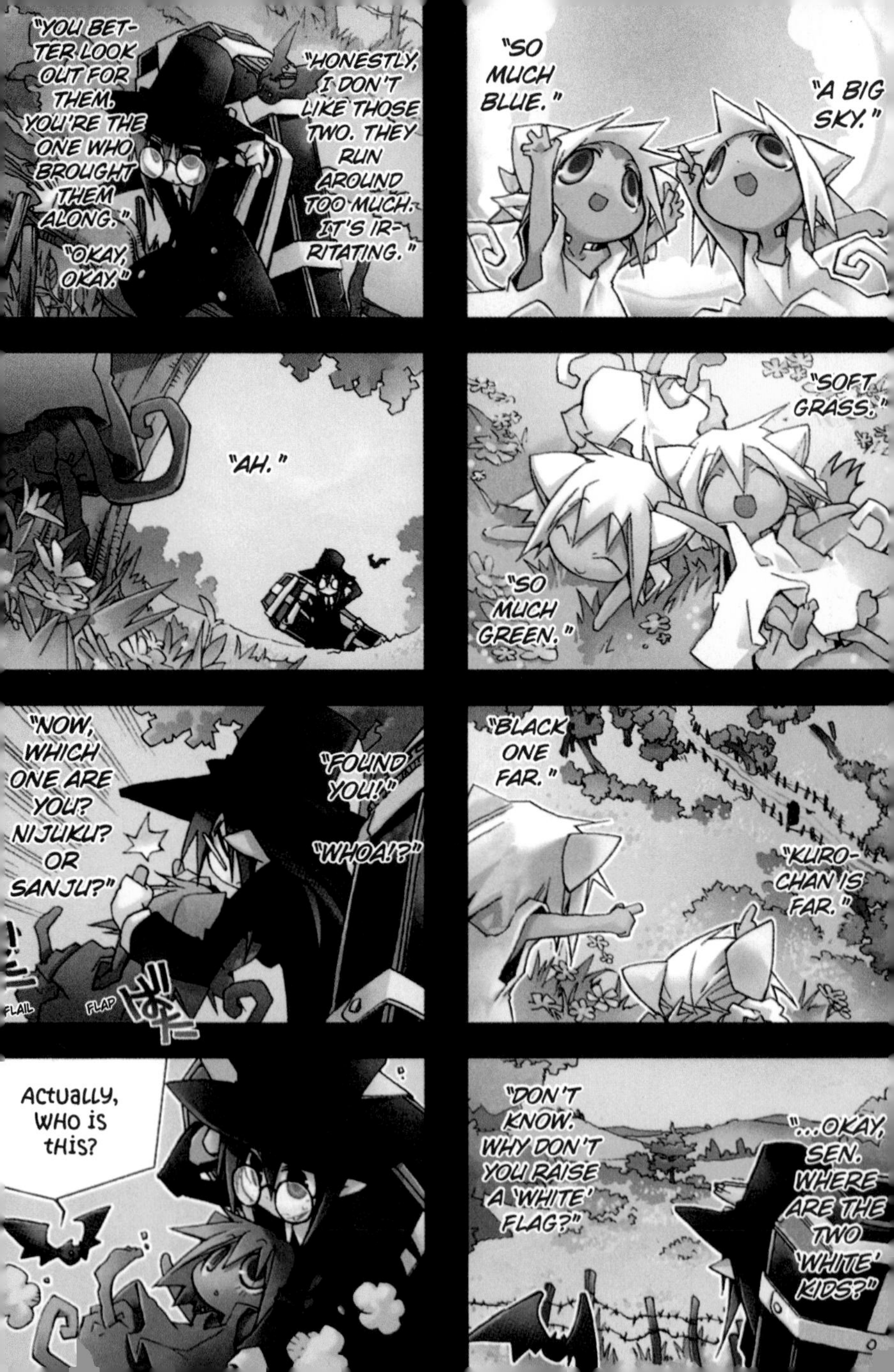
"A BIG SKY."
"SO MUCH BLUE."
"HONESTLY, I DON'T LIKE THOSE TWO. THEY RUN AROUND TOO MUCH. IT'S IR-RITATING."
"YOU BET-TER LOOK OUT FOR THEM. YOU'RE THE ONE WHO BROUGHT THEM ALONG."
"OKAY, OKAY."
"SOFT GRASS."
"SO MUCH GREEN."
"AH."
"BLACK ONE FAR."
"KURO-CHAN IS FAR."
"FOUND YOU!"
"WHOA!?"
"NOW, WHICH ONE ARE YOU? NIJUKU? OR SANJU?"
FLAP
FLAIL
"...OKAY, SEN. WHERE ARE THE TWO 'WHITE' KIDS?"
"DON'T KNOW. WHY DON'T YOU RAISE A 'WHITE' FLAG?"
Actually, who is this?

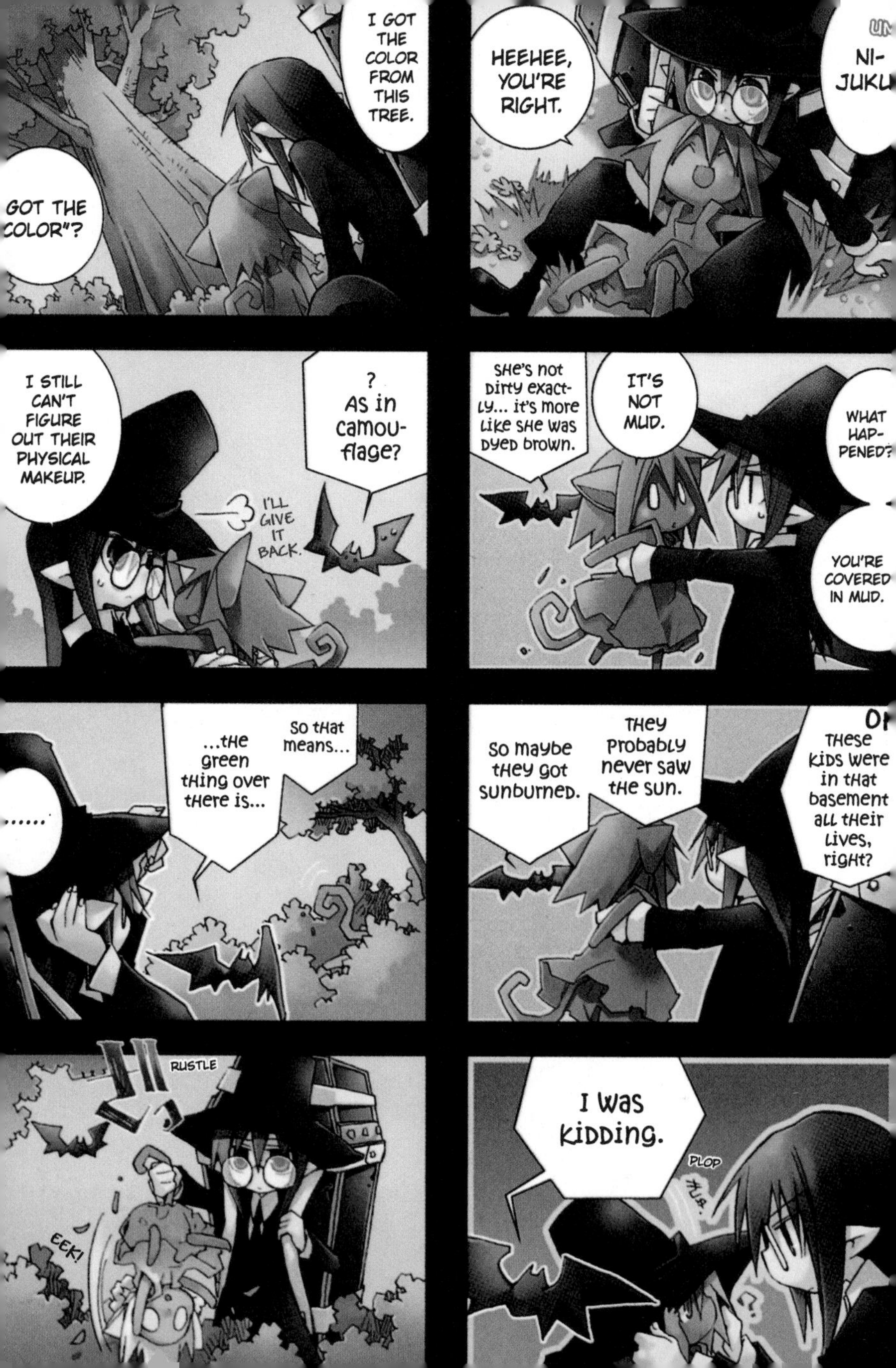
NI-JUKU
HEEHEE, YOU'RE RIGHT.
I GOT THE COLOR FROM THIS TREE.
GOT THE COLOR"?
WHAT HAP-PENED?
YOU'RE COVERED IN MUD.
IT'S NOT MUD.
SHE'S not Dirty exact-ly... it's more like SHE was Dyed brown.
? As in camou-flage?
I'LL GIVE IT BACK.
I STILL CAN'T FIGURE OUT THEIR PHYSICAL MAKEUP.
These kids were in that basement all their lives, right?
They probably never saw the sun.
So maybe they got sunburned.
So that means...
...the green thing over there is...
......
I was kidding.
PLOP
RUSTLE
EEK!

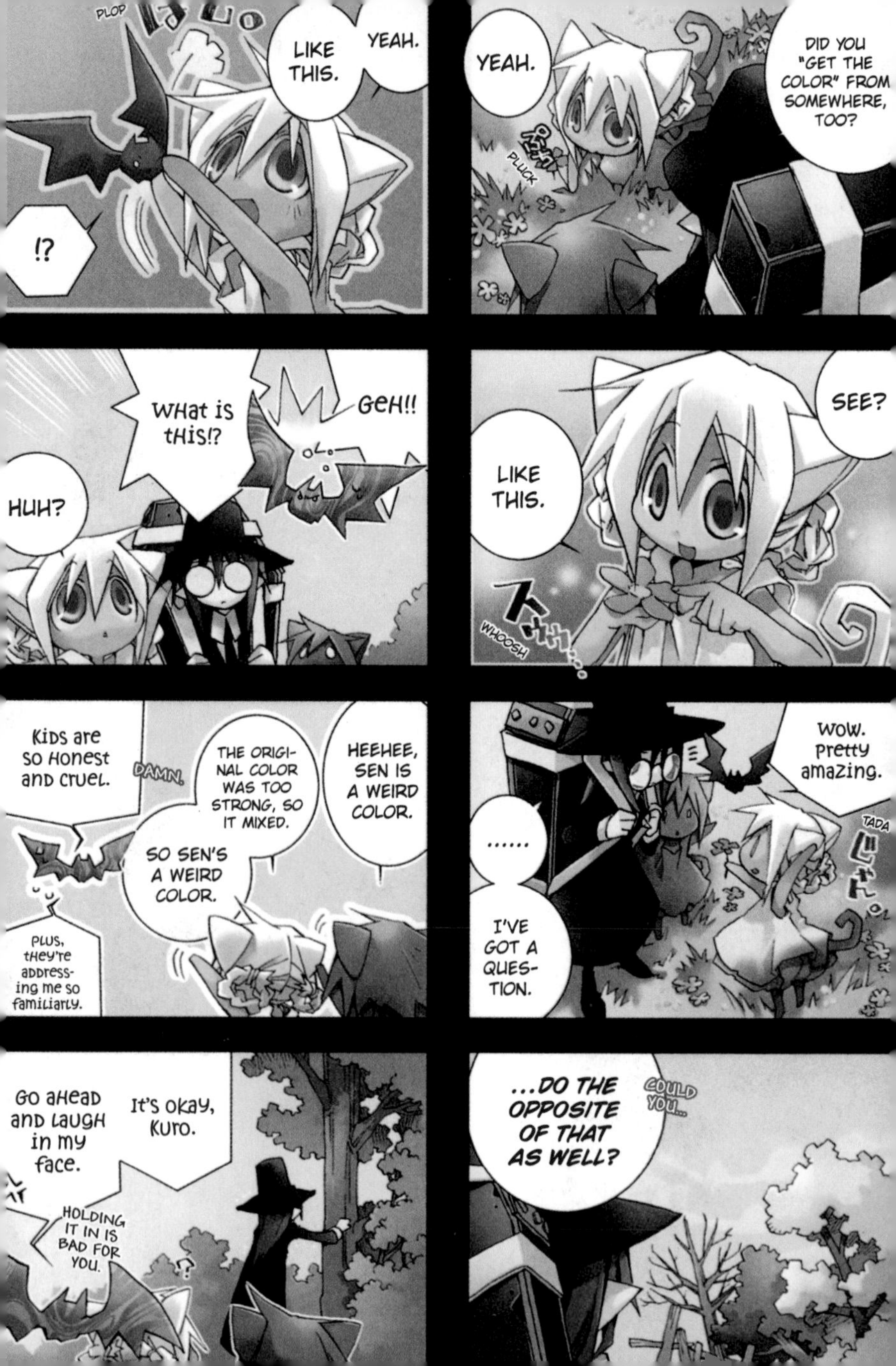
DID YOU "GET THE COLOR" FROM SOMEWHERE, TOO?
YEAH.
PLUCK
YEAH.
LIKE THIS.
PLOP
!?
SEE?
LIKE THIS.
WHOOSH
GEH!!
WHAT IS THIS!?
HUH?
WOW. PRETTY AMAZING.
TADA
......
I'VE GOT A QUES-TION.
HEEHEE, SEN IS A WEIRD COLOR.
THE ORIGI-NAL COLOR WAS TOO STRONG, SO IT MIXED.
SO SEN'S A WEIRD COLOR.
KIDS ARE SO HONEST AND CRUEL.
DAMN.
PLUS, THEY'RE ADDRESS-ING ME SO FAMILIARLY.
COULD YOU...
...DO THE OPPOSITE OF THAT AS WELL?
IT'S OKAY, KURO.
GO AHEAD AND LAUGH IN MY FACE.
HOLDING IT IN IS BAD FOR YOU.

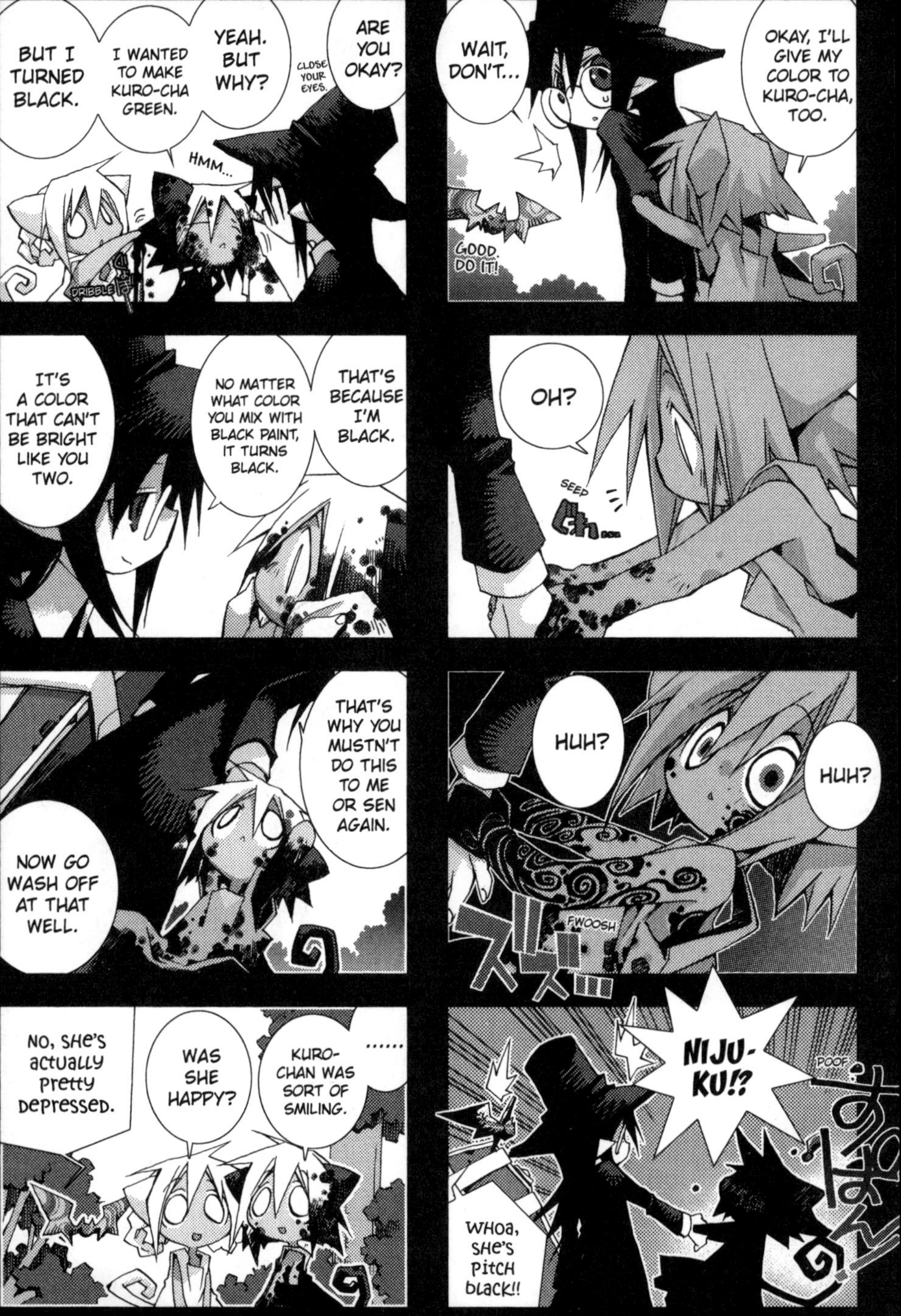
ARE YOU OKAY?
CLOSE YOUR EYES.
YEAH. BUT WHY?
I WANTED TO MAKE KURO-CHA GREEN.
BUT I TURNED BLACK.
HMM...
DRIBBLE
THAT'S BECAUSE I'M BLACK.
NO MATTER WHAT COLOR YOU MIX WITH BLACK PAINT, IT TURNS BLACK.
IT'S A COLOR THAT CAN'T BE BRIGHT LIKE YOU TWO.
THAT'S WHY YOU MUSTN'T DO THIS TO ME OR SEN AGAIN.
NOW GO WASH OFF AT THAT WELL.
......
KURO-CHAN WAS SORT OF SMILING.
WAS SHE HAPPY?
No, SHE's actually pretty Depressed.
OKAY, I'LL GIVE MY COLOR TO KURO-CHA, TOO.
WAIT, DON'T...
GOOD. DO IT!
OH?
SEEP
HUH?
HUH?
FWOOSH
POOF
NIJU-KU!?
WHoa, SHe's PitCH bLack!!

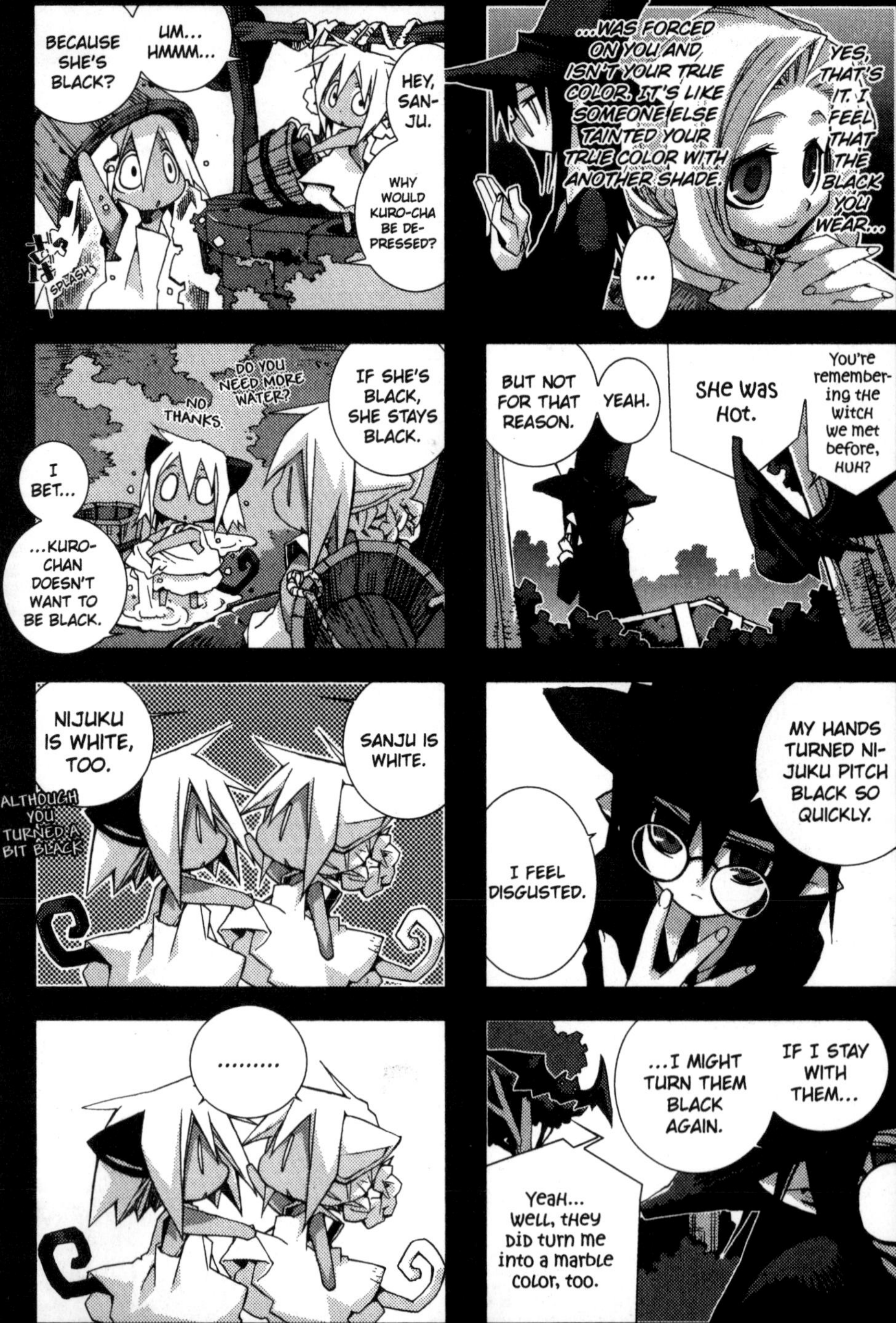
YES, THAT'S IT. I FEEL THAT THE BLACK YOU WEAR...
...WAS FORCED ON YOU AND ISN'T YOUR TRUE COLOR. IT'S LIKE SOMEONE ELSE TAINTED YOUR TRUE COLOR WITH ANOTHER SHADE.
...
HEY, SANJU.
WHY WOULD KURO-CHA BE DEPRESSED?
UM... HMMM...
BECAUSE SHE'S BLACK?
SPLASH
You're remembering the witch we met before, huh?
She was hot.
YEAH.
BUT NOT FOR THAT REASON.
IF SHE'S BLACK, SHE STAYS BLACK.
DO YOU NEED MORE WATER?
NO THANKS.
I BET...
...KURO-CHAN DOESN'T WANT TO BE BLACK.
MY HANDS TURNED NIJUKU PITCH BLACK SO QUICKLY.
I FEEL DISGUSTED.
SANJU IS WHITE.
NIJUKU IS WHITE, TOO.
ALTHOUGH YOU TURNED A BIT BLACK
IF I STAY WITH THEM...
...I MIGHT TURN THEM BLACK AGAIN.
Yeah... well, they did turn me into a marble color, too.
....

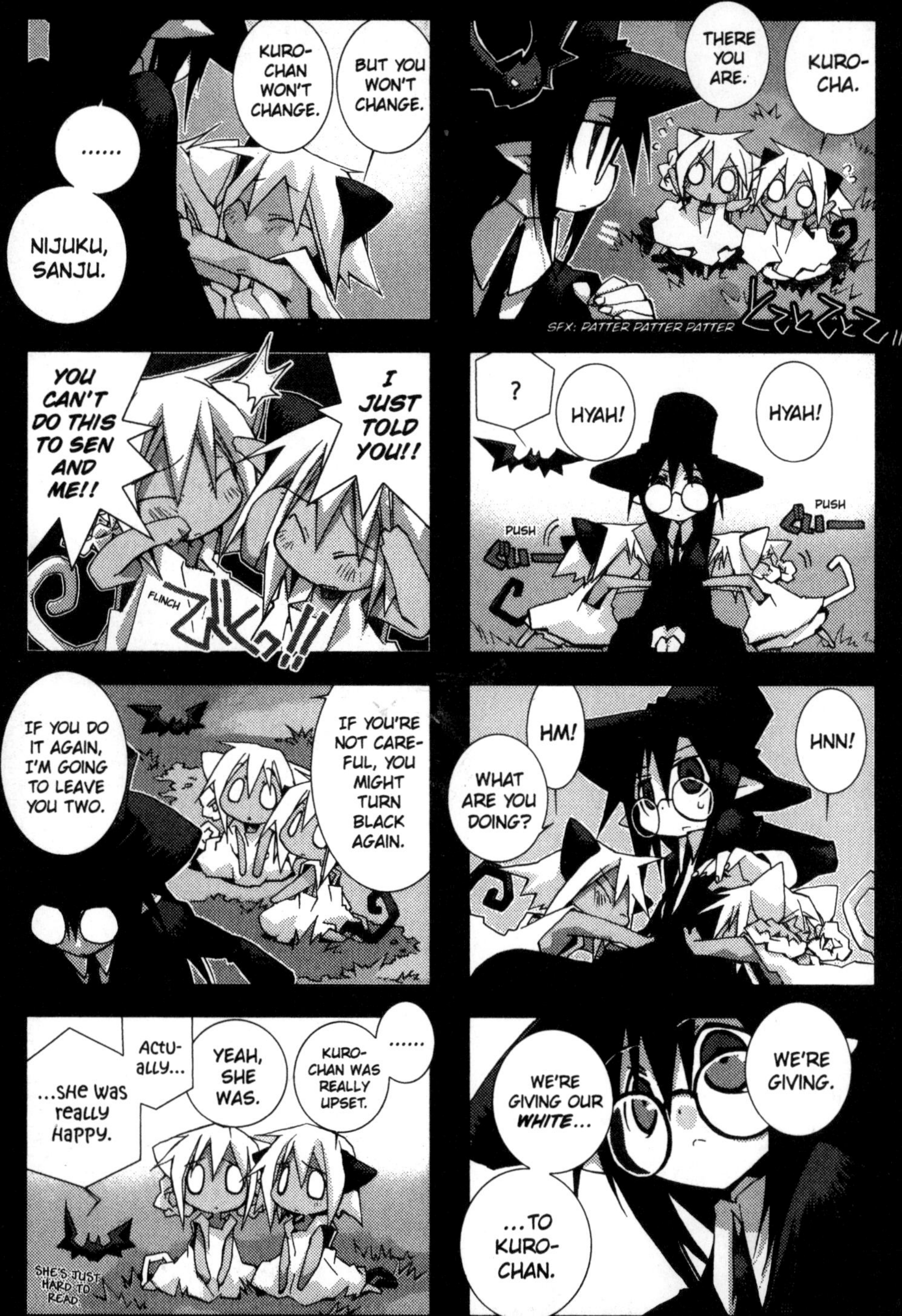
KURO-CHA.
THERE YOU ARE.
SFX: PATTER PATTER PATTER
BUT YOU WON'T CHANGE.
KURO-CHAN WON'T CHANGE.
......
NIJUKU, SANJU.
HYAH!
HYAH!
?
PUSH
PUSH
I JUST TOLD YOU!!
YOU CAN'T DO THIS TO SEN AND ME!!
FLINCH
HNN!
HM!
WHAT ARE YOU DOING?
IF YOU'RE NOT CAREFUL, YOU MIGHT TURN BLACK AGAIN.
IF YOU DO IT AGAIN, I'M GOING TO LEAVE YOU TWO.
WE'RE GIVING.
WE'RE GIVING OUR WHITE...
...TO KURO-CHAN.
......
KURO-CHAN WAS REALLY UPSET.
YEAH, SHE WAS.
Actually...
...she was really happy.
SHE'S JUST HARD TO READ.

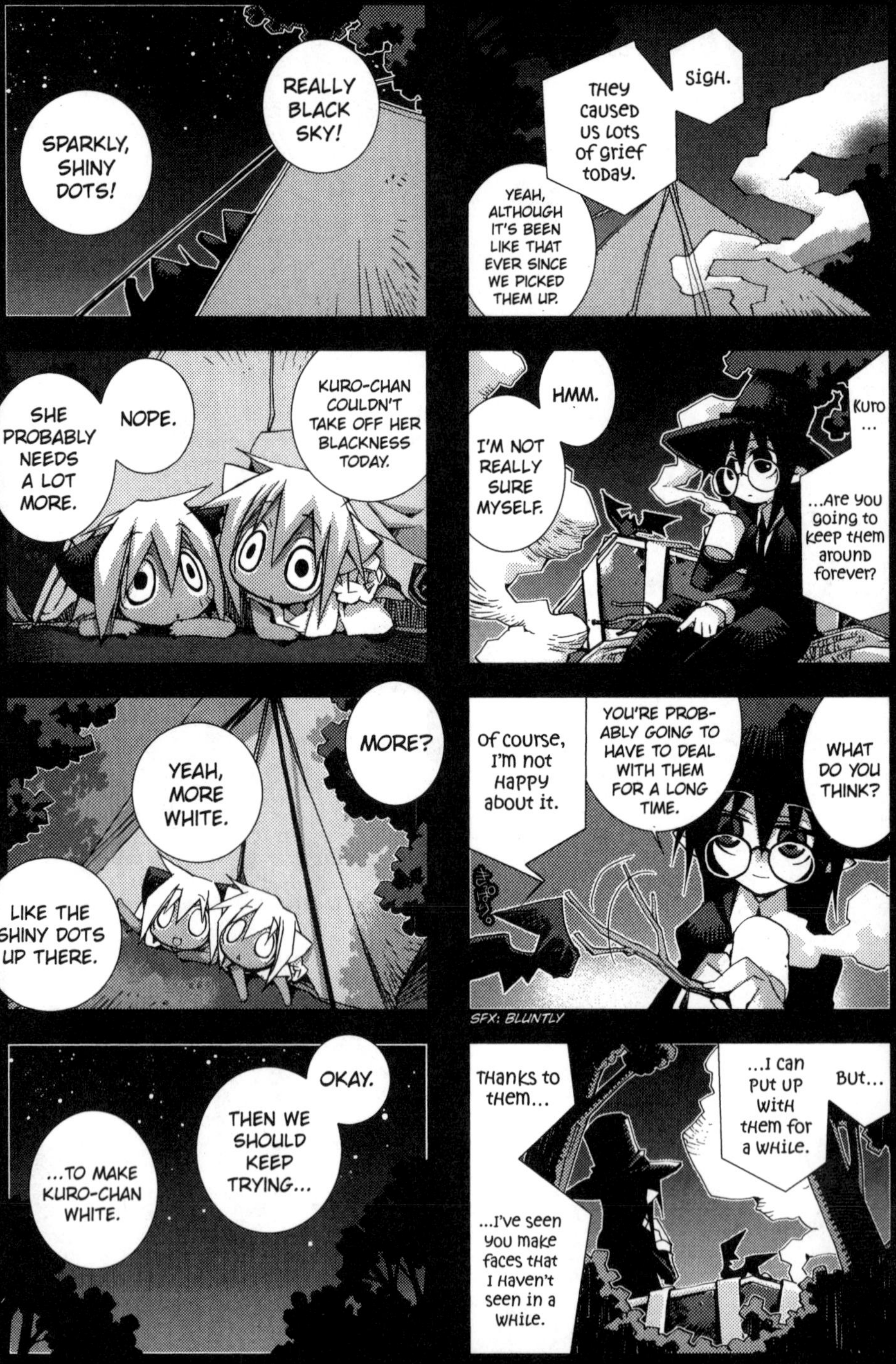
SIGH.
THEY CAUSED US LOTS OF GRIEF TODAY.
YEAH, ALTHOUGH IT'S BEEN LIKE THAT EVER SINCE WE PICKED THEM UP.
REALLY BLACK SKY!
SPARKLY, SHINY DOTS!
Kuro...
...Are you going to keep them around forever?
HMM.
I'M NOT REALLY SURE MYSELF.
KURO-CHAN COULDN'T TAKE OFF HER BLACKNESS TODAY.
NOPE.
SHE PROBABLY NEEDS A LOT MORE.
WHAT DO YOU THINK?
YOU'RE PROB-ABLY GOING TO HAVE TO DEAL WITH THEM FOR A LONG TIME.
Of course, I'm not happy about it.
SFX: BLUNTLY
MORE?
YEAH, MORE WHITE.
LIKE THE SHINY DOTS UP THERE.
But...
...I can put up with them for a while.
Thanks to them...
...I've seen you make faces that I haven't seen in a while.
OKAY.
THEN WE SHOULD KEEP TRYING...
...TO MAKE KURO-CHAN WHITE.

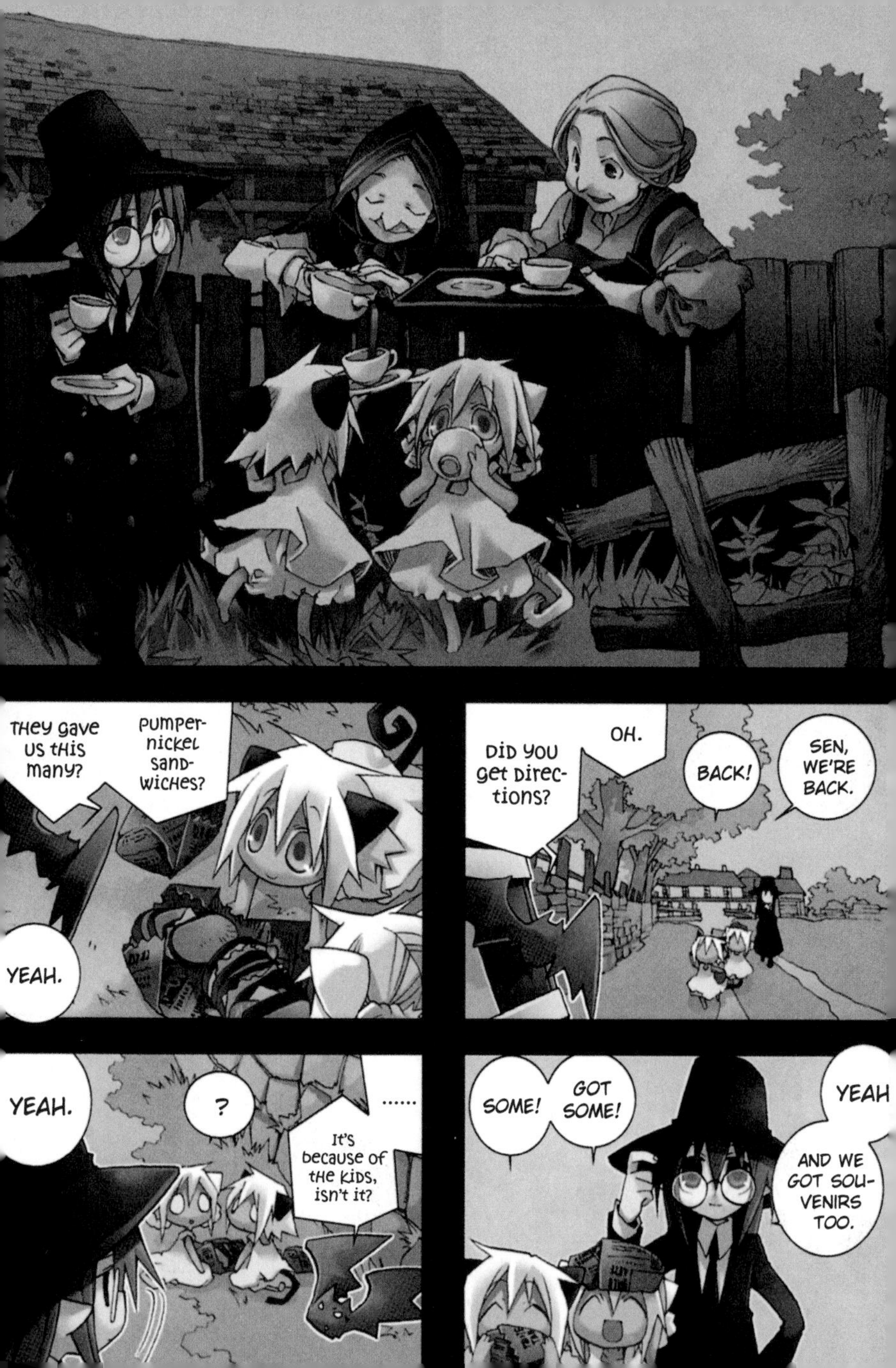
SEN, WE'RE BACK.
BACK!
OH.
DID YOU GET DIREC-TIONS?
PUMPER-NICKEL SAND-WICHES?
THEY GAVE US THIS MANY?
YEAH.
YEAH
AND WE GOT SOU-VENIRS TOO.
GOT SOME!
SOME!
......
?
YEAH.
It's because of the kids, isn't it?

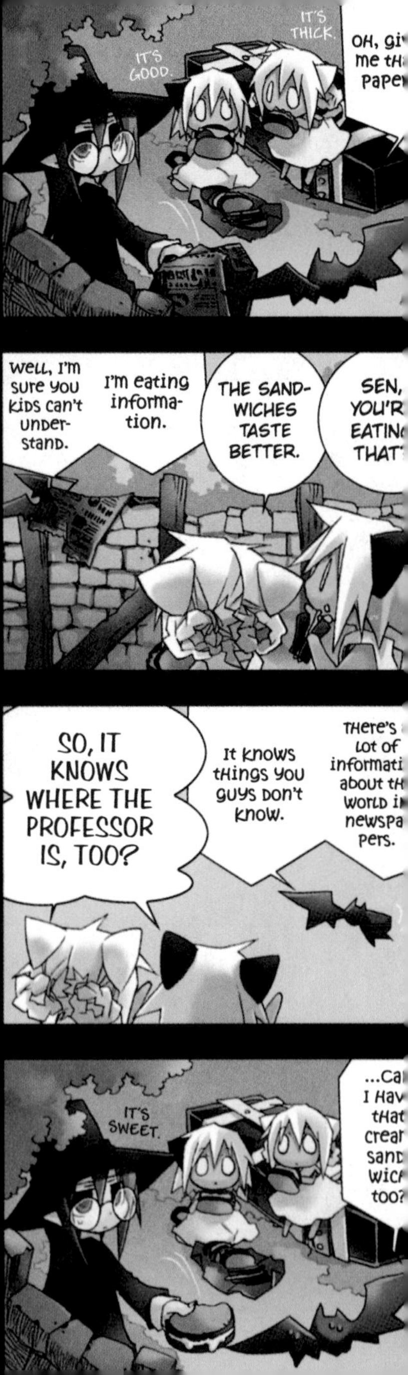

OH, GI
ME TH
PAPE
IT'S THICK.
IT'S GOOD.
SEN, YOU'R EATIN THAT
THE SANDWICHES TASTE BETTER.
I'm eating information.
Well, I'm sure you kids can't understand.
There's lot of informati about th world i newspapers.
It knows things you guys don't know.
SO, IT KNOWS WHERE THE PROFESSOR IS, TOO?
...Ca I Hav that crear sand wic too?
IT'S SWEET.

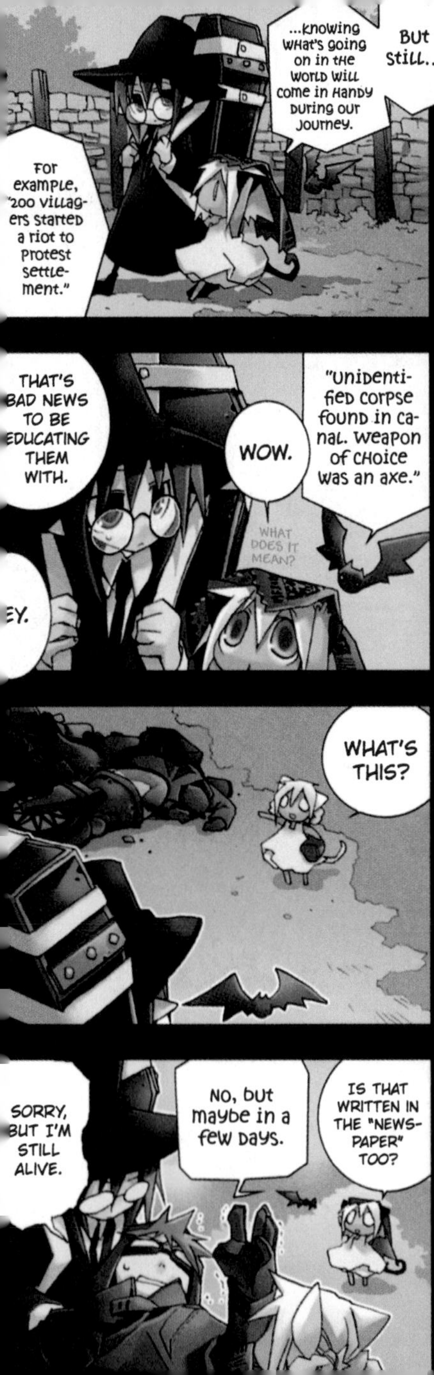

But still...
...knowing what's going on in the world will come in handy during our journey.
For example, "200 villagers started a riot to protest settlement."
"Unidentified corpse found in canal. Weapon of choice was an axe."
WOW.
WHAT DOES IT MEAN?
THAT'S BAD NEWS TO BE EDUCATING THEM WITH.
EY.
WHAT'S THIS?
IS THAT WRITTEN IN THE "NEWSPAPER" TOO?
No, but maybe in a few days.
SORRY, BUT I'M STILL ALIVE.

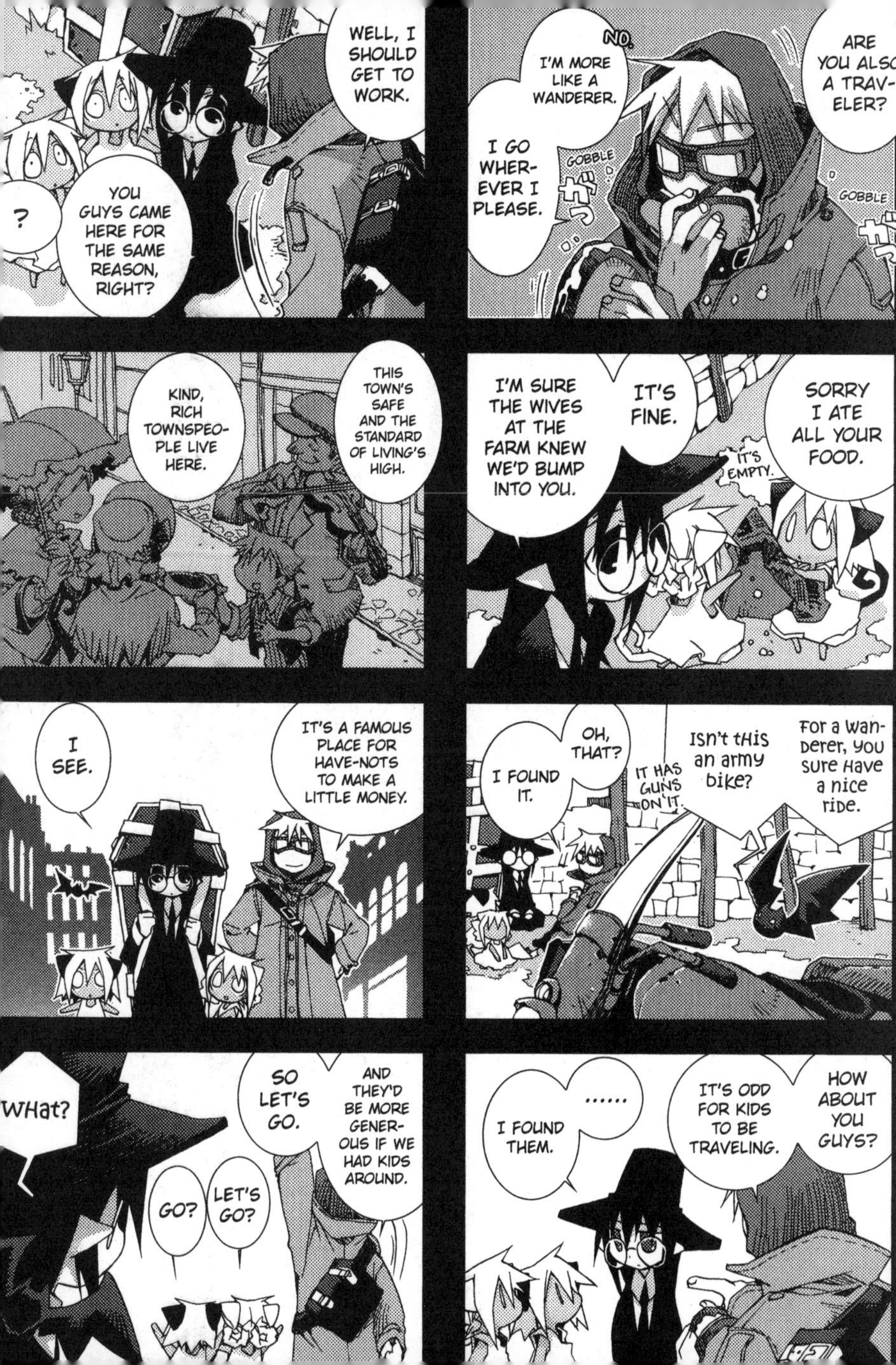
ARE YOU ALSO A TRAVELER?
NO.
I'M MORE LIKE A WANDERER.
I GO WHEREVER I PLEASE.
GOBBLE
GOBBLE
WELL, I SHOULD GET TO WORK.
YOU GUYS CAME HERE FOR THE SAME REASON, RIGHT?
?
SORRY I ATE ALL YOUR FOOD.
IT'S EMPTY.
IT'S FINE.
I'M SURE THE WIVES AT THE FARM KNEW WE'D BUMP INTO YOU.
THIS TOWN'S SAFE AND THE STANDARD OF LIVING'S HIGH.
KIND, RICH TOWNSPEOPLE LIVE HERE.
For a wanderer, you sure have a nice ride.
Isn't this an army bike?
IT HAS GUNS ON IT.
OH, THAT?
I FOUND IT.
IT'S A FAMOUS PLACE FOR HAVE-NOTS TO MAKE A LITTLE MONEY.
I SEE.
HOW ABOUT YOU GUYS?
IT'S ODD FOR KIDS TO BE TRAVELING.
......
I FOUND THEM.
AND THEY'D BE MORE GENEROUS IF WE HAD KIDS AROUND.
SO LET'S GO.
LET'S GO?
GO?
WHat?

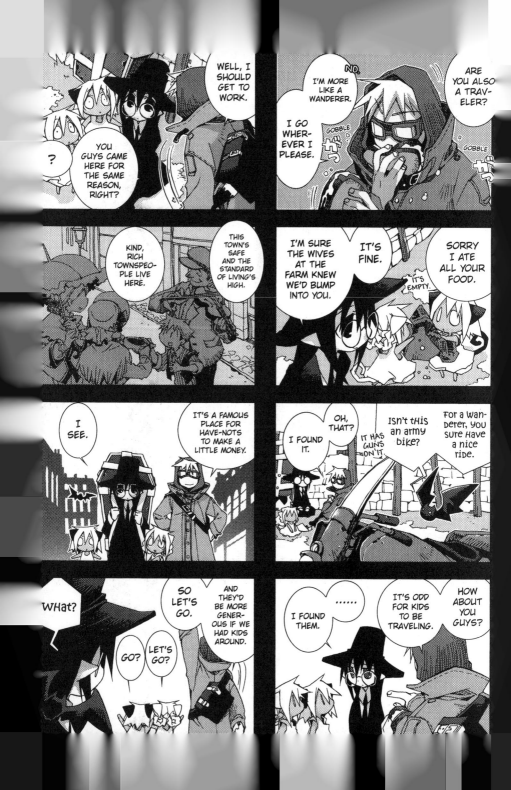

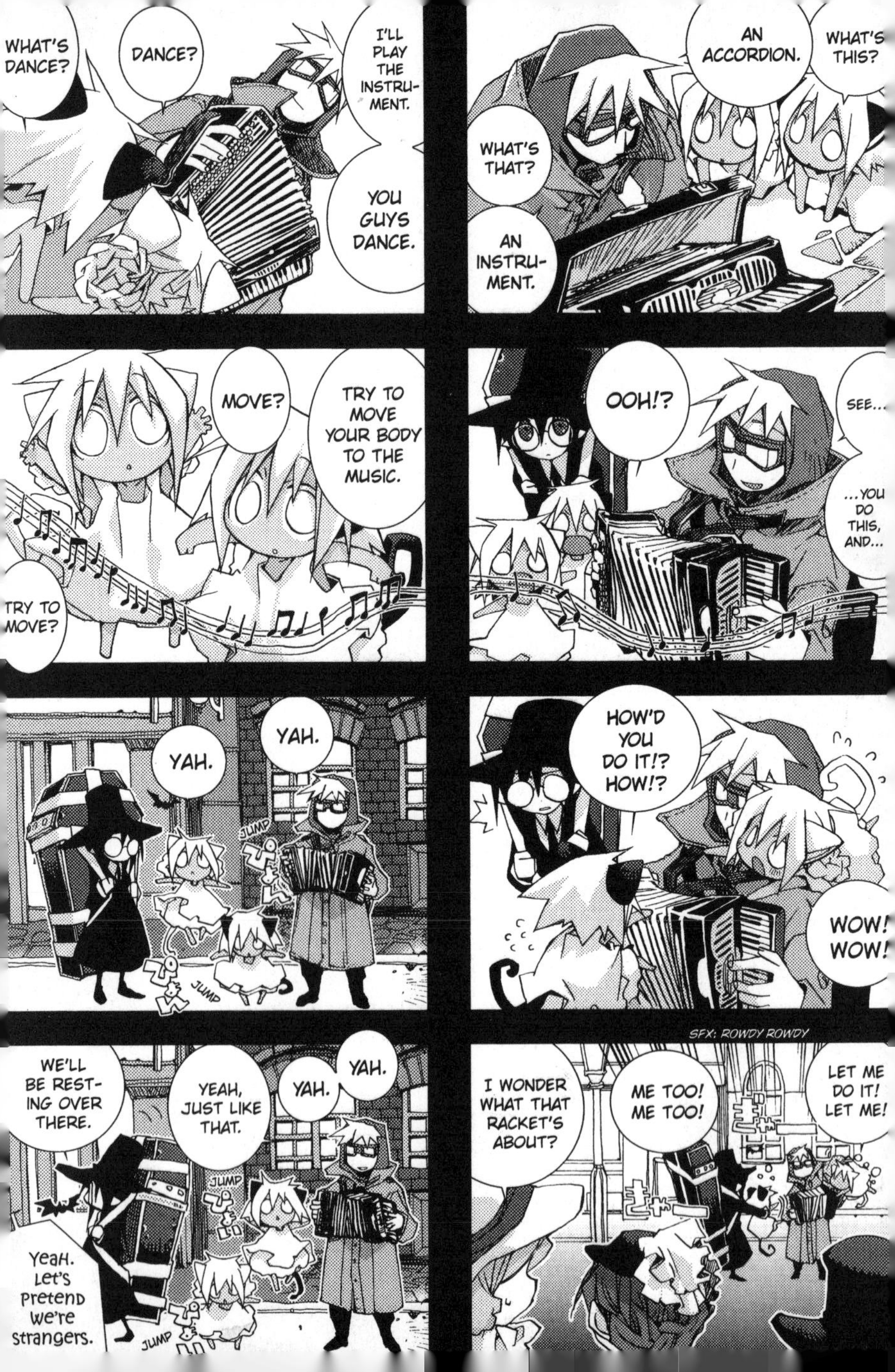
WHAT'S THIS?
AN ACCORDION.
WHAT'S THAT?
AN INSTRUMENT.
SEE...
...YOU DO THIS, AND...
OOH!?
WOW! WOW!
HOW'D YOU DO IT!? HOW!?
SFX: ROWDY ROWDY
LET ME DO IT! LET ME!
ME TOO! ME TOO!
I WONDER WHAT THAT RACKET'S ABOUT?
I'LL PLAY THE INSTRUMENT.
YOU GUYS DANCE.
DANCE?
WHAT'S DANCE?
TRY TO MOVE YOUR BODY TO THE MUSIC.
MOVE?
TRY TO MOVE?
YAH.
YAH.
JUMP
JUMP
YAH.
YAH.
YEAH, JUST LIKE THAT.
WE'LL BE RESTING OVER THERE.
Yeah. Let's pretend we're strangers.
JUMP
JUMP

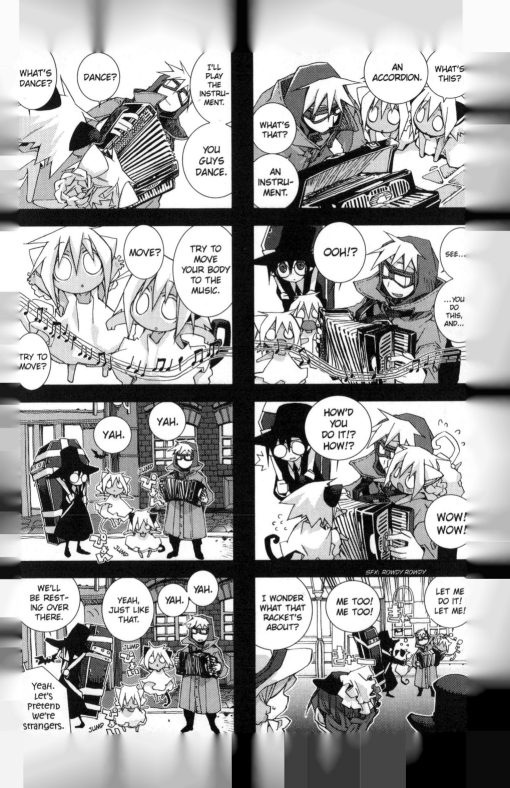

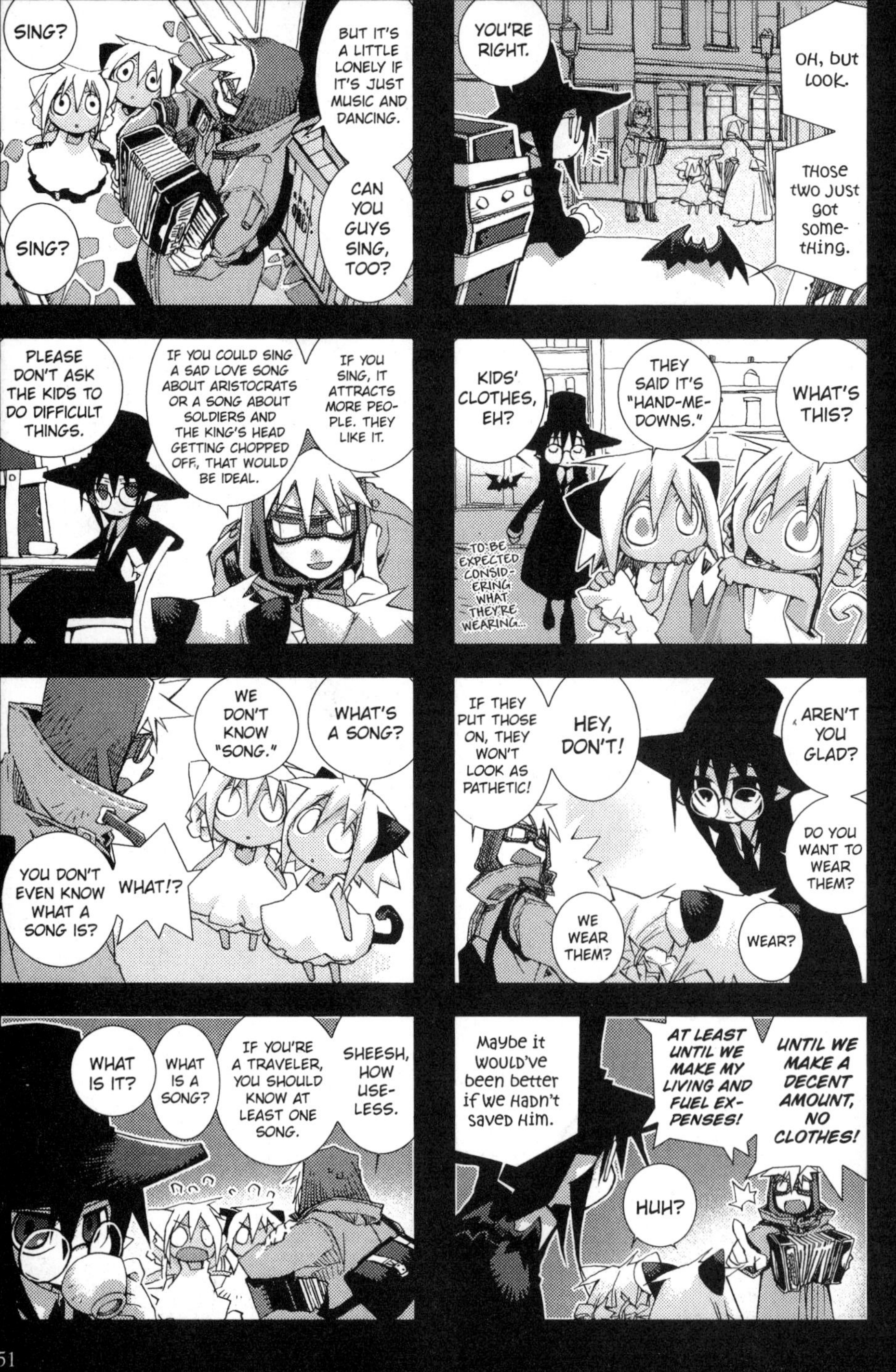
OH, but look.
YOU'RE RIGHT.
THOSE two JUST got some-thing.
BUT IT'S A LITTLE LONELY IF IT'S JUST MUSIC AND DANCING.
SING?
CAN YOU GUYS SING, TOO?
SING?
WHAT'S THIS?
THEY SAID IT'S "HAND-ME-DOWNS."
KIDS' CLOTHES, EH?
TO BE EXPECTED CONSID-ERING WHAT THEY'RE WEARING...
IF YOU SING, IT ATTRACTS MORE PEO-PLE. THEY LIKE IT.
IF YOU COULD SING A SAD LOVE SONG ABOUT ARISTOCRATS OR A SONG ABOUT SOLDIERS AND THE KING'S HEAD GETTING CHOPPED OFF, THAT WOULD BE IDEAL.
PLEASE DON'T ASK THE KIDS TO DO DIFFICULT THINGS.
AREN'T YOU GLAD?
HEY, DON'T!
IF THEY PUT THOSE ON, THEY WON'T LOOK AS PATHETIC!
DO YOU WANT TO WEAR THEM?
WEAR?
WE WEAR THEM?
WHAT'S A SONG?
WE DON'T KNOW "SONG."
WHAT!?
YOU DON'T EVEN KNOW WHAT A SONG IS?
UNTIL WE MAKE A DECENT AMOUNT, NO CLOTHES!
AT LEAST UNTIL WE MAKE MY LIVING AND FUEL EX-PENSES!
Maybe it would've been better if we hadn't saved him.
HUH?
SHEESH, HOW USE-LESS.
IF YOU'RE A TRAVELER, YOU SHOULD KNOW AT LEAST ONE SONG.
WHAT IS A SONG?
WHAT IS IT?

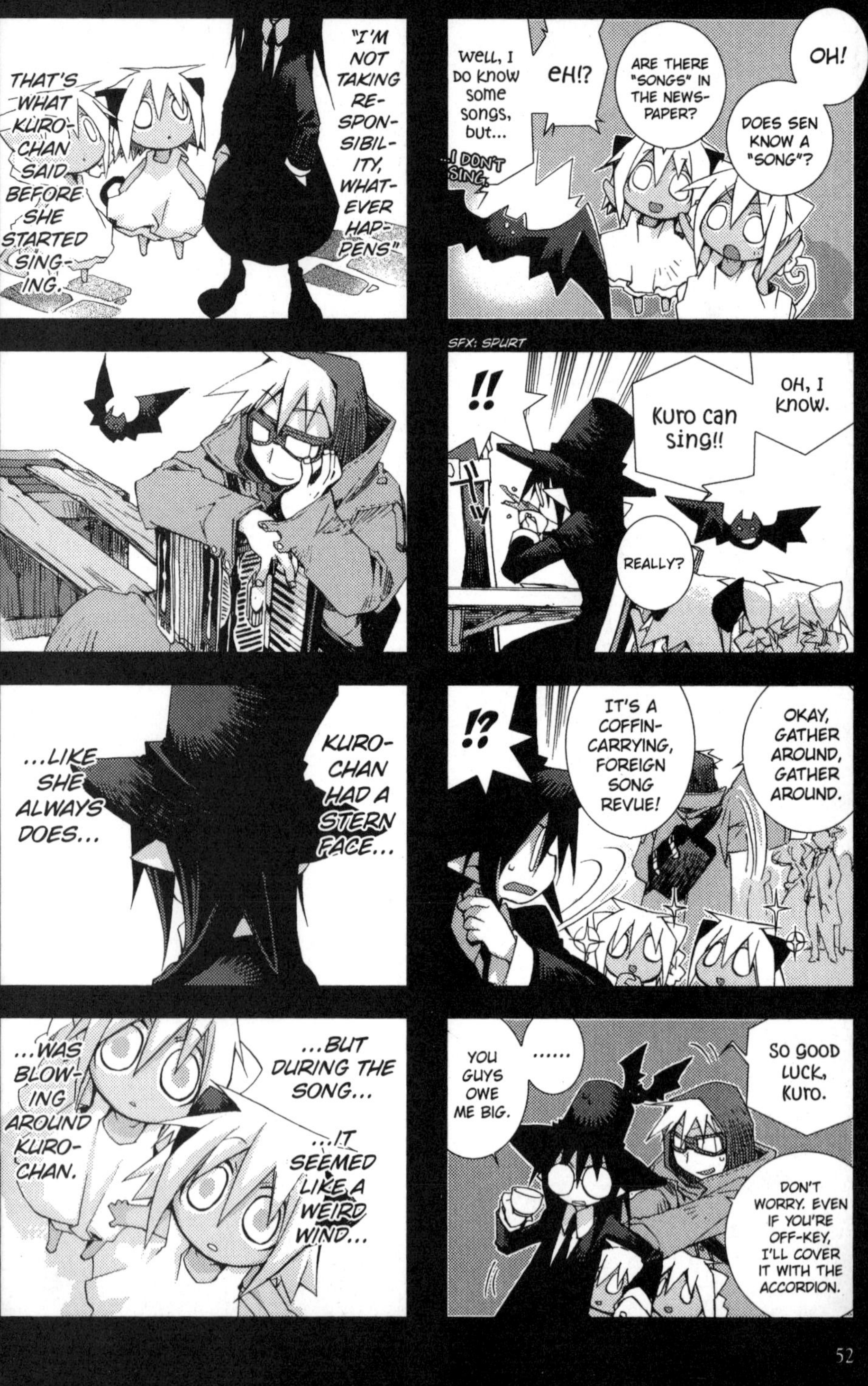
OH!
DOES SEN KNOW A "SONG"?
ARE THERE "SONGS" IN THE NEWSPAPER?
EH!?
Well, I do know some songs, but...
...I DON'T SING.
SFX: SPURT
OH, I KNOW.
Kuro can sing!!
!!
REALLY?
OKAY, GATHER AROUND, GATHER AROUND.
IT'S A COFFIN-CARRYING, FOREIGN SONG REVUE!
!?
So good luck, Kuro.
......
YOU GUYS OWE ME BIG.
DON'T WORRY. EVEN IF YOU'RE OFF-KEY, I'LL COVER IT WITH THE ACCORDION.
"I'M NOT TAKING RESPONSIBILITY, WHATEVER HAPPENS"
THAT'S WHAT KURO-CHAN SAID BEFORE SHE STARTED SINGING.
KURO-CHAN HAD A STERN FACE...
...LIKE SHE ALWAYS DOES...
...BUT DURING THE SONG...
...IT SEEMED LIKE A WEIRD WIND...
...WAS BLOWING AROUND KURO-CHAN.

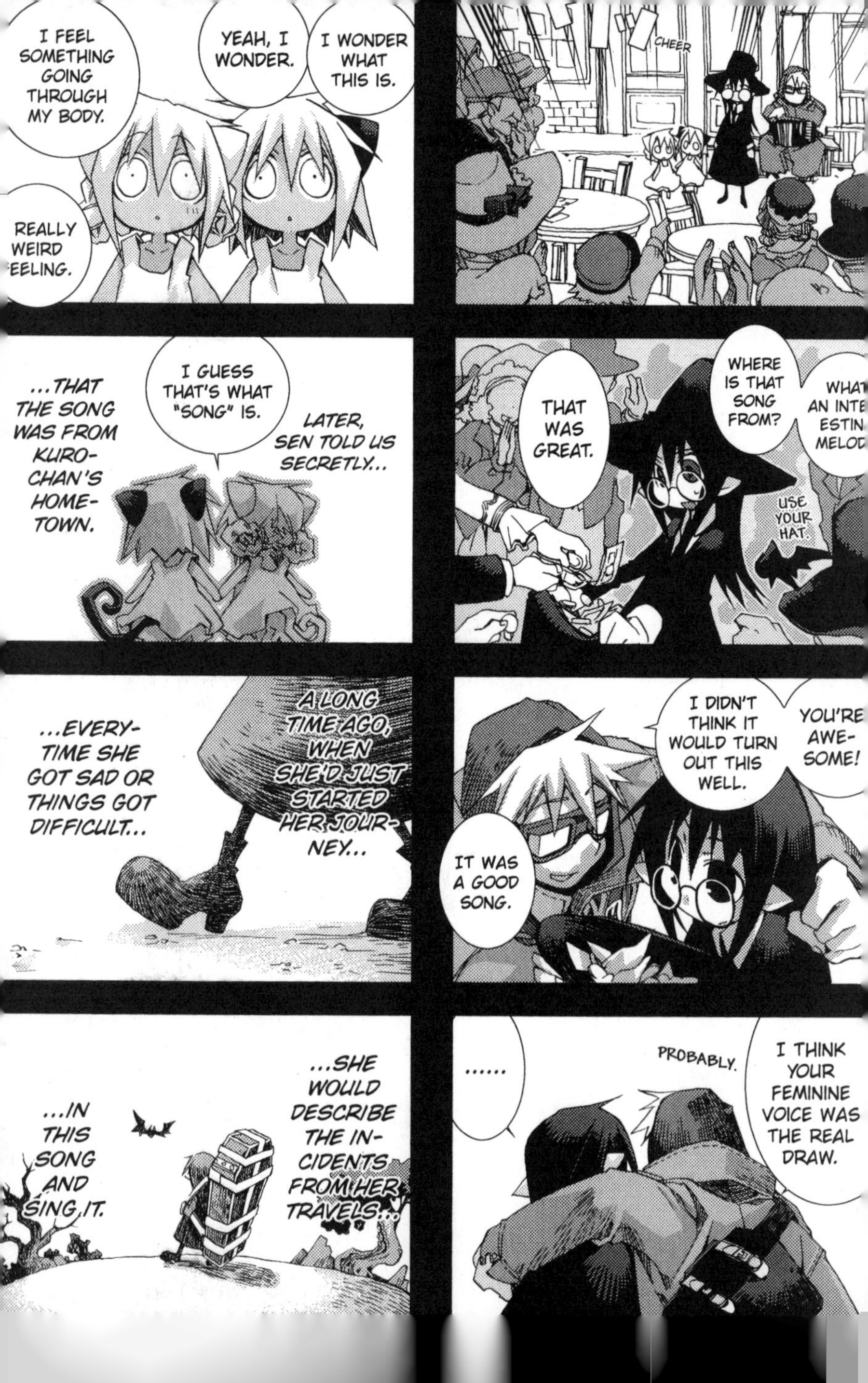
CHEER
I WONDER WHAT THIS IS.
YEAH, I WONDER.
I FEEL SOMETHING GOING THROUGH MY BODY.
REALLY WEIRD FEELING.
WHAT AN INTE ESTIN MELOD
WHERE IS THAT SONG FROM?
THAT WAS GREAT.
USE YOUR HAT.
LATER, SEN TOLD US SECRETLY...
I GUESS THAT'S WHAT "SONG" IS.
...THAT THE SONG WAS FROM KURO-CHAN'S HOME-TOWN.
YOU'RE AWE-SOME!
I DIDN'T THINK IT WOULD TURN OUT THIS WELL.
IT WAS A GOOD SONG.
A LONG TIME AGO, WHEN SHE'D JUST STARTED HER JOUR-NEY...
...EVERY-TIME SHE GOT SAD OR THINGS GOT DIFFICULT...
I THINK YOUR FEMININE VOICE WAS THE REAL DRAW.
PROBABLY.
......
...SHE WOULD DESCRIBE THE IN-CIDENTS FROM HER TRAVELS...
...IN THIS SONG AND SING IT.

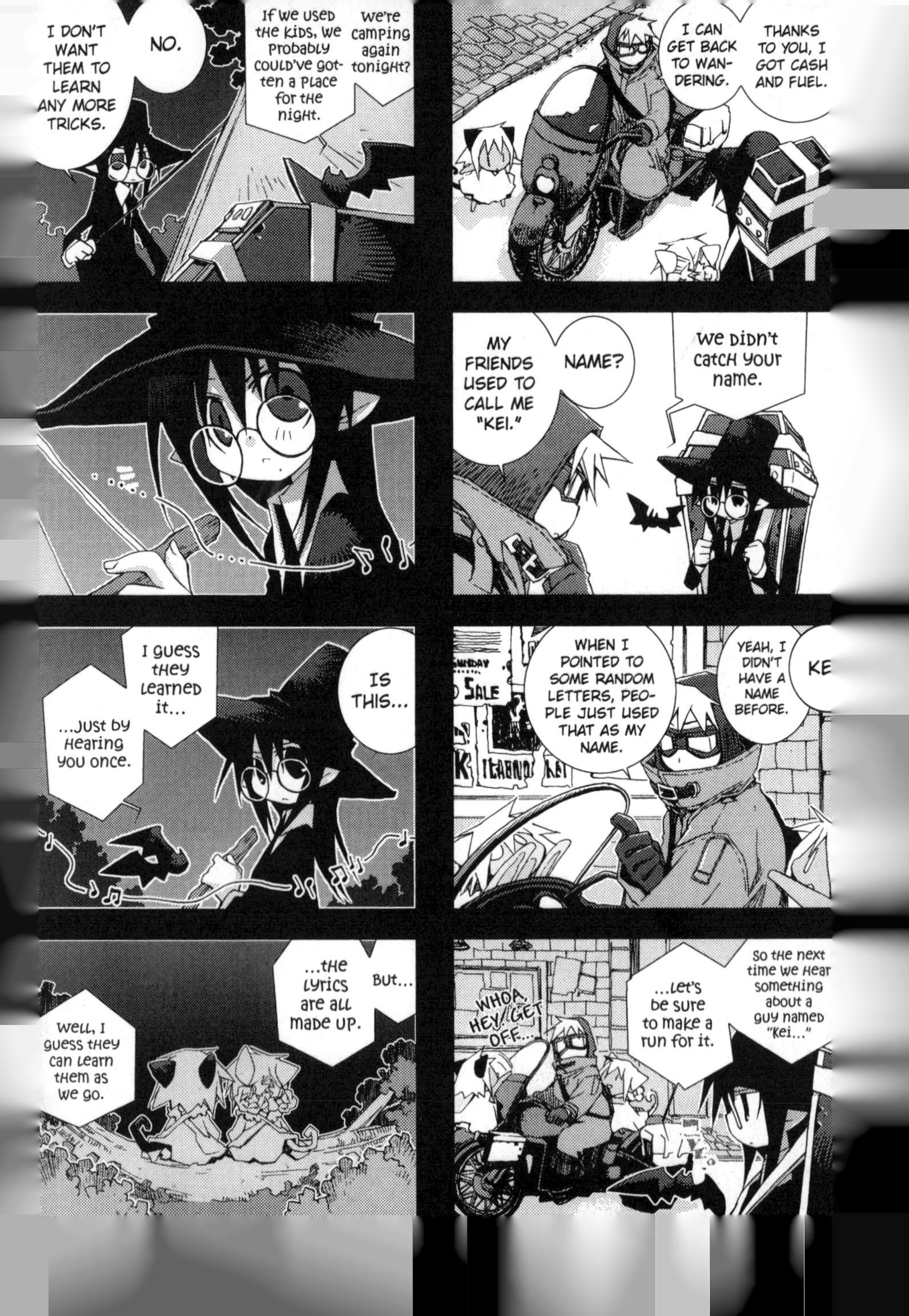
THANKS TO YOU, I GOT CASH AND FUEL.
I CAN GET BACK TO WAN-DERING.
We didn't catch your name.
NAME?
MY FRIENDS USED TO CALL ME "KEI."
KE
YEAH, I DIDN'T HAVE A NAME BEFORE.
WHEN I POINTED TO SOME RANDOM LETTERS, PEO-PLE JUST USED THAT AS MY NAME.
So the next time we hear something about a guy named "Kei..."
...let's be sure to make a run for it.
WHOA, HEY! GET OFF...
We're camping again tonight?
If we used the kids, we probably could've got-ten a place for the night.
NO.
I DON'T WANT THEM TO LEARN ANY MORE TRICKS.
IS THIS...
I guess they learned it...
...just by hearing you once.
But...
...the lyrics are all made up.
Well, I guess they can learn them as we go.

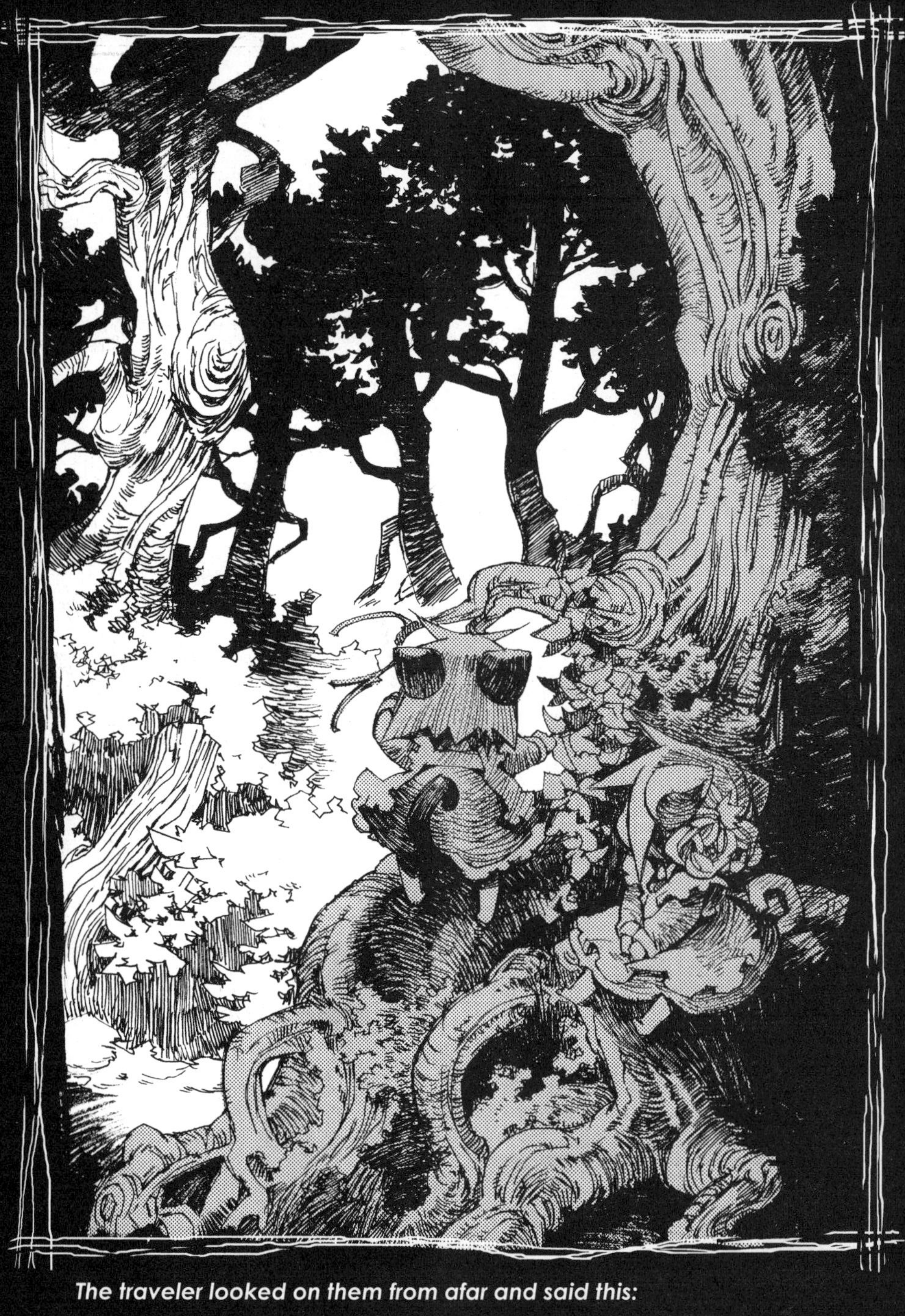

The traveler looked on them from afar and said this:

"But I probably can't do more for them than the Professor can do now."

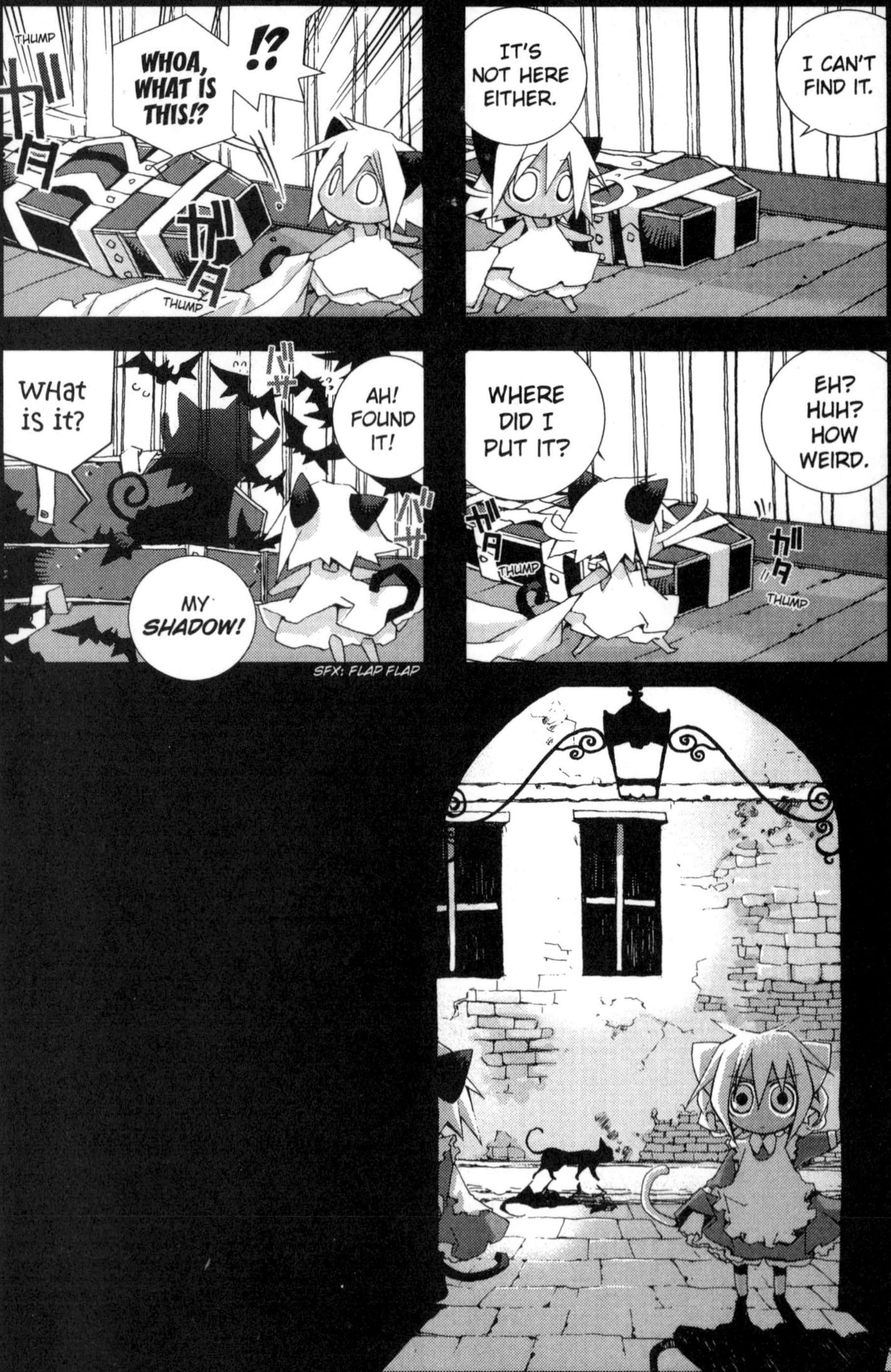
I CAN'T FIND IT.
IT'S NOT HERE EITHER.
!?
WHOA, WHAT IS THIS!?
ガタ
THUMP
ガタ
THUMP
EH? HUH? HOW WEIRD.
WHERE DID I PUT IT?
ガタ
THUMP
ガタ
THUMP
バサ
バサ
AH! FOUND IT!
WHAt is it?
MY SHADOW!
SFX: FLAP FLAP

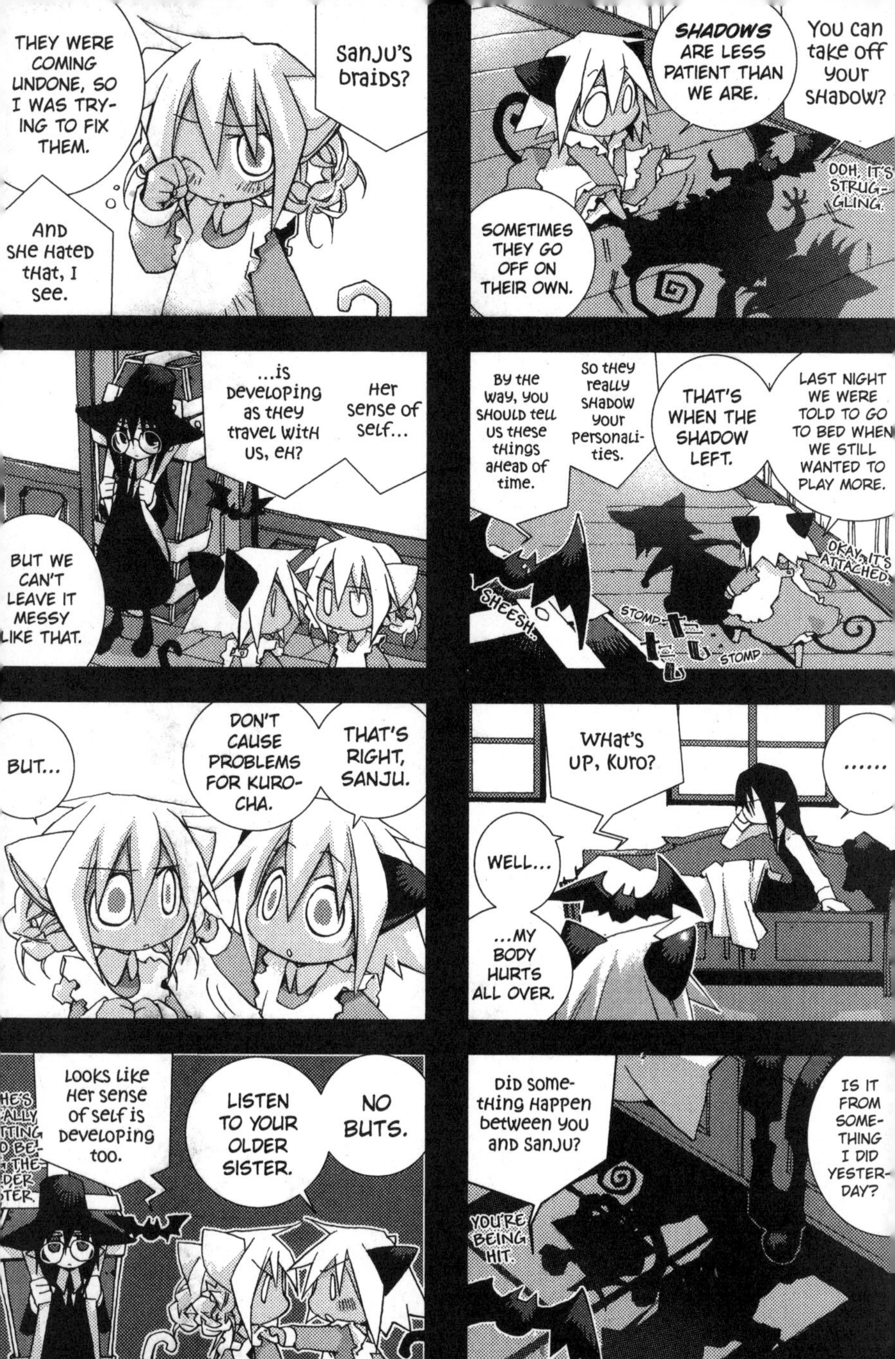
You can take off your shadow?
SHADOWS ARE LESS PATIENT THAN WE ARE.
OOH, IT'S STRUGGLING.
SOMETIMES THEY GO OFF ON THEIR OWN.
Sanju's braids?
THEY WERE COMING UNDONE, SO I WAS TRYING TO FIX THEM.
And she hated that, I see.
LAST NIGHT WE WERE TOLD TO GO TO BED WHEN WE STILL WANTED TO PLAY MORE.
THAT'S WHEN THE SHADOW LEFT.
So they really shadow your personalities.
By the way, you should tell us these things ahead of time.
OKAY, IT'S ATTACHED.
STOMP
SHEESH..
STOMP
Her sense of self...
...is developing as they travel with us, eh?
BUT WE CAN'T LEAVE IT MESSY LIKE THAT.
......
What's up, Kuro?
WELL...
...MY BODY HURTS ALL OVER.
THAT'S RIGHT, SANJU.
DON'T CAUSE PROBLEMS FOR KURO-CHA.
BUT...
IS IT FROM SOMETHING I DID YESTERDAY?
Did something happen between you and Sanju?
YOU'RE BEING HIT.
NO BUTS.
LISTEN TO YOUR OLDER SISTER.
Looks like her sense of self is developing too.

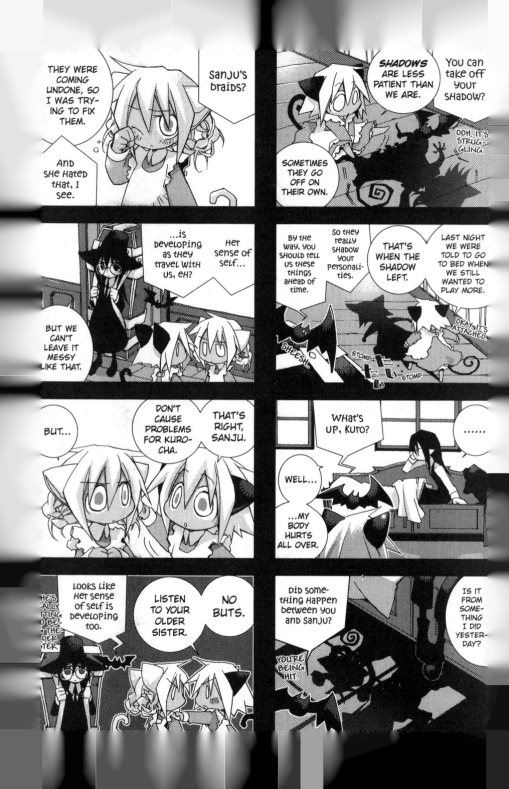

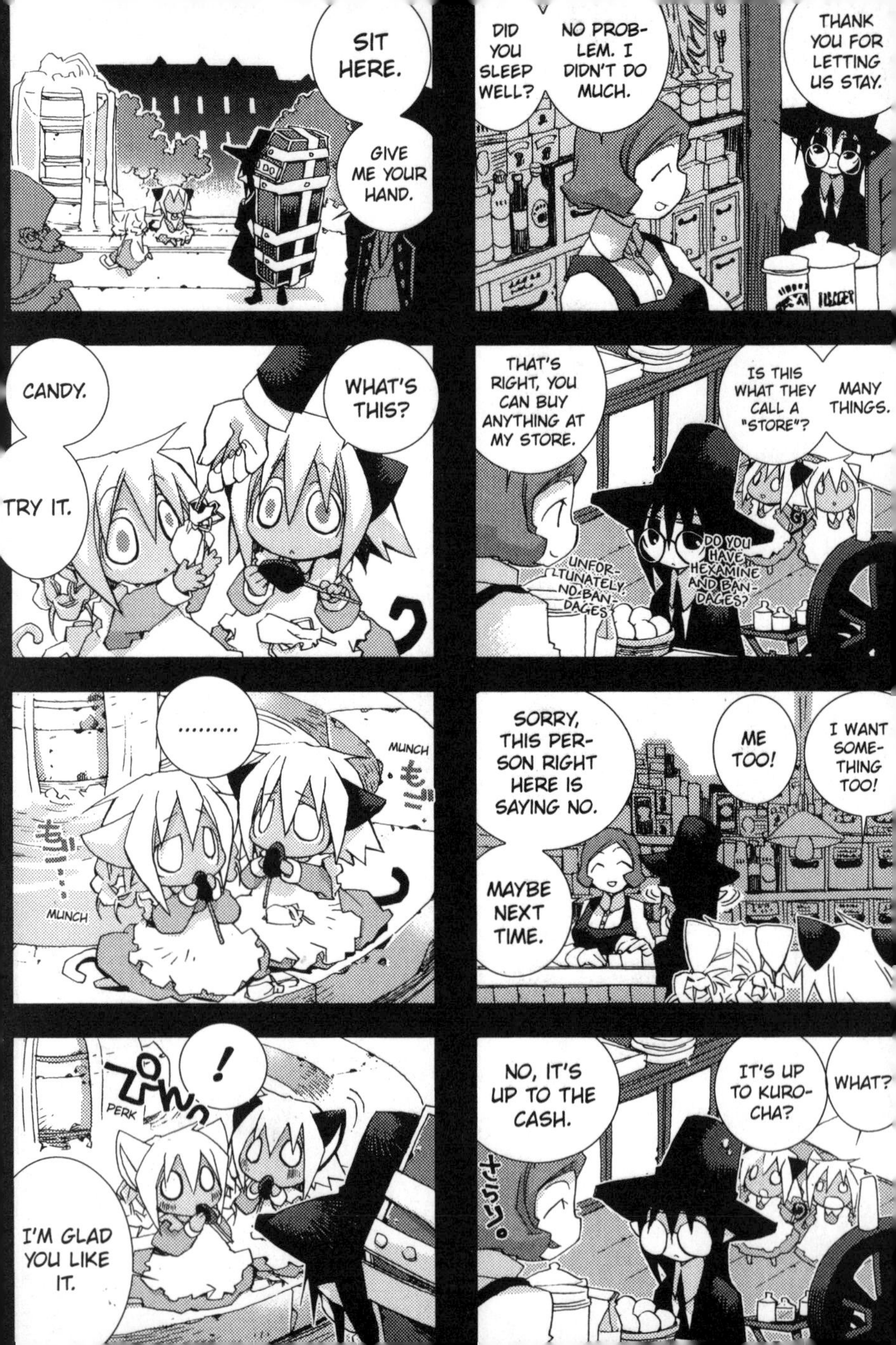
THANK YOU FOR LETTING US STAY.
NO PROBLEM. I DIDN'T DO MUCH.
DID YOU SLEEP WELL?
MANY THINGS.
IS THIS WHAT THEY CALL A "STORE"?
THAT'S RIGHT, YOU CAN BUY ANYTHING AT MY STORE.
DO YOU HAVE HEXAMINE AND BANDAGES?
UNFORTUNATELY, NO BANDAGES.
I WANT SOMETHING TOO!
ME TOO!
SORRY, THIS PERSON RIGHT HERE IS SAYING NO.
MAYBE NEXT TIME.
WHAT?
IT'S UP TO KURO-CHA?
NO, IT'S UP TO THE CASH.
SIT HERE.
GIVE ME YOUR HAND.
WHAT'S THIS?
CANDY.
TRY IT.
....
MUNCH
MUNCH
!
PERK
I'M GLAD YOU LIKE IT.

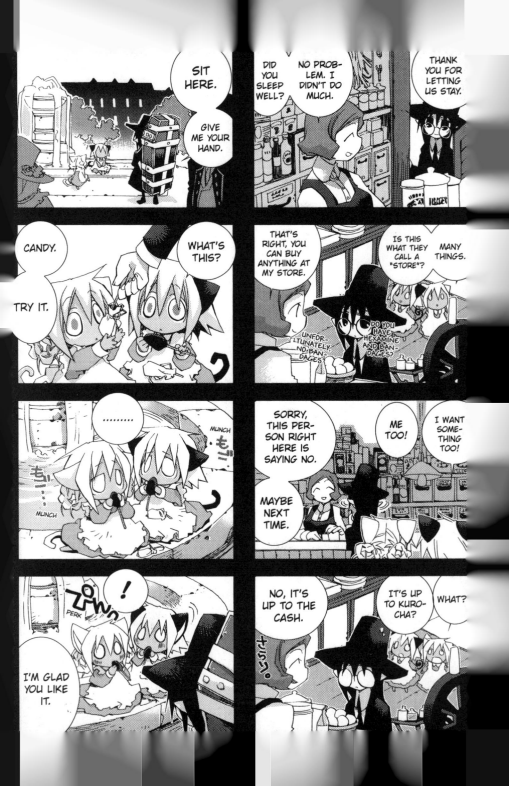

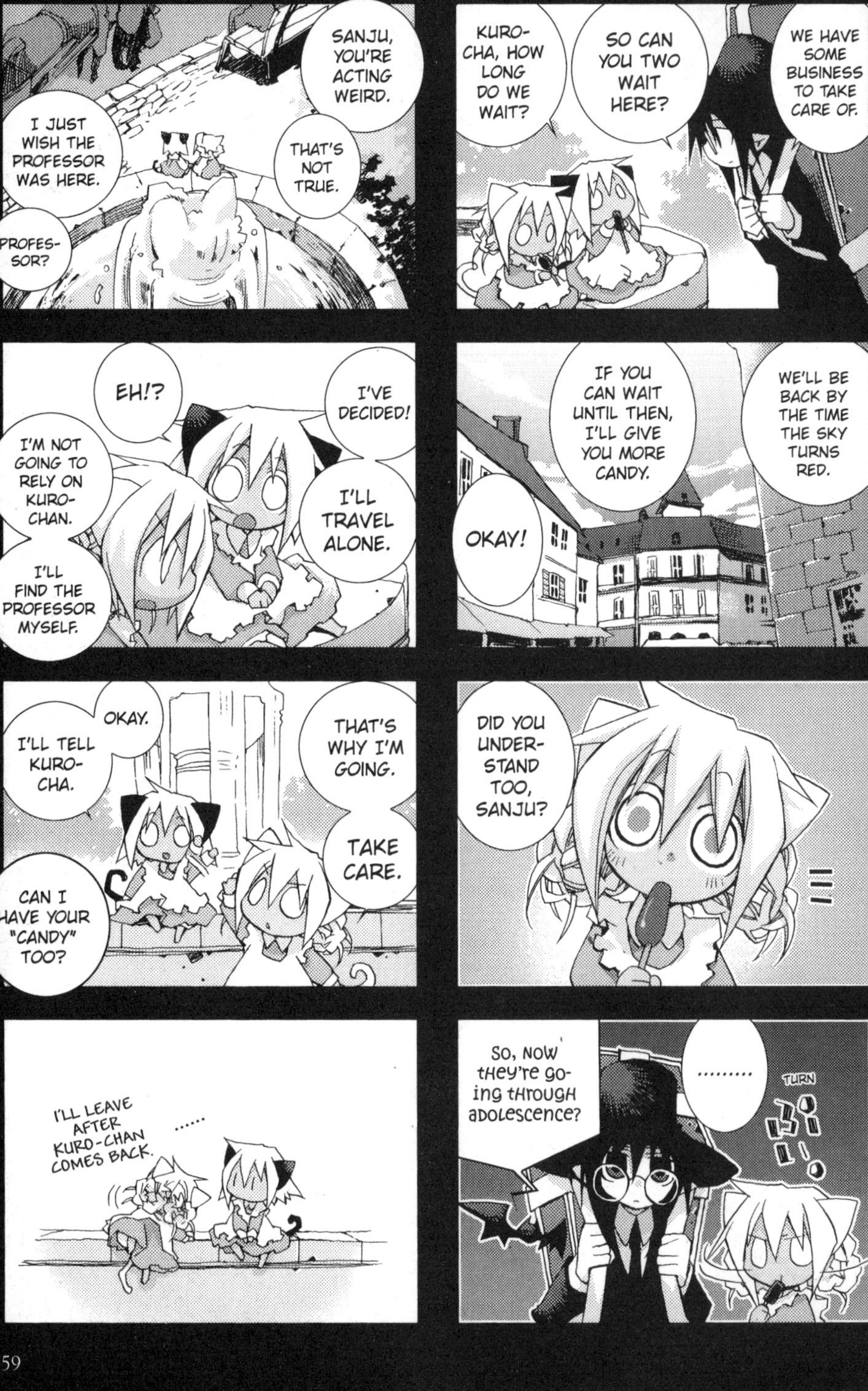
WE HAVE SOME BUSINESS TO TAKE CARE OF.
SO CAN YOU TWO WAIT HERE?
KURO-CHA, HOW LONG DO WE WAIT?
SANJU, YOU'RE ACTING WEIRD.
THAT'S NOT TRUE.
I JUST WISH THE PROFESSOR WAS HERE.
PROFES-SOR?
WE'LL BE BACK BY THE TIME THE SKY TURNS RED.
IF YOU CAN WAIT UNTIL THEN, I'LL GIVE YOU MORE CANDY.
OKAY!
I'VE DECIDED!
EH!?
I'LL TRAVEL ALONE.
I'M NOT GOING TO RELY ON KURO-CHAN.
I'LL FIND THE PROFESSOR MYSELF.
DID YOU UNDERSTAND TOO, SANJU?
THAT'S WHY I'M GOING.
OKAY.
I'LL TELL KURO-CHA.
TAKE CARE.
CAN I HAVE YOUR "CANDY" TOO?
....
TURN
SO, NOW THEY'RE GO-ING THROUGH ADOLESCENCE?
......
I'LL LEAVE AFTER KURO-CHAN COMES BACK.

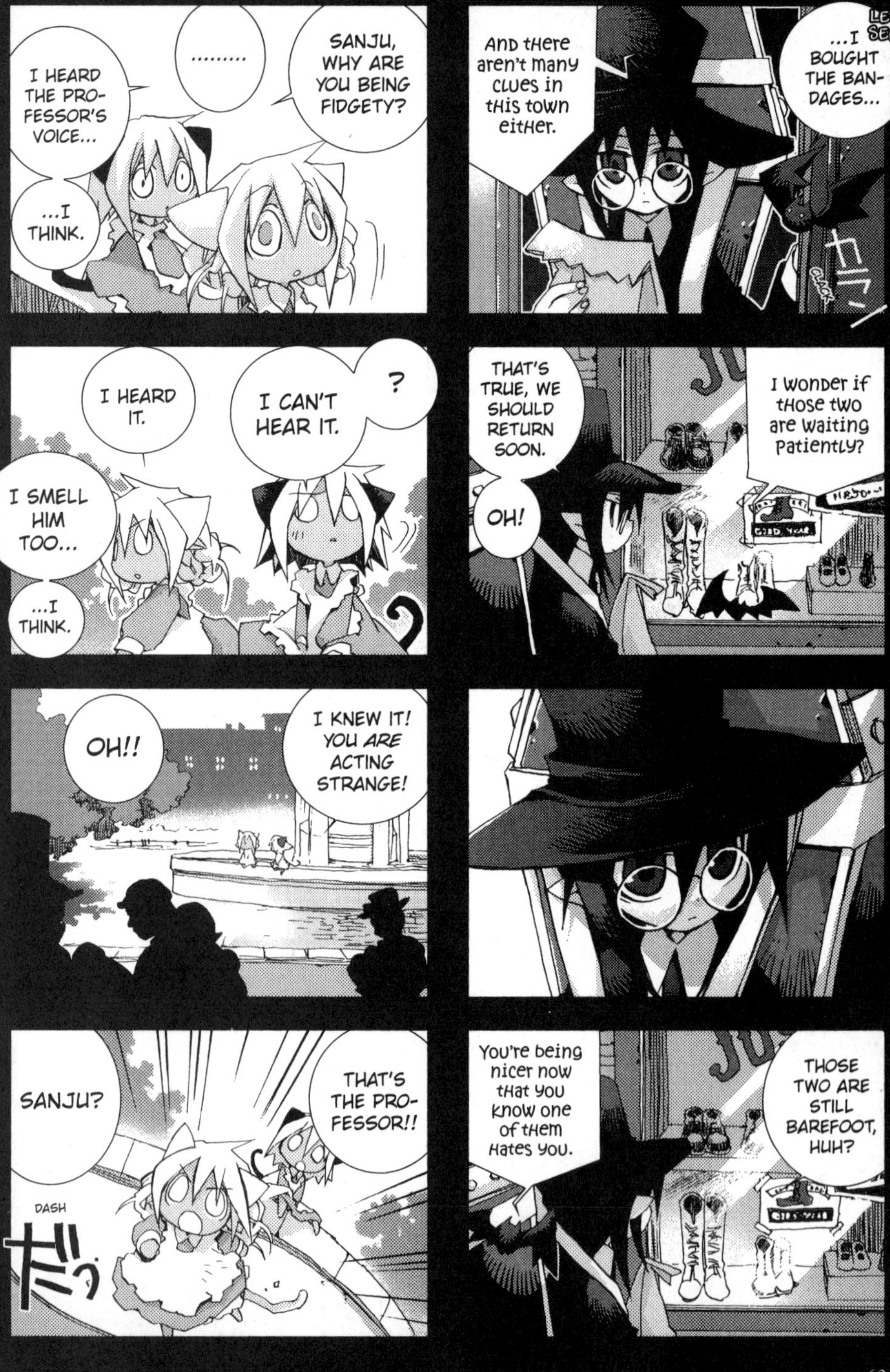
LET'S SEE...
...I BOUGHT THE BANDAGES...
And there aren't many clues in this town either.
CLACK
I wonder if those two are waiting patiently?
THAT'S TRUE, WE SHOULD RETURN SOON.
OH!
THOSE TWO ARE STILL BAREFOOT, HUH?
You're being nicer now that you know one of them Hates you.
SANJU, WHY ARE YOU BEING FIDGETY?
....
I HEARD THE PROFESSOR'S VOICE...
...I THINK.
?
I CAN'T HEAR IT.
I HEARD IT.
I SMELL HIM TOO...
...I THINK.
I KNEW IT! YOU ARE ACTING STRANGE!
OH!!
THAT'S THE PROFESSOR!!
SANJU?
DASH

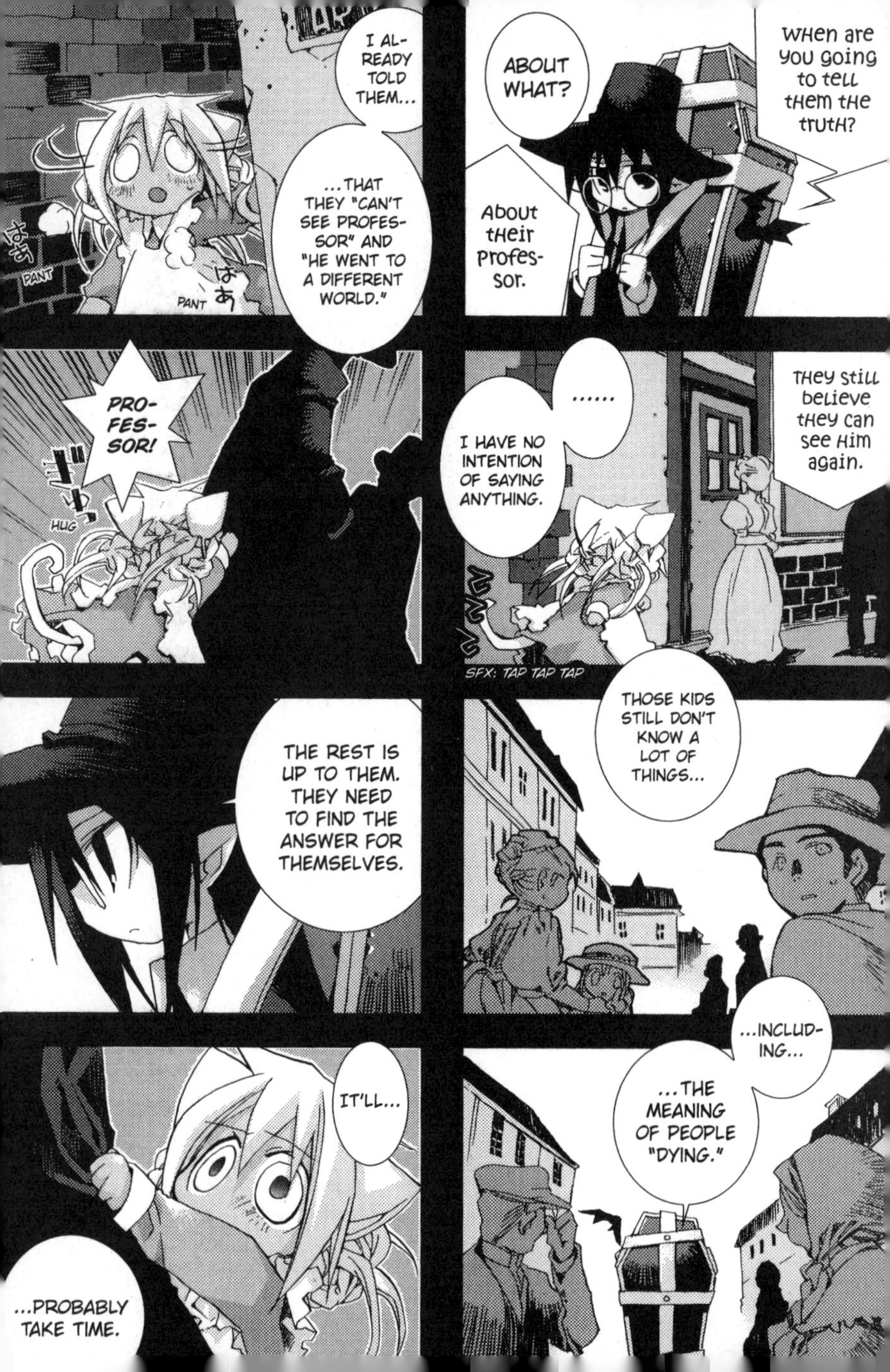
When are you going to tell them the truth?
ABOUT WHAT?
About their profes-sor.
I AL-READY TOLD THEM...
...THAT THEY "CAN'T SEE PROFES-SOR" AND "HE WENT TO A DIFFERENT WORLD."
はあ PANT
はあ PANT
They still believe they can see him again.
......
I HAVE NO INTENTION OF SAYING ANYTHING.
SFX: TAP TAP TAP
PRO-FES-SOR!
HUG
THOSE KIDS STILL DON'T KNOW A LOT OF THINGS...
THE REST IS UP TO THEM. THEY NEED TO FIND THE ANSWER FOR THEMSELVES.
...INCLUD-ING...
...THE MEANING OF PEOPLE "DYING."
IT'LL...
...PROBABLY TAKE TIME.

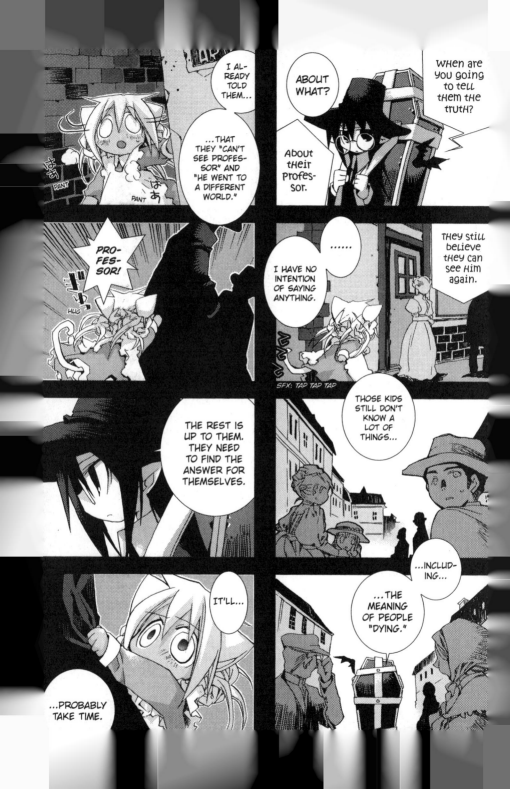

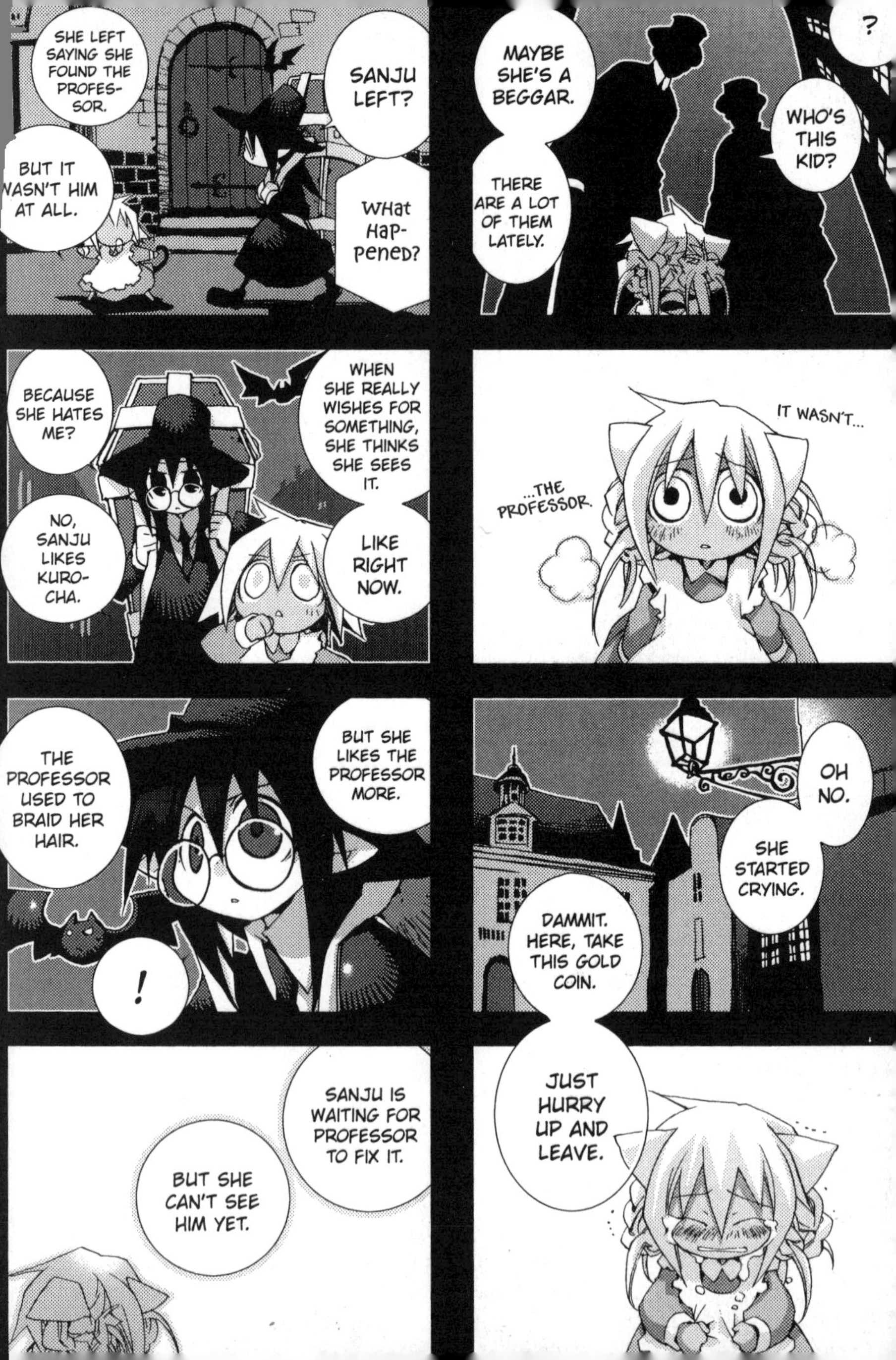
?
WHO'S THIS KID?
MAYBE SHE'S A BEGGAR.
THERE ARE A LOT OF THEM LATELY.
SANJU LEFT?
What Hap-pened?
SHE LEFT SAYING SHE FOUND THE PROFES-SOR.
BUT IT WASN'T HIM AT ALL.
IT WASN'T...
...THE PROFESSOR.
WHEN SHE REALLY WISHES FOR SOMETHING, SHE THINKS SHE SEES IT.
LIKE RIGHT NOW.
BECAUSE SHE HATES ME?
NO, SANJU LIKES KURO-CHA.
OH NO.
SHE STARTED CRYING.
DAMMIT. HERE, TAKE THIS GOLD COIN.
BUT SHE LIKES THE PROFESSOR MORE.
THE PROFESSOR USED TO BRAID HER HAIR.
!
JUST HURRY UP AND LEAVE.
SANJU IS WAITING FOR PROFESSOR TO FIX IT.
BUT SHE CAN'T SEE HIM YET.

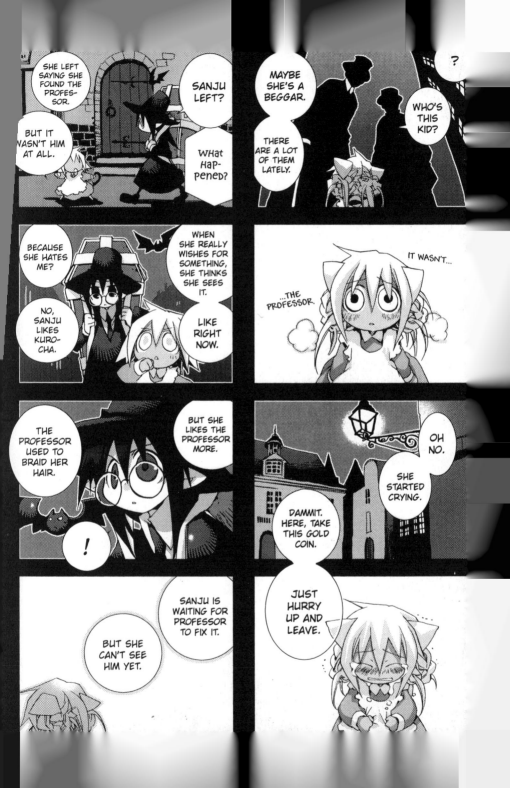

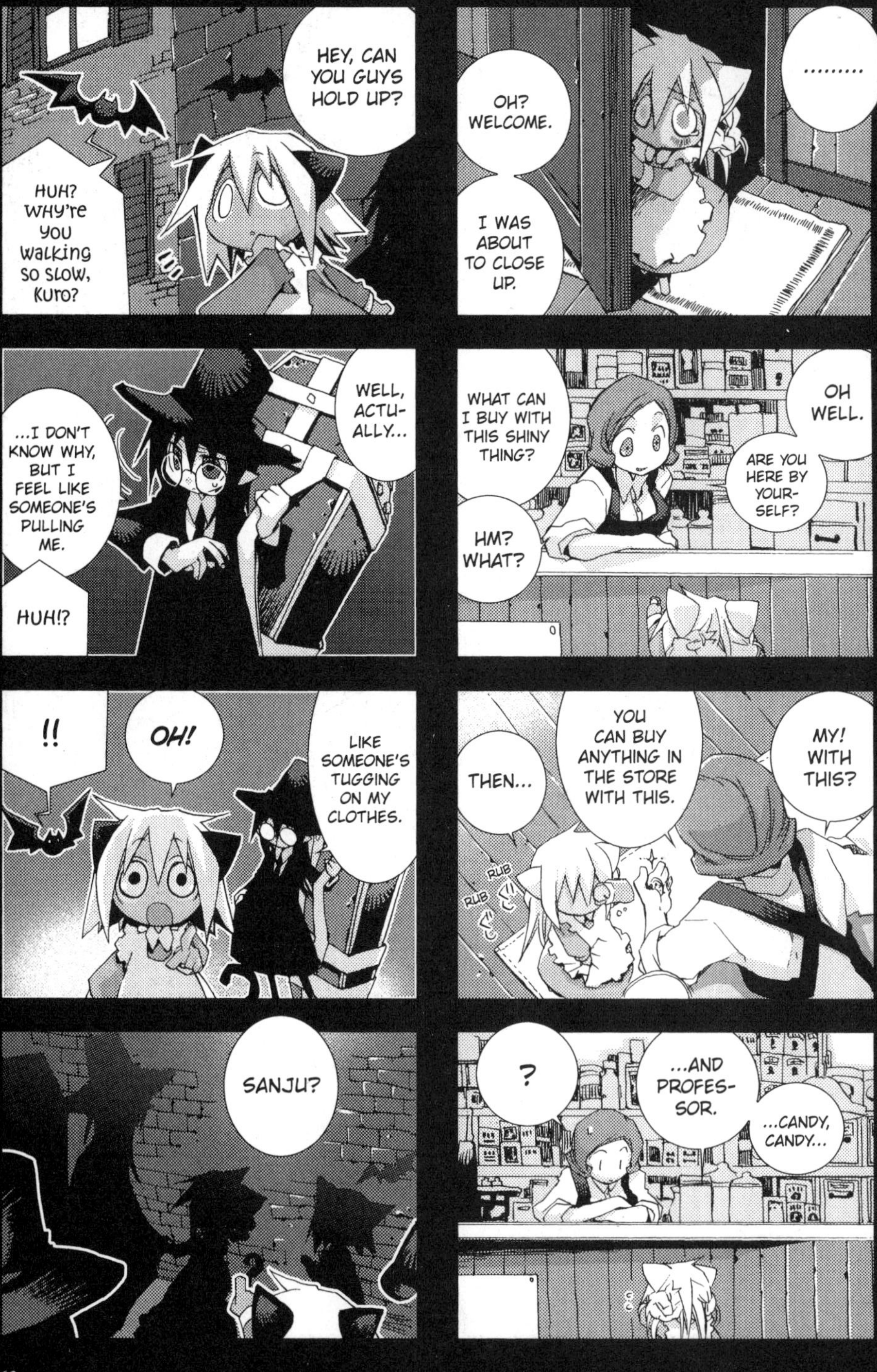
....
OH? WELCOME.
I WAS ABOUT TO CLOSE UP.
HEY, CAN YOU GUYS HOLD UP?
HUH? WHY're YOU walking SO SLOW, Kuro?
OH WELL.
ARE YOU HERE BY YOUR-SELF?
WHAT CAN I BUY WITH THIS SHINY THING?
HM? WHAT?
WELL, ACTU-ALLY...
...I DON'T KNOW WHY, BUT I FEEL LIKE SOMEONE'S PULLING ME.
HUH!?
MY! WITH THIS?
YOU CAN BUY ANYTHING IN THE STORE WITH THIS.
THEN...
RUB RUB
LIKE SOMEONE'S TUGGING ON MY CLOTHES.
OH!
!!
...CANDY, CANDY...
...AND PROFES-SOR.
?
SANJU?

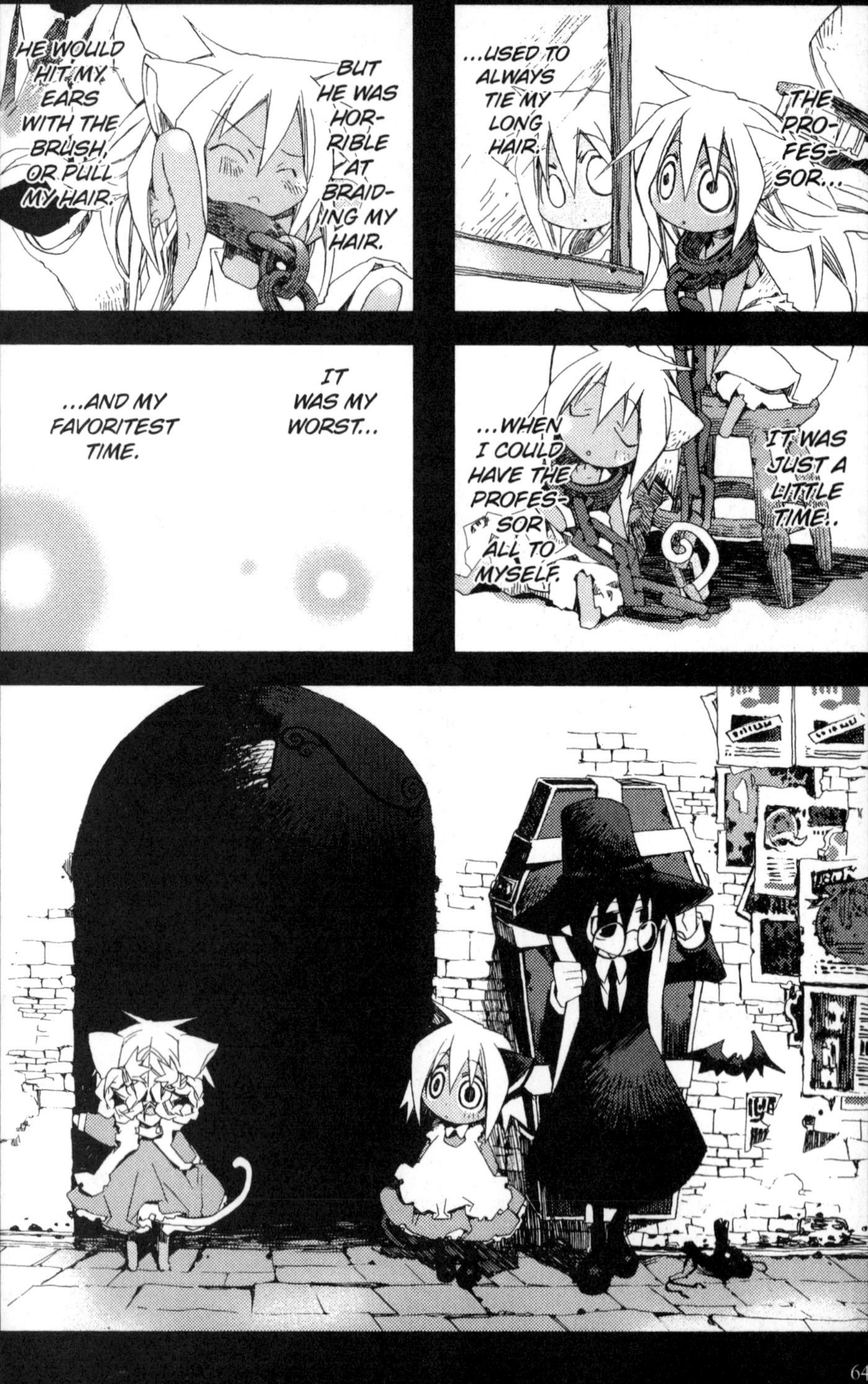
THE PRO-FES-SOR...
...USED TO ALWAYS TIE MY LONG HAIR.
BUT HE WAS HOR-RIBLE AT BRAID-ING MY HAIR.
HE WOULD HIT MY EARS WITH THE BRUSH, OR PULL MY HAIR.
IT WAS JUST A LITTLE TIME...
...WHEN I COULD HAVE THE PROFES-SOR ALL TO MYSELF.
IT WAS MY WORST...
...AND MY FAVORITEST TIME.

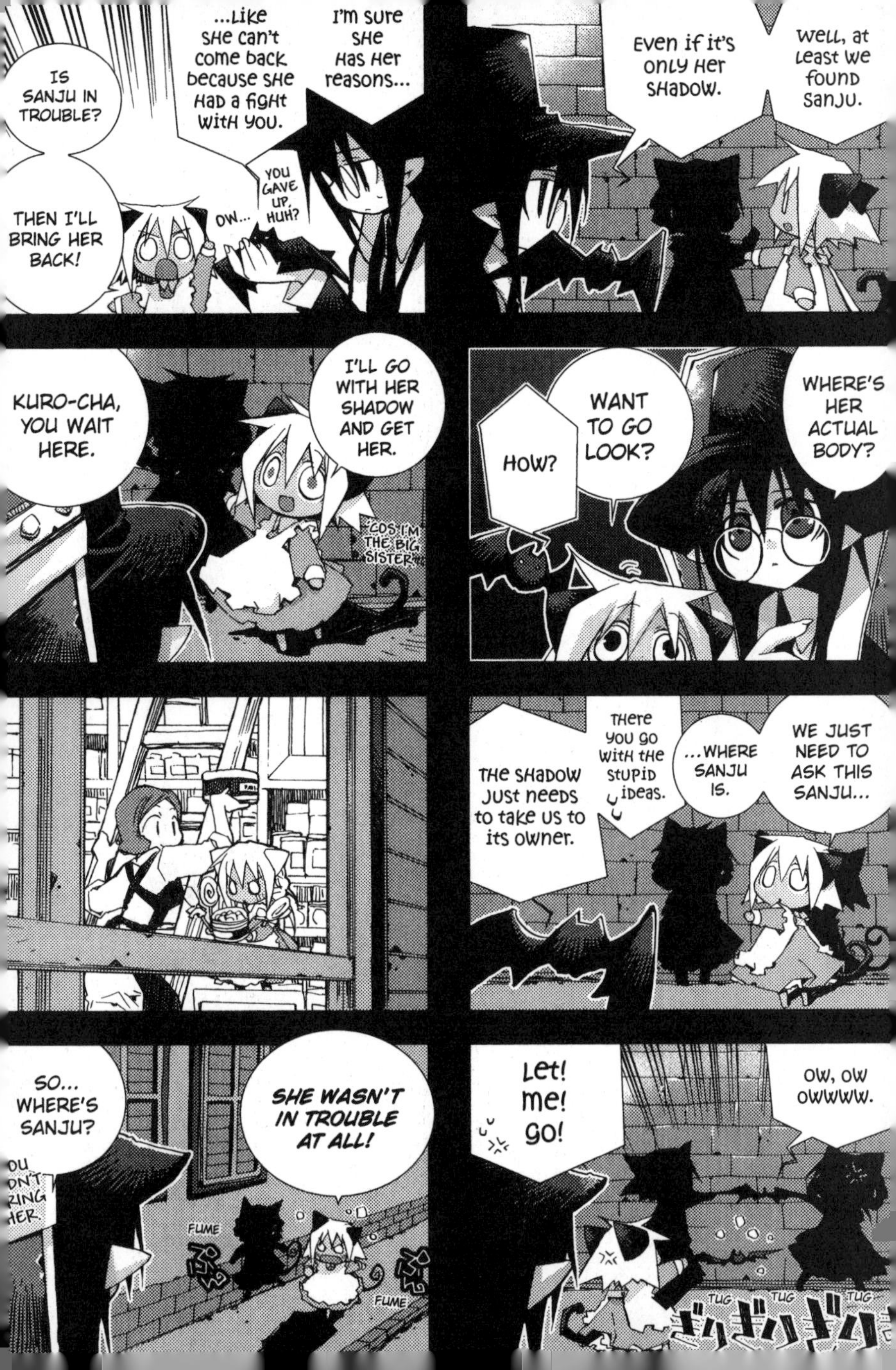
WELL, at Least we found Sanju.
Even if it's only Her SHADOW.
WHERE'S HER ACTUAL BODY?
WANT TO GO LOOK?
HOW?
WE JUST NEED TO ASK THIS SANJU...
...WHERE SANJU IS.
There you go with the stupid ideas.
The shadow just needs to take us to its owner.
OW, OW OWWWW.
Let! me! go!
TUG
TUG
TUG
I'm sure SHE Has Her reasons...
...Like SHE can't come back because SHE Had a fight with you.
YOU GAVE UP, HUH?
OW...
IS SANJU IN TROUBLE?
THEN I'LL BRING HER BACK!
I'LL GO WITH HER SHADOW AND GET HER.
'COS I'M THE BIG SISTER
KURO-CHA, YOU WAIT HERE.
SHE WASN'T IN TROUBLE AT ALL!
FUME
FUME
SO... WHERE'S SANJU?

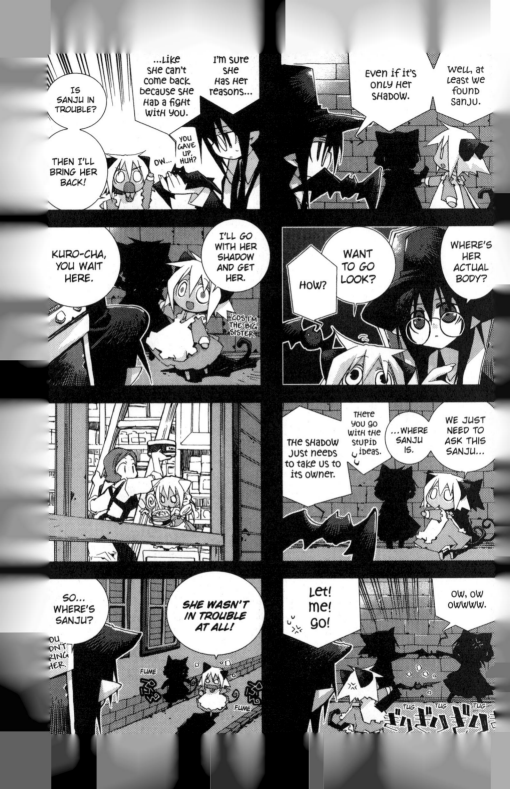

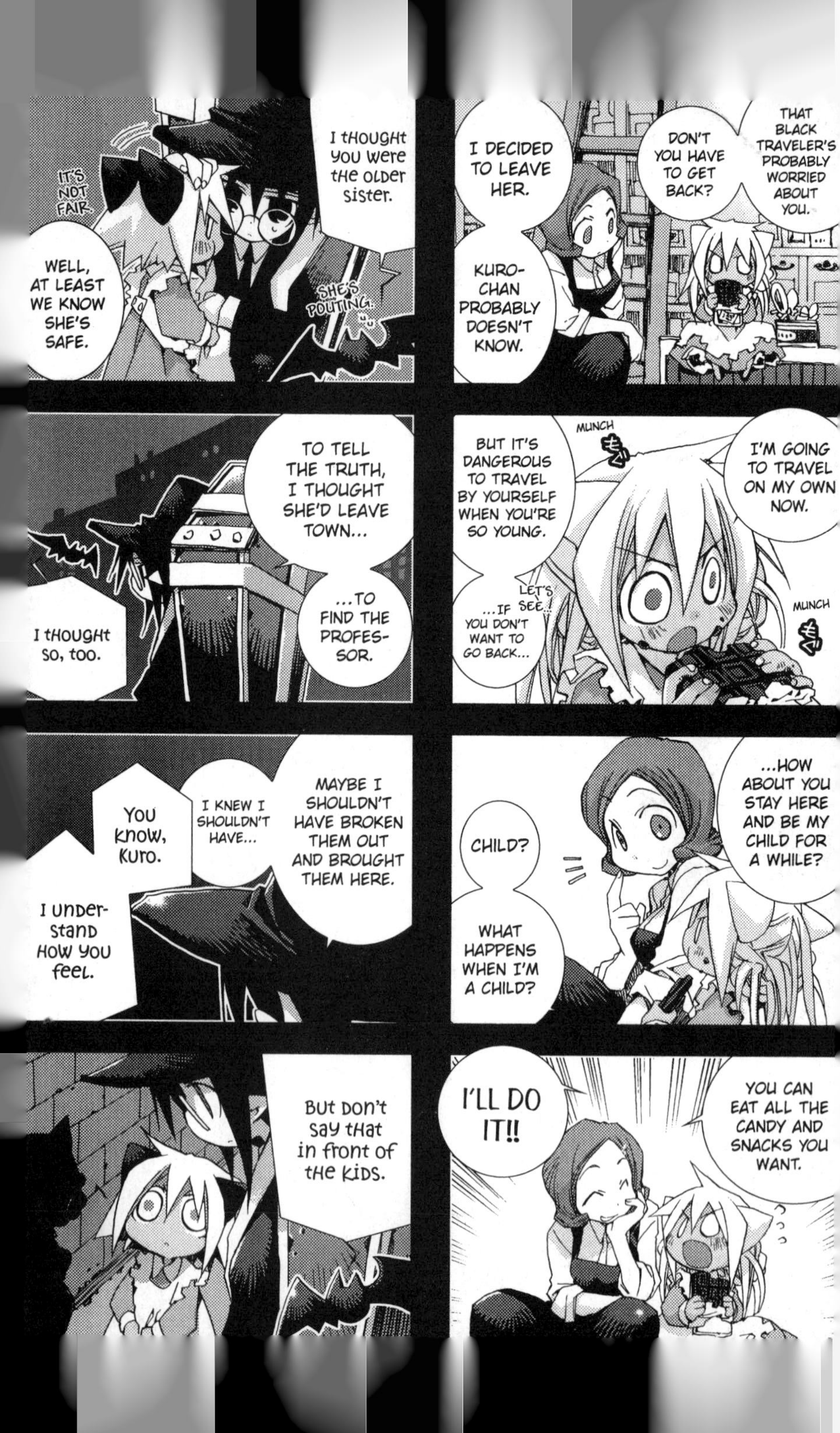
THAT BLACK TRAVELER'S PROBABLY WORRIED ABOUT YOU.
DON'T YOU HAVE TO GET BACK?
I DECIDED TO LEAVE HER.
KURO-CHAN PROBABLY DOESN'T KNOW.
I thought you were the older sister.
IT'S NOT FAIR
SHE'S POUTING.
WELL, AT LEAST WE KNOW SHE'S SAFE.
MUNCH
I'M GOING TO TRAVEL ON MY OWN NOW.
BUT IT'S DANGEROUS TO TRAVEL BY YOURSELF WHEN YOU'RE SO YOUNG.
MUNCH
LET'S SEE...
...IF YOU DON'T WANT TO GO BACK...
TO TELL THE TRUTH, I THOUGHT SHE'D LEAVE TOWN...
...TO FIND THE PROFES-SOR.
I thought so, too.
...HOW ABOUT YOU STAY HERE AND BE MY CHILD FOR A WHILE?
CHILD?
WHAT HAPPENS WHEN I'M A CHILD?
MAYBE I SHOULDN'T HAVE BROKEN THEM OUT AND BROUGHT THEM HERE.
I KNEW I SHOULDN'T HAVE...
You know, Kuro.
I under-stand how you feel.
YOU CAN EAT ALL THE CANDY AND SNACKS YOU WANT.
I'LL DO IT!!
But don't say that in front of the kids.

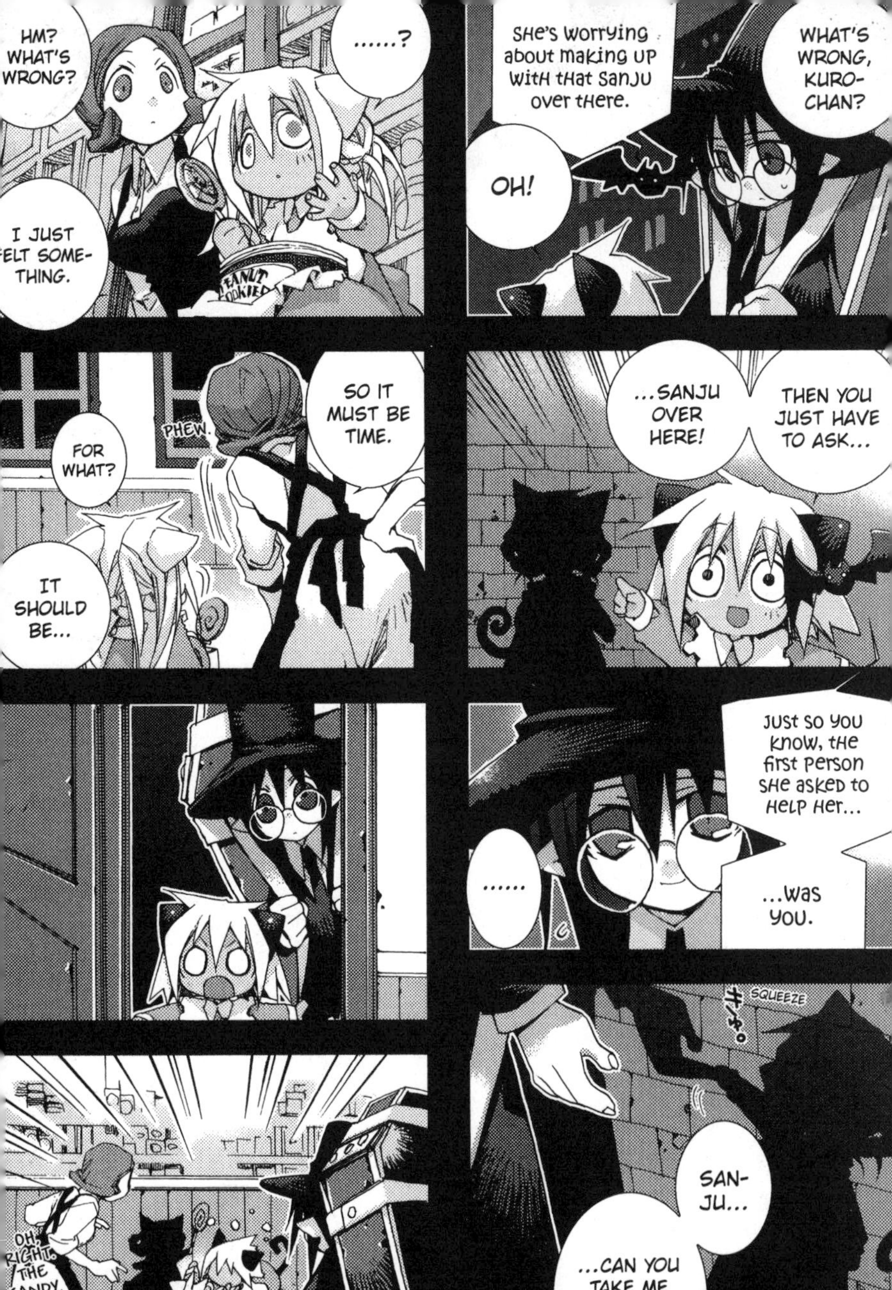
WHAT'S WRONG, KURO-CHAN?
SHE'S WORRYING ABOUT MAKING UP WITH THAT SANJU OVER THERE.
OH!
......?
HM? WHAT'S WRONG?
I JUST FELT SOME-THING.
PEANUT COOKIES
THEN YOU JUST HAVE TO ASK...
...SANJU OVER HERE!
SO IT MUST BE TIME.
PHEW.
FOR WHAT?
IT SHOULD BE...
JUST SO YOU KNOW, THE FIRST PERSON SHE ASKED TO HELP HER...
......
...WAS YOU.
SQUEEZE
SAN-JU...
...CAN YOU TAKE ME TO WHERE YOU ARE?
OH, RIGHT. THE CANDY.

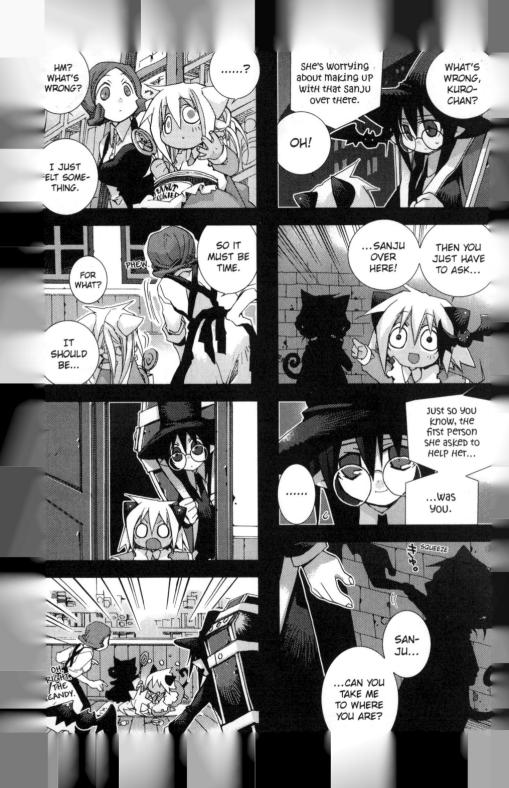

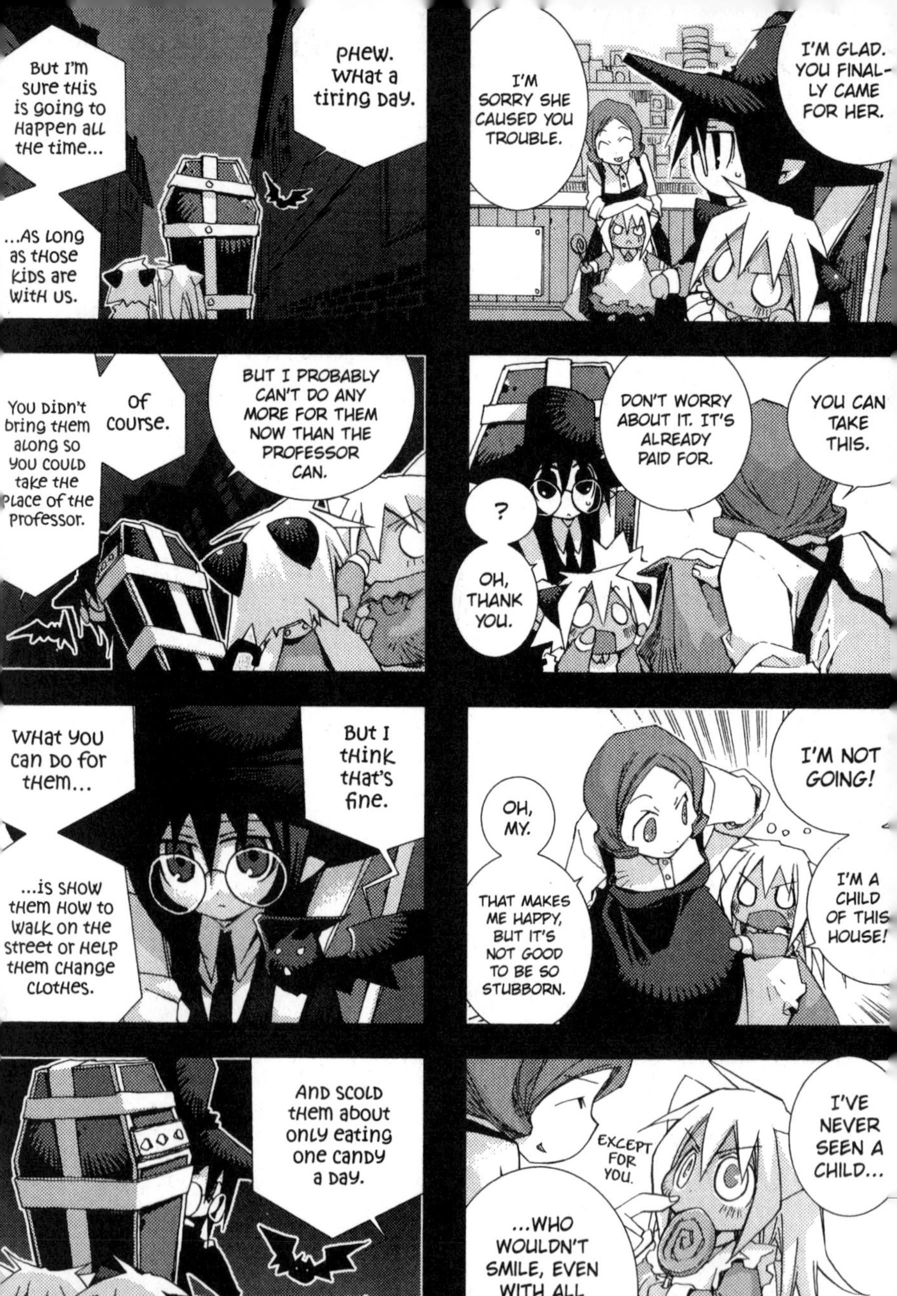
I'M GLAD. YOU FINALLY CAME FOR HER.
I'M SORRY SHE CAUSED YOU TROUBLE.
YOU CAN TAKE THIS.
DON'T WORRY ABOUT IT. IT'S ALREADY PAID FOR.
?
OH, THANK YOU.
I'M NOT GOING!
I'M A CHILD OF THIS HOUSE!
OH, MY.
THAT MAKES ME HAPPY, BUT IT'S NOT GOOD TO BE SO STUBBORN.
I'VE NEVER SEEN A CHILD...
EXCEPT FOR YOU.
...WHO WOULDN'T SMILE, EVEN WITH ALL THE CANDY IN MY STORE.
Phew. What a tiring day.
But I'm sure this is going to happen all the time...
...as long as those kids are with us.
BUT I PROBABLY CAN'T DO ANY MORE FOR THEM NOW THAN THE PROFESSOR CAN.
Of course.
You didn't bring them along so you could take the place of the Professor.
But I think that's fine.
What you can do for them...
...is show them how to walk on the street or help them change clothes.
And scold them about only eating one candy a day.
STRICTLY...

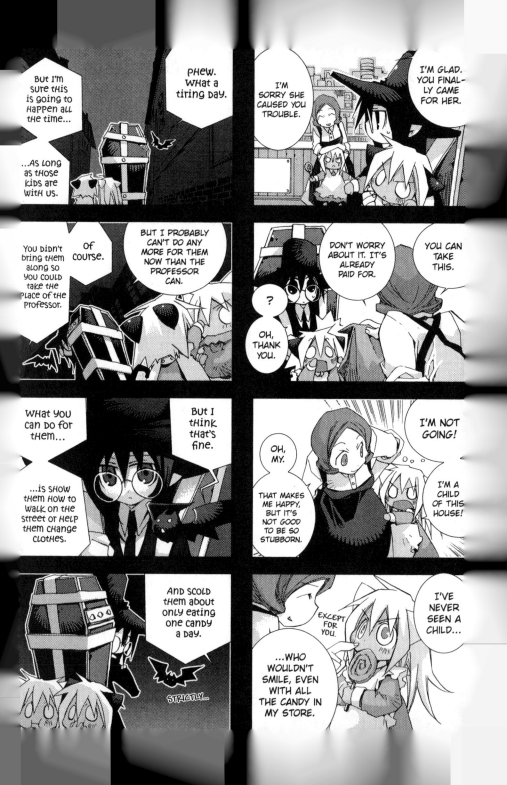

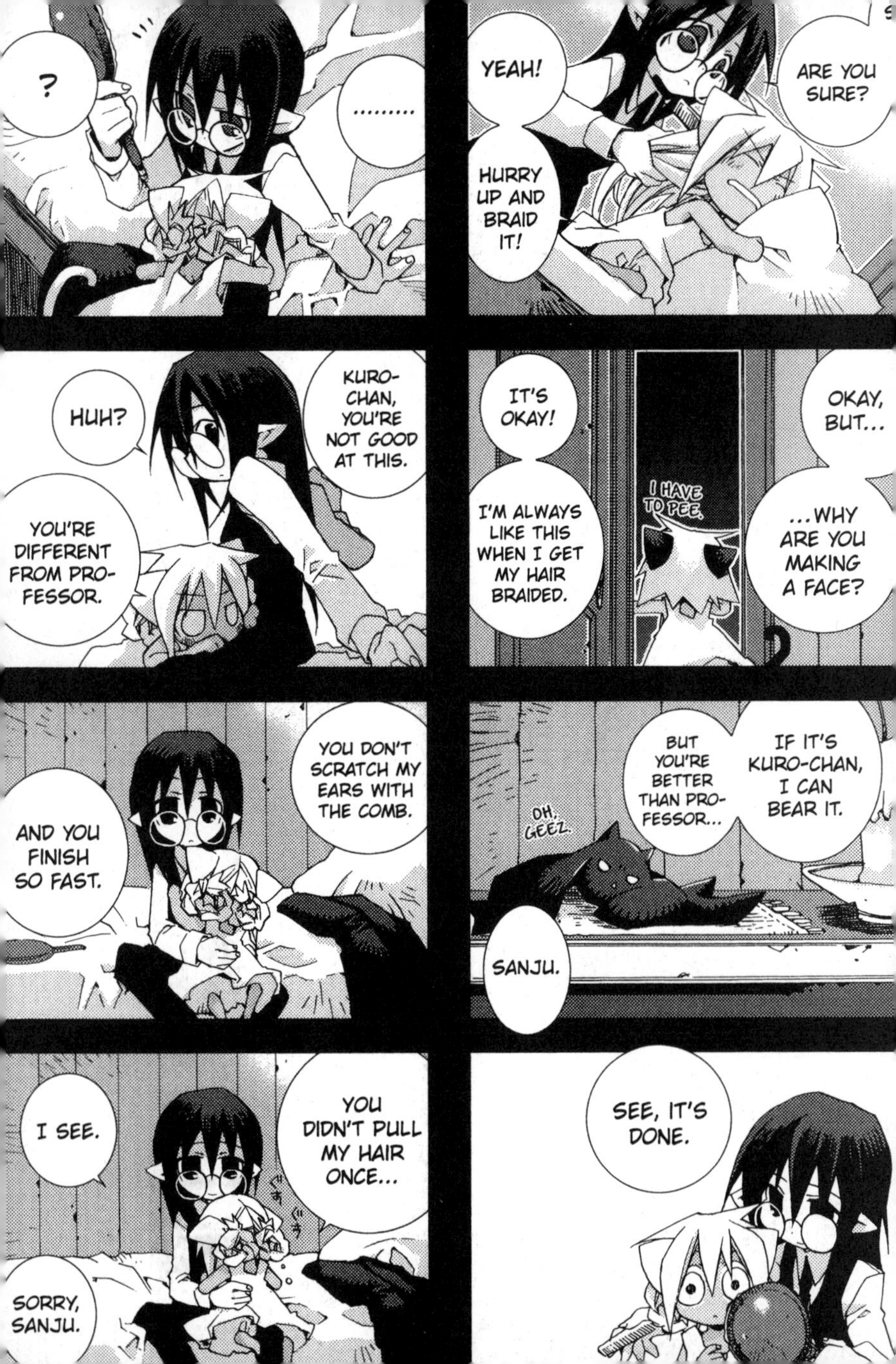
ARE YOU SURE?
YEAH!
HURRY UP AND BRAID IT!
....
?
OKAY, BUT...
...WHY ARE YOU MAKING A FACE?
IT'S OKAY!
I'M ALWAYS LIKE THIS WHEN I GET MY HAIR BRAIDED.
I HAVE TO PEE.
KURO-CHAN, YOU'RE NOT GOOD AT THIS.
HUH?
YOU'RE DIFFERENT FROM PRO-FESSOR.
IF IT'S KURO-CHAN, I CAN BEAR IT.
BUT YOU'RE BETTER THAN PRO-FESSOR...
OH, GEEZ.
SANJU.
YOU DON'T SCRATCH MY EARS WITH THE COMB.
AND YOU FINISH SO FAST.
SEE, IT'S DONE.
YOU DIDN'T PULL MY HAIR ONCE...
I SEE.
SORRY, SANJU.

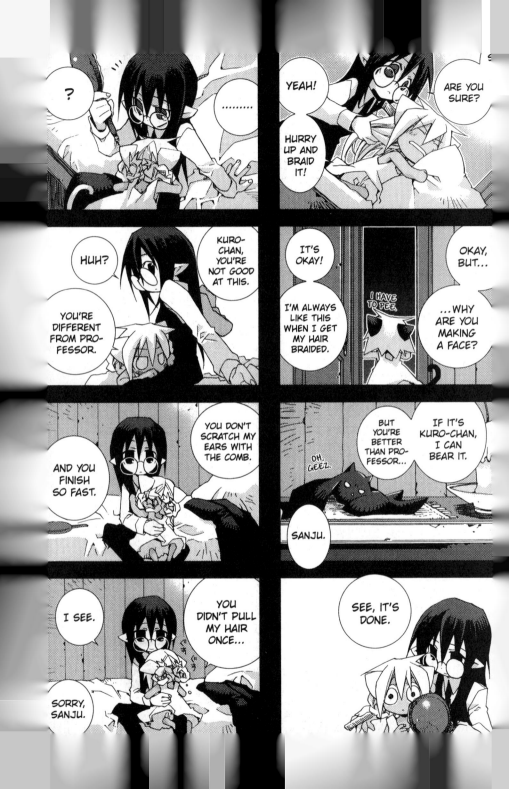

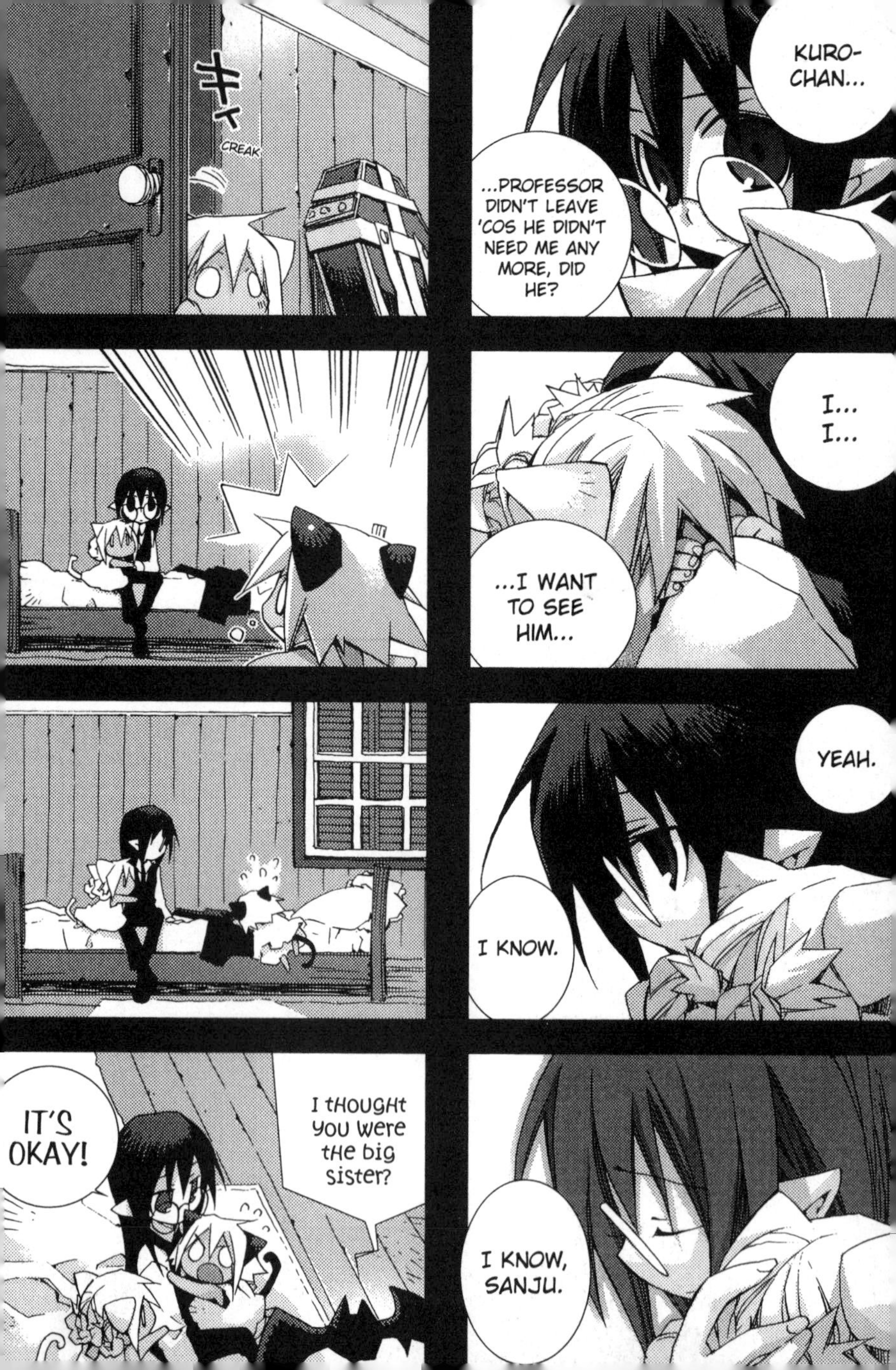
KURO-CHAN...
...PROFESSOR DIDN'T LEAVE 'COS HE DIDN'T NEED ME ANY MORE, DID HE?
キィ
CREAK
I... I...
...I WANT TO SEE HIM...
YEAH.
I KNOW.
I KNOW, SANJU.
I tHOUGHt you were tHe big sister?
IT'S OKAY!

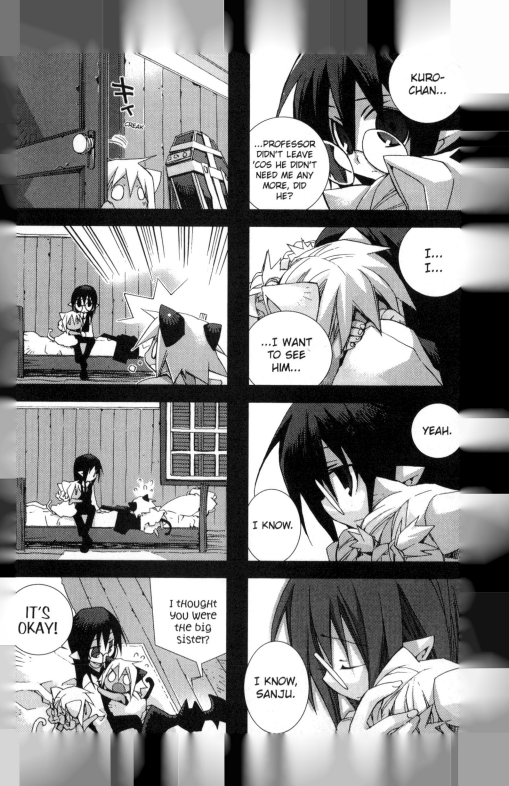

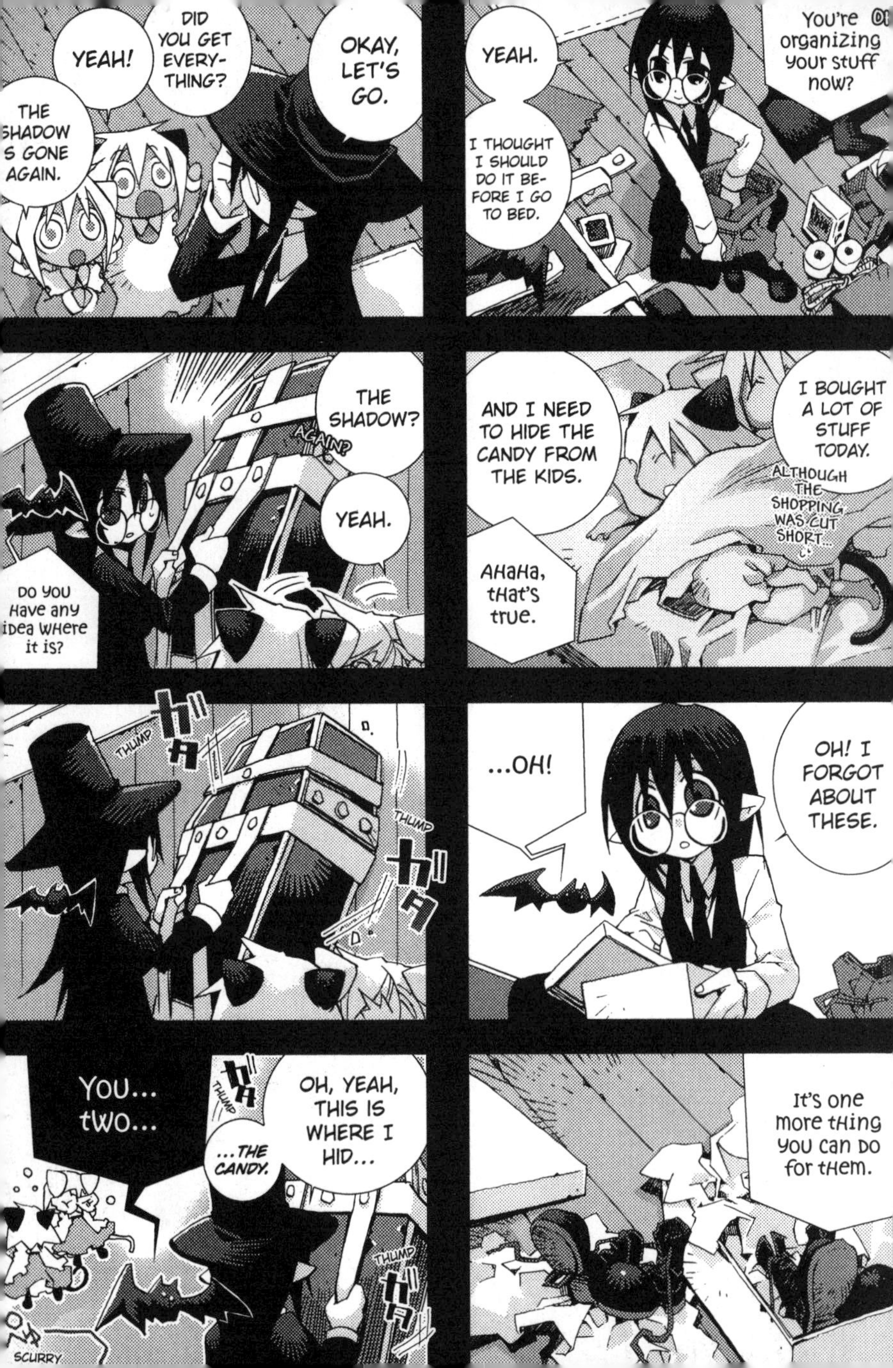
You're organizing your stuff now?
YEAH.
I THOUGHT I SHOULD DO IT BEFORE I GO TO BED.
OKAY, LET'S GO.
DID YOU GET EVERYTHING?
YEAH!
THE SHADOW S GONE AGAIN.
I BOUGHT A LOT OF STUFF TODAY.
ALTHOUGH THE SHOPPING WAS CUT SHORT...
AND I NEED TO HIDE THE CANDY FROM THE KIDS.
AHaHa, tHat's true.
THE SHADOW?
AGAIN?
YEAH.
DO YOU Have any idea WHere it is?
OH! I FORGOT ABOUT THESE.
...OH!
THUMP
THUMP
It's one more tHing you can do for tHem.
OH, YEAH, THIS IS WHERE I HID...
...THE CANDY.
THUMP
YOU... tWO...
THUMP
SCURRY

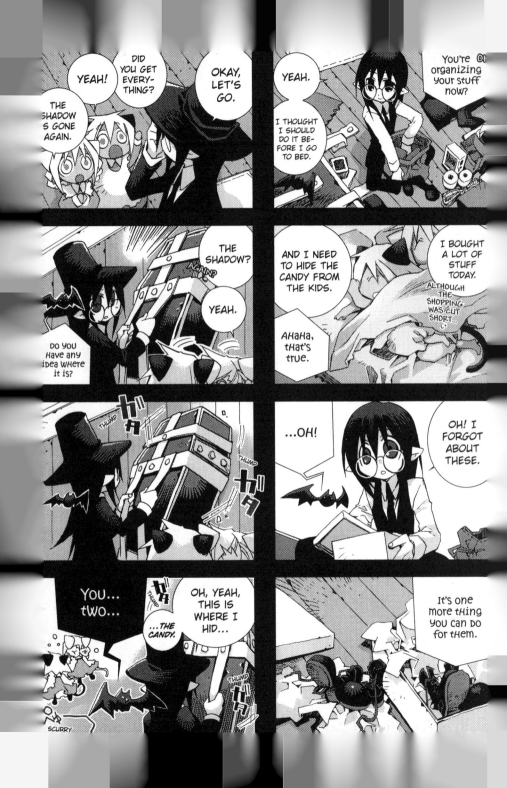

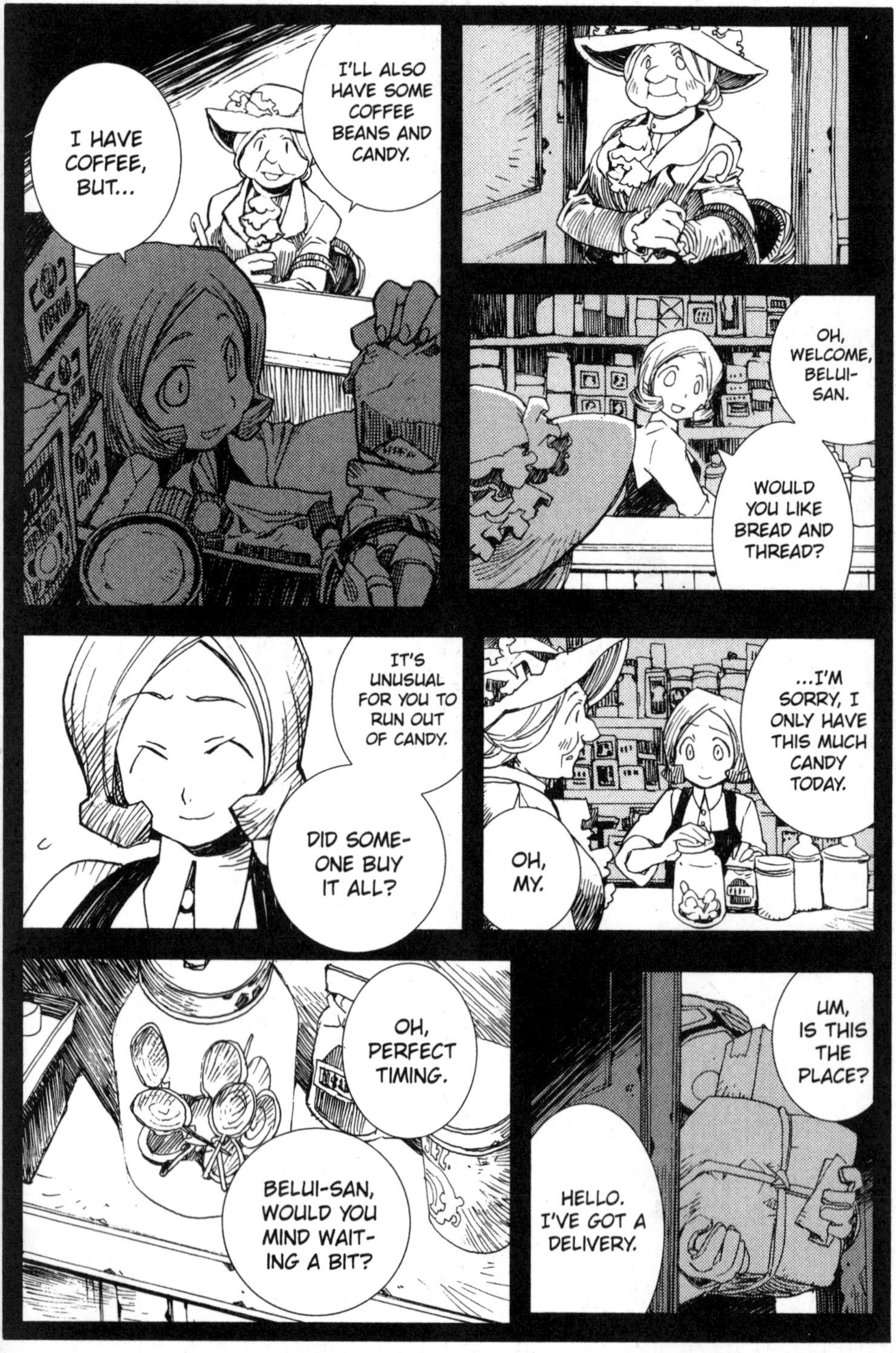
OH, WELCOME, BELUI-SAN.
WOULD YOU LIKE BREAD AND THREAD?
I'LL ALSO HAVE SOME COFFEE BEANS AND CANDY.
I HAVE COFFEE, BUT...
...I'M SORRY, I ONLY HAVE THIS MUCH CANDY TODAY.
OH, MY.
IT'S UNUSUAL FOR YOU TO RUN OUT OF CANDY.
DID SOME-ONE BUY IT ALL?
UM, IS THIS THE PLACE?
HELLO. I'VE GOT A DELIVERY.
OH, PERFECT TIMING.
BELUI-SAN, WOULD YOU MIND WAIT-ING A BIT?

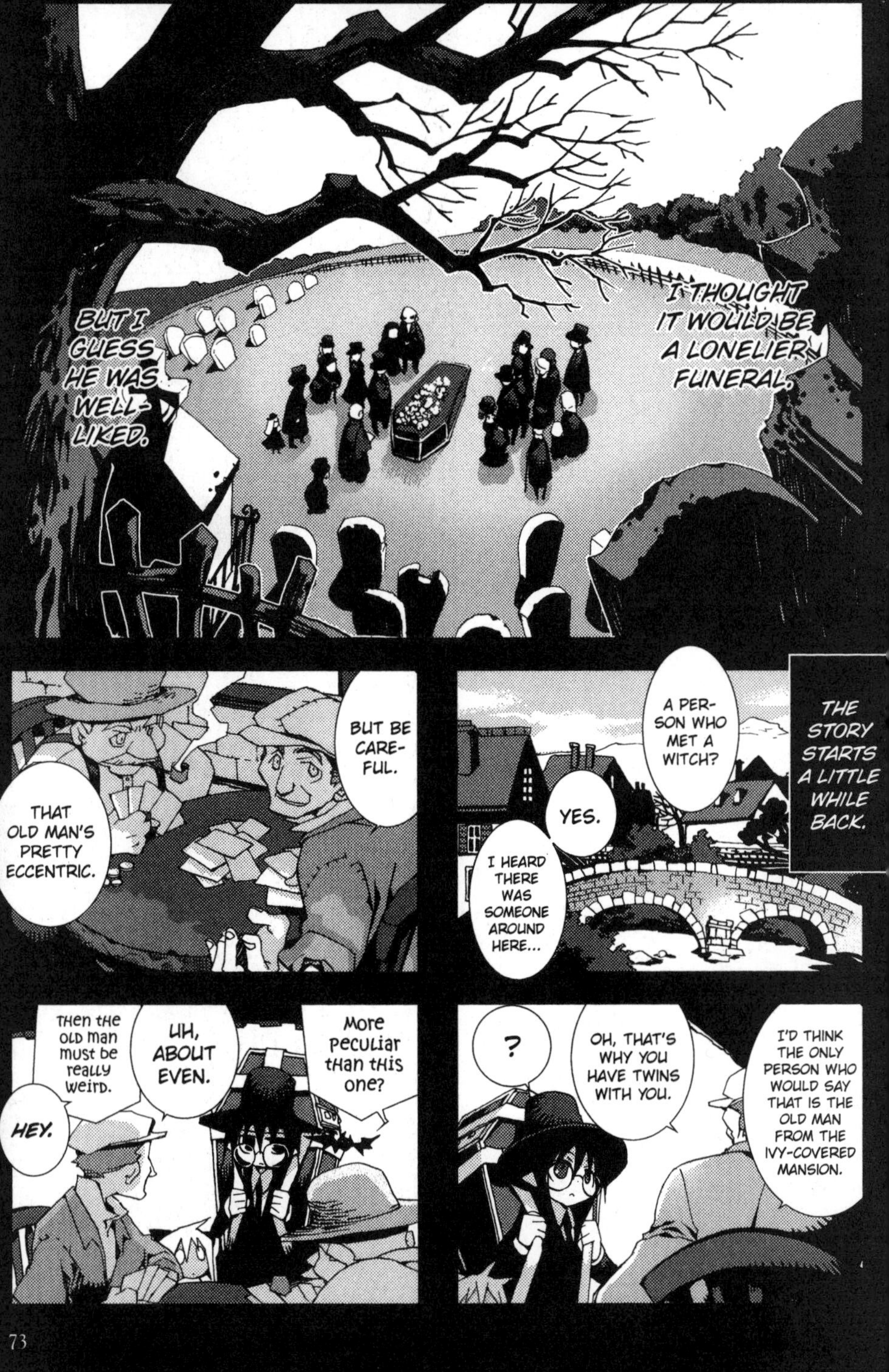
I THOUGHT IT WOULD BE A LONELIER FUNERAL.
BUT I GUESS HE WAS WELL-LIKED.
THE STORY STARTS A LITTLE WHILE BACK.
A PERSON WHO MET A WITCH?
YES.
I HEARD THERE WAS SOMEONE AROUND HERE...
BUT BE CAREFUL.
THAT OLD MAN'S PRETTY ECCENTRIC.
I'D THINK THE ONLY PERSON WHO WOULD SAY THAT IS THE OLD MAN FROM THE IVY-COVERED MANSION.
OH, THAT'S WHY YOU HAVE TWINS WITH YOU.
?
More peculiar than this one?
UH, ABOUT EVEN.
Then the old man must be really weird.
HEY.

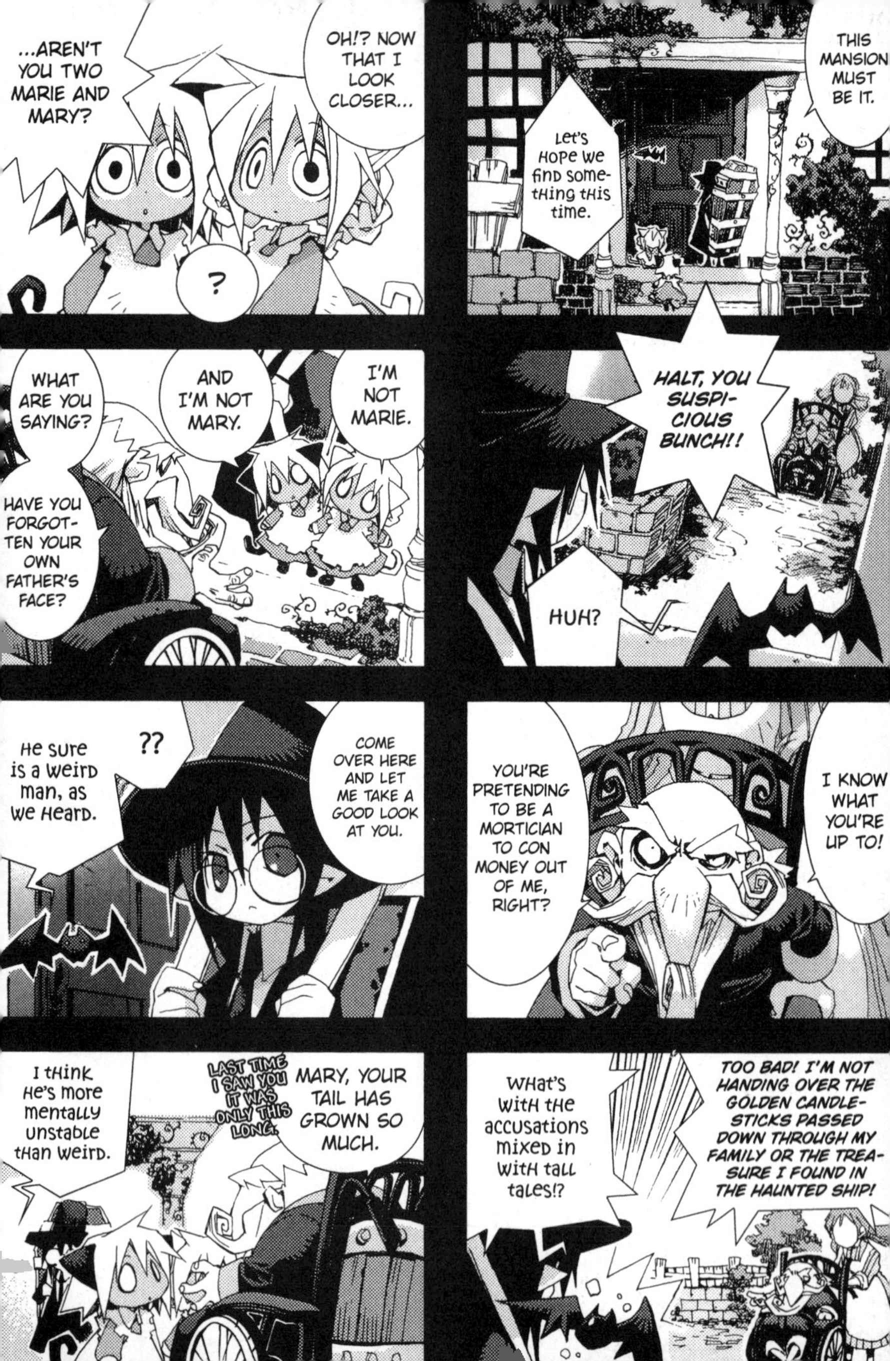
THIS MANSION MUST BE IT.
Let's hope we find something this time.
OH!? NOW THAT I LOOK CLOSER...
...AREN'T YOU TWO MARIE AND MARY?
?
HALT, YOU SUSPICIOUS BUNCH!!
HUH?
I'M NOT MARIE.
AND I'M NOT MARY.
WHAT ARE YOU SAYING?
HAVE YOU FORGOTTEN YOUR OWN FATHER'S FACE?
I KNOW WHAT YOU'RE UP TO!
YOU'RE PRETENDING TO BE A MORTICIAN TO CON MONEY OUT OF ME, RIGHT?
COME OVER HERE AND LET ME TAKE A GOOD LOOK AT YOU.
??
He sure is a weird man, as we heard.
TOO BAD! I'M NOT HANDING OVER THE GOLDEN CANDLESTICKS PASSED DOWN THROUGH MY FAMILY OR THE TREASURE I FOUND IN THE HAUNTED SHIP!
What's with the accusations mixed in with tall tales!?
MARY, YOUR TAIL HAS GROWN SO MUCH.
LAST TIME I SAW YOU IT WAS ONLY THIS LONG.
I think he's more mentally unstable than weird.

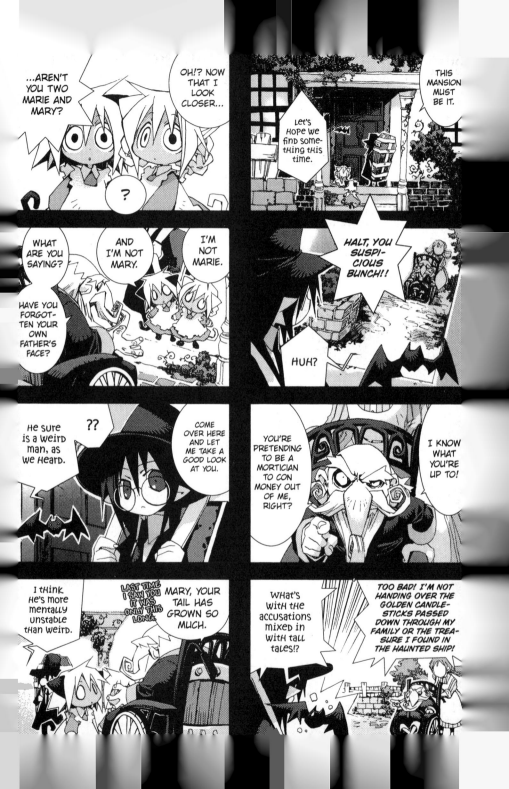

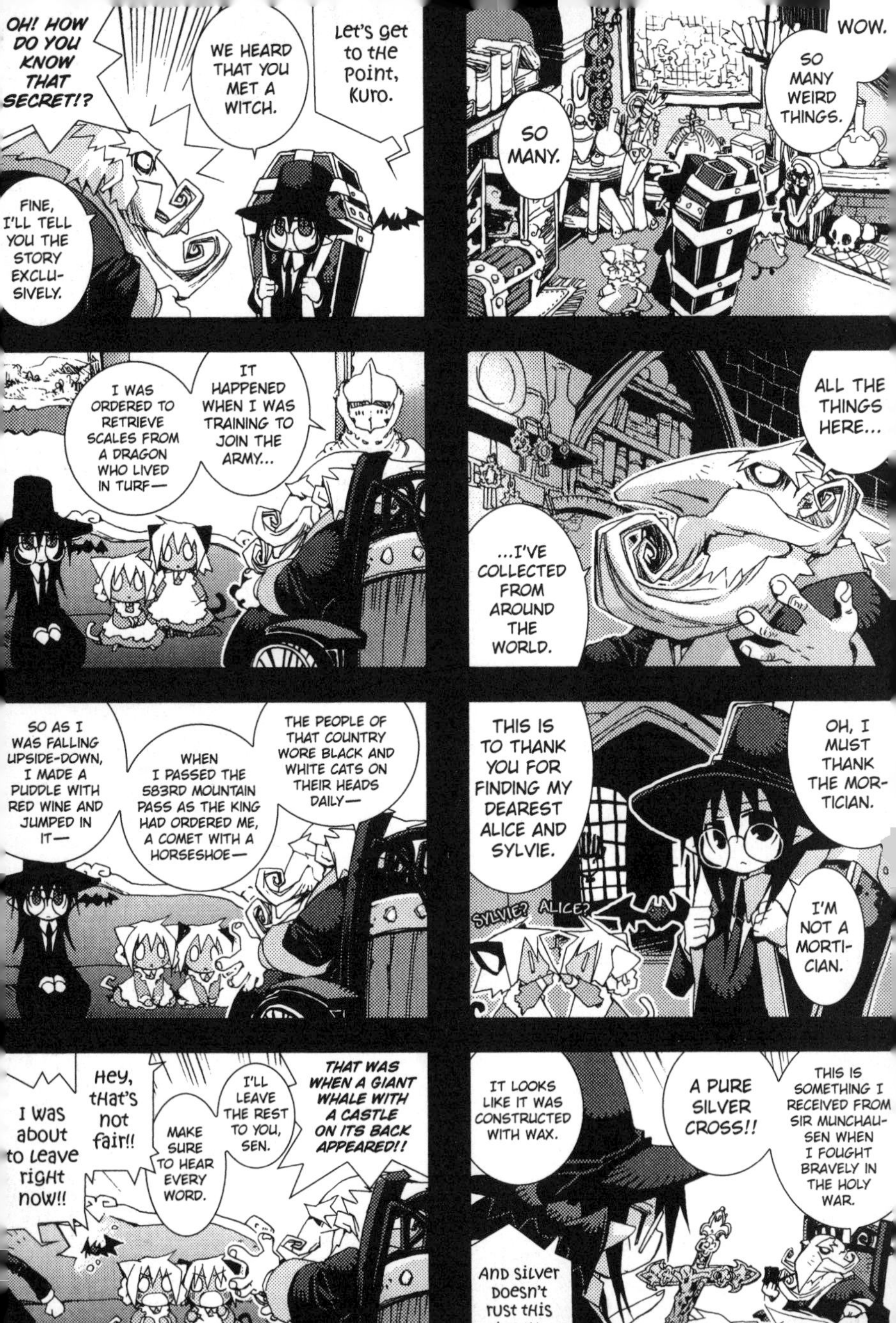
WOW.
SO MANY WEIRD THINGS.
SO MANY.
ALL THE THINGS HERE...
...I'VE COLLECTED FROM AROUND THE WORLD.
OH, I MUST THANK THE MORTICIAN.
THIS IS TO THANK YOU FOR FINDING MY DEAREST ALICE AND SYLVIE.
I'M NOT A MORTICIAN.
SYLVIE? ALICE?
THIS IS SOMETHING I RECEIVED FROM SIR MUNCHAUSEN WHEN I FOUGHT BRAVELY IN THE HOLY WAR.
A PURE SILVER CROSS!!
IT LOOKS LIKE IT WAS CONSTRUCTED WITH WAX.
And silver doesn't rust this badly, does it?
Let's get to the point, Kuro.
WE HEARD THAT YOU MET A WITCH.
OH! HOW DO YOU KNOW THAT SECRET!?
FINE, I'LL TELL YOU THE STORY EXCLUSIVELY.
IT HAPPENED WHEN I WAS TRAINING TO JOIN THE ARMY...
I WAS ORDERED TO RETRIEVE SCALES FROM A DRAGON WHO LIVED IN TURF—
THE PEOPLE OF THAT COUNTRY WORE BLACK AND WHITE CATS ON THEIR HEADS DAILY—
WHEN I PASSED THE 583RD MOUNTAIN PASS AS THE KING HAD ORDERED ME, A COMET WITH A HORSESHOE—
SO AS I WAS FALLING UPSIDE-DOWN, I MADE A PUDDLE WITH RED WINE AND JUMPED IN IT—
THAT WAS WHEN A GIANT WHALE WITH A CASTLE ON ITS BACK APPEARED!!
I'LL LEAVE THE REST TO YOU, SEN.
MAKE SURE TO HEAR EVERY WORD.
Hey, that's not fair!!
I was about to leave right now!!

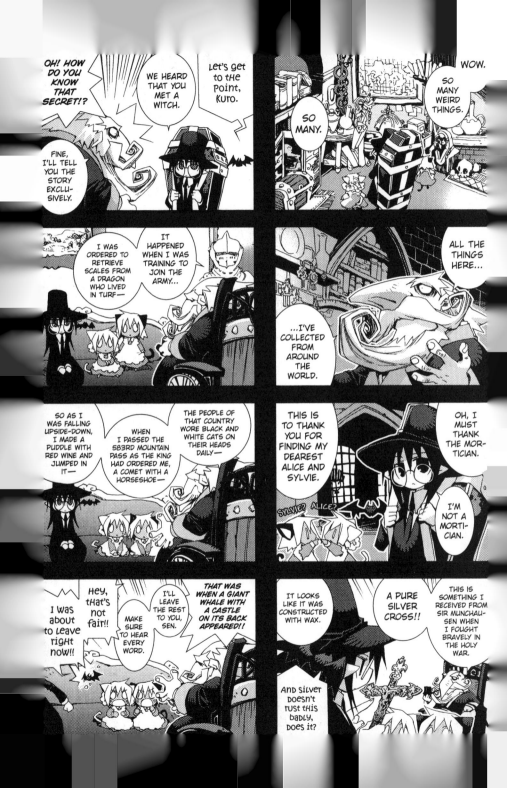

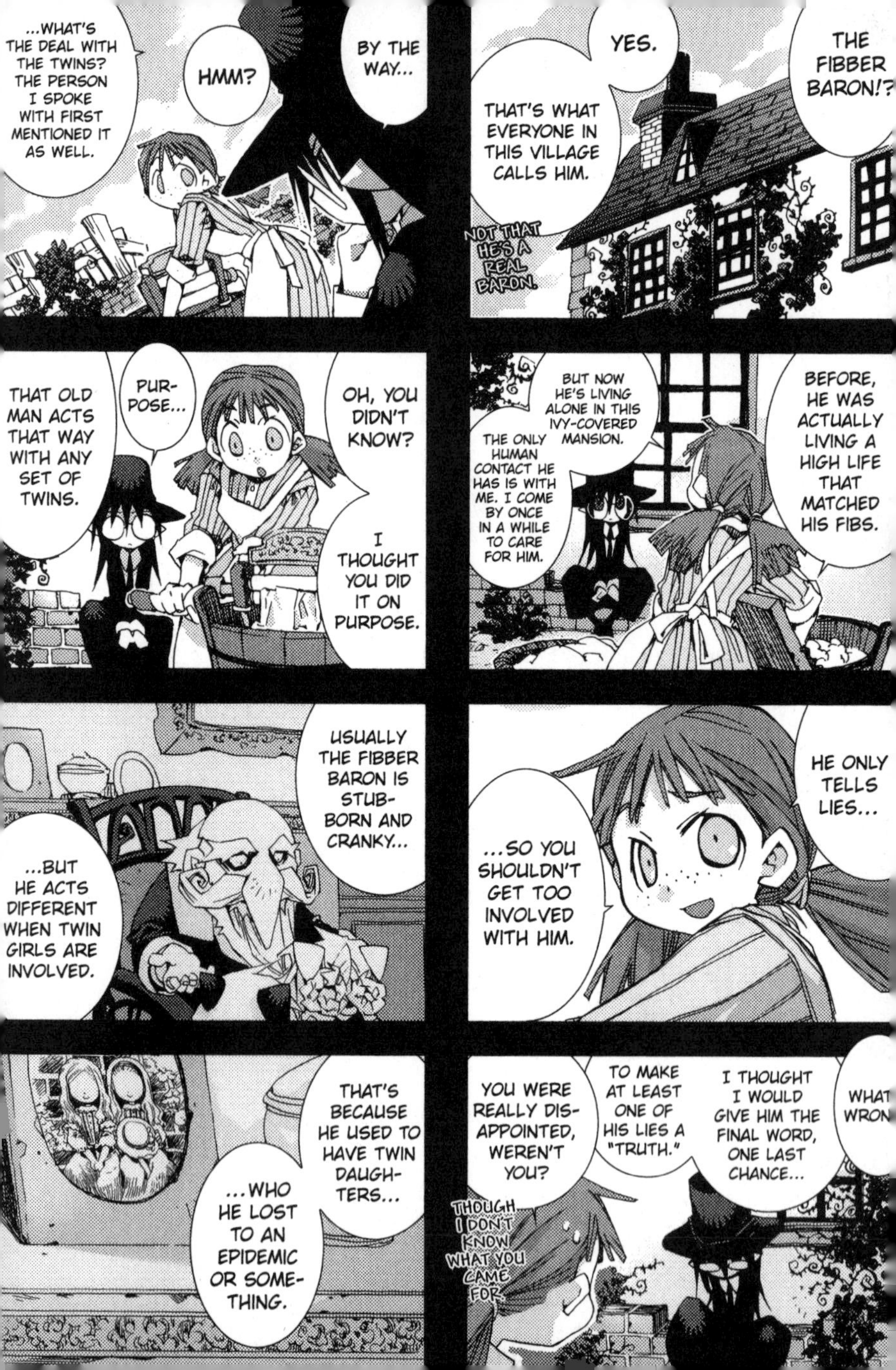
THE FIBBER BARON!?
YES.
THAT'S WHAT EVERYONE IN THIS VILLAGE CALLS HIM.
NOT THAT HE'S A REAL BARON.
BY THE WAY...
HMM?
...WHAT'S THE DEAL WITH THE TWINS? THE PERSON I SPOKE WITH FIRST MENTIONED IT AS WELL.
BEFORE, HE WAS ACTUALLY LIVING A HIGH LIFE THAT MATCHED HIS FIBS.
BUT NOW HE'S LIVING ALONE IN THIS IVY-COVERED MANSION.
THE ONLY HUMAN CONTACT HE HAS IS WITH ME. I COME BY ONCE IN A WHILE TO CARE FOR HIM.
OH, YOU DIDN'T KNOW?
I THOUGHT YOU DID IT ON PURPOSE.
PUR-POSE...
THAT OLD MAN ACTS THAT WAY WITH ANY SET OF TWINS.
HE ONLY TELLS LIES...
...SO YOU SHOULDN'T GET TOO INVOLVED WITH HIM.
USUALLY THE FIBBER BARON IS STUB-BORN AND CRANKY...
...BUT HE ACTS DIFFERENT WHEN TWIN GIRLS ARE INVOLVED.
WHAT WRON
I THOUGHT I WOULD GIVE HIM THE FINAL WORD, ONE LAST CHANCE...
TO MAKE AT LEAST ONE OF HIS LIES A "TRUTH."
YOU WERE REALLY DIS-APPOINTED, WEREN'T YOU?
THOUGH I DON'T KNOW WHAT YOU CAME FOR.
THAT'S BECAUSE HE USED TO HAVE TWIN DAUGH-TERS...
...WHO HE LOST TO AN EPIDEMIC OR SOME-THING.

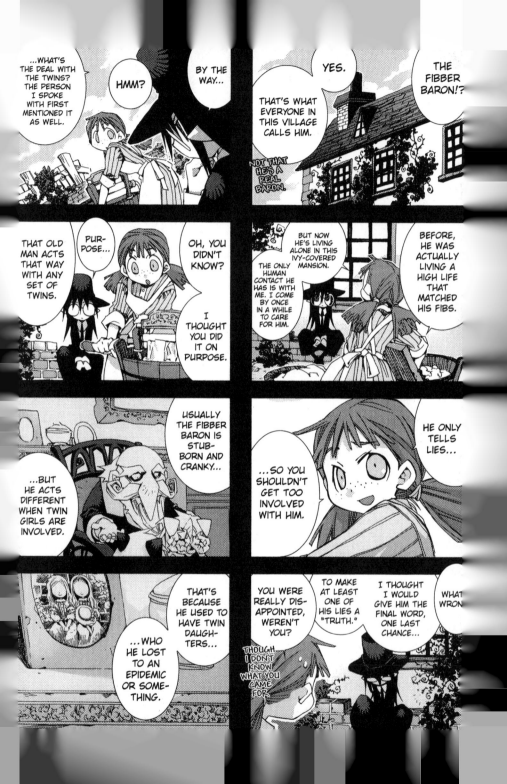

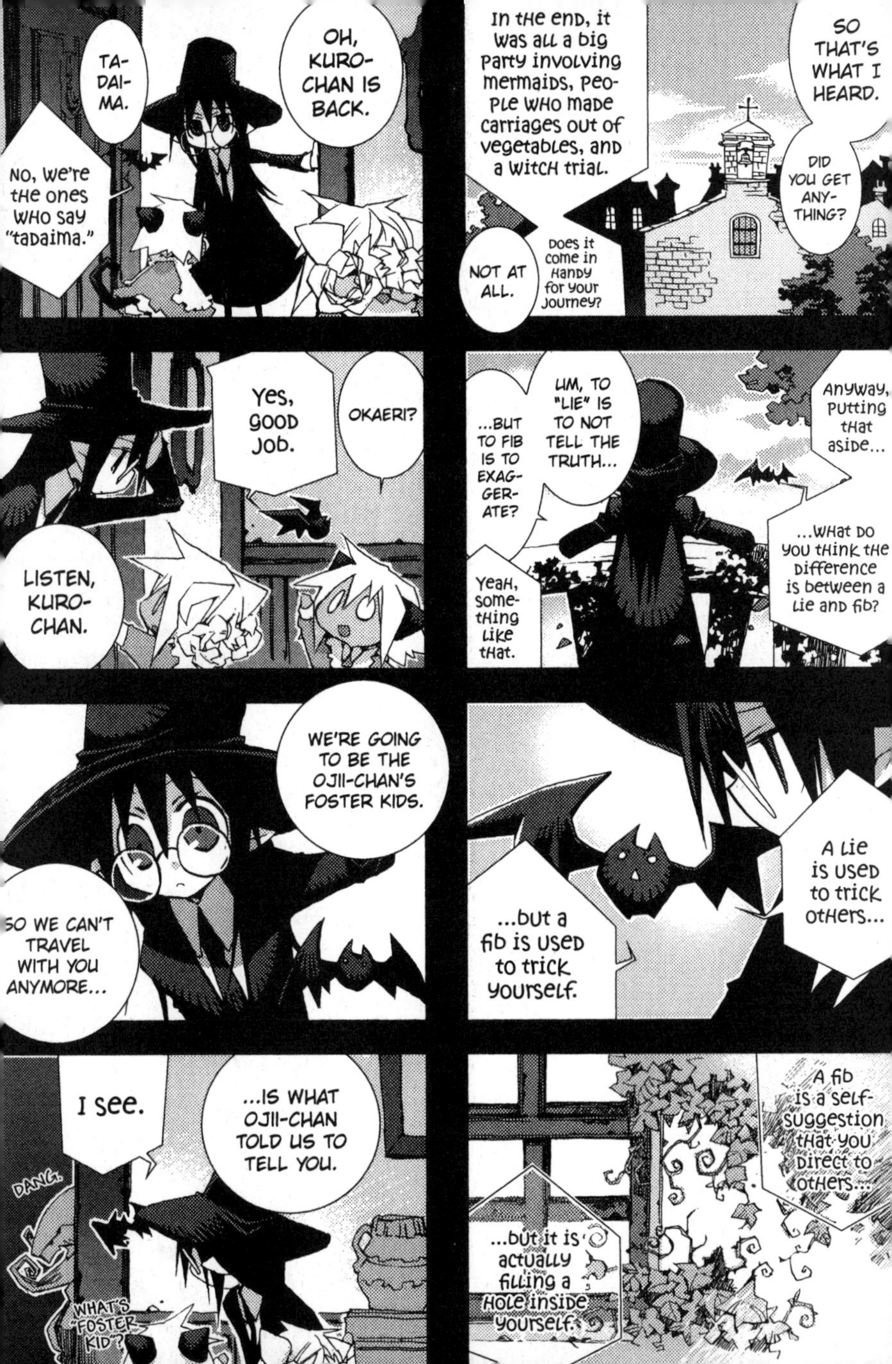
In the end, it was all a big party involving mermaids, people who made carriages out of vegetables, and a witch trial.
SO THAT'S WHAT I HEARD.
DID YOU GET ANYTHING?
Does it come in handy for your journey?
NOT AT ALL.
Anyway, putting that aside...
...What do you think the difference is between a lie and fib?
UM, TO "LIE" IS TO NOT TELL THE TRUTH...
...BUT TO FIB IS TO EXAGGERATE?
Yeah, something like that.
A lie is used to trick others...
...but a fib is used to trick yourself.
A fib is a self-suggestion that you direct to others...
...but it is actually filling a hole inside yourself.
OH, KURO-CHAN IS BACK.
TA-DAI-MA.
No, we're the ones who say "tadaima."
OKAERI?
Yes, good job.
LISTEN, KURO-CHAN.
WE'RE GOING TO BE THE OJII-CHAN'S FOSTER KIDS.
SO WE CAN'T TRAVEL WITH YOU ANYMORE...
...IS WHAT OJII-CHAN TOLD US TO TELL YOU.
I see.
DANG.
WHAT'S "FOSTER KID"?

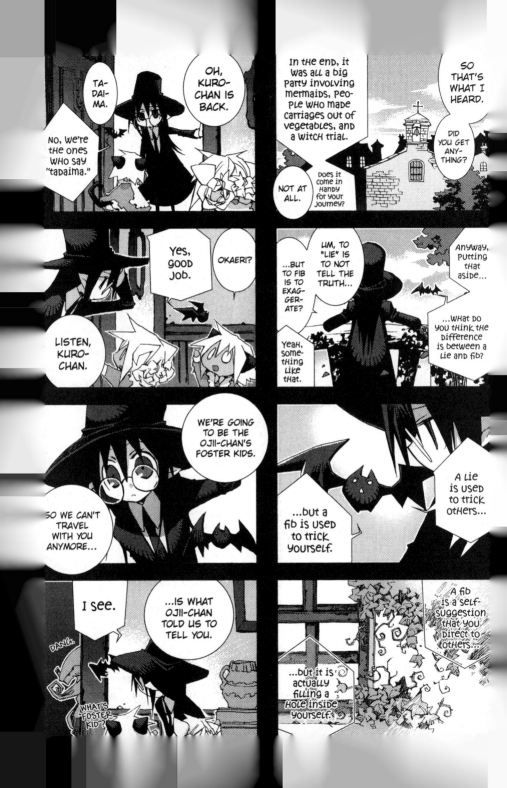

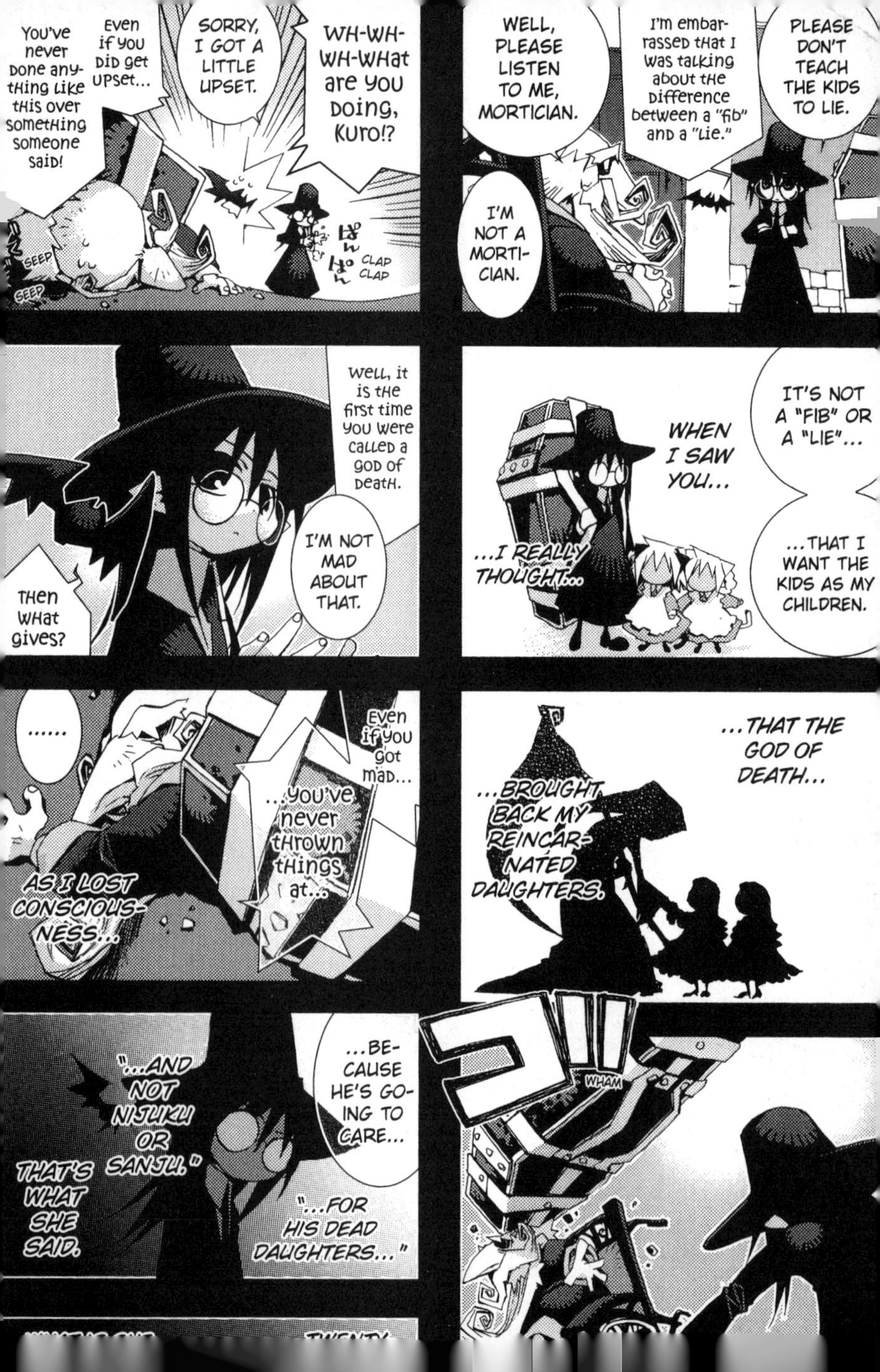
PLEASE DON'T TEACH THE KIDS TO LIE.
I'm embarrassed that I was talking about the difference between a "fib" and a "lie."
WELL, PLEASE LISTEN TO ME, MORTICIAN.
I'M NOT A MORTICIAN.
WH-WH-WH-WHat are you doing, Kuro!?
SORRY, I GOT A LITTLE UPSET.
Even if you did get upset...
You've never done anything like this over something someone said!
CLAP CLAP
SEEP
SEEP
IT'S NOT A "FIB" OR A "LIE"...
...THAT I WANT THE KIDS AS MY CHILDREN.
WHEN I SAW YOU...
...I REALLY THOUGHT...
Well, it is the first time you were called a god of death.
I'M NOT MAD ABOUT THAT.
Then what gives?
...THAT THE GOD OF DEATH...
...BROUGHT BACK MY REINCARNATED DAUGHTERS.
Even if you got mad...
...you've never thrown things at...
......
AS I LOST CONSCIOUSNESS...
WHAM
...BECAUSE HE'S GOING TO CARE...
"...FOR HIS DEAD DAUGHTERS..."
"...AND NOT NIJUKU OR SANJU."
THAT'S WHAT SHE SAID.

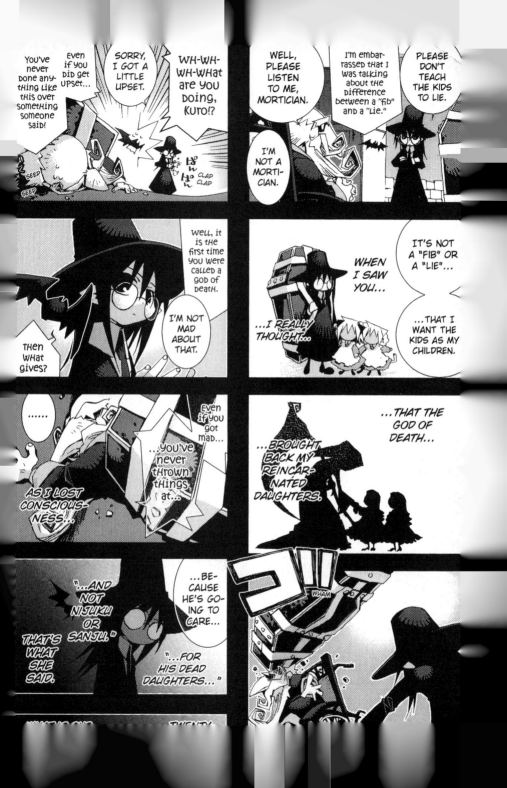

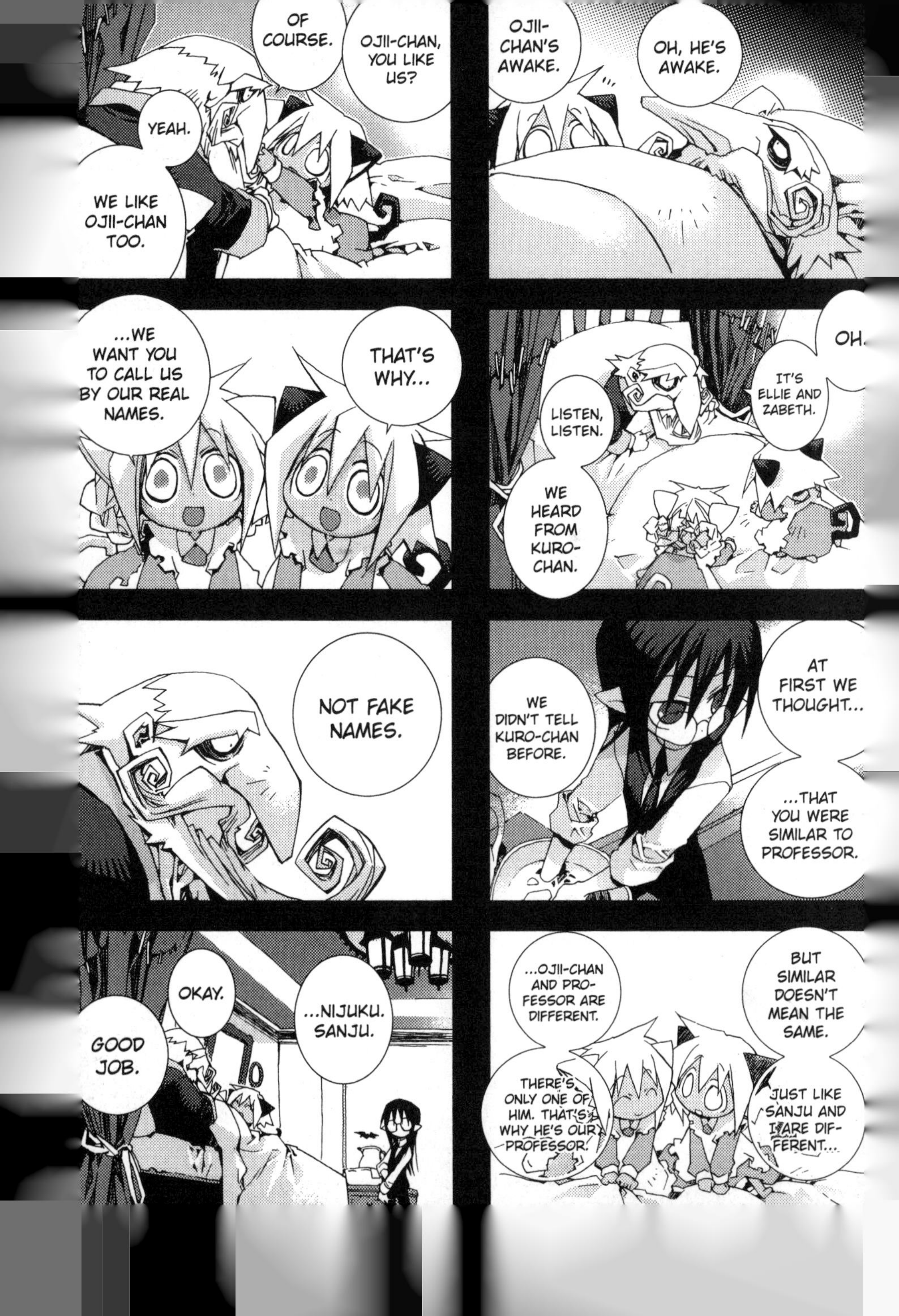
OH, HE'S AWAKE.
OJII-CHAN'S AWAKE.
OJII-CHAN, YOU LIKE US?
OF COURSE.
YEAH.
WE LIKE OJII-CHAN TOO.
OH.
IT'S ELLIE AND ZABETH.
LISTEN, LISTEN.
WE HEARD FROM KURO-CHAN.
THAT'S WHY...
...WE WANT YOU TO CALL US BY OUR REAL NAMES.
AT FIRST WE THOUGHT...
...THAT YOU WERE SIMILAR TO PROFESSOR.
WE DIDN'T TELL KURO-CHAN BEFORE.
NOT FAKE NAMES.
BUT SIMILAR DOESN'T MEAN THE SAME.
...OJII-CHAN AND PROFESSOR ARE DIFFERENT.
JUST LIKE SANJU AND I ARE DIFFERENT...
THERE'S ONLY ONE OF HIM. THAT'S WHY HE'S OUR PROFESSOR.
...NIJUKU. SANJU.
OKAY.
GOOD JOB.

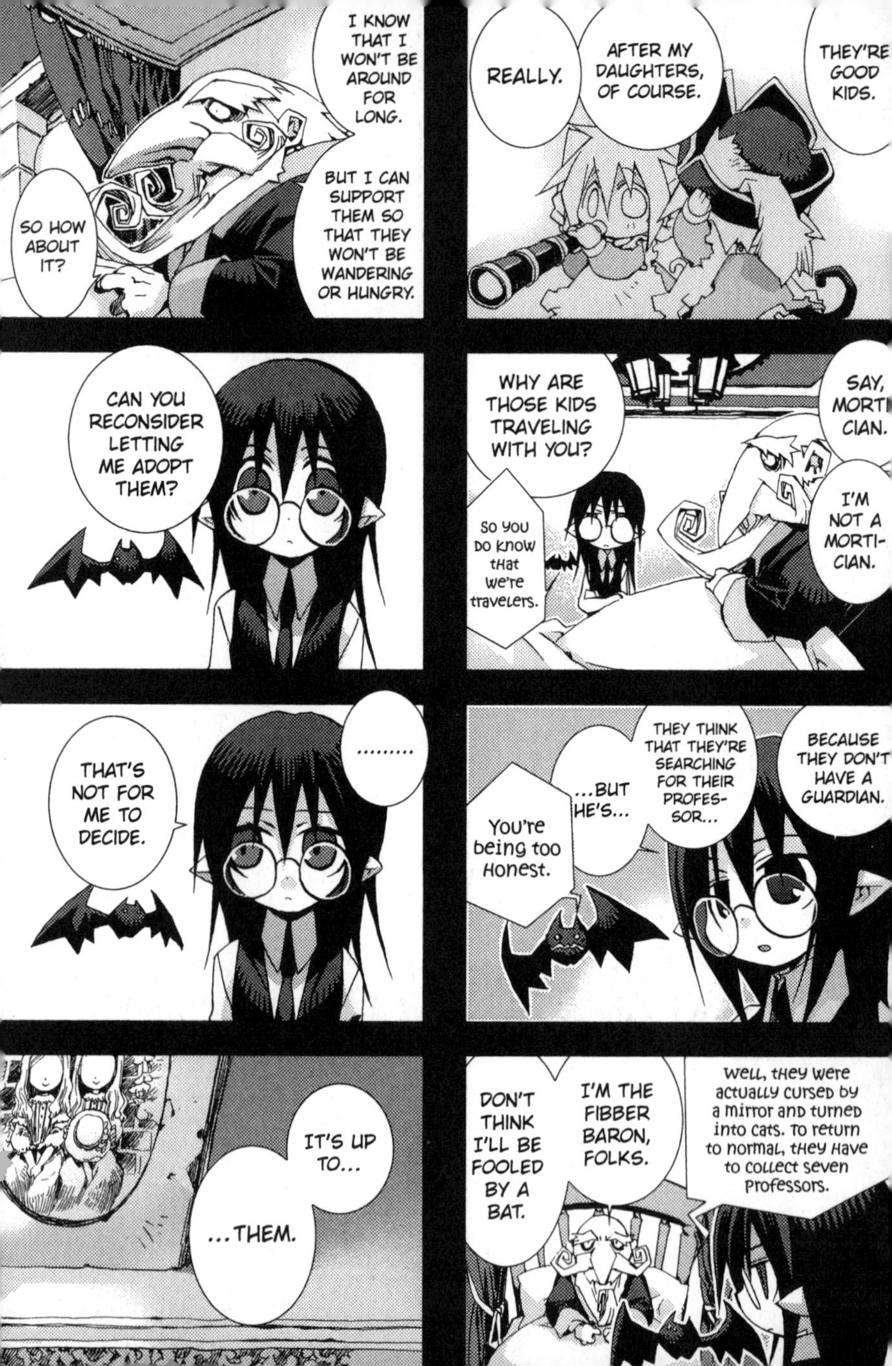
THEY'RE GOOD KIDS.
AFTER MY DAUGHTERS, OF COURSE.
REALLY.
I KNOW THAT I WON'T BE AROUND FOR LONG.
BUT I CAN SUPPORT THEM SO THAT THEY WON'T BE WANDERING OR HUNGRY.
SO HOW ABOUT IT?
SAY, MORTICIAN.
I'M NOT A MORTICIAN.
WHY ARE THOSE KIDS TRAVELING WITH YOU?
So you do know that we're travelers.
CAN YOU RECONSIDER LETTING ME ADOPT THEM?
BECAUSE THEY DON'T HAVE A GUARDIAN.
THEY THINK THAT THEY'RE SEARCHING FOR THEIR PROFESSOR...
...BUT HE'S...
You're being too Honest.
....
THAT'S NOT FOR ME TO DECIDE.
Well, they were actually cursed by a mirror and turned into cats. To return to normal, they have to collect seven Professors.
I'M THE FIBBER BARON, FOLKS.
DON'T THINK I'LL BE FOOLED BY A BAT.
IT'S UP TO...
...THEM.

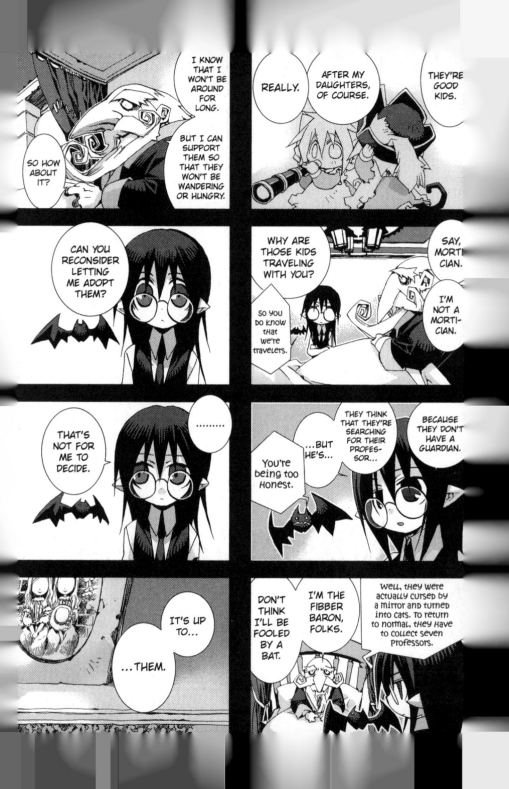

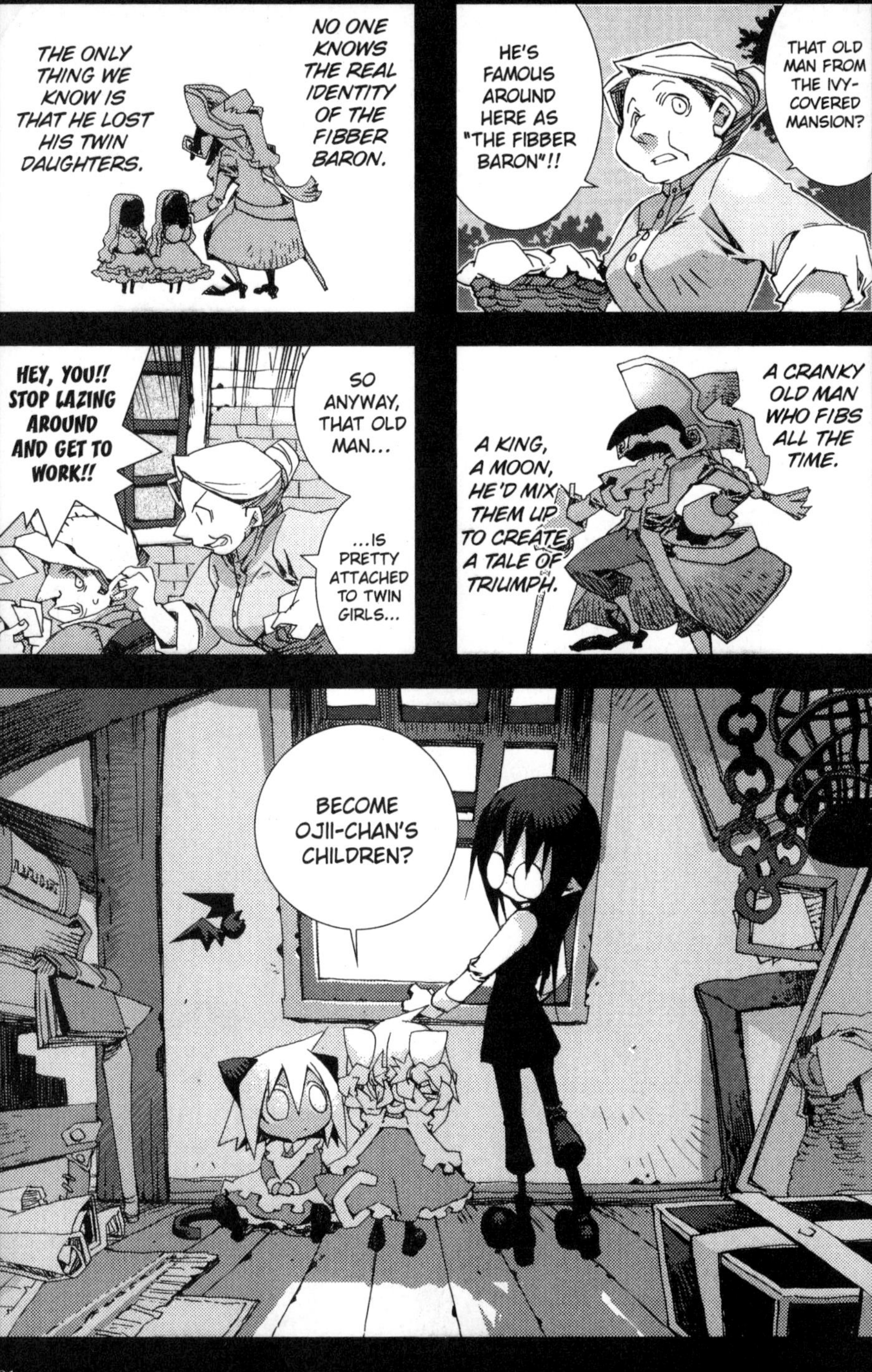
THAT OLD MAN FROM THE IVY-COVERED MANSION?
HE'S FAMOUS AROUND HERE AS "THE FIBBER BARON"!!
NO ONE KNOWS THE REAL IDENTITY OF THE FIBBER BARON.
THE ONLY THING WE KNOW IS THAT HE LOST HIS TWIN DAUGHTERS.
A CRANKY OLD MAN WHO FIBS ALL THE TIME.
A KING, A MOON, HE'D MIX THEM UP TO CREATE A TALE OF TRIUMPH.
SO ANYWAY, THAT OLD MAN...
...IS PRETTY ATTACHED TO TWIN GIRLS...
HEY, YOU!! STOP LAZING AROUND AND GET TO WORK!!
BECOME OJII-CHAN'S CHILDREN?

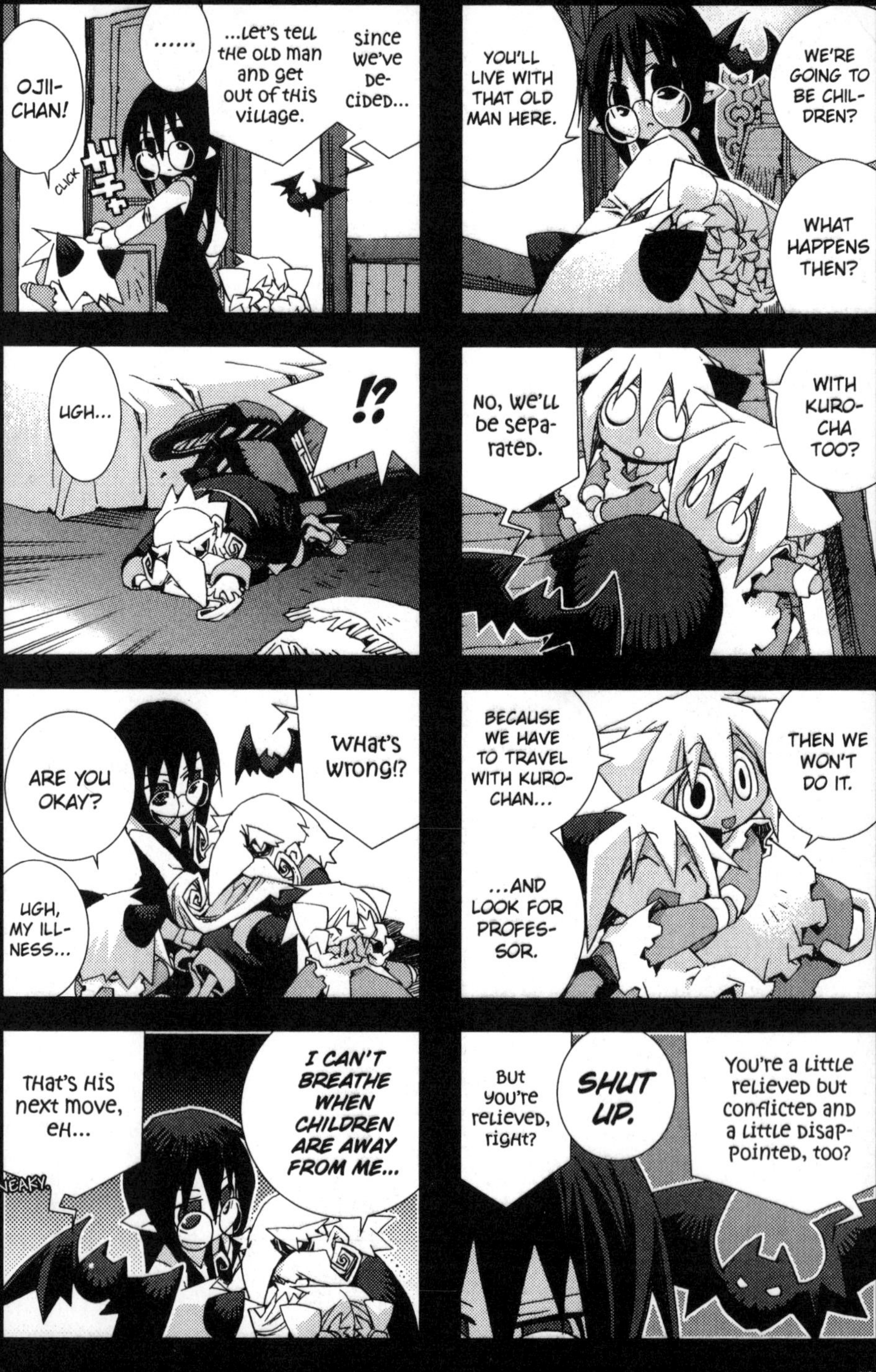
WE'RE GOING TO BE CHILDREN?
YOU'LL LIVE WITH THAT OLD MAN HERE.
WHAT HAPPENS THEN?
Since we've decided...
...let's tell the old man and get out of this village.
......
OJII-CHAN!
ガチャ
CLICK
WITH KURO-CHA TOO?
No, we'll be separated.
!?
UGH...
THEN WE WON'T DO IT.
BECAUSE WE HAVE TO TRAVEL WITH KURO-CHAN...
...AND LOOK FOR PROFESSOR.
What's wrong!?
ARE YOU OKAY?
UGH, MY ILLNESS...
You're a little relieved but conflicted and a little disappointed, too?
SHUT UP.
But you're relieved, right?
I CAN'T BREATHE WHEN CHILDREN ARE AWAY FROM ME...
That's his next move, eh...
SNEAKY.

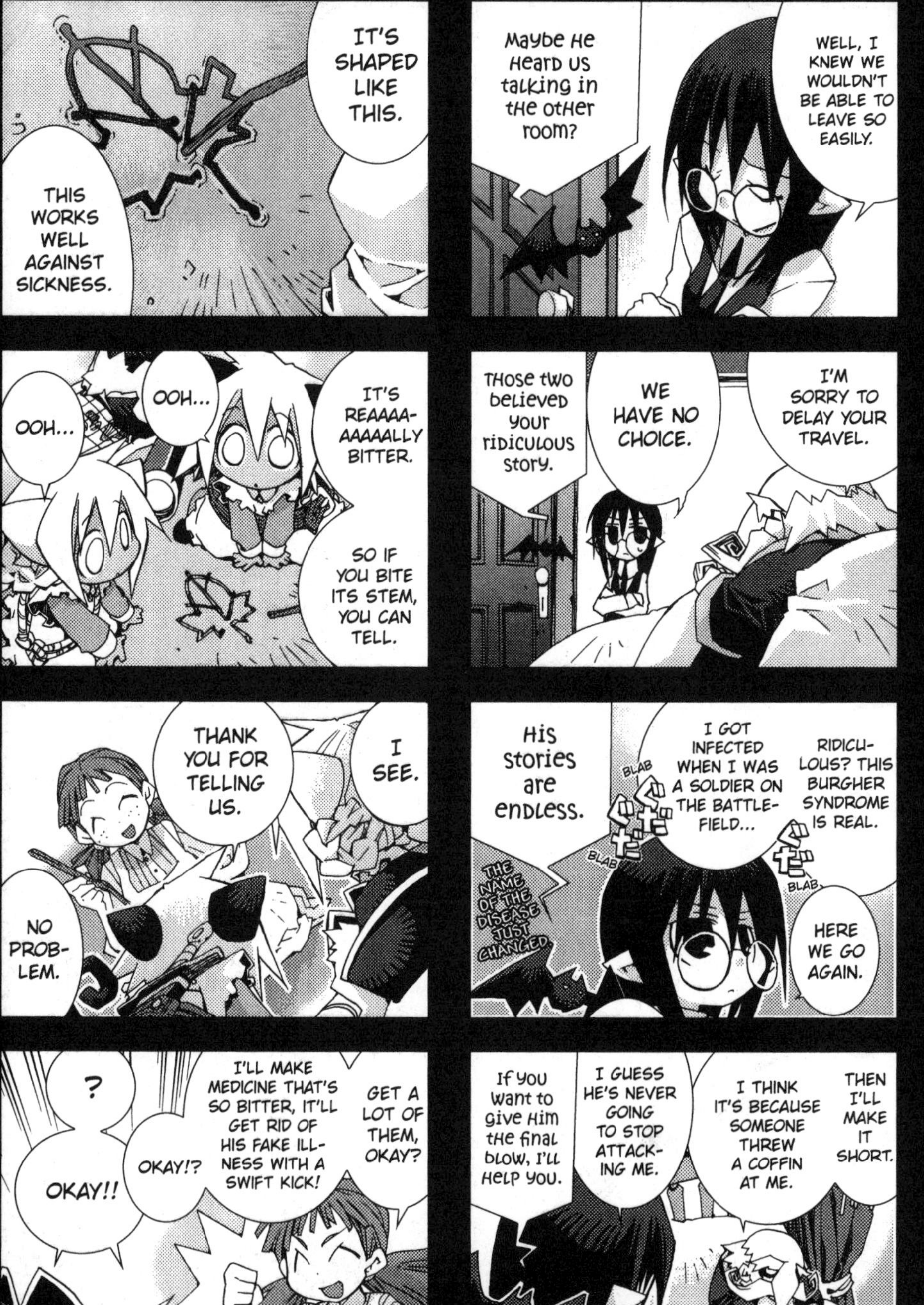
WELL, I KNEW WE WOULDN'T BE ABLE TO LEAVE SO EASILY.
Maybe He Heard US talking in the other room?
IT'S SHAPED LIKE THIS.
THIS WORKS WELL AGAINST SICKNESS.
I'M SORRY TO DELAY YOUR TRAVEL.
WE HAVE NO CHOICE.
THOSE two believed your ridiculous story.
IT'S REAAAAA-AAAAALLY BITTER.
SO IF YOU BITE ITS STEM, YOU CAN TELL.
OOH...
OOH...
RIDICU-LOUS? THIS BURGHER SYNDROME IS REAL.
BLAB
I GOT INFECTED WHEN I WAS A SOLDIER ON THE BATTLE-FIELD...
BLAB
BLAB
His stories are endless.
HERE WE GO AGAIN.
THE NAME OF THE DISEASE JUST CHANGED.
I SEE.
THANK YOU FOR TELLING US.
NO PROB-LEM.
THEN I'LL MAKE IT SHORT.
I THINK IT'S BECAUSE SOMEONE THREW A COFFIN AT ME.
I GUESS HE'S NEVER GOING TO STOP ATTACK-ING ME.
If you want to give Him the final blow, I'll Help you.
GET A LOT OF THEM, OKAY?
I'LL MAKE MEDICINE THAT'S SO BITTER, IT'LL GET RID OF HIS FAKE ILL-NESS WITH A SWIFT KICK!
OKAY!?
?
OKAY!!

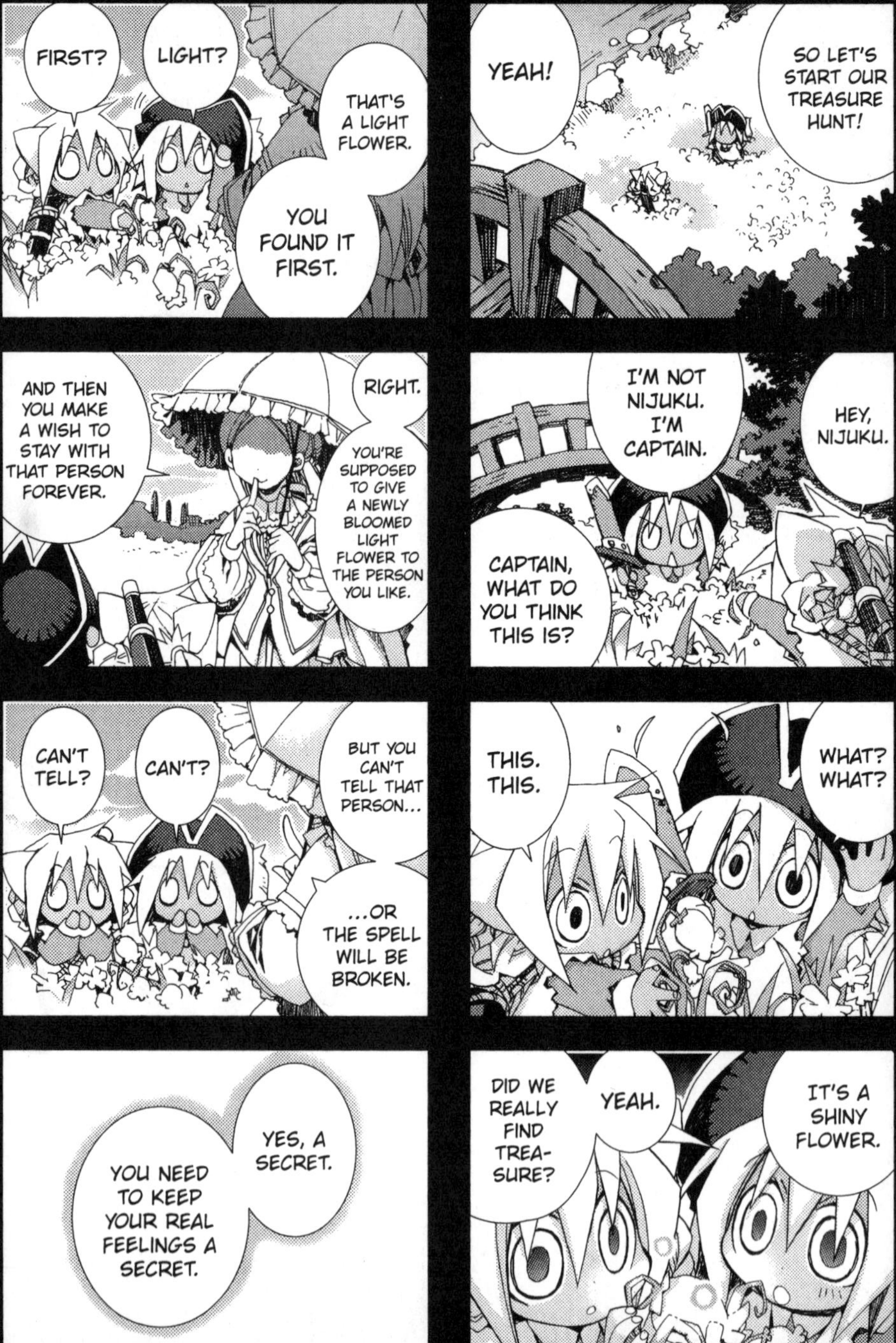
SO LET'S START OUR TREASURE HUNT!
YEAH!
THAT'S A LIGHT FLOWER.
YOU FOUND IT FIRST.
LIGHT?
FIRST?
HEY, NIJUKU.
I'M NOT NIJUKU. I'M CAPTAIN.
CAPTAIN, WHAT DO YOU THINK THIS IS?
RIGHT.
YOU'RE SUPPOSED TO GIVE A NEWLY BLOOMED LIGHT FLOWER TO THE PERSON YOU LIKE.
AND THEN YOU MAKE A WISH TO STAY WITH THAT PERSON FOREVER.
WHAT? WHAT?
THIS. THIS.
BUT YOU CAN'T TELL THAT PERSON...
...OR THE SPELL WILL BE BROKEN.
CAN'T?
CAN'T TELL?
IT'S A SHINY FLOWER.
YEAH.
DID WE REALLY FIND TREA-SURE?
YES, A SECRET.
YOU NEED TO KEEP YOUR REAL FEELINGS A SECRET.

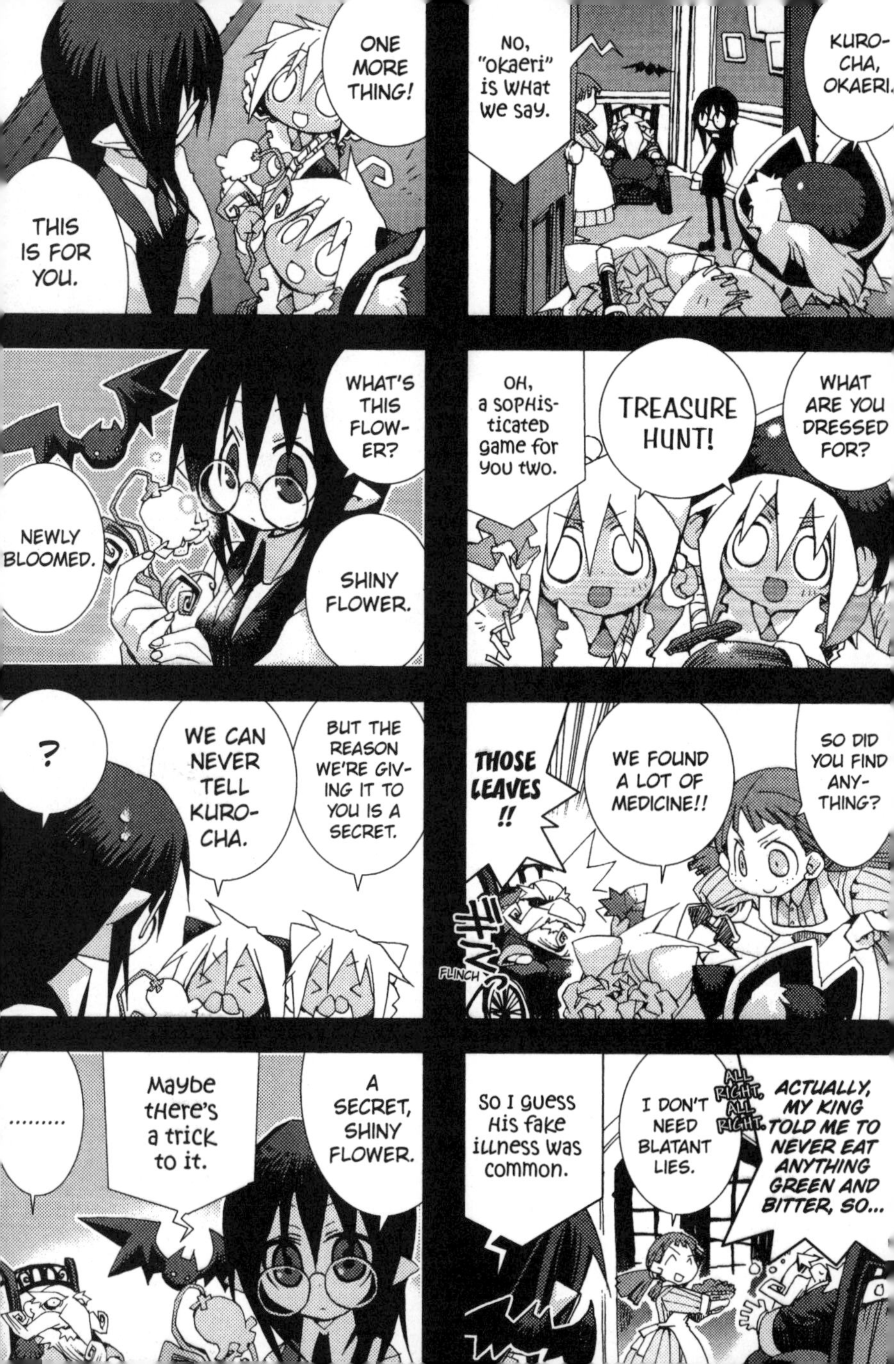

KURO-CHA, OKAERI.
NO, "okaeri" is WHAt we say.
ONE MORE THING!
THIS IS FOR YOU.
WHAT ARE YOU DRESSED FOR?
TREASURE HUNT!
OH, a sophisticated game for you two.
WHAT'S THIS FLOWER?
SHINY FLOWER.
NEWLY BLOOMED.
SO DID YOU FIND ANYTHING?
WE FOUND A LOT OF MEDICINE!!
THOSE LEAVES!!
FLINCH
BUT THE REASON WE'RE GIVING IT TO YOU IS A SECRET.
WE CAN NEVER TELL KURO-CHA.
?
ACTUALLY, MY KING TOLD ME TO NEVER EAT ANYTHING GREEN AND BITTER, SO...
ALL RIGHT, ALL RIGHT.
I DON'T NEED BLATANT LIES.
So I guess His fake illness was common.
A SECRET, SHINY FLOWER.
Maybe there's a trick to it.
....

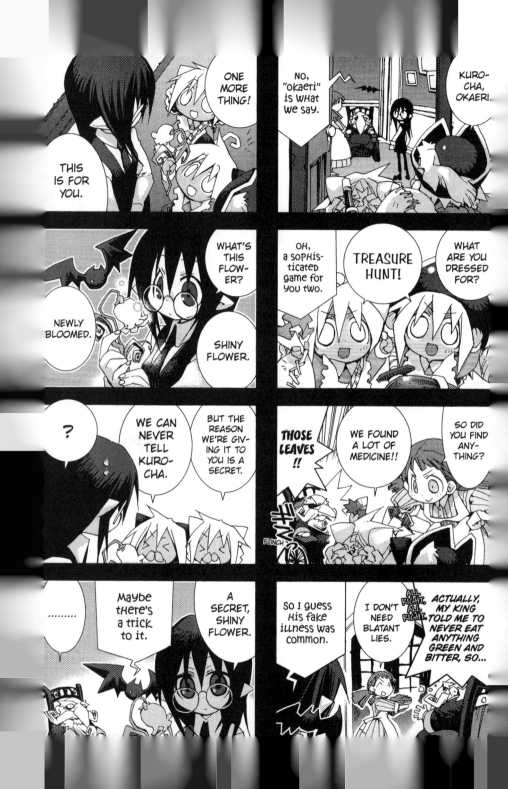

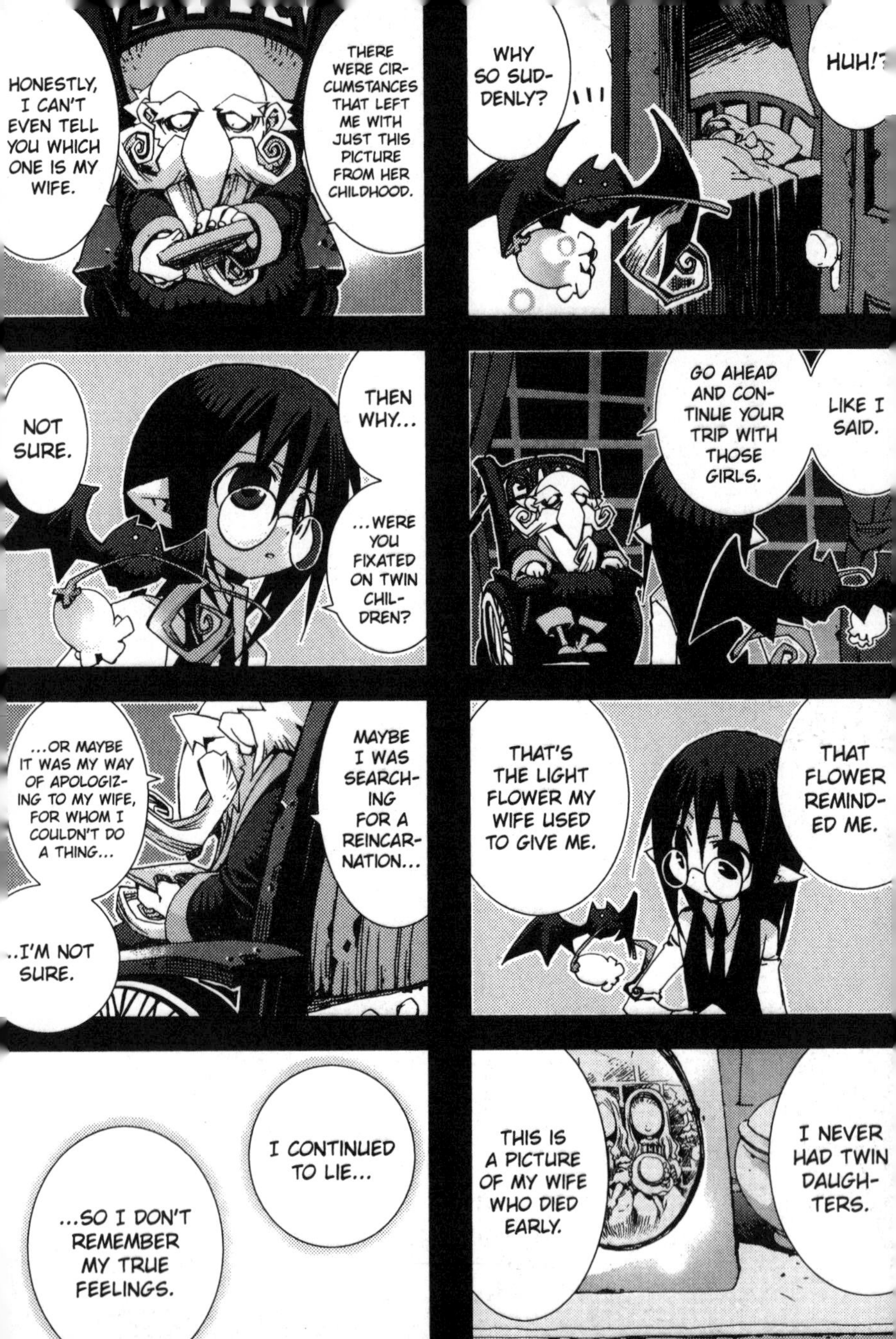
HUH!?
WHY SO SUDDENLY?
THERE WERE CIRCUMSTANCES THAT LEFT ME WITH JUST THIS PICTURE FROM HER CHILDHOOD.
HONESTLY, I CAN'T EVEN TELL YOU WHICH ONE IS MY WIFE.
LIKE I SAID.
GO AHEAD AND CONTINUE YOUR TRIP WITH THOSE GIRLS.
THEN WHY...
...WERE YOU FIXATED ON TWIN CHILDREN?
NOT SURE.
THAT FLOWER REMINDED ME.
THAT'S THE LIGHT FLOWER MY WIFE USED TO GIVE ME.
MAYBE I WAS SEARCHING FOR A REINCARNATION...
...OR MAYBE IT WAS MY WAY OF APOLOGIZING TO MY WIFE, FOR WHOM I COULDN'T DO A THING...
..I'M NOT SURE.
I NEVER HAD TWIN DAUGHTERS.
THIS IS A PICTURE OF MY WIFE WHO DIED EARLY.
I CONTINUED TO LIE...
...SO I DON'T REMEMBER MY TRUE FEELINGS.

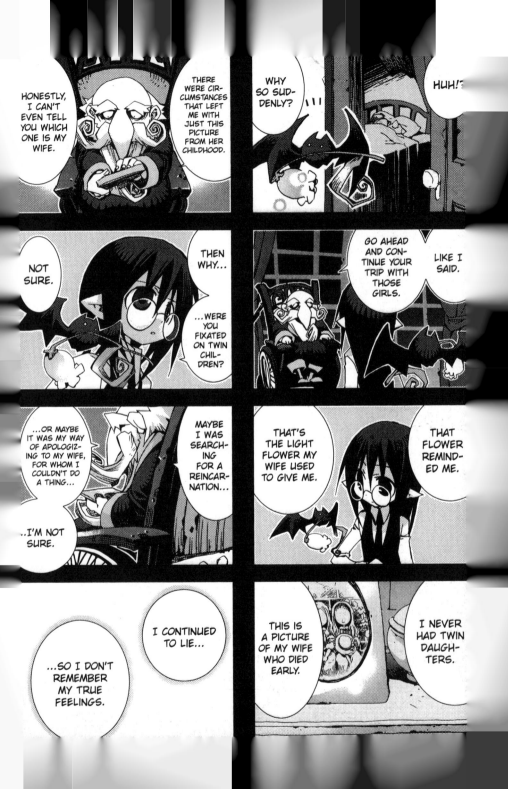

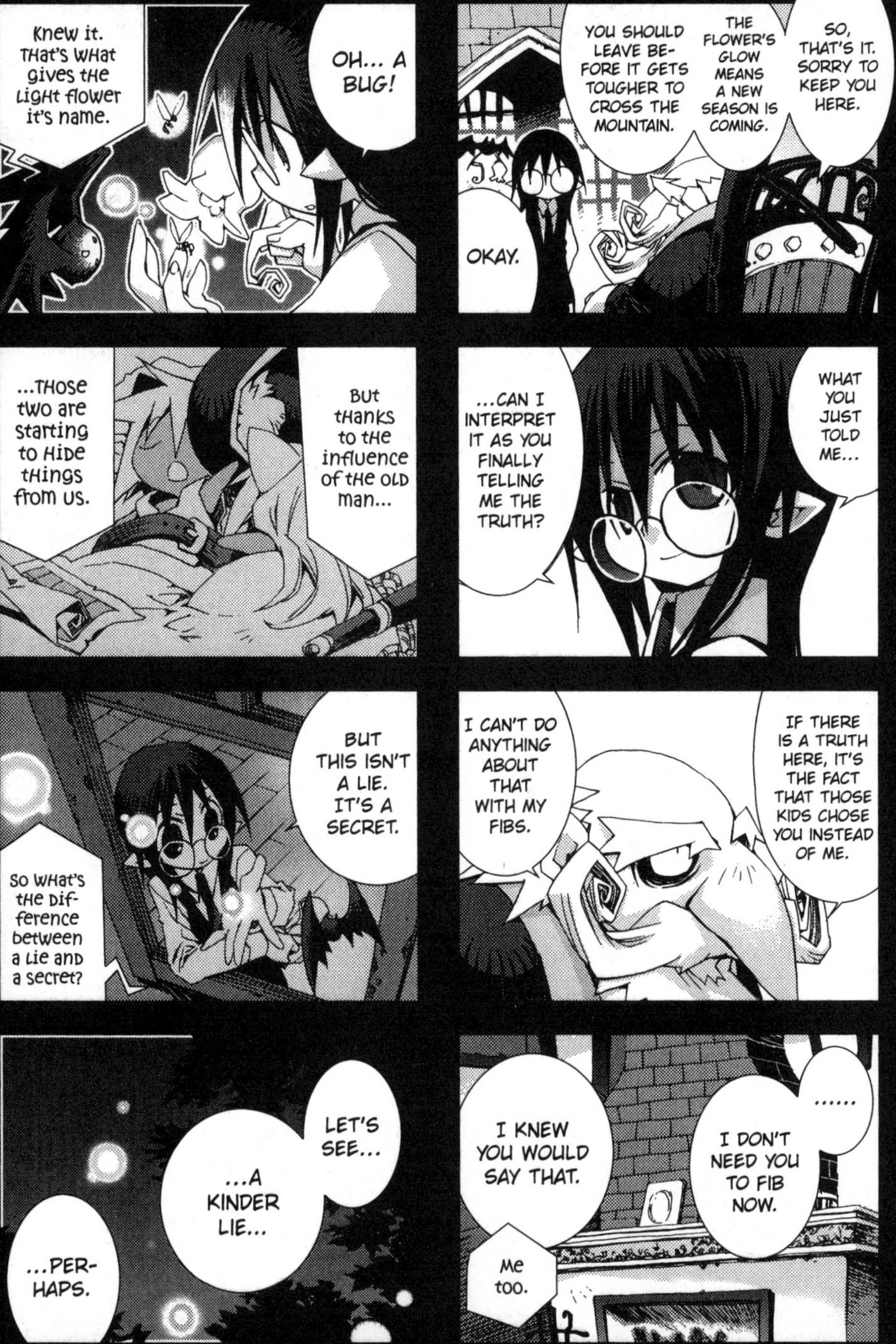
SO, THAT'S IT. SORRY TO KEEP YOU HERE.
THE FLOWER'S GLOW MEANS A NEW SEASON IS COMING.
YOU SHOULD LEAVE BE-FORE IT GETS TOUGHER TO CROSS THE MOUNTAIN.
OKAY.
OH... A BUG!
Knew it. That's what gives the light flower it's name.
WHAT YOU JUST TOLD ME...
...CAN I INTERPRET IT AS YOU FINALLY TELLING ME THE TRUTH?
But thanks to the influence of the old man...
...those two are starting to hide things from us.
IF THERE IS A TRUTH HERE, IT'S THE FACT THAT THOSE KIDS CHOSE YOU INSTEAD OF ME.
I CAN'T DO ANYTHING ABOUT THAT WITH MY FIBS.
BUT THIS ISN'T A LIE. IT'S A SECRET.
So what's the dif-ference between a lie and a secret?
......
I DON'T NEED YOU TO FIB NOW.
I KNEW YOU WOULD SAY THAT.
Me too.
LET'S SEE...
...A KINDER LIE...
...PER-HAPS.

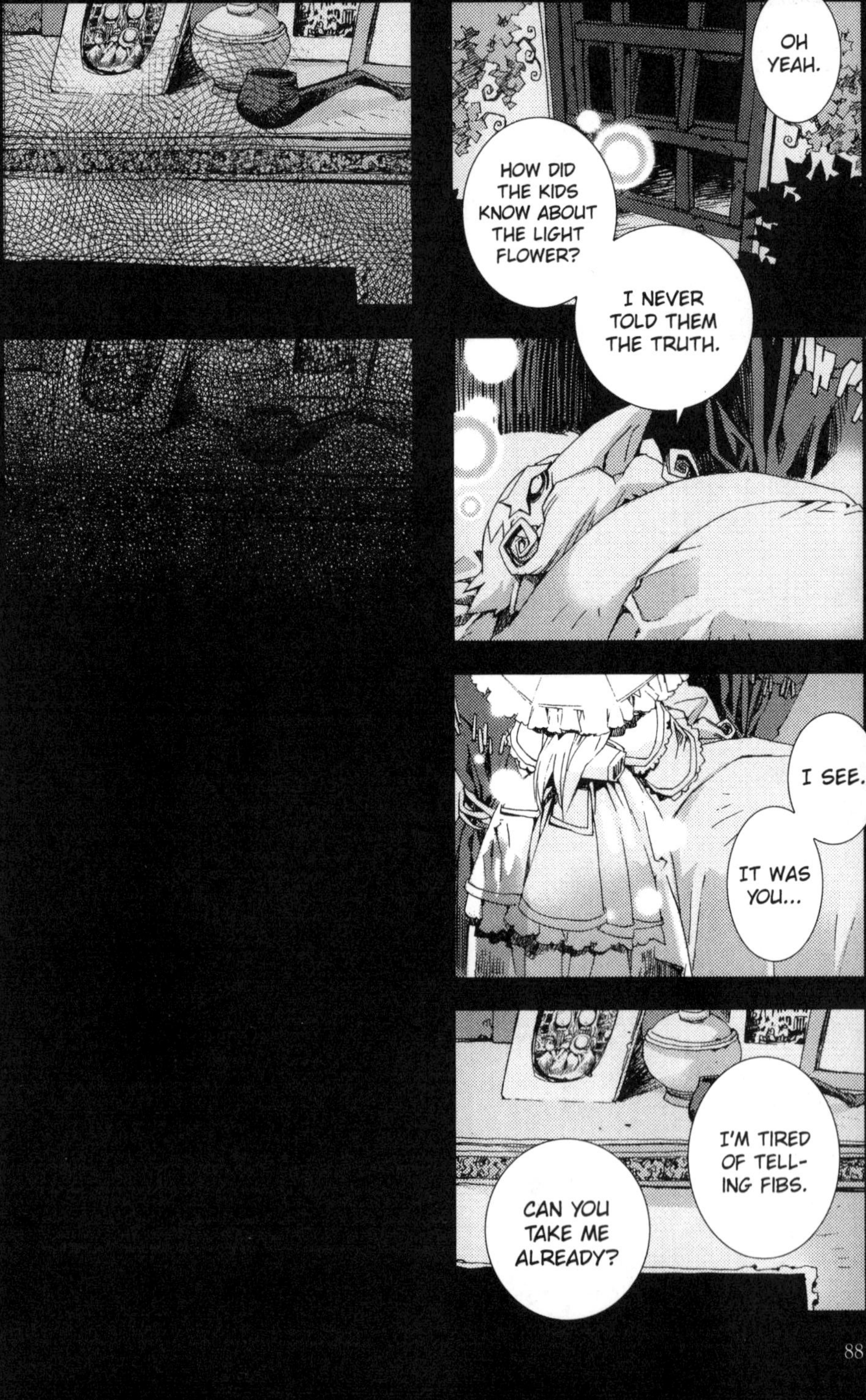
OH YEAH.
HOW DID THE KIDS KNOW ABOUT THE LIGHT FLOWER?
I NEVER TOLD THEM THE TRUTH.
I SEE.
IT WAS YOU...
I'M TIRED OF TELL-ING FIBS.
CAN YOU TAKE ME ALREADY?

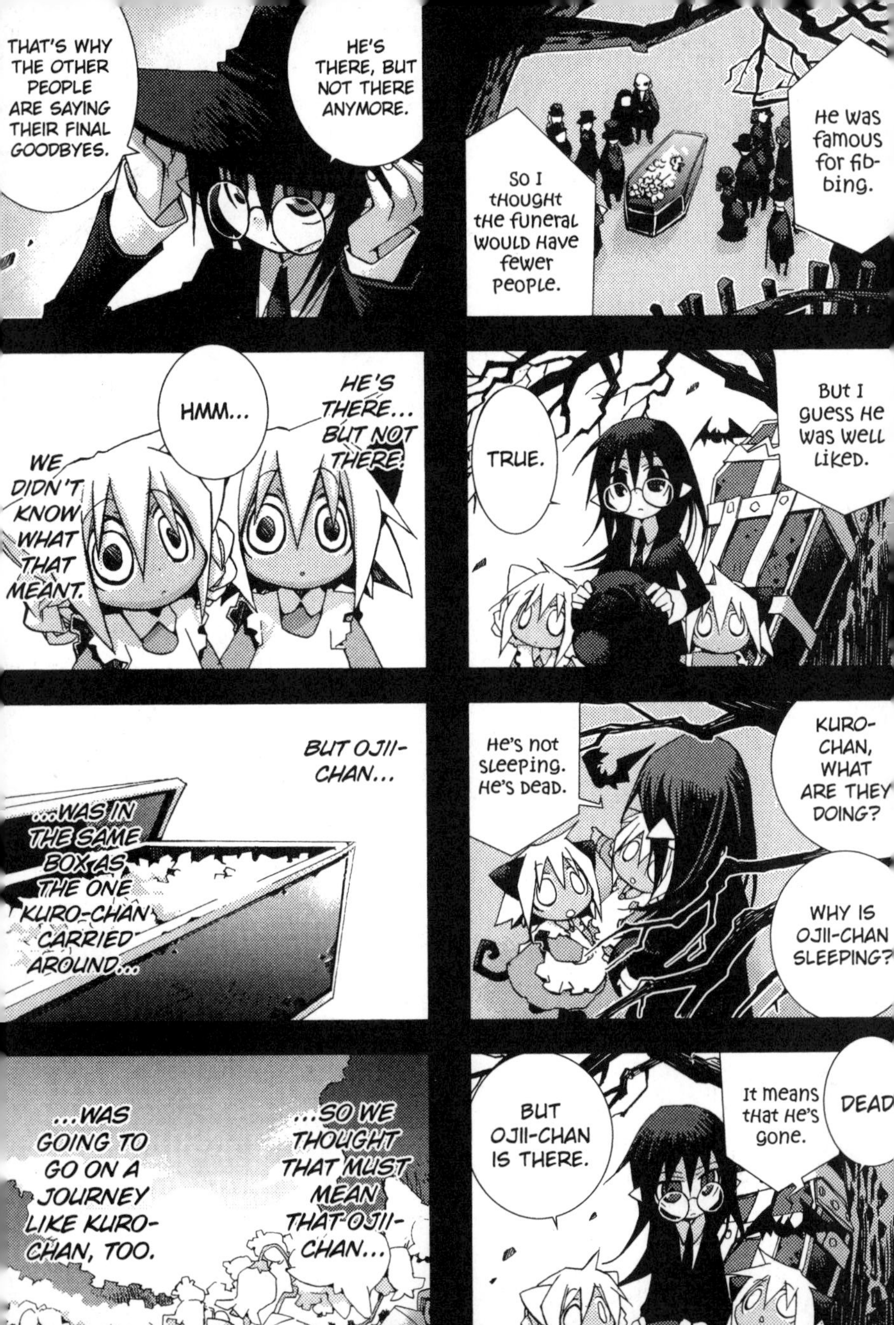
He was famous for fib-bing.
So I thought the funeral would have fewer people.
HE'S THERE, BUT NOT THERE ANYMORE.
THAT'S WHY THE OTHER PEOPLE ARE SAYING THEIR FINAL GOODBYES.
But I guess he was well liked.
TRUE.
HE'S THERE... BUT NOT THERE.
HMM...
WE DIDN'T KNOW WHAT THAT MEANT.
KURO-CHAN, WHAT ARE THEY DOING?
WHY IS OJII-CHAN SLEEPING?
He's not sleeping. He's dead.
BUT OJII-CHAN...
...WAS IN THE SAME BOX AS THE ONE KURO-CHAN CARRIED AROUND...
DEAD
It means that he's gone.
BUT OJII-CHAN IS THERE.
...SO WE THOUGHT THAT MUST MEAN THAT OJII-CHAN...
...WAS GOING TO GO ON A JOURNEY LIKE KURO-CHAN, TOO.

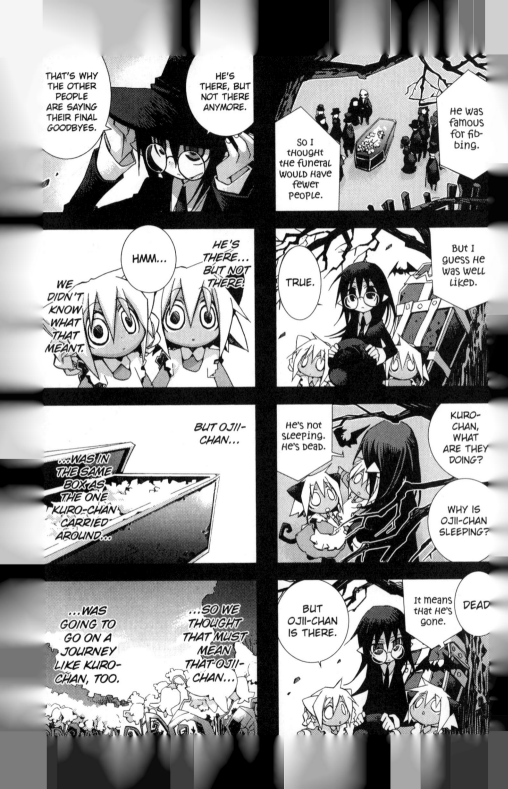

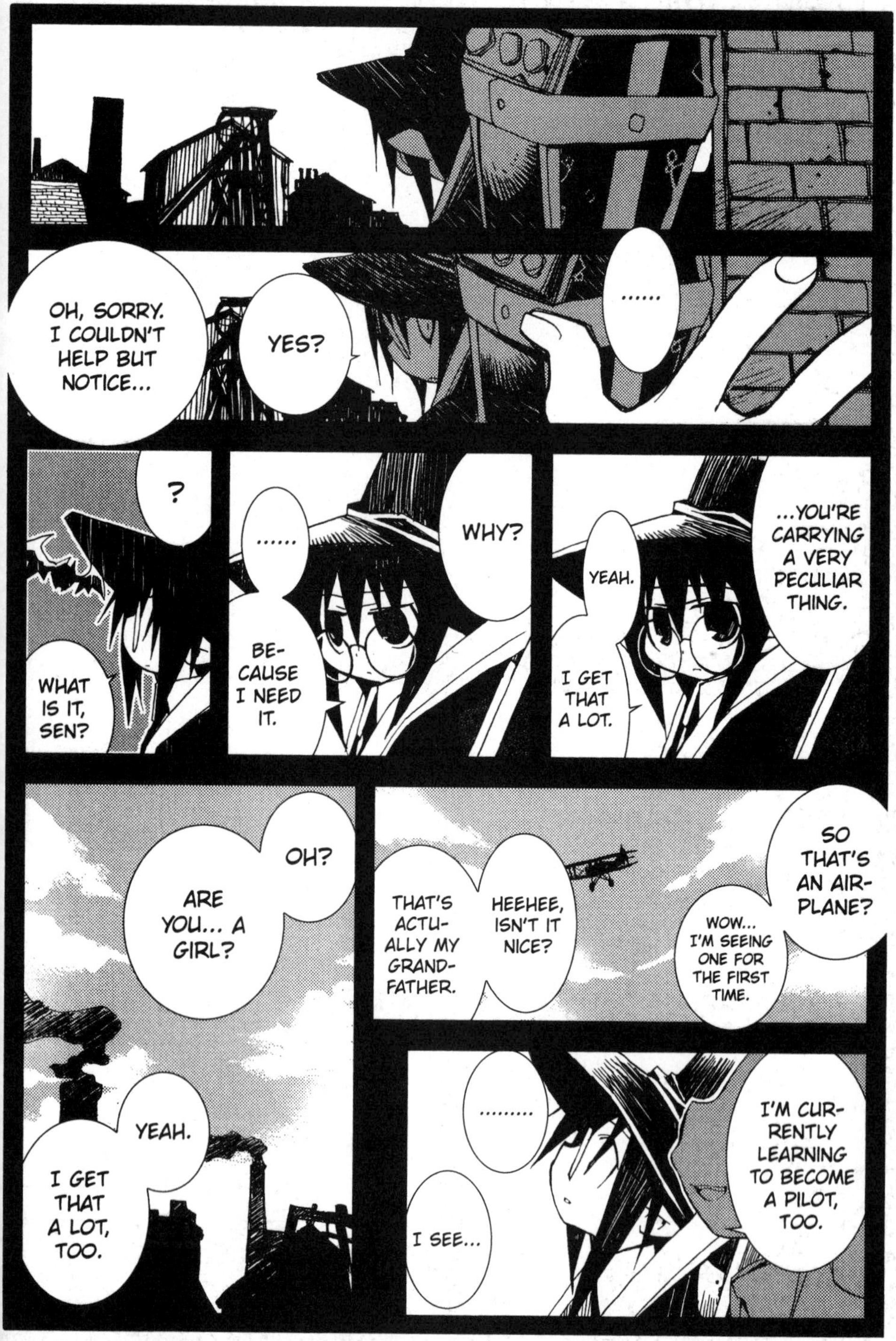
......
YES?
OH, SORRY. I COULDN'T HELP BUT NOTICE...
...YOU'RE CARRYING A VERY PECULIAR THING.
YEAH.
I GET THAT A LOT.
WHY?
......
BECAUSE I NEED IT.
?
WHAT IS IT, SEN?
SO THAT'S AN AIRPLANE?
WOW... I'M SEEING ONE FOR THE FIRST TIME.
HEEHEE, ISN'T IT NICE?
THAT'S ACTUALLY MY GRANDFATHER.
I'M CURRENTLY LEARNING TO BECOME A PILOT, TOO.
....
I SEE...
OH?
ARE YOU... A GIRL?
YEAH.
I GET THAT A LOT, TOO.

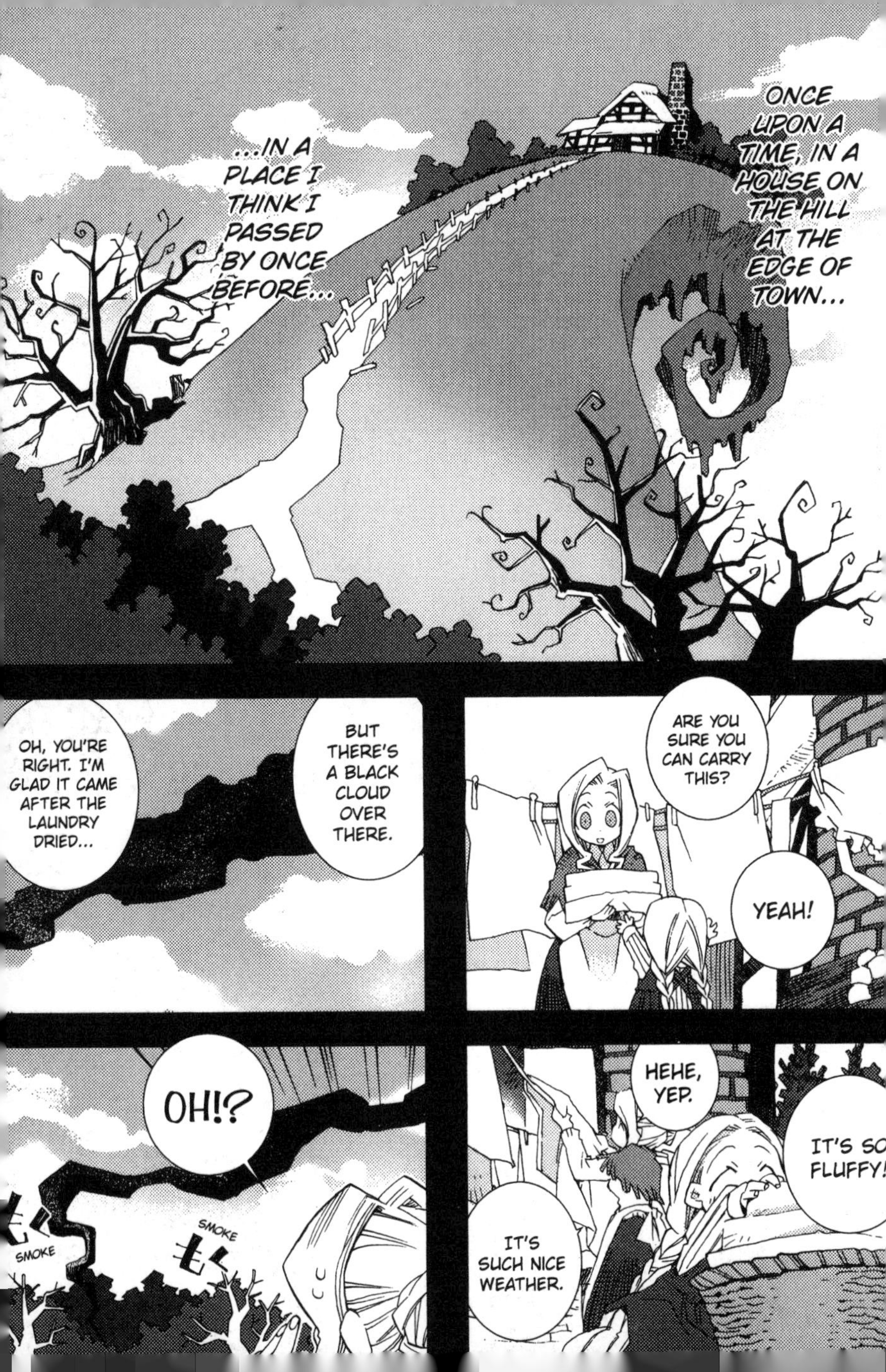
ONCE UPON A TIME, IN A HOUSE ON THE HILL AT THE EDGE OF TOWN...
...IN A PLACE I THINK I PASSED BY ONCE BEFORE...
ARE YOU SURE YOU CAN CARRY THIS?
YEAH!
BUT THERE'S A BLACK CLOUD OVER THERE.
OH, YOU'RE RIGHT. I'M GLAD IT CAME AFTER THE LAUNDRY DRIED...
IT'S SO FLUFFY!
HEHE, YEP.
IT'S SUCH NICE WEATHER.
OH!?
SMOKE
SMOKE

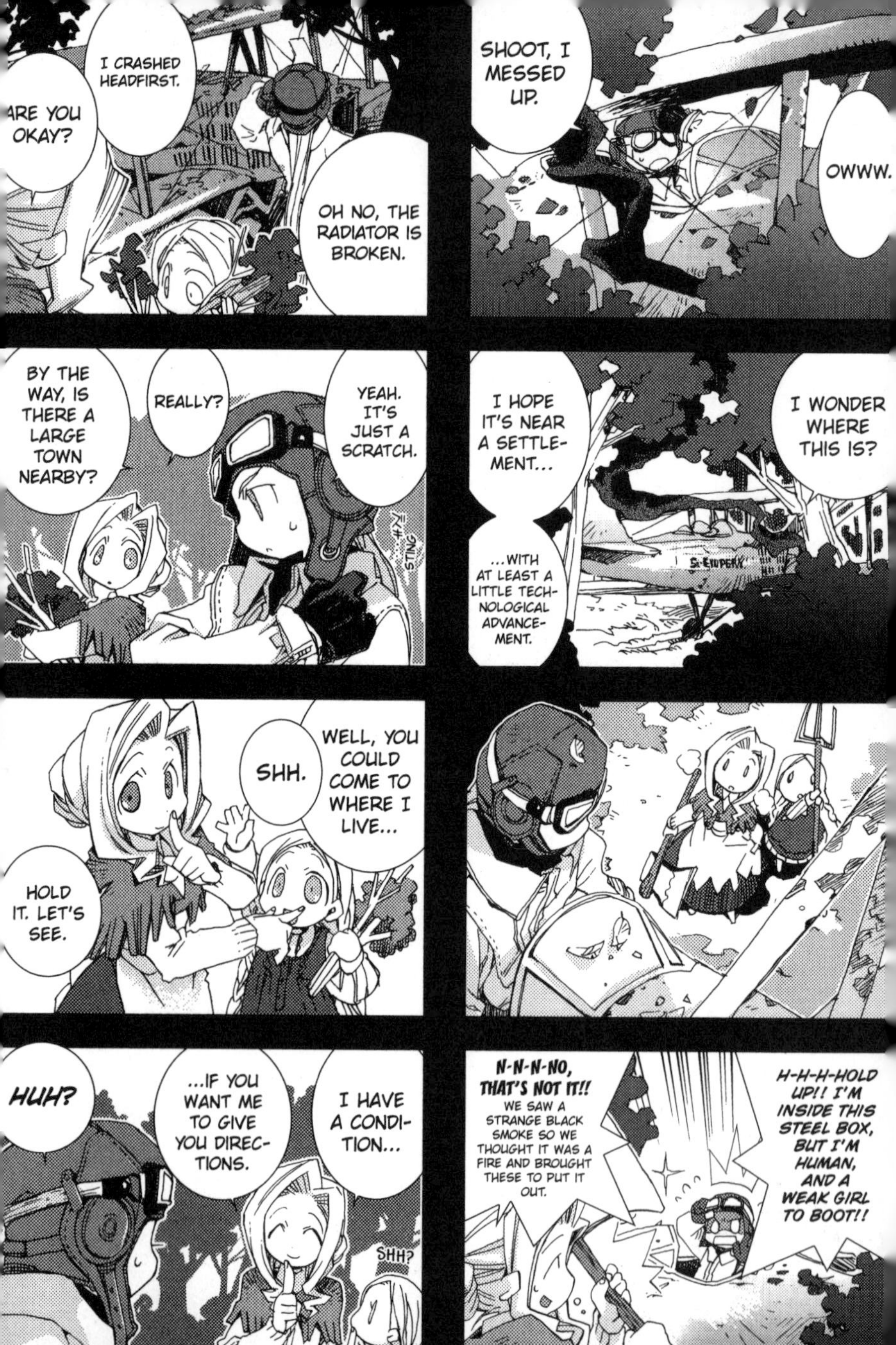
OWWW.
SHOOT, I MESSED UP.
OH NO, THE RADIATOR IS BROKEN.
I CRASHED HEADFIRST.
ARE YOU OKAY?
I WONDER WHERE THIS IS?
I HOPE IT'S NEAR A SETTLE-MENT...
...WITH AT LEAST A LITTLE TECH-NOLOGICAL ADVANCE-MENT.
YEAH. IT'S JUST A SCRATCH.
STING
REALLY?
BY THE WAY, IS THERE A LARGE TOWN NEARBY?
WELL, YOU COULD COME TO WHERE I LIVE...
SHH.
HOLD IT. LET'S SEE.
H-H-H-HOLD UP!! I'M INSIDE THIS STEEL BOX, BUT I'M HUMAN, AND A WEAK GIRL TO BOOT!!
N-N-N-NO, THAT'S NOT IT!!
WE SAW A STRANGE BLACK SMOKE SO WE THOUGHT IT WAS A FIRE AND BROUGHT THESE TO PUT IT OUT.
I HAVE A CONDI-TION...
...IF YOU WANT ME TO GIVE YOU DIREC-TIONS.
HUH?
SHH?

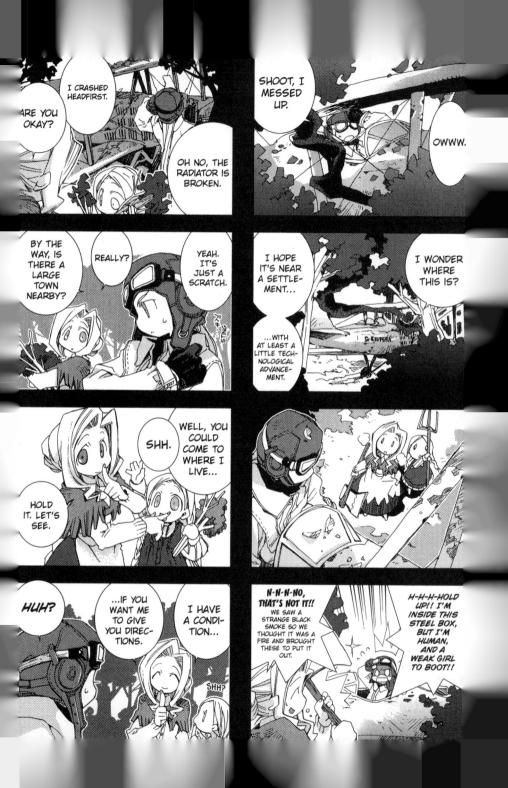

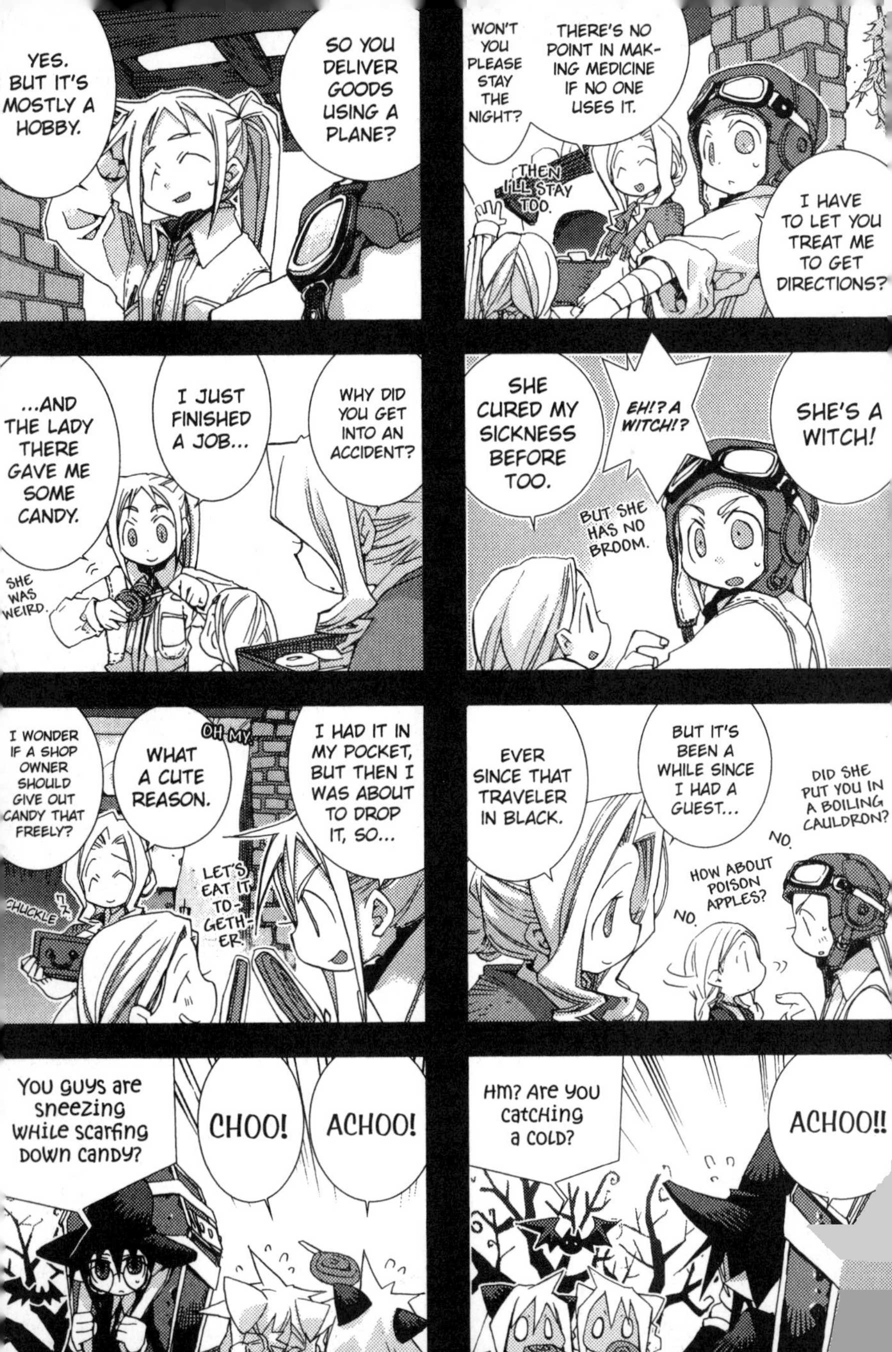
I HAVE TO LET YOU TREAT ME TO GET DIRECTIONS?
THERE'S NO POINT IN MAK-ING MEDICINE IF NO ONE USES IT.
WON'T YOU PLEASE STAY THE NIGHT?
THEN I'LL STAY TOO.
SHE'S A WITCH!
EH!? A WITCH!?
SHE CURED MY SICKNESS BEFORE TOO.
BUT SHE HAS NO BROOM.
DID SHE PUT YOU IN A BOILING CAULDRON?
NO.
BUT IT'S BEEN A WHILE SINCE I HAD A GUEST...
EVER SINCE THAT TRAVELER IN BLACK.
HOW ABOUT POISON APPLES?
NO.
ACHOO!!
Hm? Are you catching a cold?
SO YOU DELIVER GOODS USING A PLANE?
YES. BUT IT'S MOSTLY A HOBBY.
WHY DID YOU GET INTO AN ACCIDENT?
I JUST FINISHED A JOB...
...AND THE LADY THERE GAVE ME SOME CANDY.
SHE WAS WEIRD.
I HAD IT IN MY POCKET, BUT THEN I WAS ABOUT TO DROP IT, SO...
LET'S EAT IT TO-GETH-ER.
OH MY.
WHAT A CUTE REASON.
I WONDER IF A SHOP OWNER SHOULD GIVE OUT CANDY THAT FREELY?
CHUCKLE
ACHOO!
CHOO!
You guys are sneezing while scarfing down candy?

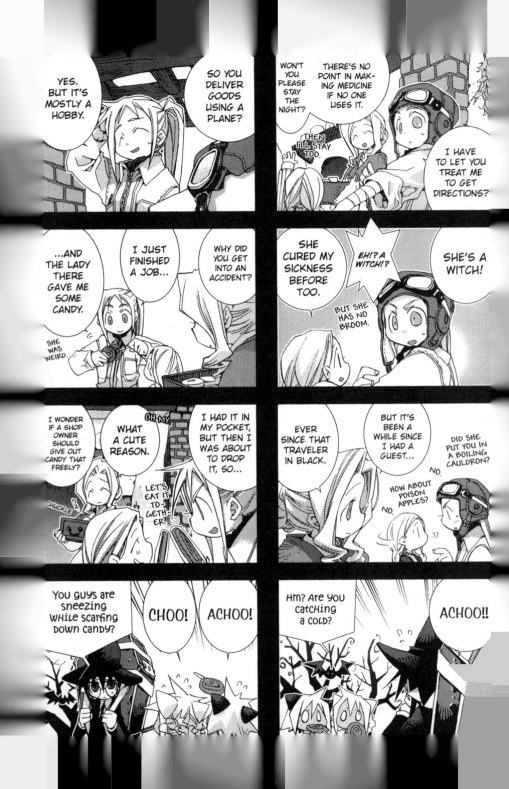

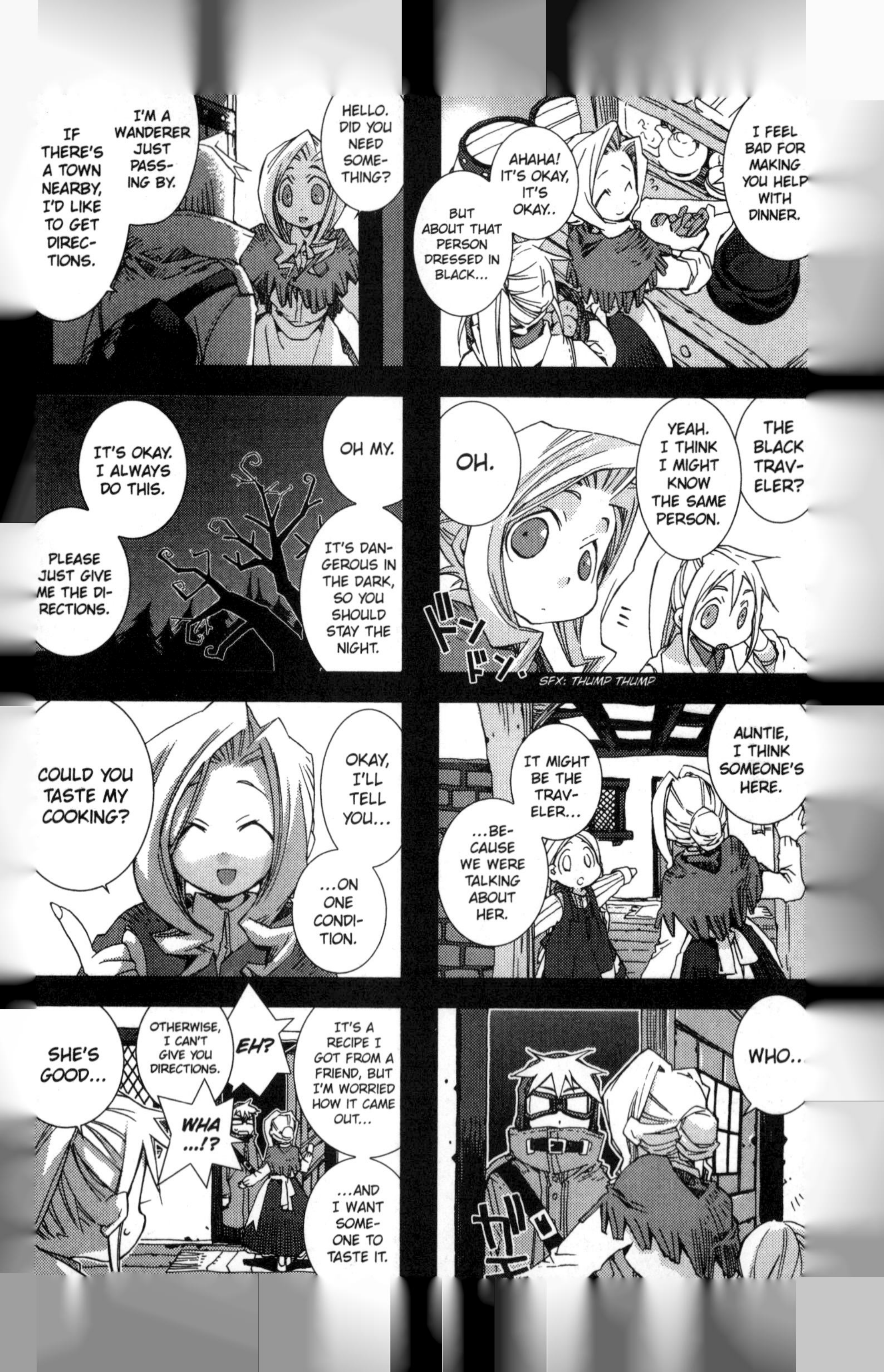
I FEEL BAD FOR MAKING YOU HELP WITH DINNER.
AHAHA! IT'S OKAY, IT'S OKAY..
BUT ABOUT THAT PERSON DRESSED IN BLACK...
THE BLACK TRAVELER?
YEAH. I THINK I MIGHT KNOW THE SAME PERSON.
OH.
SFX: THUMP THUMP
AUNTIE, I THINK SOMEONE'S HERE.
IT MIGHT BE THE TRAVELER...
...BECAUSE WE WERE TALKING ABOUT HER.
WHO...
HELLO. DID YOU NEED SOMETHING?
I'M A WANDERER JUST PASSING BY.
IF THERE'S A TOWN NEARBY, I'D LIKE TO GET DIRECTIONS.
OH MY.
IT'S DANGEROUS IN THE DARK, SO YOU SHOULD STAY THE NIGHT.
IT'S OKAY. I ALWAYS DO THIS.
PLEASE JUST GIVE ME THE DIRECTIONS.
OKAY, I'LL TELL YOU...
...ON ONE CONDITION.
COULD YOU TASTE MY COOKING?
IT'S A RECIPE I GOT FROM A FRIEND, BUT I'M WORRIED HOW IT CAME OUT...
...AND I WANT SOMEONE TO TASTE IT.
EH?
OTHERWISE, I CAN'T GIVE YOU DIRECTIONS.
WHA...!?
SHE'S GOOD...

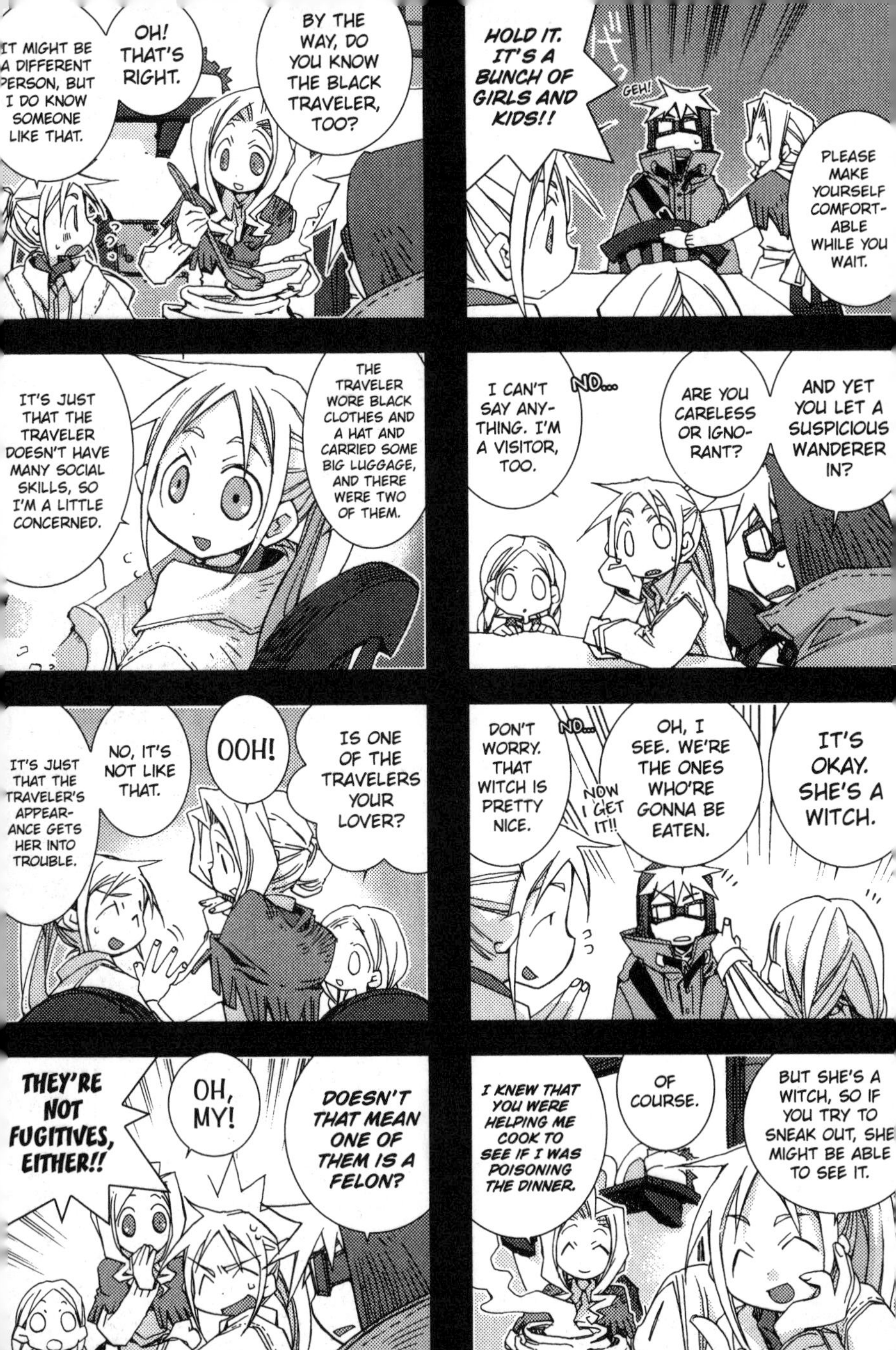
PLEASE MAKE YOURSELF COMFORT-ABLE WHILE YOU WAIT.
GEH!
HOLD IT. IT'S A BUNCH OF GIRLS AND KIDS!!
AND YET YOU LET A SUSPICIOUS WANDERER IN?
ARE YOU CARELESS OR IGNO-RANT?
NO...
I CAN'T SAY ANY-THING. I'M A VISITOR, TOO.
IT'S OKAY. SHE'S A WITCH.
OH, I SEE. WE'RE THE ONES WHO'RE GONNA BE EATEN.
NOW I GET IT!!
NO...
DON'T WORRY. THAT WITCH IS PRETTY NICE.
BUT SHE'S A WITCH, SO IF YOU TRY TO SNEAK OUT, SHE MIGHT BE ABLE TO SEE IT.
OF COURSE.
I KNEW THAT YOU WERE HELPING ME COOK TO SEE IF I WAS POISONING THE DINNER.
BY THE WAY, DO YOU KNOW THE BLACK TRAVELER, TOO?
OH! THAT'S RIGHT.
IT MIGHT BE A DIFFERENT PERSON, BUT I DO KNOW SOMEONE LIKE THAT.
THE TRAVELER WORE BLACK CLOTHES AND A HAT AND CARRIED SOME BIG LUGGAGE, AND THERE WERE TWO OF THEM.
IT'S JUST THAT THE TRAVELER DOESN'T HAVE MANY SOCIAL SKILLS, SO I'M A LITTLE CONCERNED.
IS ONE OF THE TRAVELERS YOUR LOVER?
OOH!
NO, IT'S NOT LIKE THAT.
IT'S JUST THAT THE TRAVELER'S APPEAR-ANCE GETS HER INTO TROUBLE.
DOESN'T THAT MEAN ONE OF THEM IS A FELON?
OH, MY!
THEY'RE NOT FUGITIVES, EITHER!!

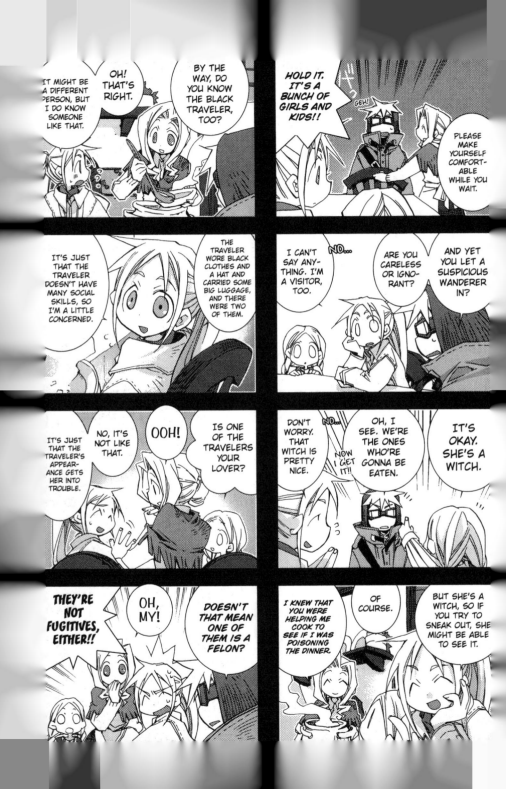

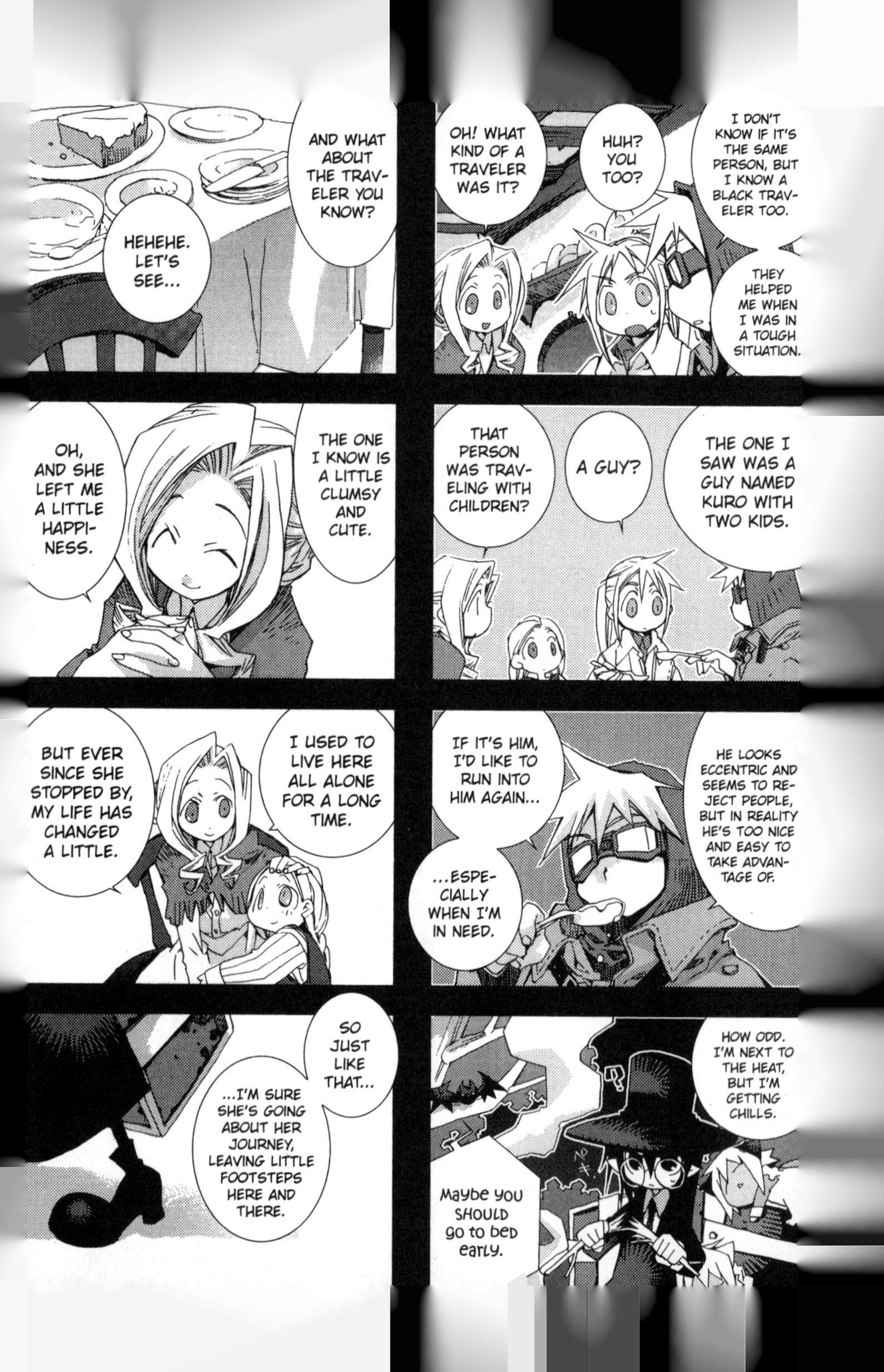
I DON'T KNOW IF IT'S THE SAME PERSON, BUT I KNOW A BLACK TRAVELER TOO.
THEY HELPED ME WHEN I WAS IN A TOUGH SITUATION.
HUH? YOU TOO?
OH! WHAT KIND OF A TRAVELER WAS IT?
AND WHAT ABOUT THE TRAVELER YOU KNOW?
HEHEHE. LET'S SEE...
THE ONE I SAW WAS A GUY NAMED KURO WITH TWO KIDS.
A GUY?
THAT PERSON WAS TRAVELING WITH CHILDREN?
THE ONE I KNOW IS A LITTLE CLUMSY AND CUTE.
OH, AND SHE LEFT ME A LITTLE HAPPINESS.
HE LOOKS ECCENTRIC AND SEEMS TO REJECT PEOPLE, BUT IN REALITY HE'S TOO NICE AND EASY TO TAKE ADVANTAGE OF.
IF IT'S HIM, I'D LIKE TO RUN INTO HIM AGAIN...
...ESPECIALLY WHEN I'M IN NEED.
I USED TO LIVE HERE ALL ALONE FOR A LONG TIME.
BUT EVER SINCE SHE STOPPED BY, MY LIFE HAS CHANGED A LITTLE.
HOW ODD. I'M NEXT TO THE HEAT, BUT I'M GETTING CHILLS.
Maybe you SHOULD go to bed early.
SO JUST LIKE THAT...
...I'M SURE SHE'S GOING ABOUT HER JOURNEY, LEAVING LITTLE FOOTSTEPS HERE AND THERE.

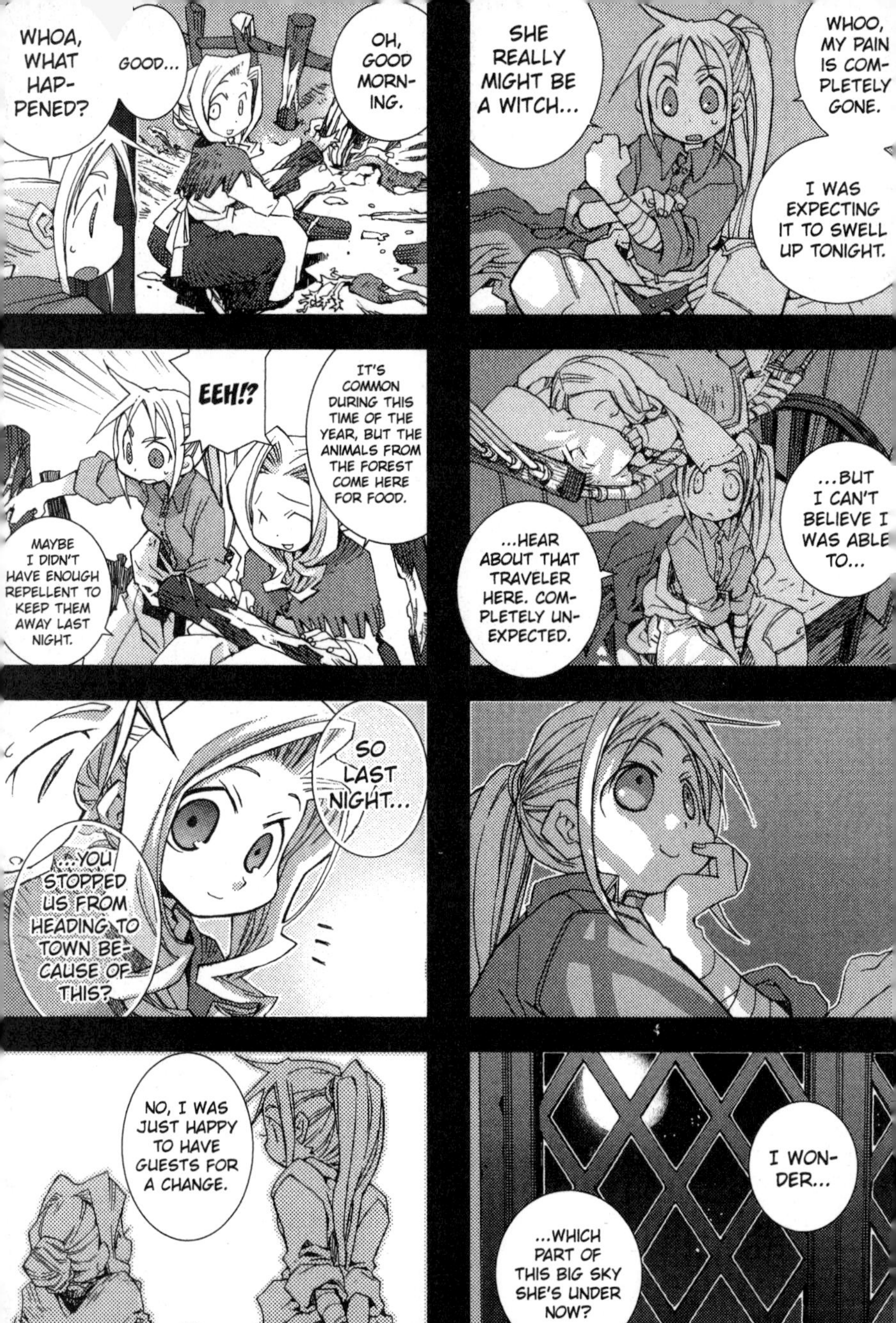
WHOO, MY PAIN IS COMPLETELY GONE.
I WAS EXPECTING IT TO SWELL UP TONIGHT.
SHE REALLY MIGHT BE A WITCH...
OH, GOOD MORNING.
GOOD...
WHOA, WHAT HAPPENED?
...BUT I CAN'T BELIEVE I WAS ABLE TO...
...HEAR ABOUT THAT TRAVELER HERE. COMPLETELY UNEXPECTED.
IT'S COMMON DURING THIS TIME OF THE YEAR, BUT THE ANIMALS FROM THE FOREST COME HERE FOR FOOD.
EEH!?
MAYBE I DIDN'T HAVE ENOUGH REPELLENT TO KEEP THEM AWAY LAST NIGHT.
SO LAST NIGHT...
...YOU STOPPED US FROM HEADING TO TOWN BECAUSE OF THIS?
I WONDER...
...WHICH PART OF THIS BIG SKY SHE'S UNDER NOW?
NO, I WAS JUST HAPPY TO HAVE GUESTS FOR A CHANGE.

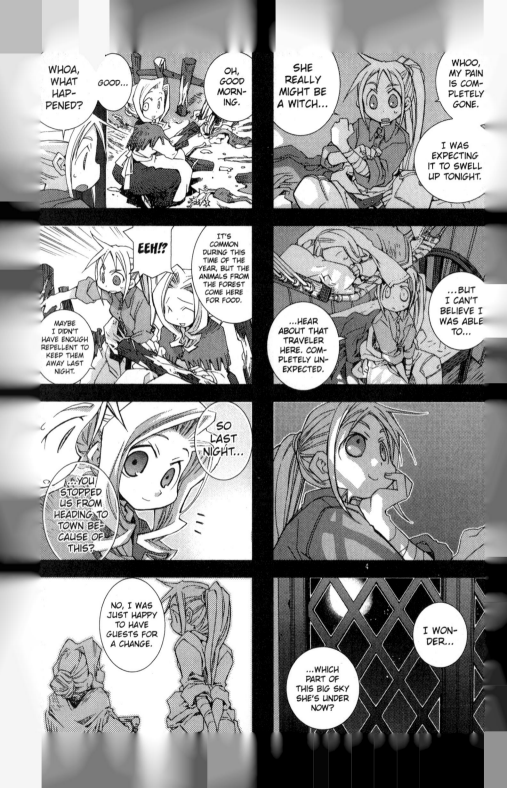

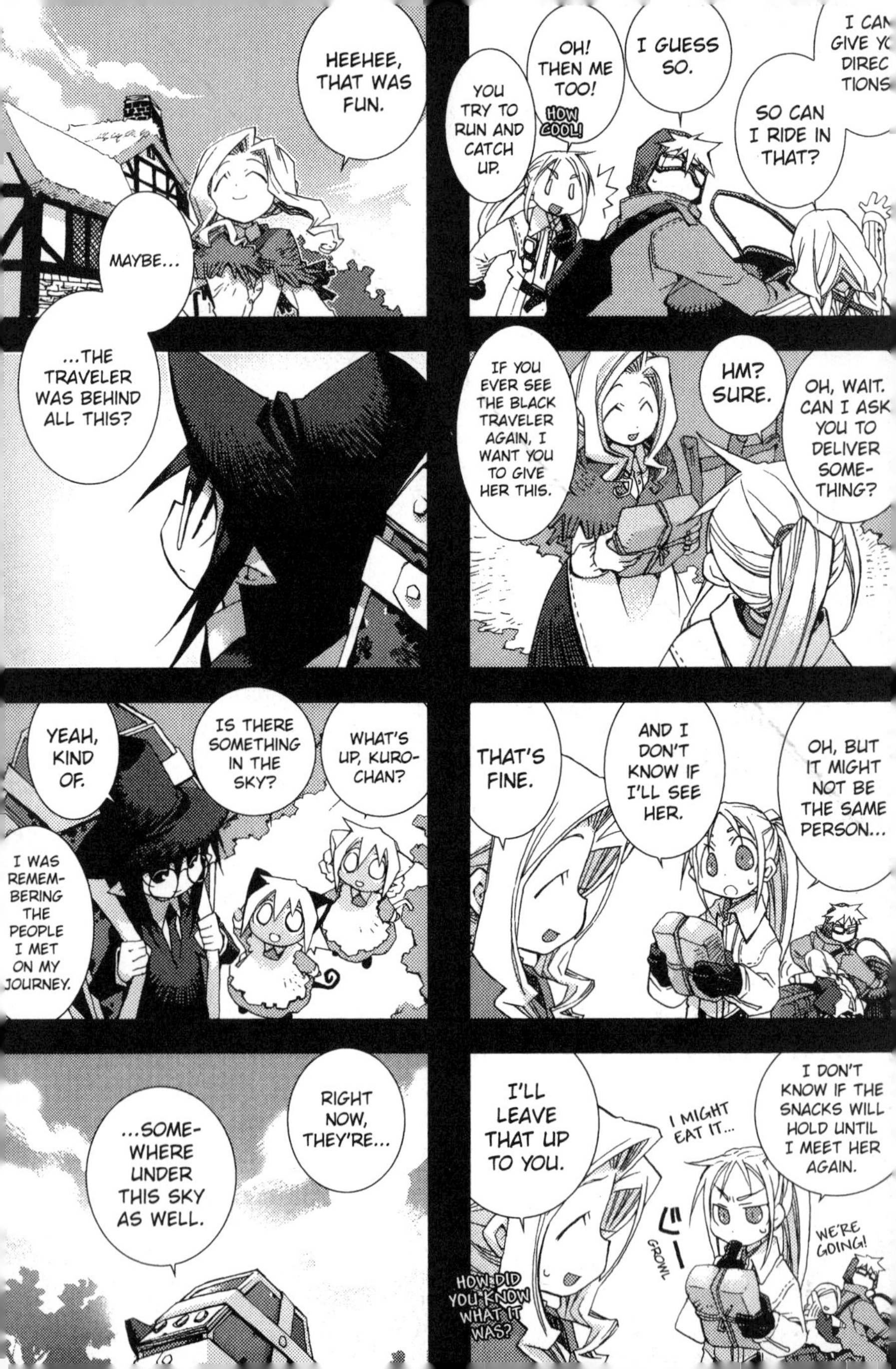
I CAN GIVE YOU DIRECTIONS.
SO CAN I RIDE IN THAT?
I GUESS SO.
OH! THEN ME TOO!
YOU TRY TO RUN AND CATCH UP.
HOW COOL!
OH, WAIT. CAN I ASK YOU TO DELIVER SOMETHING?
HM? SURE.
IF YOU EVER SEE THE BLACK TRAVELER AGAIN, I WANT YOU TO GIVE HER THIS.
OH, BUT IT MIGHT NOT BE THE SAME PERSON...
AND I DON'T KNOW IF I'LL SEE HER.
THAT'S FINE.
I DON'T KNOW IF THE SNACKS WILL HOLD UNTIL I MEET HER AGAIN.
I'LL LEAVE THAT UP TO YOU.
I MIGHT EAT IT...
WE'RE GOING!
GROWL
HOW DID YOU KNOW WHAT IT WAS?
HEEHEE, THAT WAS FUN.
MAYBE...
...THE TRAVELER WAS BEHIND ALL THIS?
WHAT'S UP, KURO-CHAN?
IS THERE SOMETHING IN THE SKY?
YEAH, KIND OF.
I WAS REMEMBERING THE PEOPLE I MET ON MY JOURNEY.
RIGHT NOW, THEY'RE...
...SOMEWHERE UNDER THIS SKY AS WELL.

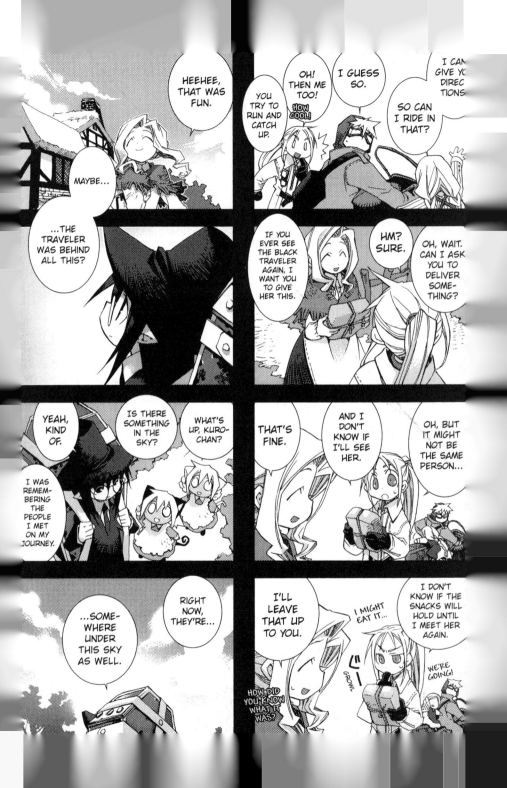

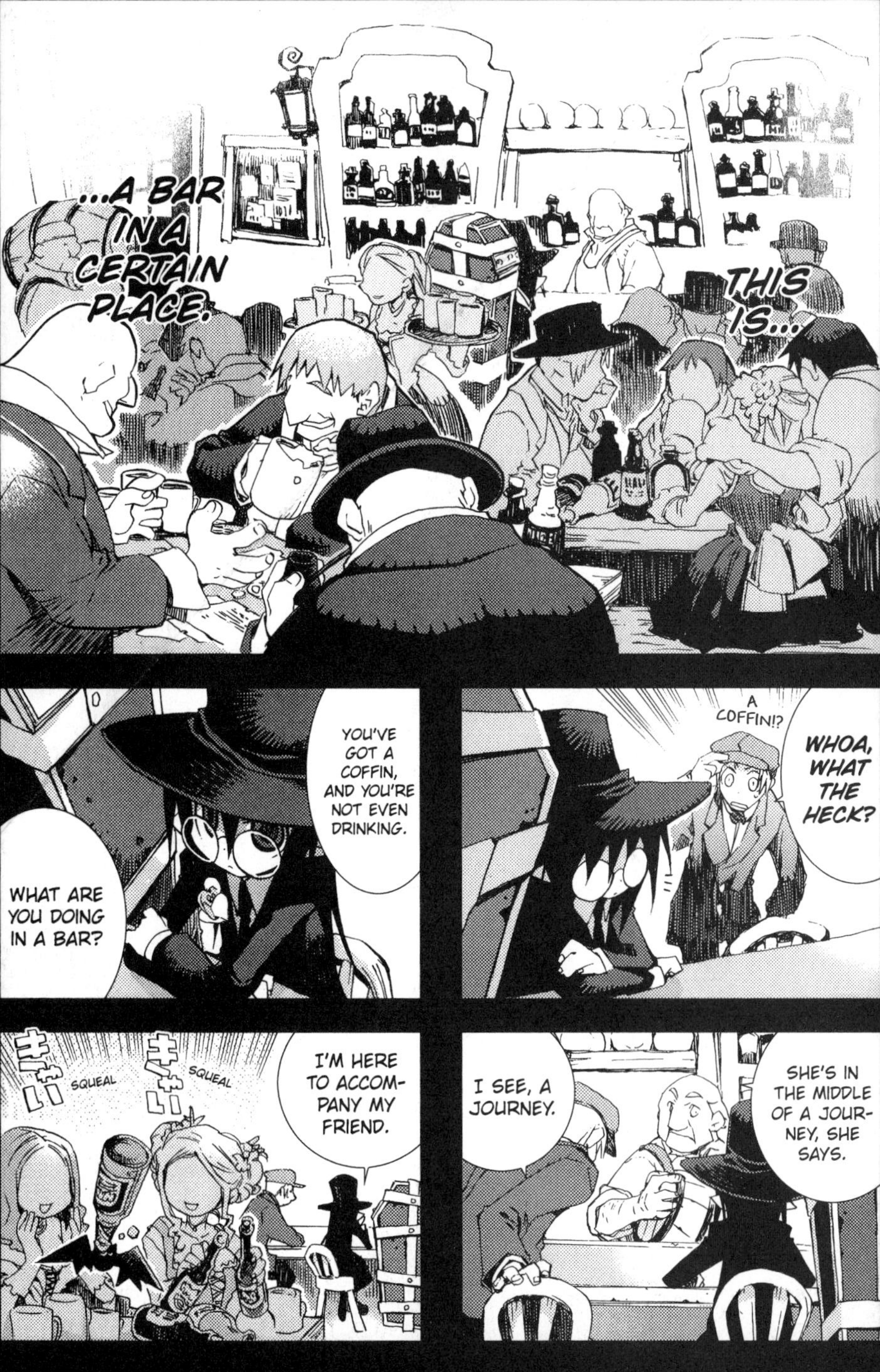
THIS IS...
...A BAR IN A CERTAIN PLACE.
WHOA, WHAT THE HECK?
A COFFIN!?
YOU'VE GOT A COFFIN, AND YOU'RE NOT EVEN DRINKING.
WHAT ARE YOU DOING IN A BAR?
SHE'S IN THE MIDDLE OF A JOURNEY, SHE SAYS.
I SEE, A JOURNEY.
I'M HERE TO ACCOMPANY MY FRIEND.
SQUEAL
SQUEAL

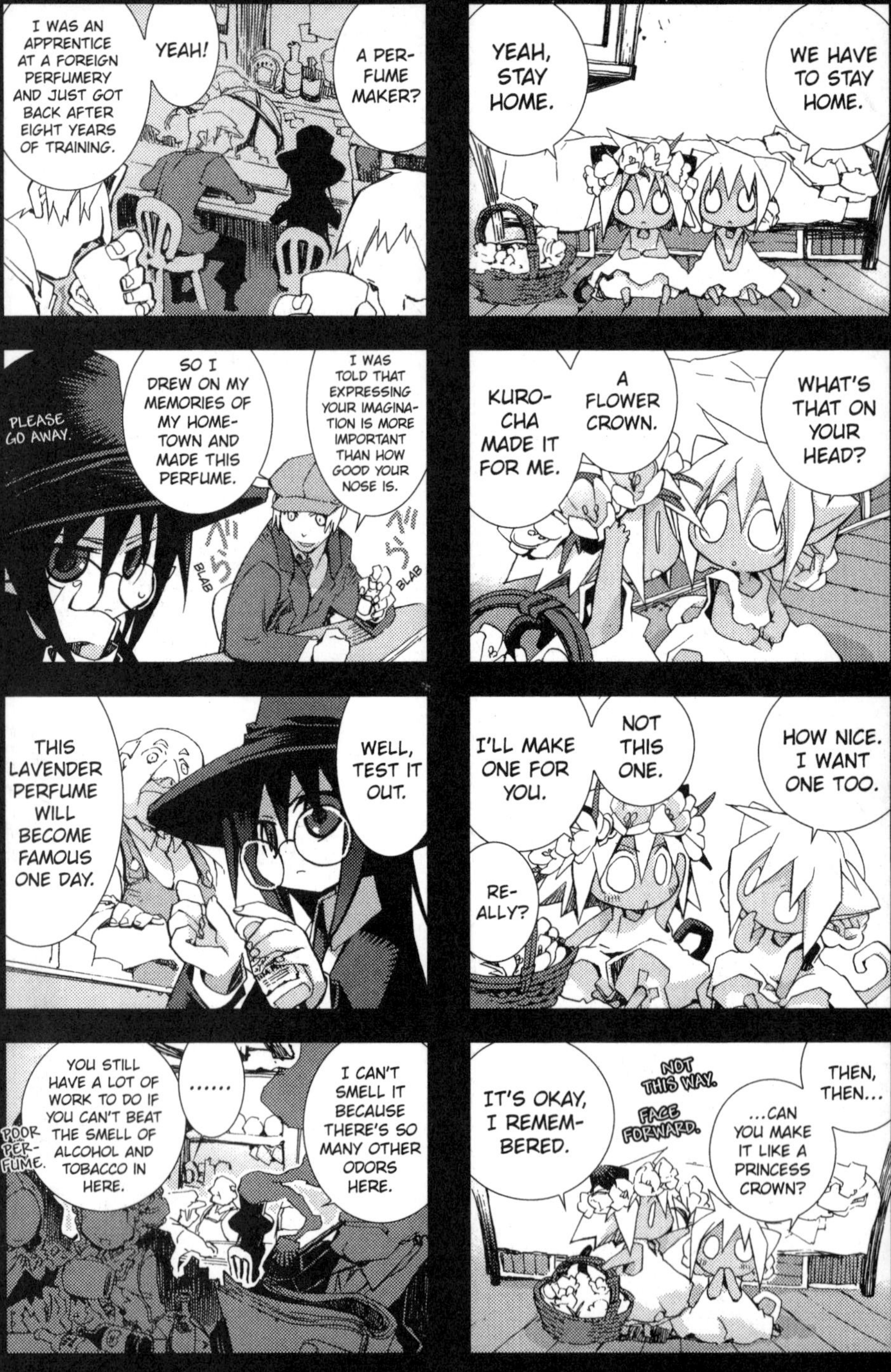
WE HAVE TO STAY HOME.
YEAH, STAY HOME.
A PERFUME MAKER?
YEAH!
I WAS AN APPRENTICE AT A FOREIGN PERFUMERY AND JUST GOT BACK AFTER EIGHT YEARS OF TRAINING.
WHAT'S THAT ON YOUR HEAD?
A FLOWER CROWN.
KURO-CHA MADE IT FOR ME.
I WAS TOLD THAT EXPRESSING YOUR IMAGINATION IS MORE IMPORTANT THAN HOW GOOD YOUR NOSE IS.
SO I DREW ON MY MEMORIES OF MY HOMETOWN AND MADE THIS PERFUME.
BLAB
BLAB
PLEASE GO AWAY.
HOW NICE. I WANT ONE TOO.
NOT THIS ONE.
I'LL MAKE ONE FOR YOU.
RE-ALLY?
WELL, TEST IT OUT.
THIS LAVENDER PERFUME WILL BECOME FAMOUS ONE DAY.
THEN, THEN...
...CAN YOU MAKE IT LIKE A PRINCESS CROWN?
NOT THIS WAY.
FACE FORWARD.
IT'S OKAY, I REMEMBERED.
I CAN'T SMELL IT BECAUSE THERE'S SO MANY OTHER ODORS HERE.
......
YOU STILL HAVE A LOT OF WORK TO DO IF YOU CAN'T BEAT THE SMELL OF ALCOHOL AND TOBACCO IN HERE.
POOR PERFUME.

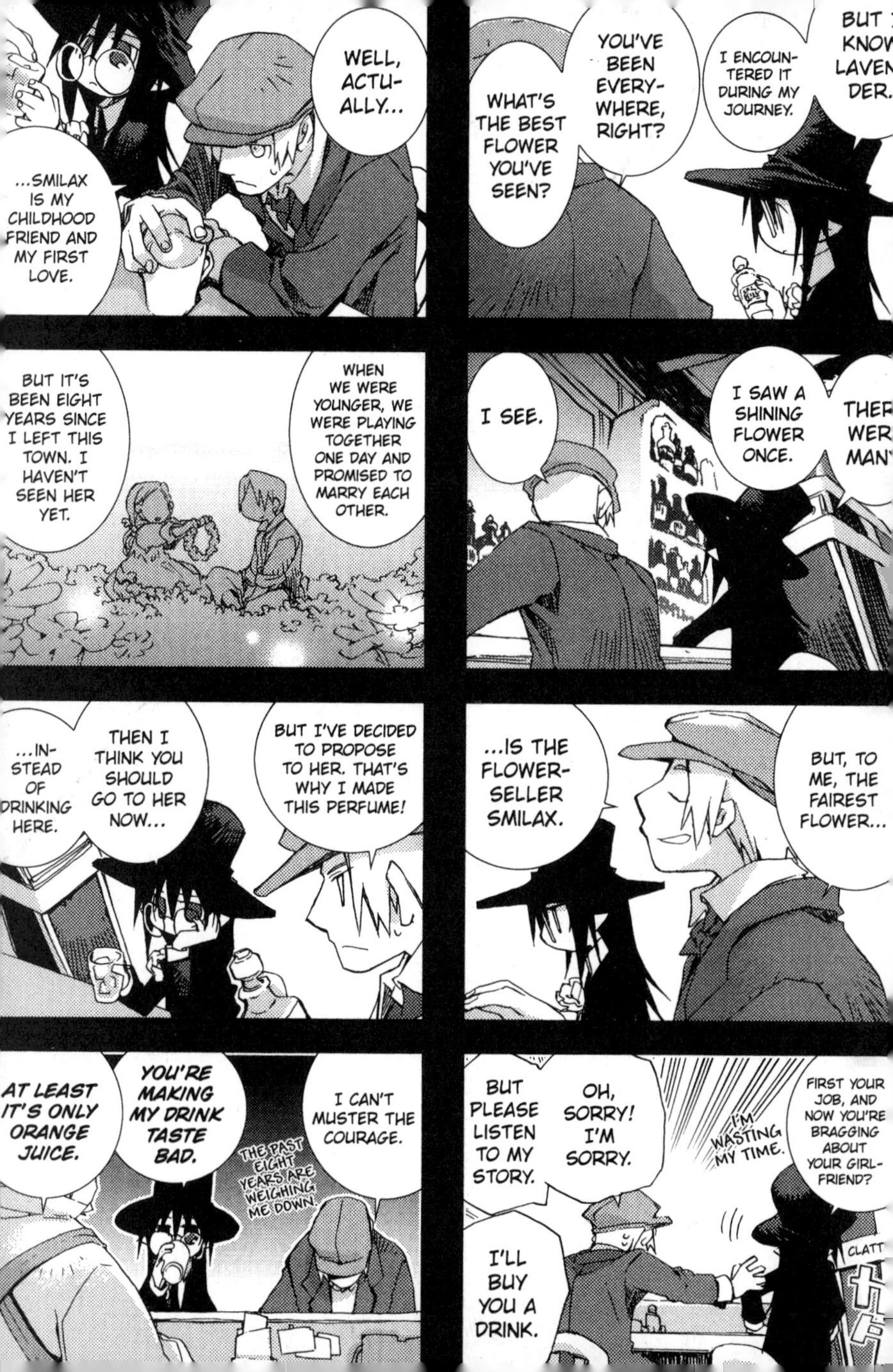
BUT I KNOW LAVEN- DER.
I ENCOUNTERED IT DURING MY JOURNEY.
YOU'VE BEEN EVERYWHERE, RIGHT?
WHAT'S THE BEST FLOWER YOU'VE SEEN?
WELL, ACTUALLY...
...SMILAX IS MY CHILDHOOD FRIEND AND MY FIRST LOVE.
THER WER MAN
I SAW A SHINING FLOWER ONCE.
I SEE.
WHEN WE WERE YOUNGER, WE WERE PLAYING TOGETHER ONE DAY AND PROMISED TO MARRY EACH OTHER.
BUT IT'S BEEN EIGHT YEARS SINCE I LEFT THIS TOWN. I HAVEN'T SEEN HER YET.
BUT, TO ME, THE FAIREST FLOWER...
...IS THE FLOWER-SELLER SMILAX.
BUT I'VE DECIDED TO PROPOSE TO HER. THAT'S WHY I MADE THIS PERFUME!
THEN I THINK YOU SHOULD GO TO HER NOW...
...INSTEAD OF DRINKING HERE.
FIRST YOUR JOB, AND NOW YOU'RE BRAGGING ABOUT YOUR GIRLFRIEND?
I'M WASTING MY TIME.
CLATT
OH, SORRY! I'M SORRY.
BUT PLEASE LISTEN TO MY STORY.
I'LL BUY YOU A DRINK.
I CAN'T MUSTER THE COURAGE.
THE PAST EIGHT YEARS ARE WEIGHING ME DOWN.
YOU'RE MAKING MY DRINK TASTE BAD.
AT LEAST IT'S ONLY ORANGE JUICE.

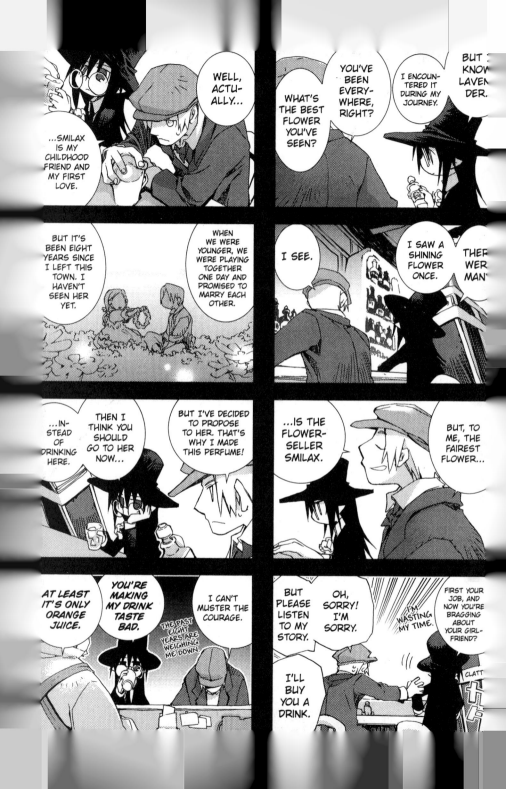

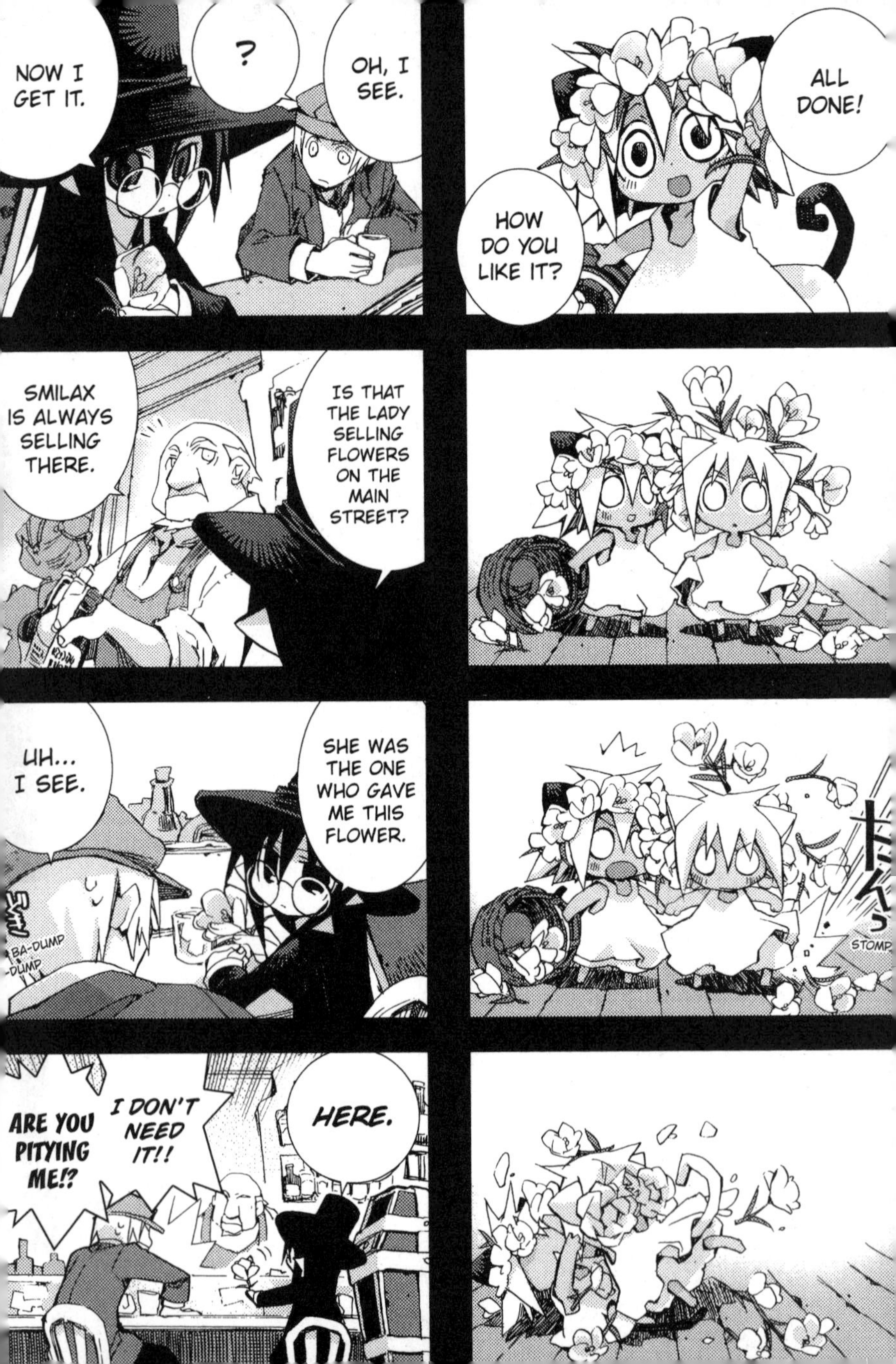
ALL DONE!
HOW DO YOU LIKE IT?
OH, I SEE.
?
NOW I GET IT.
IS THAT THE LADY SELLING FLOWERS ON THE MAIN STREET?
SMILAX IS ALWAYS SELLING THERE.
STOMP
SHE WAS THE ONE WHO GAVE ME THIS FLOWER.
UH... I SEE.
BA-DUMP
-DUMP
HERE.
I DON'T NEED IT!!
ARE YOU PITYING ME!?

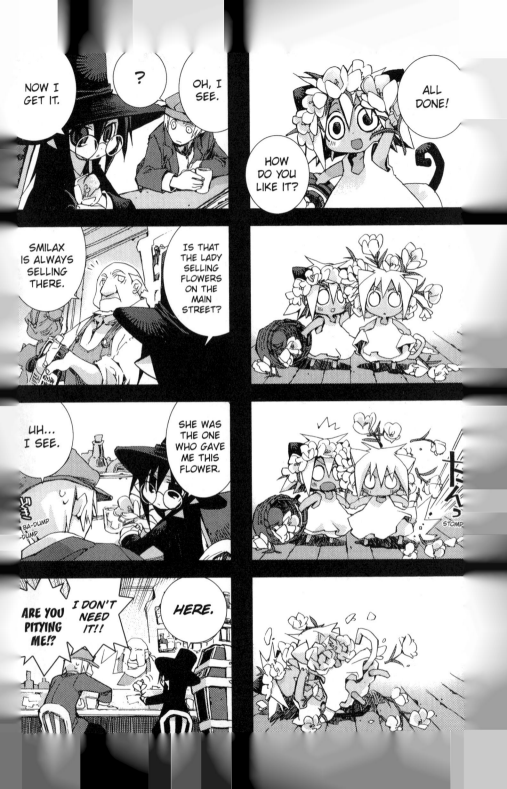

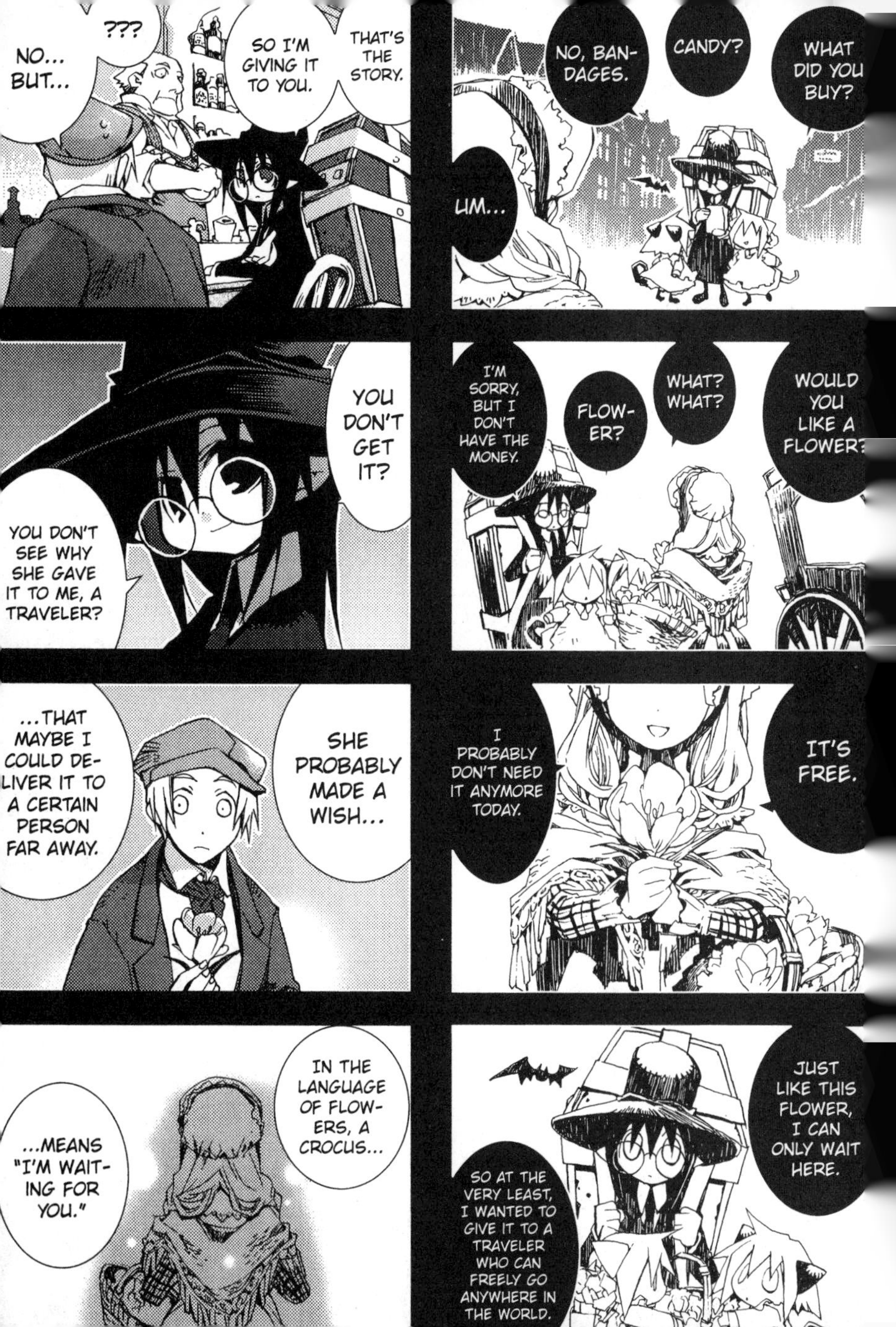
WHAT DID YOU BUY?
CANDY?
NO, BAN-DAGES.
UM...
WOULD YOU LIKE A FLOWER?
WHAT? WHAT?
FLOW-ER?
I'M SORRY, BUT I DON'T HAVE THE MONEY.
IT'S FREE.
I PROBABLY DON'T NEED IT ANYMORE TODAY.
JUST LIKE THIS FLOWER, I CAN ONLY WAIT HERE.
SO AT THE VERY LEAST, I WANTED TO GIVE IT TO A TRAVELER WHO CAN FREELY GO ANYWHERE IN THE WORLD.
THAT'S THE STORY.
SO I'M GIVING IT TO YOU.
???
NO... BUT...
YOU DON'T GET IT?
YOU DON'T SEE WHY SHE GAVE IT TO ME, A TRAVELER?
SHE PROBABLY MADE A WISH...
...THAT MAYBE I COULD DE-LIVER IT TO A CERTAIN PERSON FAR AWAY.
IN THE LANGUAGE OF FLOW-ERS, A CROCUS...
...MEANS "I'M WAIT-ING FOR YOU."

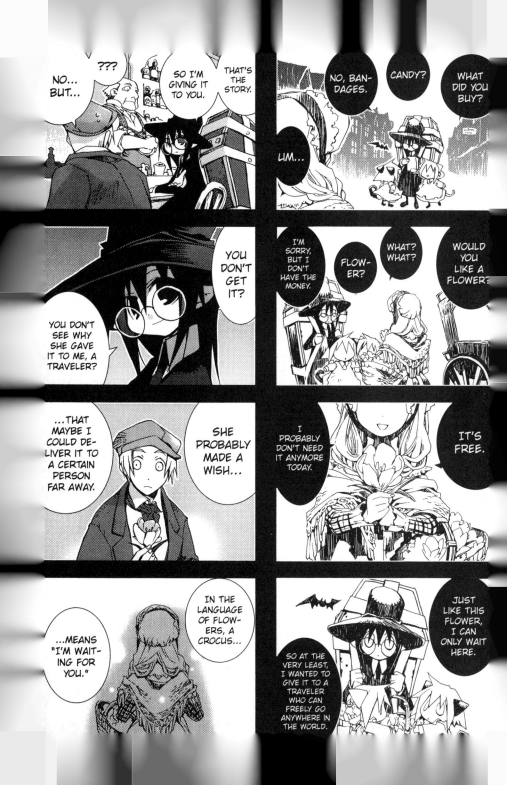

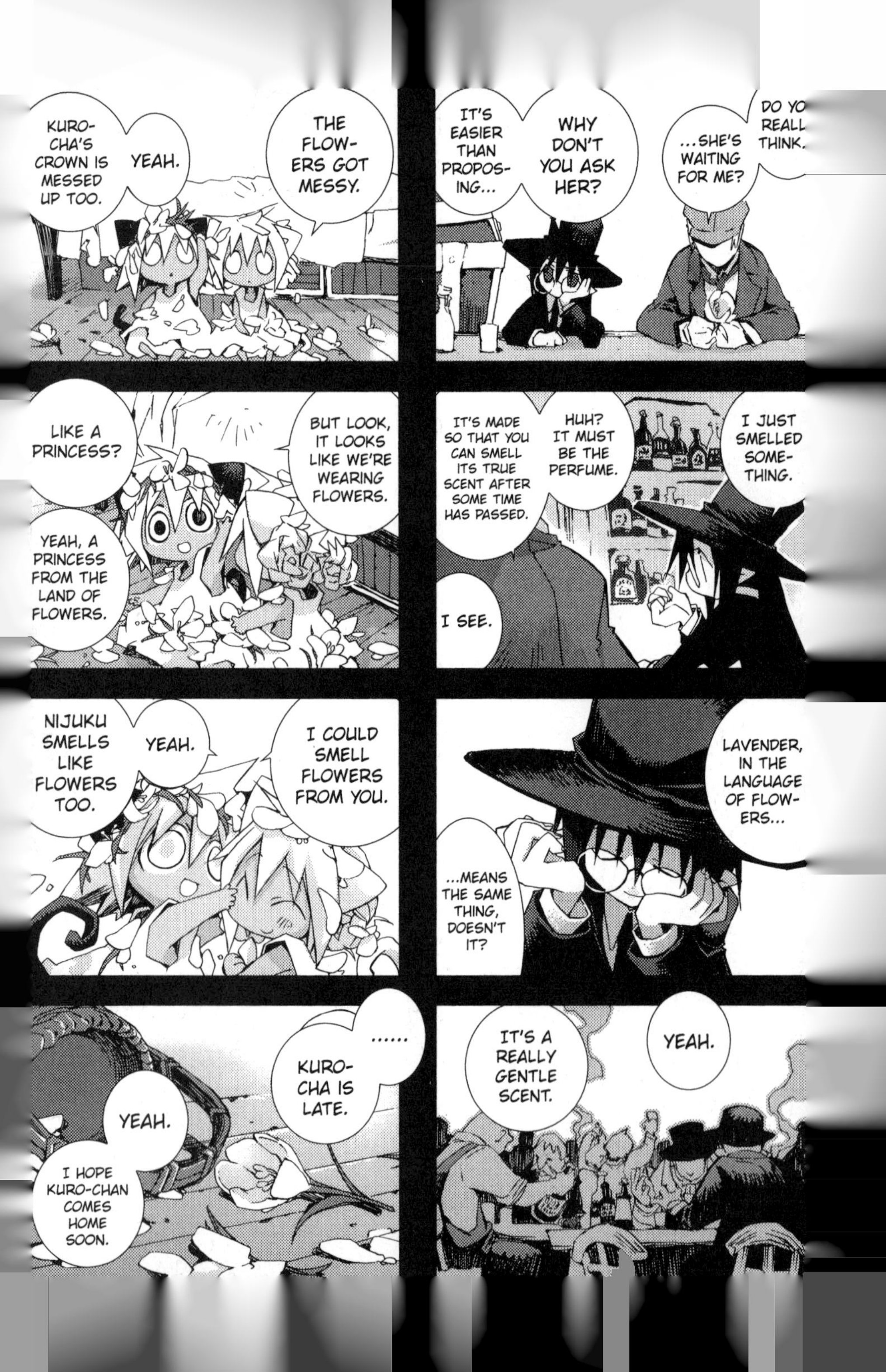
DO YO REALL THINK.
...SHE'S WAITING FOR ME?
WHY DON'T YOU ASK HER?
IT'S EASIER THAN PROPOSING...
I JUST SMELLED SOMETHING.
HUH? IT MUST BE THE PERFUME.
IT'S MADE SO THAT YOU CAN SMELL ITS TRUE SCENT AFTER SOME TIME HAS PASSED.
I SEE.
LAVENDER, IN THE LANGUAGE OF FLOWERS...
...MEANS THE SAME THING, DOESN'T IT?
YEAH.
IT'S A REALLY GENTLE SCENT.
THE FLOWERS GOT MESSY.
YEAH.
KURO-CHA'S CROWN IS MESSED UP TOO.
BUT LOOK, IT LOOKS LIKE WE'RE WEARING FLOWERS.
LIKE A PRINCESS?
YEAH, A PRINCESS FROM THE LAND OF FLOWERS.
I COULD SMELL FLOWERS FROM YOU.
YEAH.
NIJUKU SMELLS LIKE FLOWERS TOO.
......
KURO-CHA IS LATE.
YEAH.
I HOPE KURO-CHAN COMES HOME SOON.

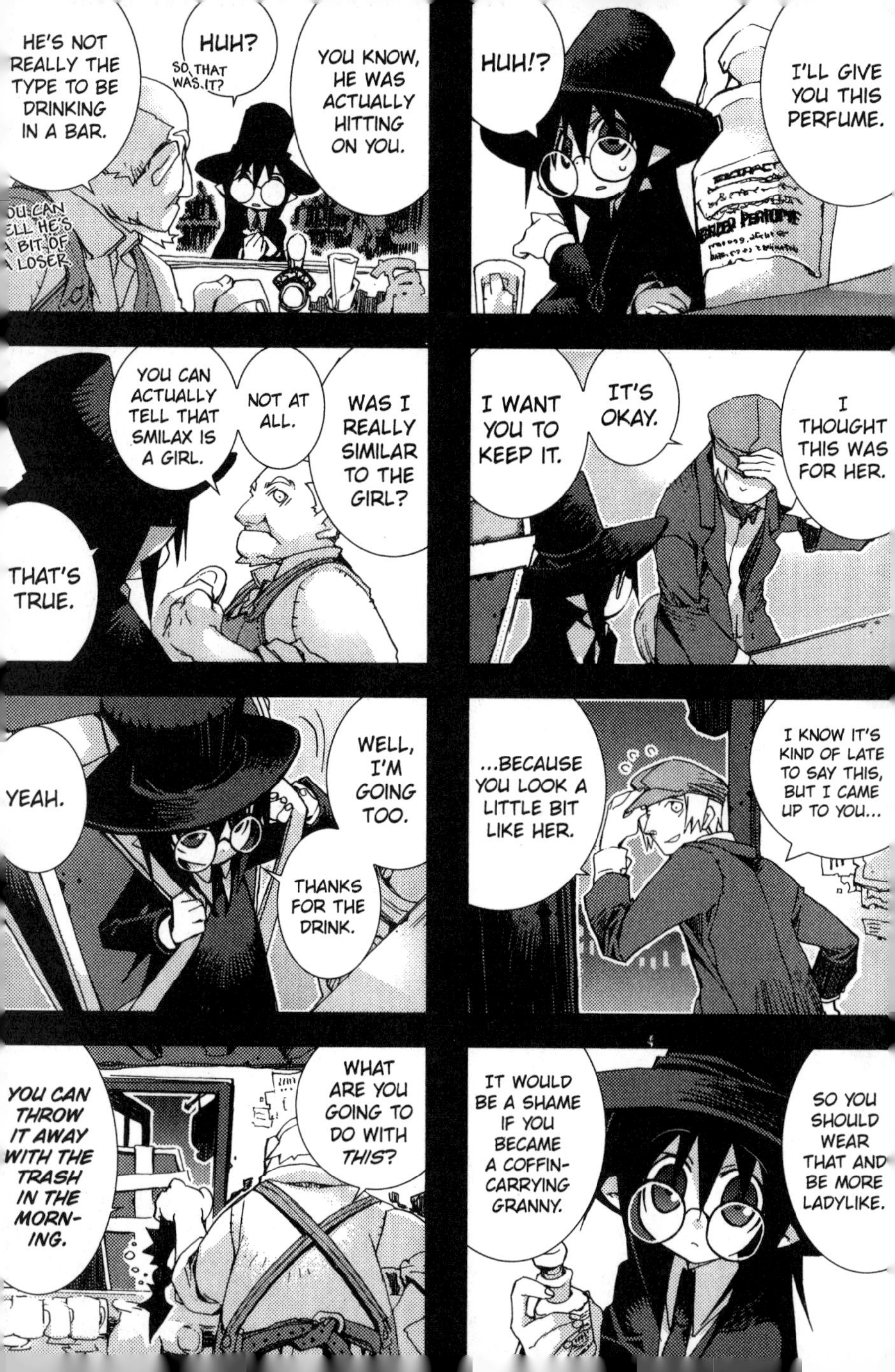
I'LL GIVE YOU THIS PERFUME.
HUH!?
YOU KNOW, HE WAS ACTUALLY HITTING ON YOU.
HUH?
SO, THAT WAS IT?
HE'S NOT REALLY THE TYPE TO BE DRINKING IN A BAR.
YOU CAN TELL HE'S A BIT OF A LOSER
I THOUGHT THIS WAS FOR HER.
IT'S OKAY.
I WANT YOU TO KEEP IT.
WAS I REALLY SIMILAR TO THE GIRL?
NOT AT ALL.
YOU CAN ACTUALLY TELL THAT SMILAX IS A GIRL.
THAT'S TRUE.
I KNOW IT'S KIND OF LATE TO SAY THIS, BUT I CAME UP TO YOU...
...BECAUSE YOU LOOK A LITTLE BIT LIKE HER.
WELL, I'M GOING TOO.
THANKS FOR THE DRINK.
YEAH.
SO YOU SHOULD WEAR THAT AND BE MORE LADYLIKE.
IT WOULD BE A SHAME IF YOU BECAME A COFFIN-CARRYING GRANNY.
WHAT ARE YOU GOING TO DO WITH THIS?
YOU CAN THROW IT AWAY WITH THE TRASH IN THE MORNING.

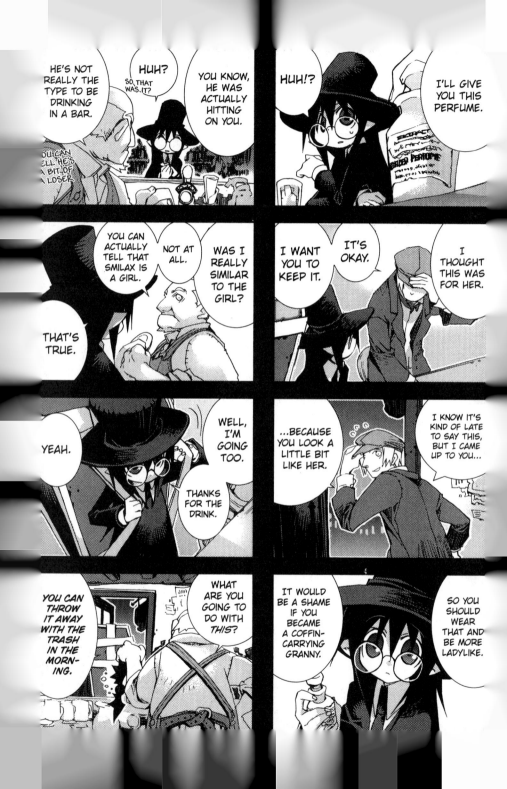

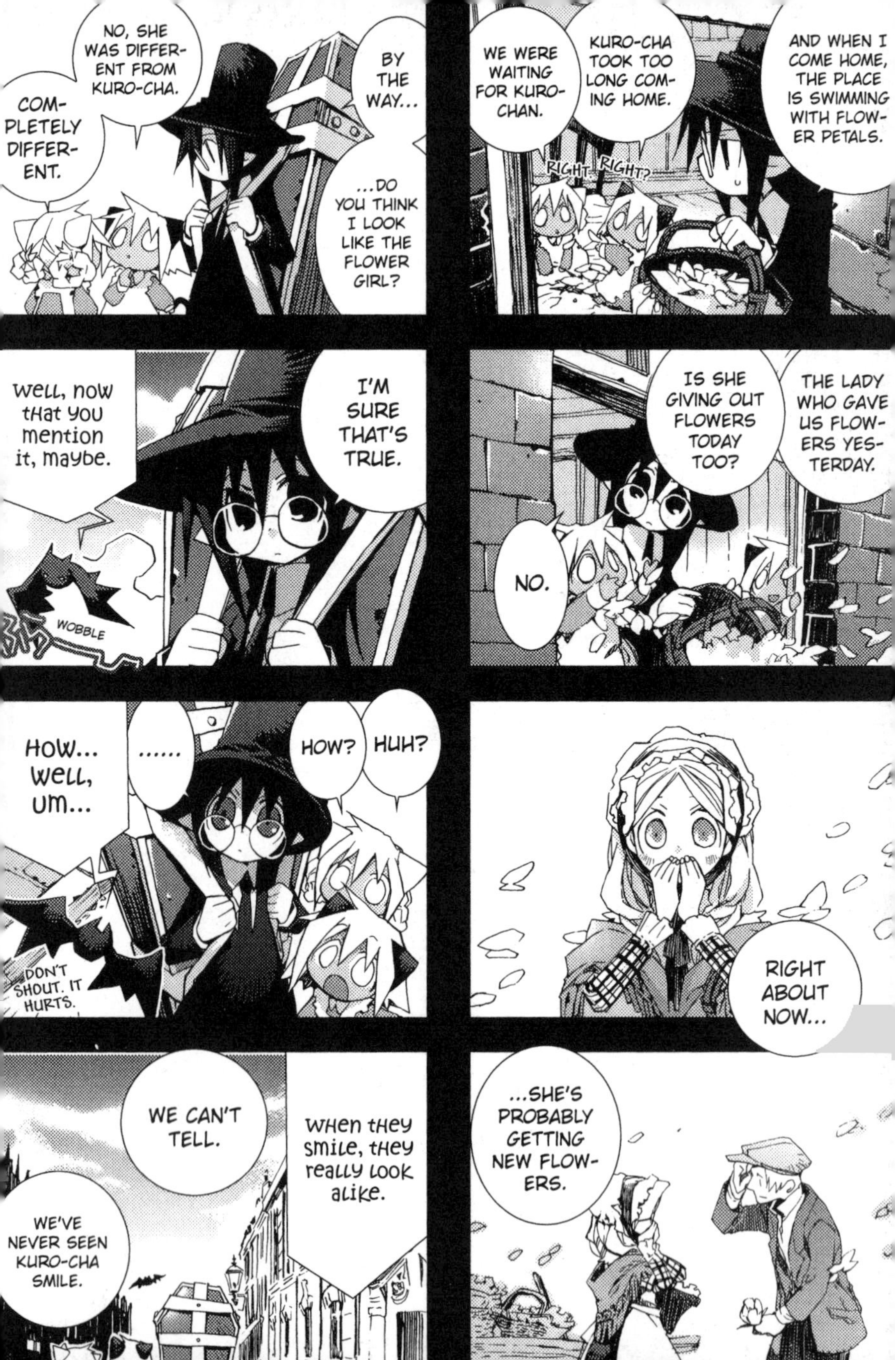
AND WHEN I COME HOME, THE PLACE IS SWIMMING WITH FLOWER PETALS.
KURO-CHA TOOK TOO LONG COMING HOME.
WE WERE WAITING FOR KURO-CHAN.
RIGHT. RIGHT?
BY THE WAY...
...DO YOU THINK I LOOK LIKE THE FLOWER GIRL?
NO, SHE WAS DIFFERENT FROM KURO-CHA.
COMPLETELY DIFFERENT.
THE LADY WHO GAVE US FLOWERS YESTERDAY.
IS SHE GIVING OUT FLOWERS TODAY TOO?
NO.
I'M SURE THAT'S TRUE.
Well, now that you mention it, maybe.
WOBBLE
RIGHT ABOUT NOW...
HUH?
HOW?
......
How... well, um...
DON'T SHOUT. IT HURTS.
...SHE'S PROBABLY GETTING NEW FLOWERS.
When they smile, they really look alike.
WE CAN'T TELL.
WE'VE NEVER SEEN KURO-CHA SMILE.

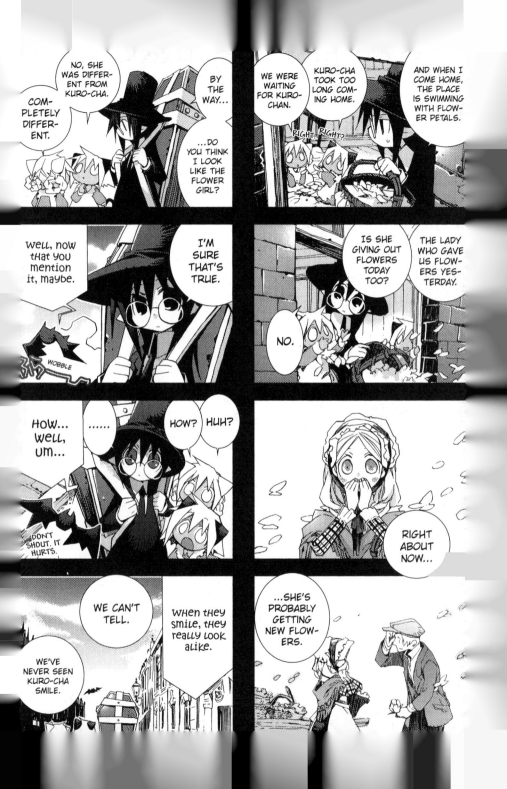

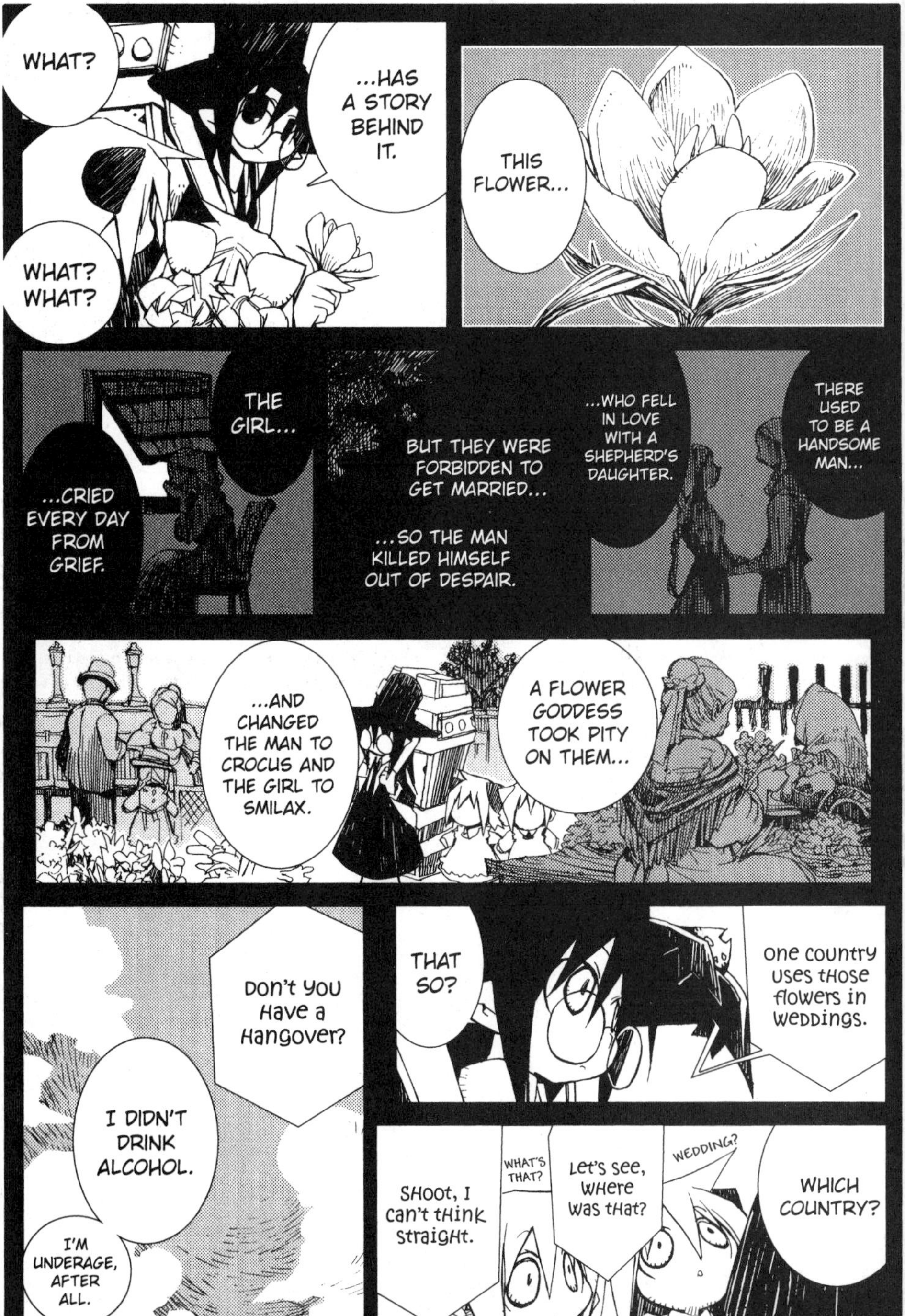
THIS FLOWER...
...HAS A STORY BEHIND IT.
WHAT?
WHAT? WHAT?
THERE USED TO BE A HANDSOME MAN...
...WHO FELL IN LOVE WITH A SHEPHERD'S DAUGHTER.
BUT THEY WERE FORBIDDEN TO GET MARRIED...
...SO THE MAN KILLED HIMSELF OUT OF DESPAIR.
THE GIRL...
...CRIED EVERY DAY FROM GRIEF.
A FLOWER GODDESS TOOK PITY ON THEM...
...AND CHANGED THE MAN TO CROCUS AND THE GIRL TO SMILAX.
One country uses those flowers in weddings.
THAT SO?
WHICH COUNTRY?
WEDDING?
Let's see, where was that?
WHAT'S THAT?
Shoot, I can't think straight.
Don't you have a hangover?
I DIDN'T DRINK ALCOHOL.
I'M UNDERAGE, AFTER ALL.

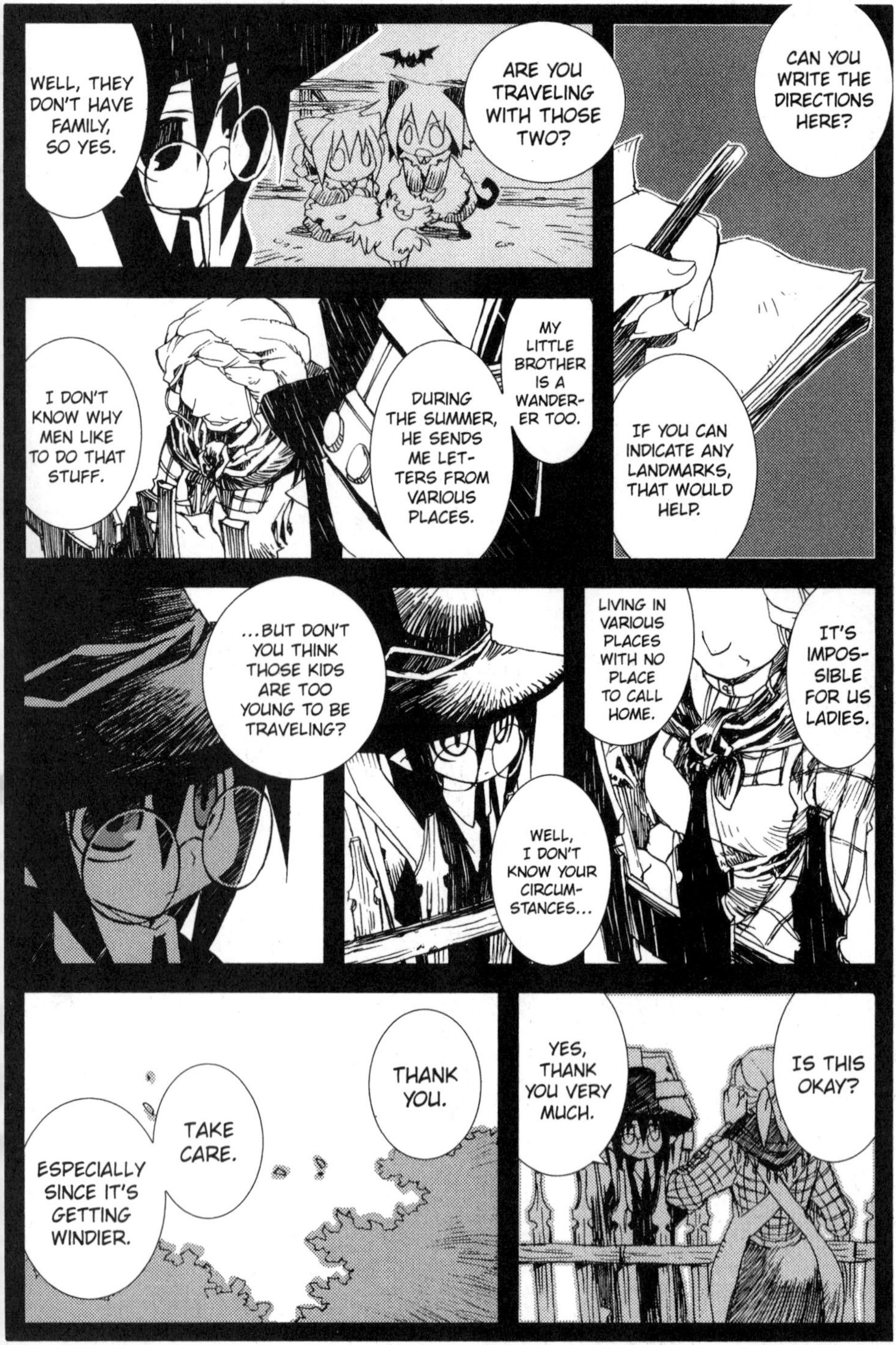
CAN YOU WRITE THE DIRECTIONS HERE?
IF YOU CAN INDICATE ANY LANDMARKS, THAT WOULD HELP.
ARE YOU TRAVELING WITH THOSE TWO?
WELL, THEY DON'T HAVE FAMILY, SO YES.
MY LITTLE BROTHER IS A WANDER-ER TOO.
DURING THE SUMMER, HE SENDS ME LET-TERS FROM VARIOUS PLACES.
I DON'T KNOW WHY MEN LIKE TO DO THAT STUFF.
LIVING IN VARIOUS PLACES WITH NO PLACE TO CALL HOME.
IT'S IMPOS-SIBLE FOR US LADIES.
WELL, I DON'T KNOW YOUR CIRCUM-STANCES...
...BUT DON'T YOU THINK THOSE KIDS ARE TOO YOUNG TO BE TRAVELING?
IS THIS OKAY?
YES, THANK YOU VERY MUCH.
THANK YOU.
TAKE CARE.
ESPECIALLY SINCE IT'S GETTING WINDIER.

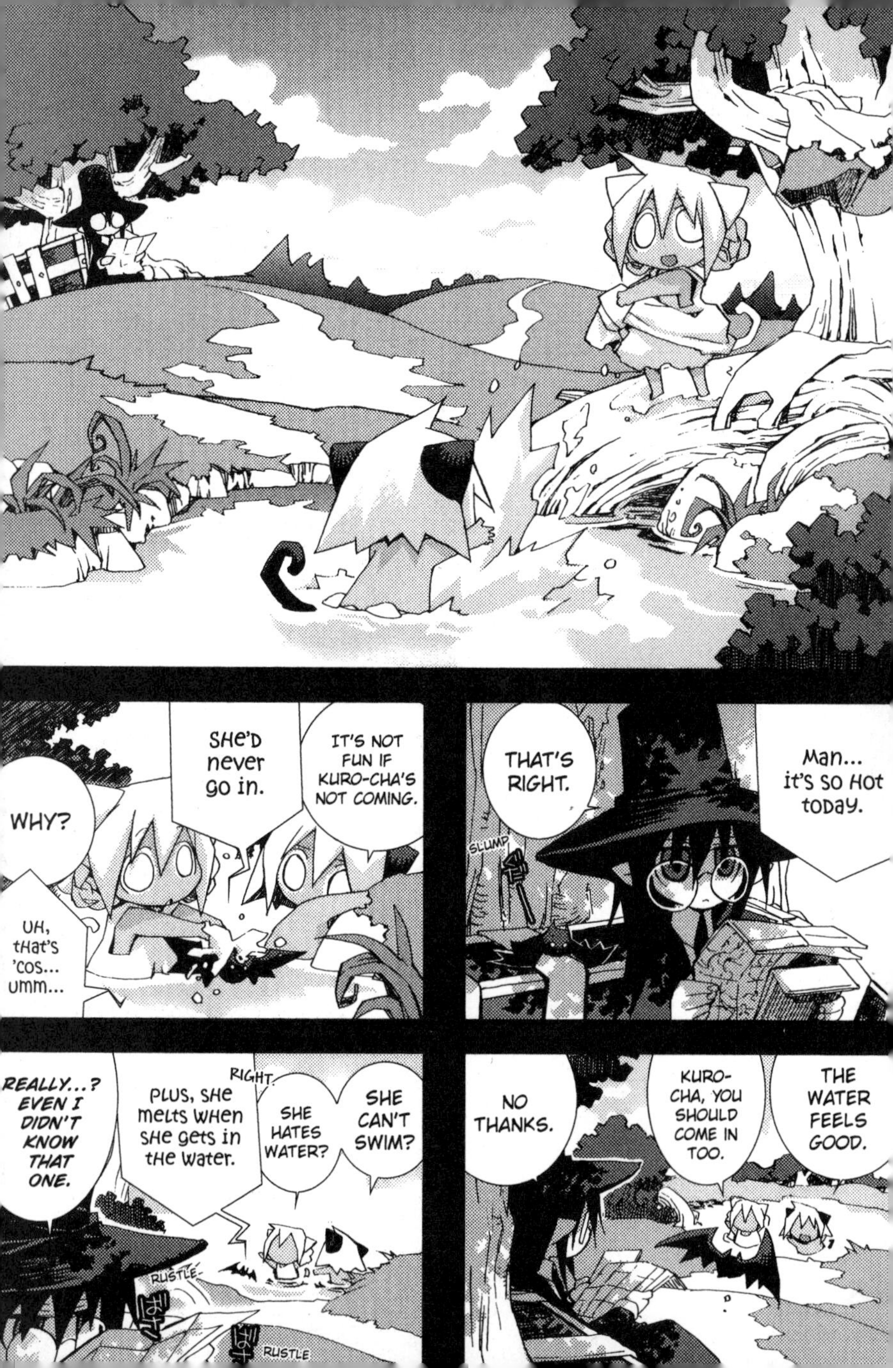
Man... it's so Hot today.
THAT'S RIGHT.
SLUMP
IT'S NOT FUN IF KURO-CHA'S NOT COMING.
SHE'D never go in.
WHY?
UH, that's 'cos... umm...
THE WATER FEELS GOOD.
KURO-CHA, YOU SHOULD COME IN TOO.
NO THANKS.
SHE CAN'T SWIM?
SHE HATES WATER?
RIGHT.
PLUS, SHE melts when she gets in the water.
REALLY...? EVEN I DIDN'T KNOW THAT ONE.
RUSTLE
RUSTLE

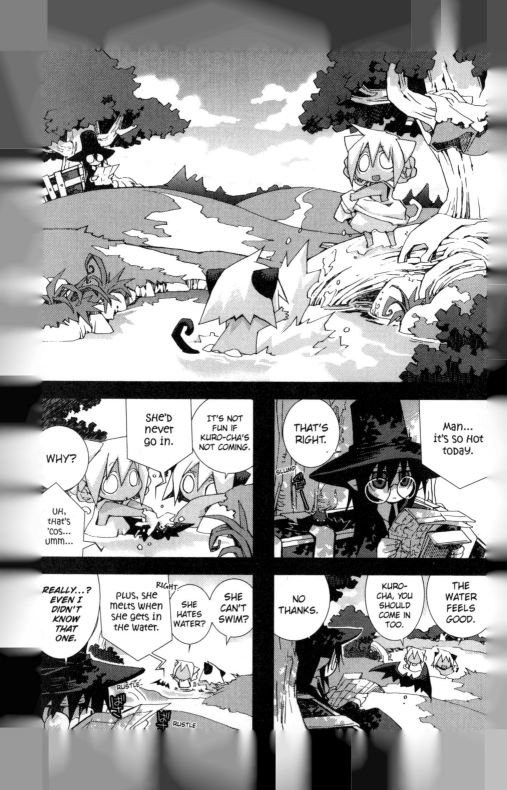

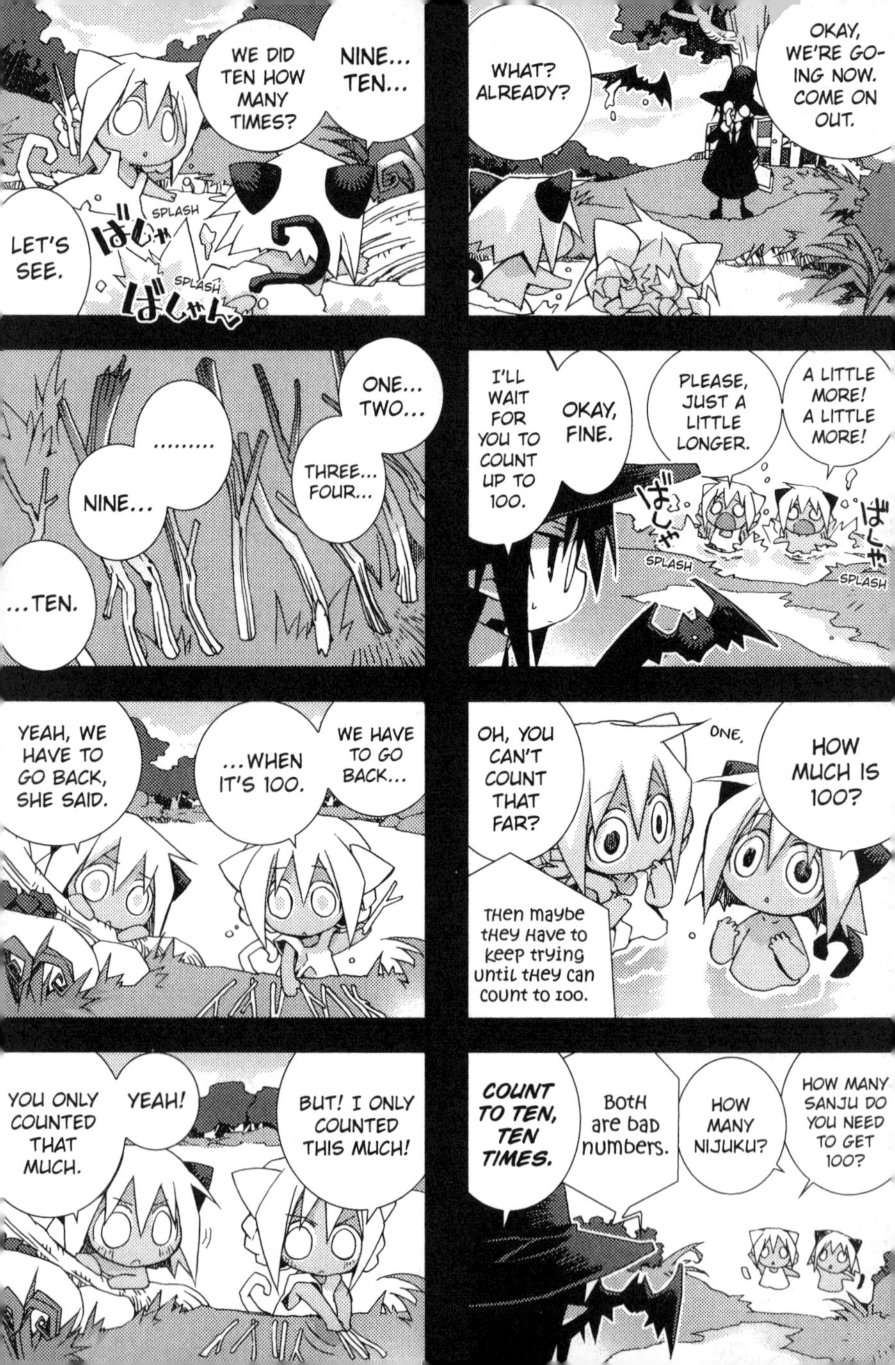
OKAY, WE'RE GO-ING NOW. COME ON OUT.
WHAT? ALREADY?
A LITTLE MORE! A LITTLE MORE!
PLEASE, JUST A LITTLE LONGER.
ばしゃ
SPLASH
ばしゃ
SPLASH
OKAY, FINE.
I'LL WAIT FOR YOU TO COUNT UP TO 100.
HOW MUCH IS 100?
ONE,
OH, YOU CAN'T COUNT THAT FAR?
Then maybe they have to keep trying until they can count to 100.
HOW MANY SANJU DO YOU NEED TO GET 100?
HOW MANY NIJUKU?
Both are bad numbers.
COUNT TO TEN, TEN TIMES.
NINE... TEN...
WE DID TEN HOW MANY TIMES?
ばしゃ
SPLASH
ばしゃん
SPLASH
LET'S SEE.
ONE... TWO...
THREE... FOUR...
....
NINE...
...TEN.
WE HAVE TO GO BACK...
...WHEN IT'S 100.
YEAH, WE HAVE TO GO BACK, SHE SAID.
BUT! I ONLY COUNTED THIS MUCH!
YEAH!
YOU ONLY COUNTED THAT MUCH.

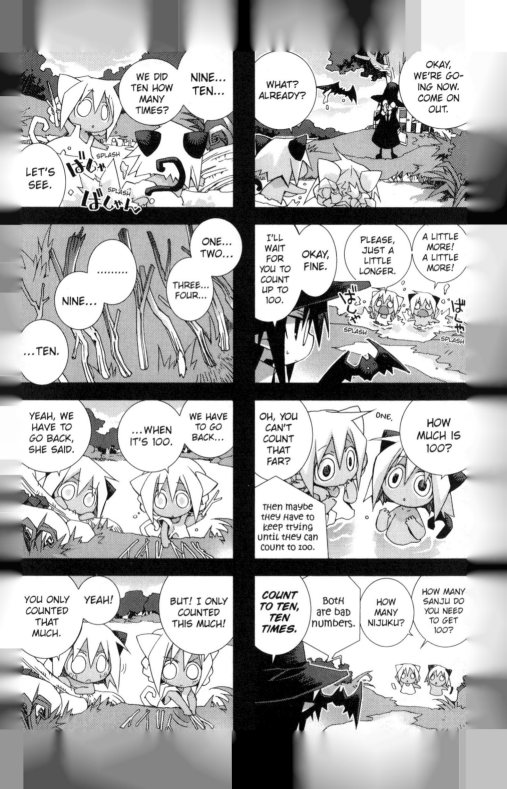

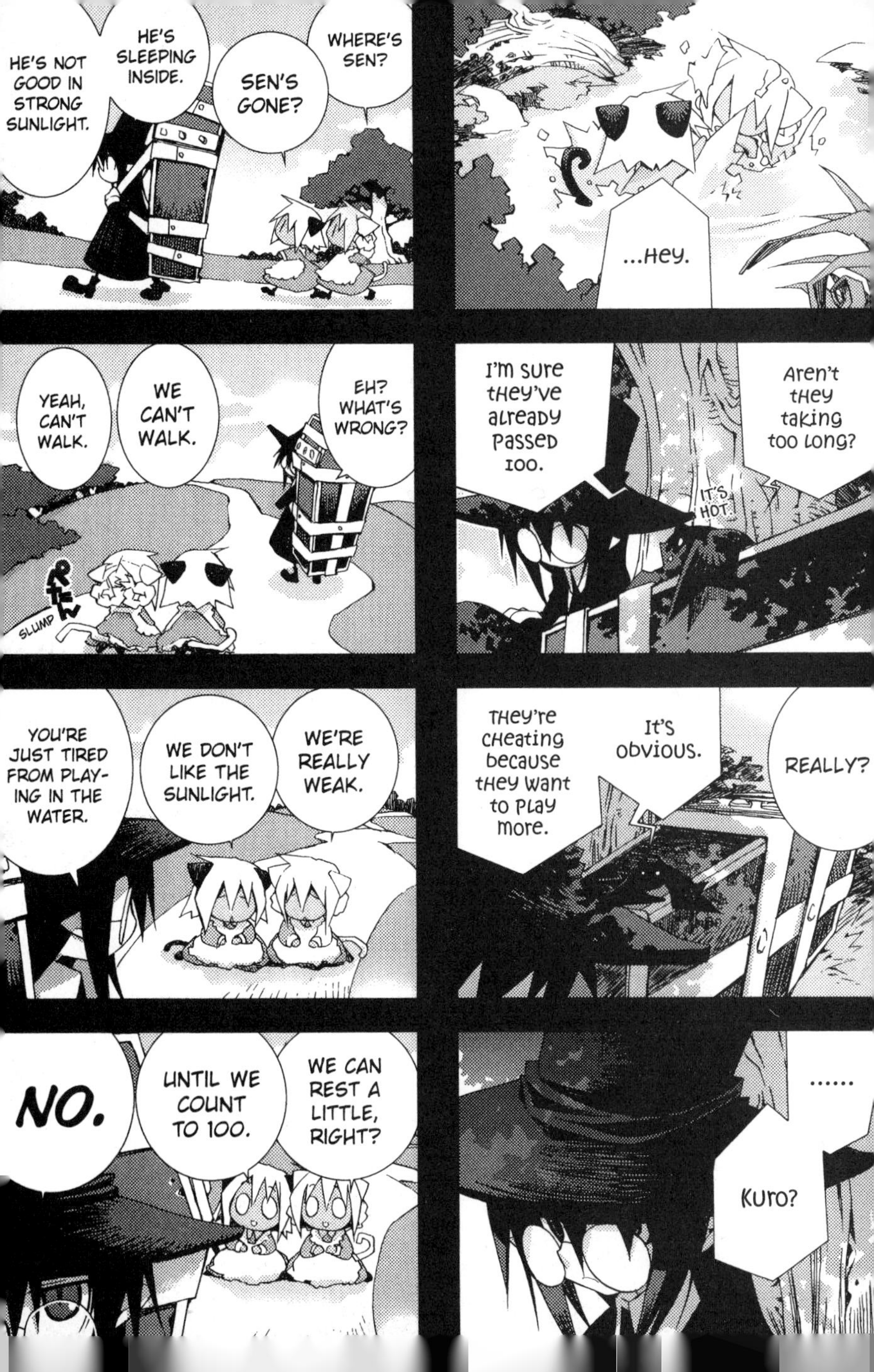
...Hey.
WHERE'S SEN?
SEN'S GONE?
HE'S SLEEPING INSIDE.
HE'S NOT GOOD IN STRONG SUNLIGHT.
Aren't they taking too long?
IT'S HOT.
I'm sure they've already passed 100.
EH? WHAT'S WRONG?
WE CAN'T WALK.
YEAH, CAN'T WALK.
SLUMP
REALLY?
It's obvious.
They're cheating because they want to play more.
WE'RE REALLY WEAK.
WE DON'T LIKE THE SUNLIGHT.
YOU'RE JUST TIRED FROM PLAY-ING IN THE WATER.
......
Kuro?
WE CAN REST A LITTLE, RIGHT?
UNTIL WE COUNT TO 100.
NO.

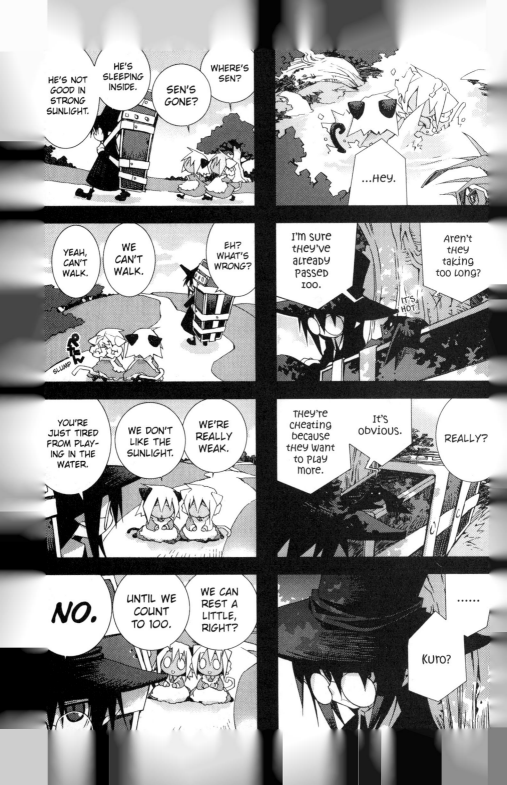

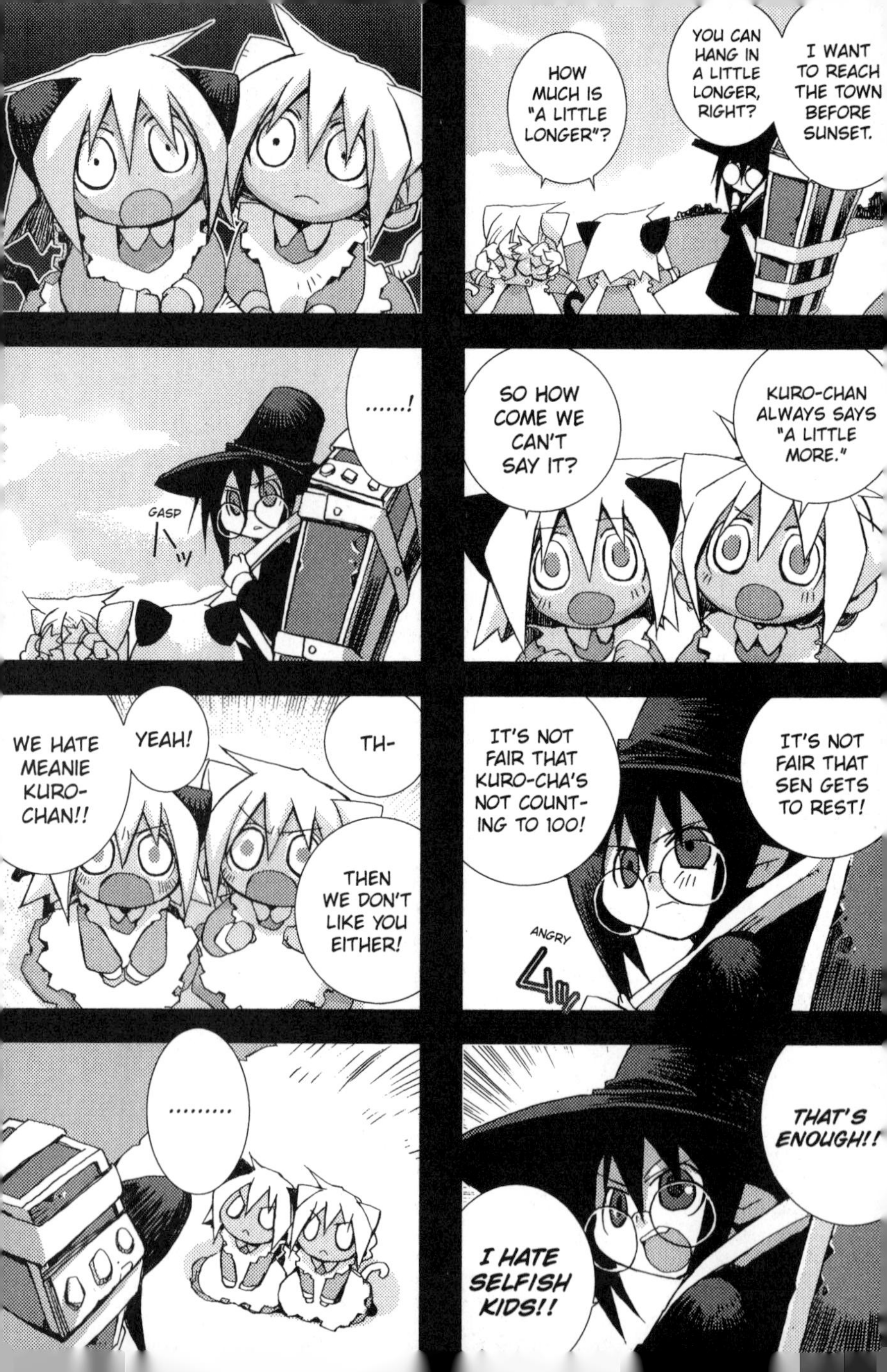
I WANT TO REACH THE TOWN BEFORE SUNSET.
YOU CAN HANG IN A LITTLE LONGER, RIGHT?
HOW MUCH IS "A LITTLE LONGER"?
KURO-CHAN ALWAYS SAYS "A LITTLE MORE."
SO HOW COME WE CAN'T SAY IT?
......!
GASP
IT'S NOT FAIR THAT SEN GETS TO REST!
IT'S NOT FAIR THAT KURO-CHA'S NOT COUNTING TO 100!
ANGRY
TH-
THEN WE DON'T LIKE YOU EITHER!
WE HATE MEANIE KURO-CHAN!!
YEAH!
THAT'S ENOUGH!!
I HATE SELFISH KIDS!!
....

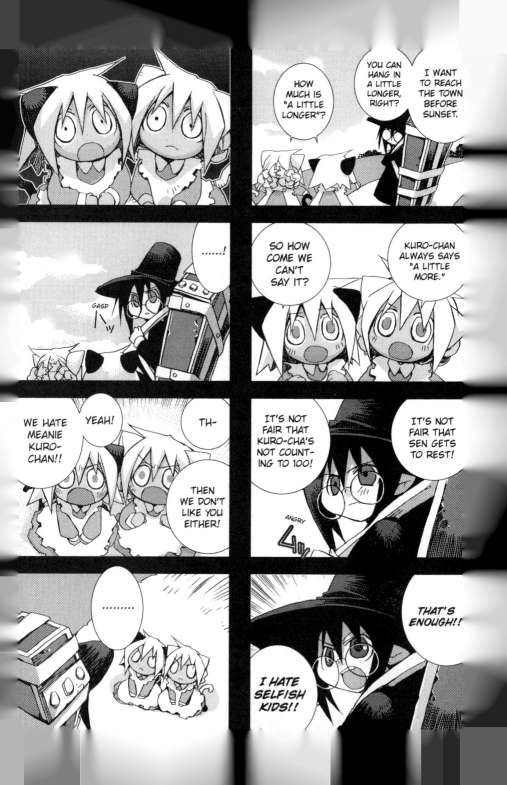

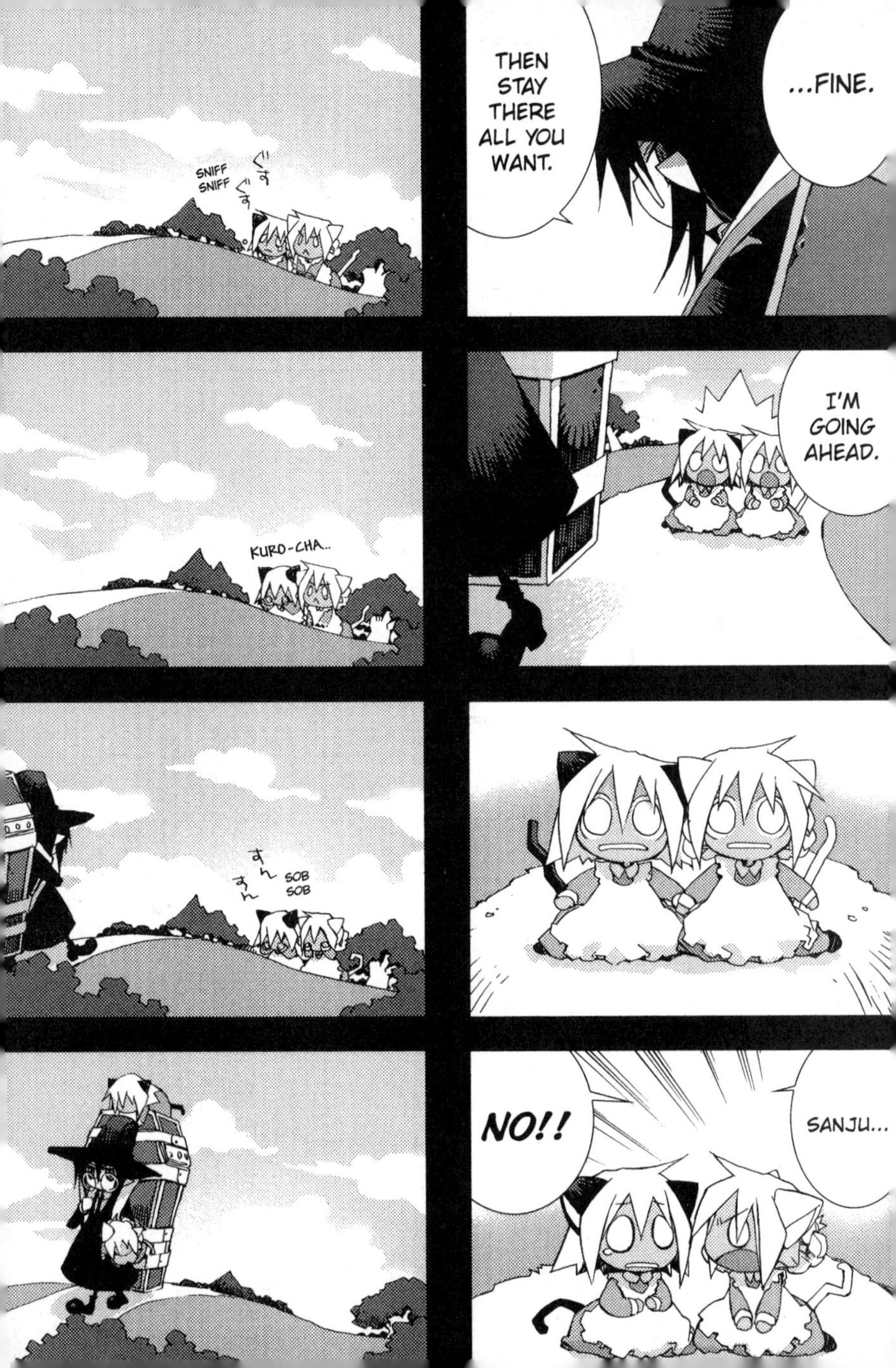
...FINE.
THEN STAY THERE ALL YOU WANT.
ぐすぐす
SNIFF SNIFF
I'M GOING AHEAD.
KURO-CHA..
すんすん
SOB SOB
SANJU...
NO!!

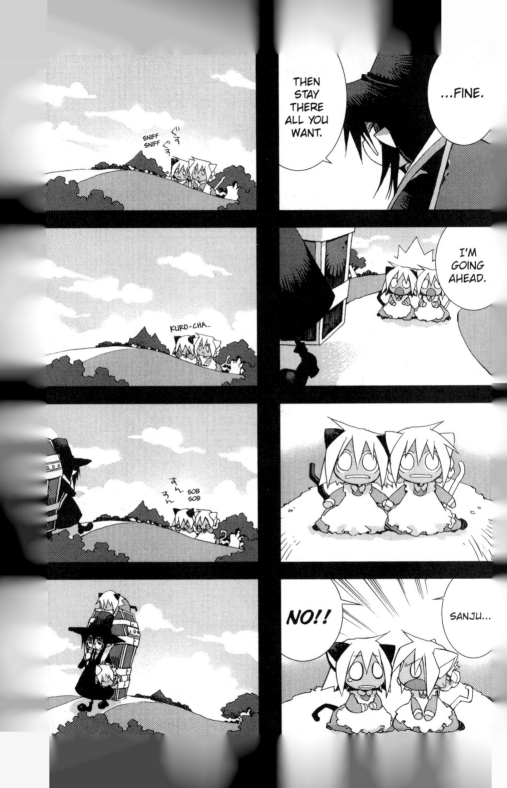

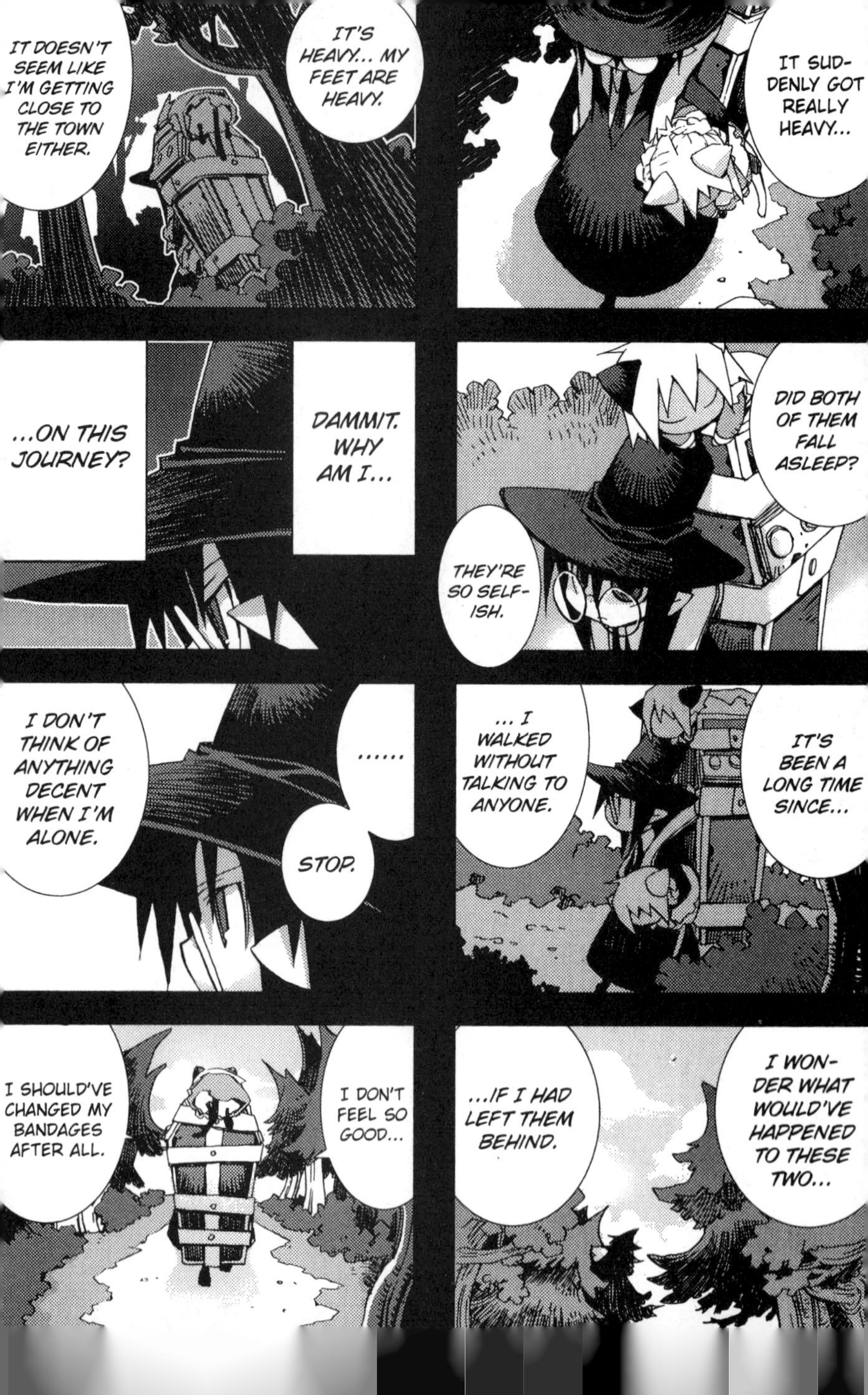
IT SUD-DENLY GOT REALLY HEAVY...
IT'S HEAVY... MY FEET ARE HEAVY.
IT DOESN'T SEEM LIKE I'M GETTING CLOSE TO THE TOWN EITHER.
DID BOTH OF THEM FALL ASLEEP?
THEY'RE SO SELF-ISH.
DAMMIT. WHY AM I...
...ON THIS JOURNEY?
IT'S BEEN A LONG TIME SINCE...
... I WALKED WITHOUT TALKING TO ANYONE.
......
STOP.
I DON'T THINK OF ANYTHING DECENT WHEN I'M ALONE.
I WON-DER WHAT WOULD'VE HAPPENED TO THESE TWO...
...IF I HAD LEFT THEM BEHIND.
I DON'T FEEL SO GOOD...
I SHOULD'VE CHANGED MY BANDAGES AFTER ALL.

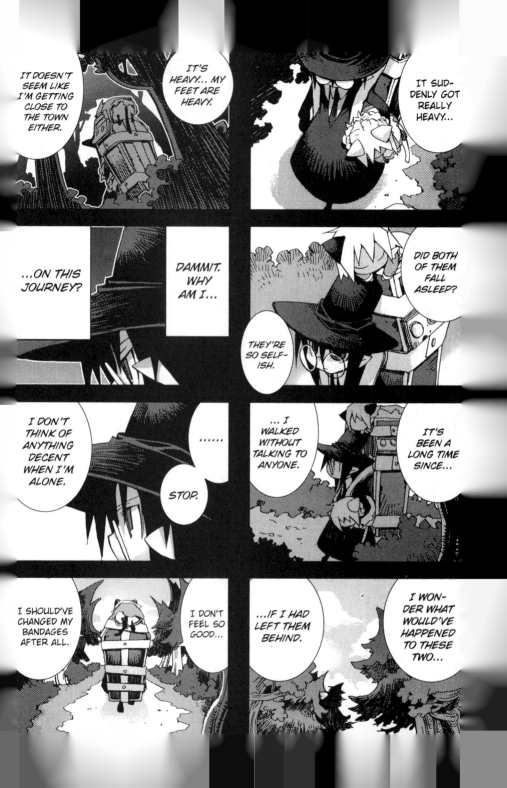

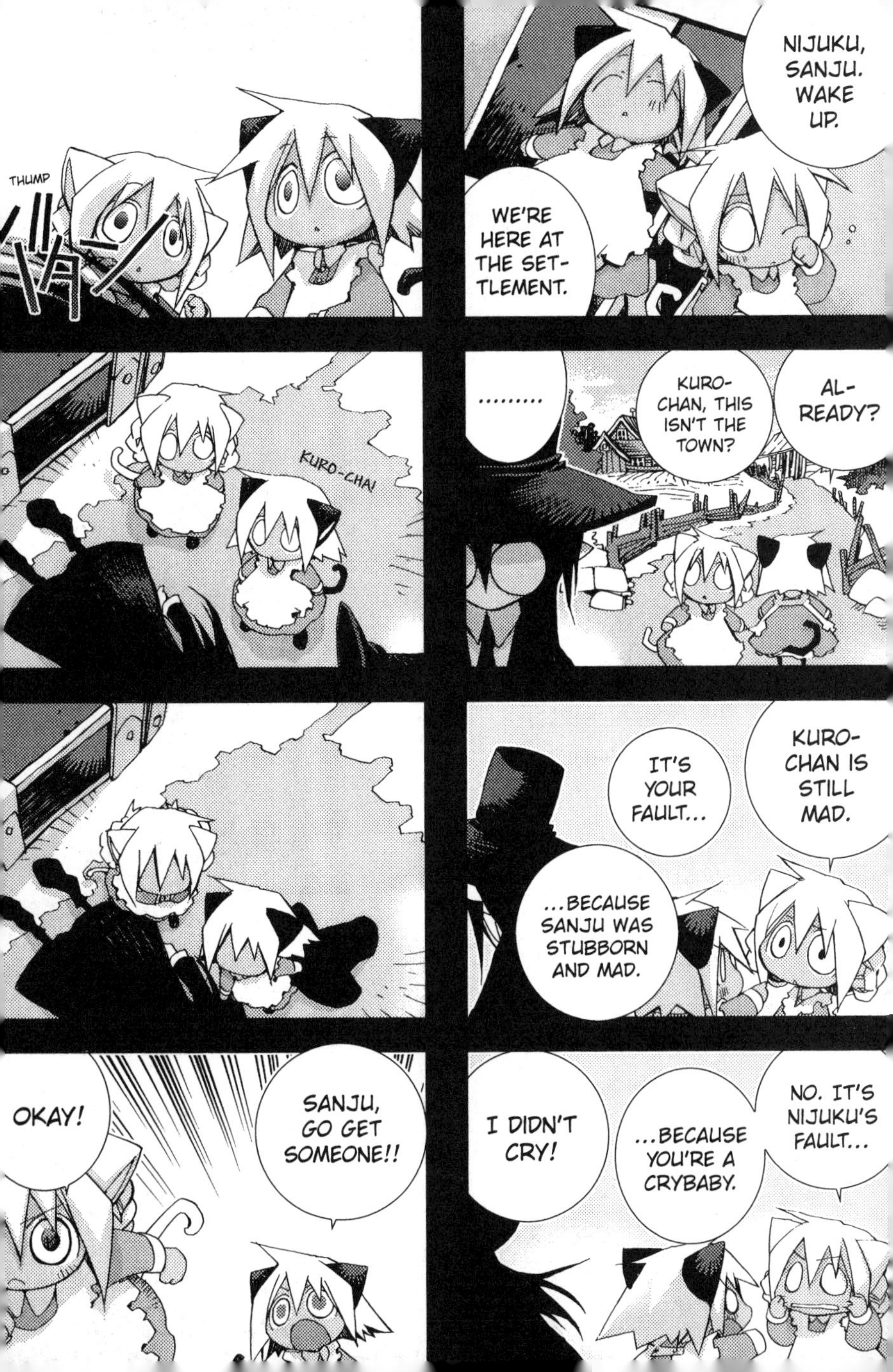
NIJUKU, SANJU. WAKE UP.
WE'RE HERE AT THE SET-TLEMENT.
THUMP
AL-READY?
KURO-CHAN, THIS ISN'T THE TOWN?
....
KURO-CHA!
KURO-CHAN IS STILL MAD.
IT'S YOUR FAULT...
...BECAUSE SANJU WAS STUBBORN AND MAD.
NO. IT'S NIJUKU'S FAULT...
...BECAUSE YOU'RE A CRYBABY.
I DIDN'T CRY!
SANJU, GO GET SOMEONE!!
OKAY!

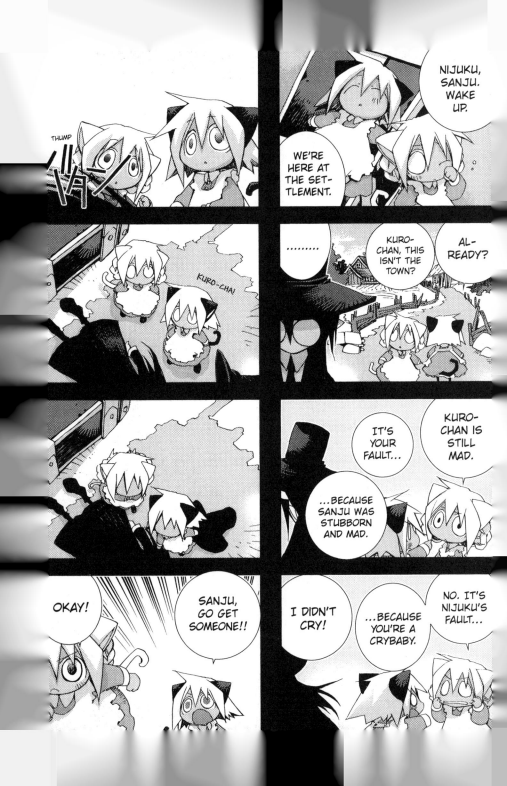

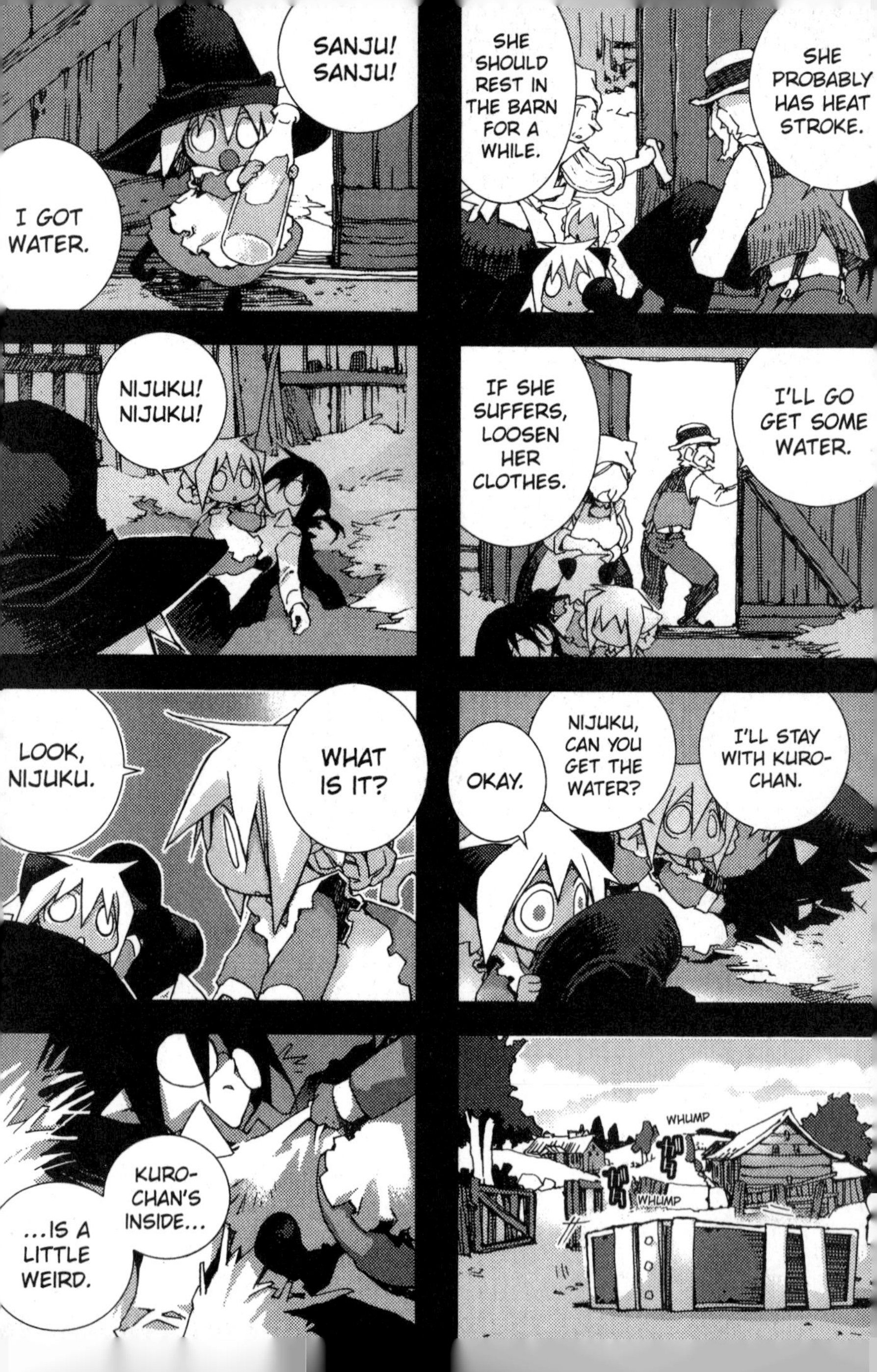
SHE PROBABLY HAS HEAT STROKE.
SHE SHOULD REST IN THE BARN FOR A WHILE.
SANJU! SANJU!
I GOT WATER.
I'LL GO GET SOME WATER.
IF SHE SUFFERS, LOOSEN HER CLOTHES.
NIJUKU! NIJUKU!
I'LL STAY WITH KURO-CHAN.
NIJUKU, CAN YOU GET THE WATER?
OKAY.
WHAT IS IT?
LOOK, NIJUKU.
WHUMP
WHUMP
KURO-CHAN'S INSIDE...
...IS A LITTLE WEIRD.

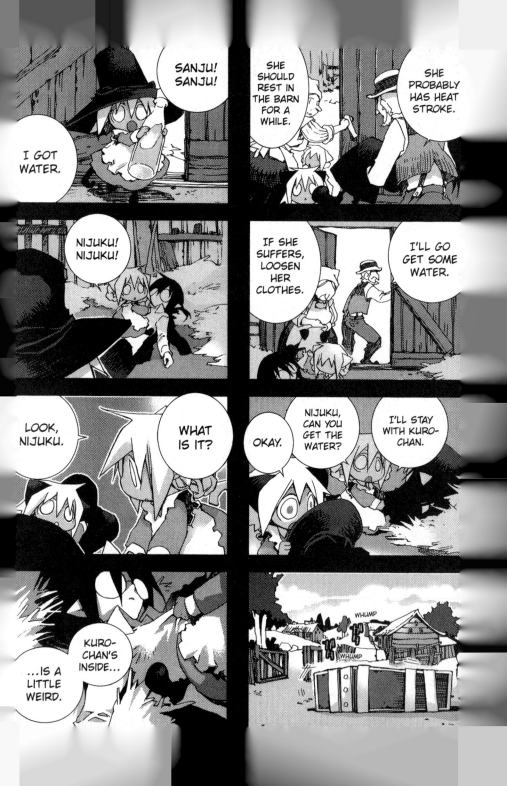

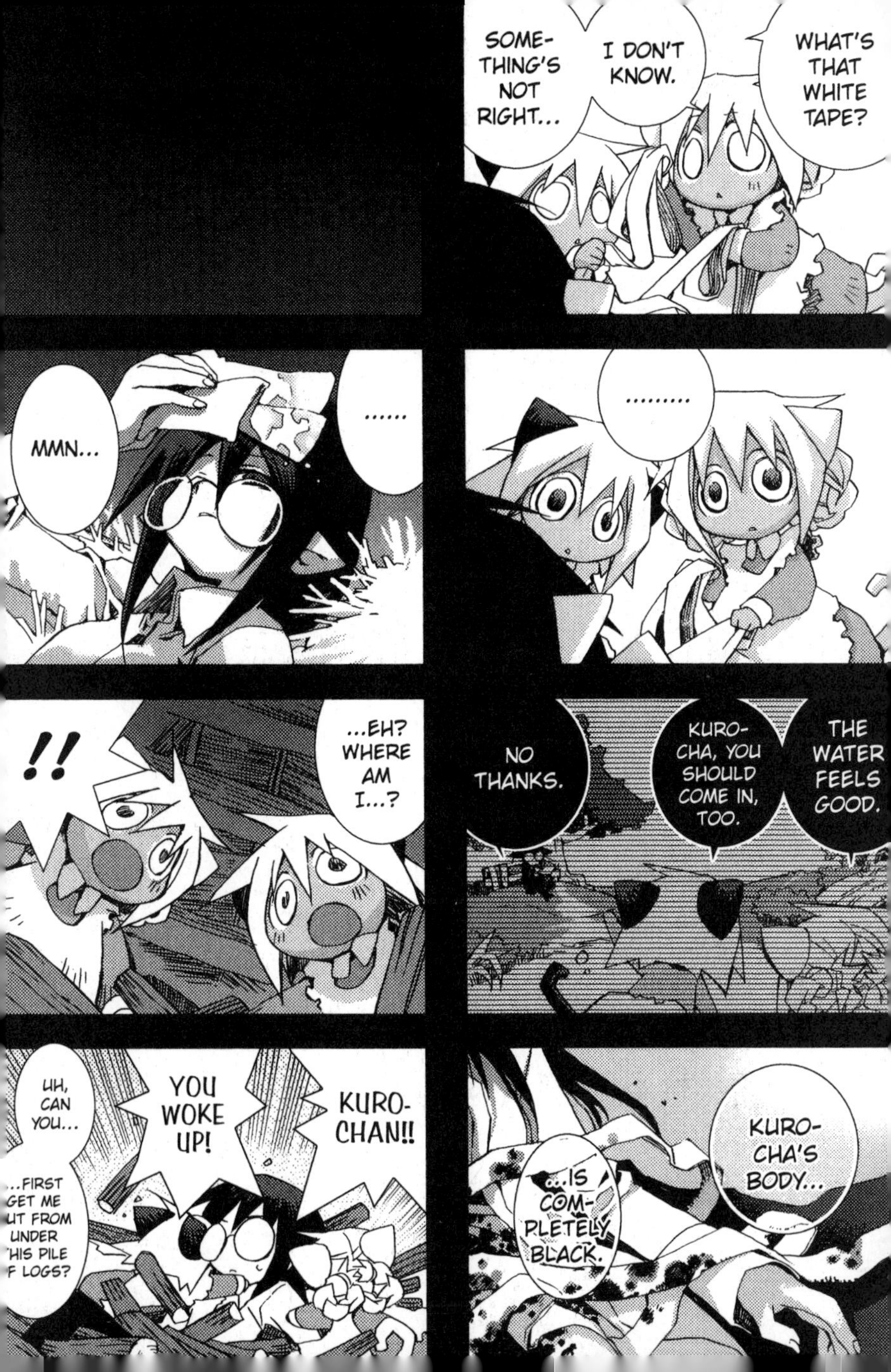
WHAT'S THAT WHITE TAPE?
I DON'T KNOW.
SOME-THING'S NOT RIGHT...
....
......
MMN...
THE WATER FEELS GOOD.
KURO-CHA, YOU SHOULD COME IN, TOO.
NO THANKS.
...EH? WHERE AM I...?
!!
KURO-CHA'S BODY...
...IS COM-PLETELY BLACK.
KURO-CHAN!!
YOU WOKE UP!
UH, CAN YOU...
...FIRST GET ME UT FROM UNDER HIS PILE F LOGS?

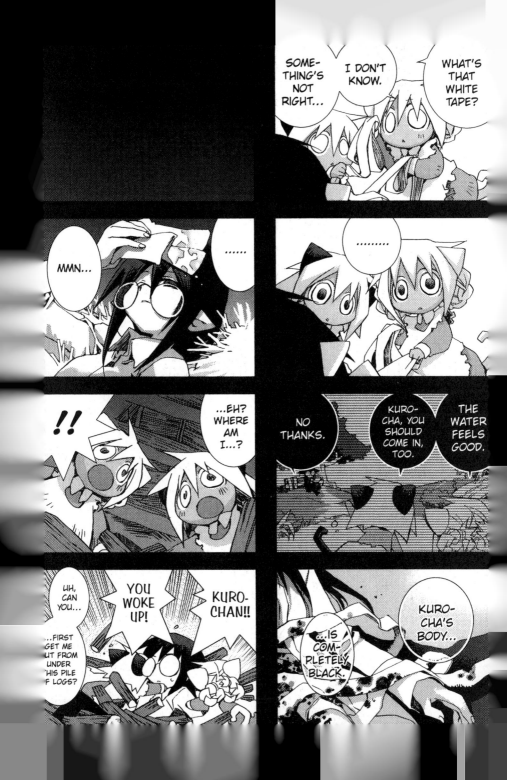

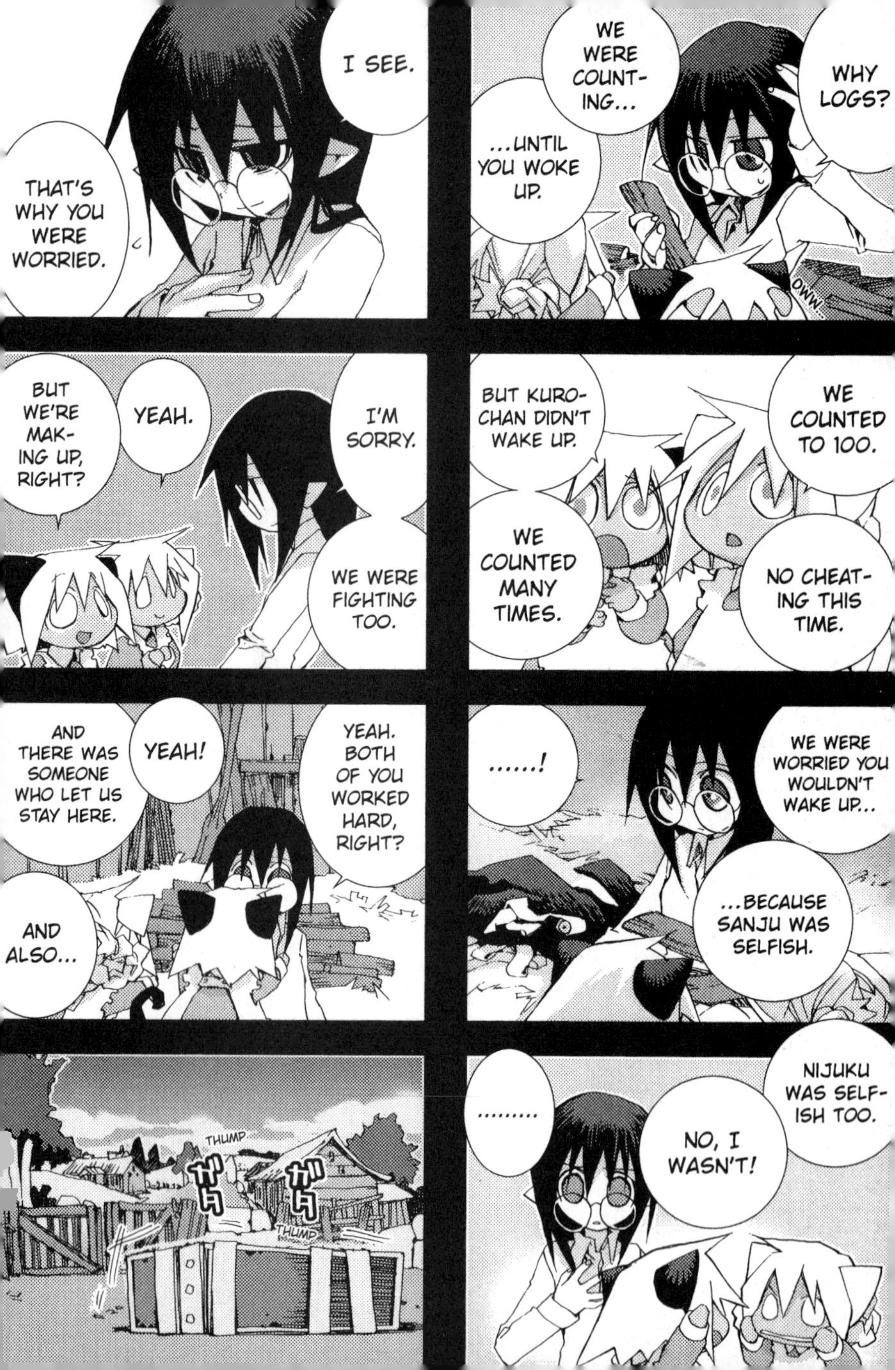
WHY LOGS?
WE WERE COUNTING...
...UNTIL YOU WOKE UP.
OWW...
I SEE.
THAT'S WHY YOU WERE WORRIED.
WE COUNTED TO 100.
BUT KURO-CHAN DIDN'T WAKE UP.
NO CHEATING THIS TIME.
WE COUNTED MANY TIMES.
I'M SORRY.
WE WERE FIGHTING TOO.
YEAH.
BUT WE'RE MAKING UP, RIGHT?
WE WERE WORRIED YOU WOULDN'T WAKE UP...
......!
...BECAUSE SANJU WAS SELFISH.
YEAH. BOTH OF YOU WORKED HARD, RIGHT?
YEAH!
AND THERE WAS SOMEONE WHO LET US STAY HERE.
AND ALSO...
NIJUKU WAS SELFISH TOO.
NO, I WASN'T!
....
THUMP
ガタ
ガタ
THUMP

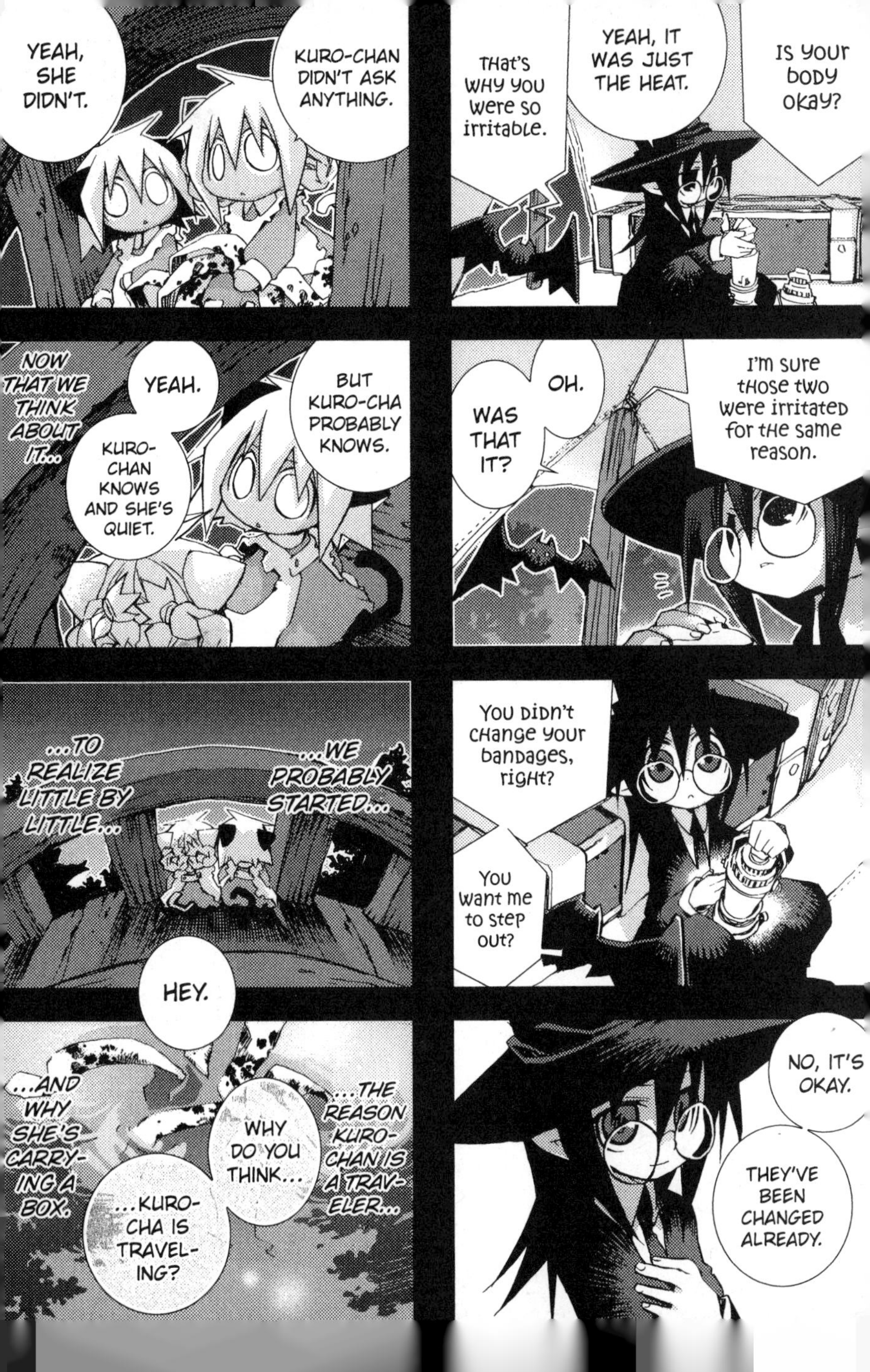
Is your body okay?
YEAH, IT WAS JUST THE HEAT.
That's why you were so irritable.
KURO-CHAN DIDN'T ASK ANYTHING.
YEAH, SHE DIDN'T.
I'm sure those two were irritated for the same reason.
OH.
WAS THAT IT?
BUT KURO-CHA PROBABLY KNOWS.
YEAH.
KURO-CHAN KNOWS AND SHE'S QUIET.
NOW THAT WE THINK ABOUT IT...
You didn't change your bandages, right?
You want me to step out?
...WE PROBABLY STARTED...
...TO REALIZE LITTLE BY LITTLE...
NO, IT'S OKAY.
THEY'VE BEEN CHANGED ALREADY.
HEY.
...THE REASON KURO-CHAN IS A TRAVELER...
WHY DO YOU THINK...
...KURO-CHA IS TRAVELING?
...AND WHY SHE'S CARRYING A BOX.

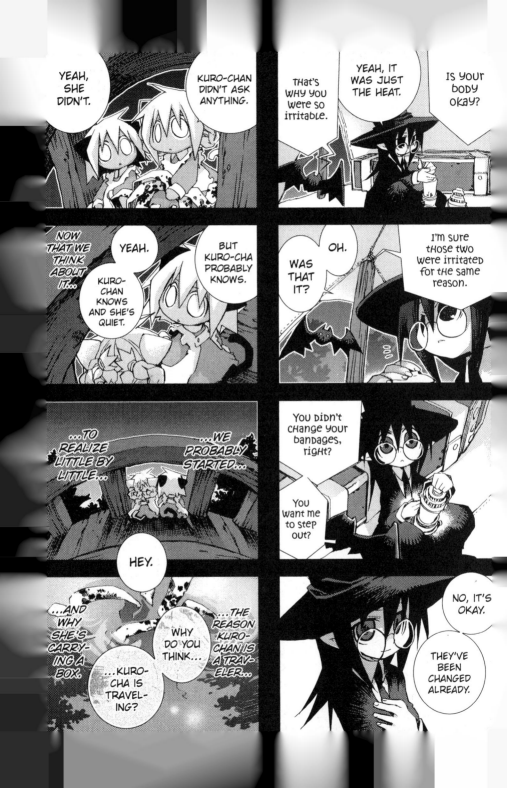

THANK YOU FOR READING SHOULDER-A-COFFIN KURO. I WOULD LIKE
TO THANK MY EDITOR AND EVERYONE INVOLVED IN MAKING THIS
BOOK. I WOULD ALSO LIKE TO THANK THOSE WHO PICKED UP THIS BOOK.

I WOULD BE HAPPY IF I COULD SEE YOU AGAIN IN THE NEXT VOLUME!

SATOKO KIYUDUKI

TRANSLATION NOTES

Page 9
Janken is the Japanese equivalent of rock-paper-scissors. Instead of saying "one, two, three," the Japanese say, "*Jan-ken-pon!*"

Page 12
Onii-san can be used as a polite term for an unrelated younger man who is or appears older than the speaker.

Page 34
Nijuku and *Sanju* are shortened terms for the numbers "twenty-nine" (*nijuuku*) and "thirty" (*sanjuu*) in Japanese.

Page 35
Kuro means "black" in Japanese.

Page 75
Sir Munchausen refers to Baron Munchausen (1720-1797), a German baron who was infamous for his tall tales.

Page 77
Tadaima is short for *tadaima modorimashita*, which translates as "I'm home." *Okaeri* is short for *okaerinasai* which translates as "Welcome back."

Page 77
Ojii-chan is an affectionate term for an elderly gentleman.

Page 93
The Japanese have a superstition that when you sneeze, it means that someone is saying something about you. If you sneeze once, someone is saying something good; if you sneeze twice, someone is saying something bad. If you sneeze three times or more, it's just a cold.

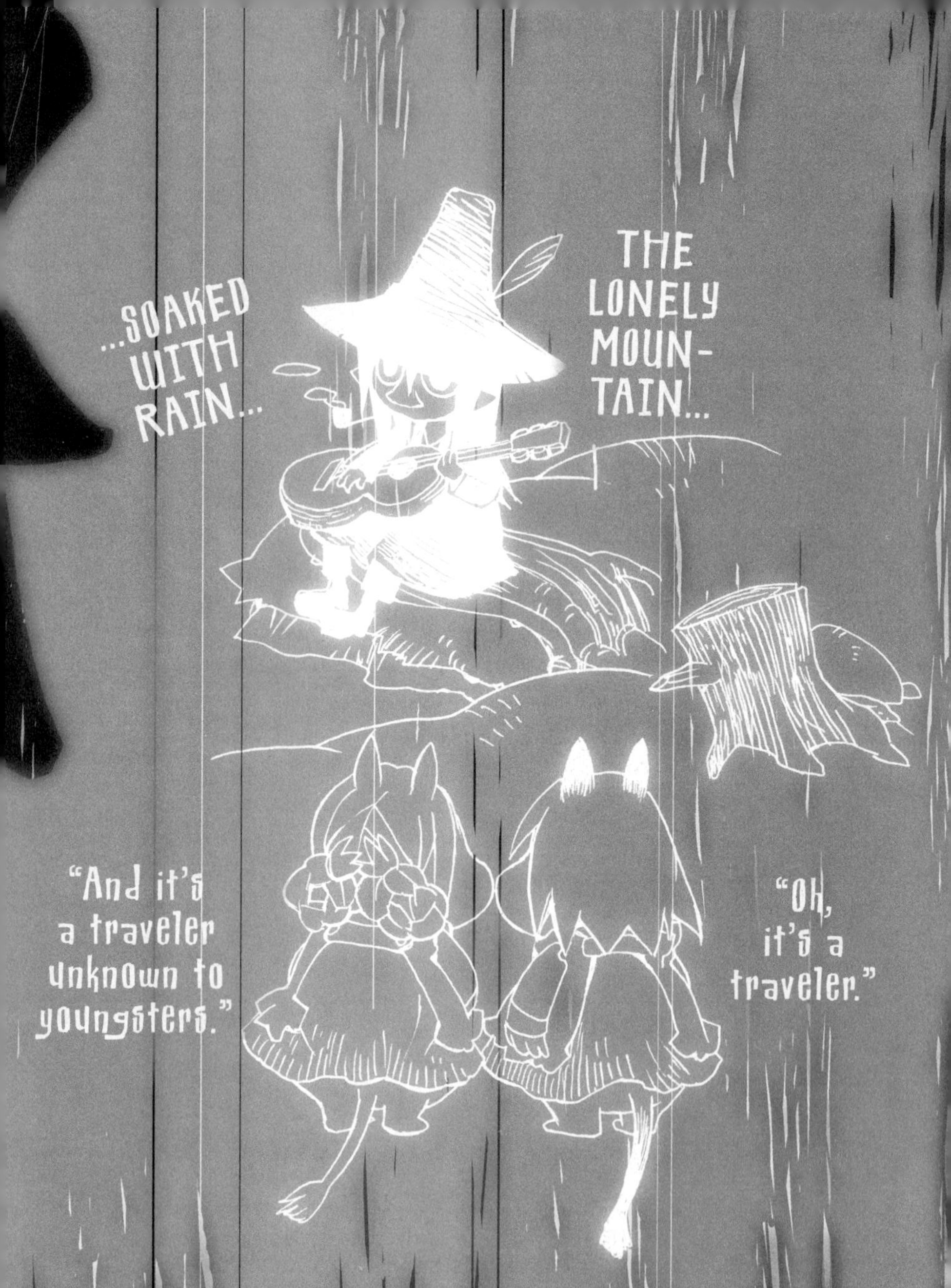
THE LONELY MOUNTAIN...
...SOAKED WITH RAIN...
"Oh, it's a traveler."
"And it's a traveler unknown to youngsters."

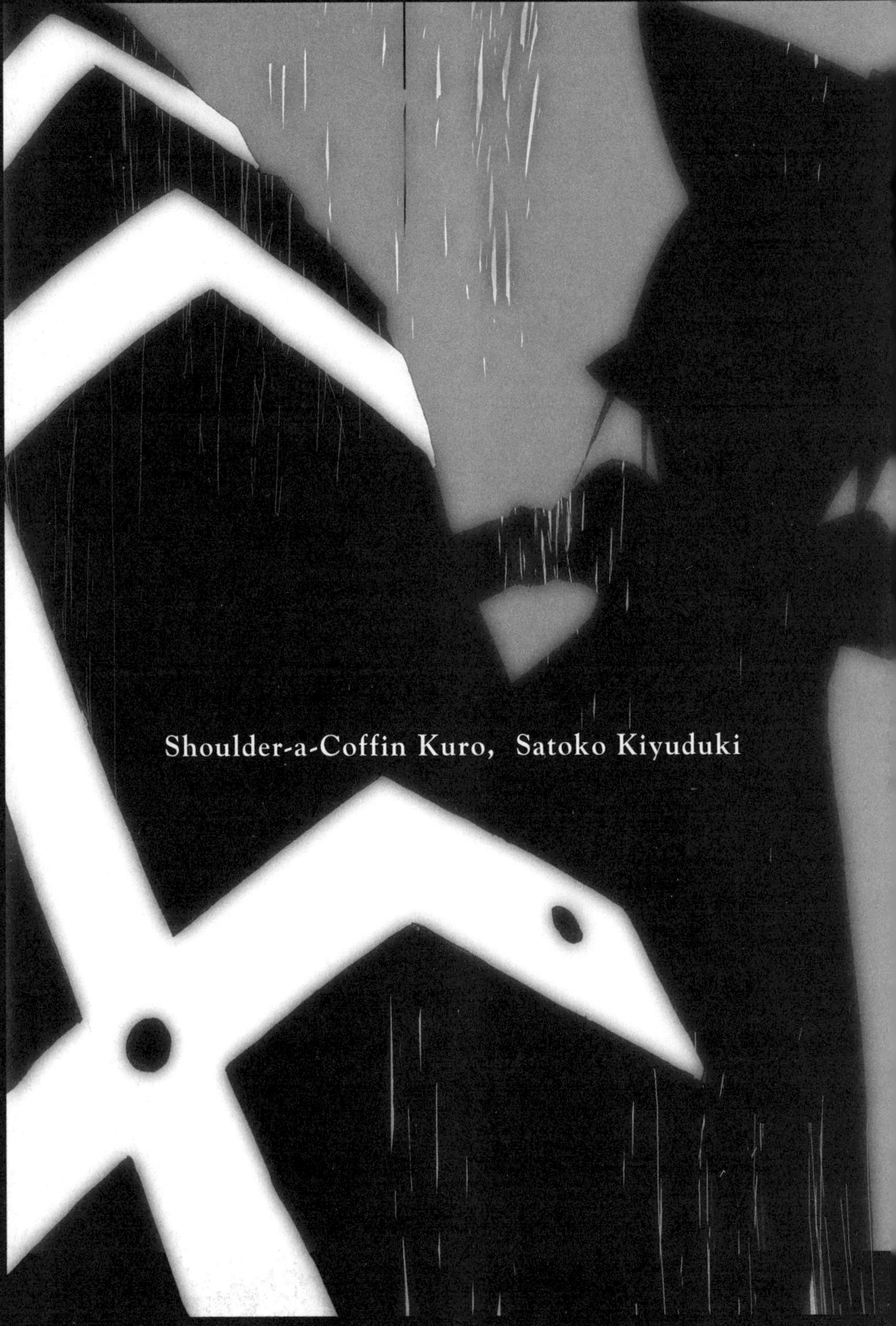
Shoulder-a-Coffin Kuro, Satoko Kiyuduki

Shoulder-a-Coffin KURO ...SPEAK!

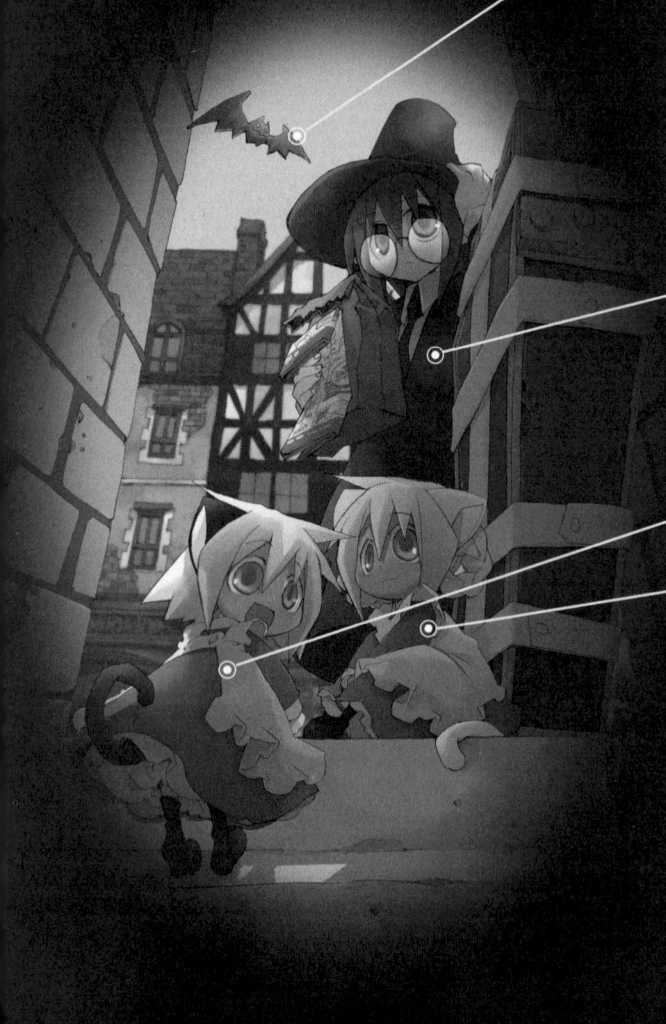

SEN is... well, Sen. Snarky to a fault, but often the voice of reason.

KURO often gets mistaken for a boy throughout her journey. While a large part of this is because of her appearance, it also has a lot to do with the way she talks in Japanese. Kuro always refers to herself with masculine pronouns and her speech is often more boyish than ladylike, just like Kuro herself!

NIJUKU and SANJU, Kuro's adorable companions, also have their own unique way of speaking. Their dialogue is written entirely in *kana*, which is made up of the two most basic writing systems of the Japanese language. This visual aid goes even further in stressing the pair's innocence and naïveté. They also speak in broken phrases, which we've tried to retain in this edition. Since one of the twins childishly refers to Kuro as "Kuro-cha," they're pretty easy to tell apart. Do you know which is which?

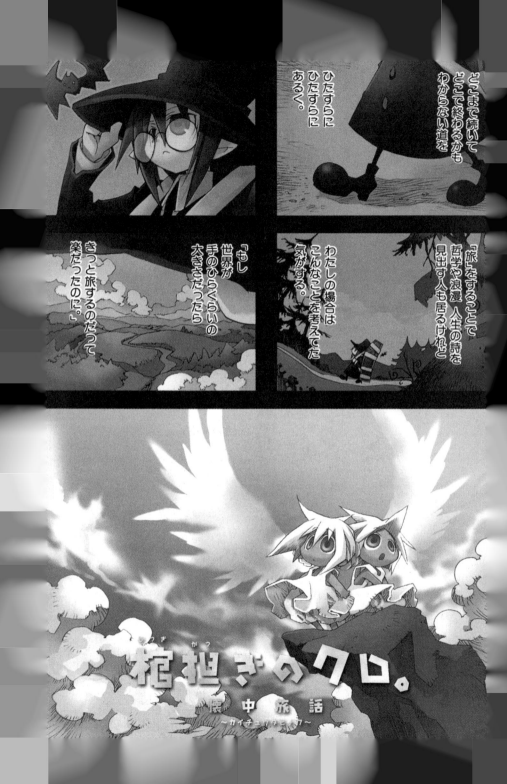

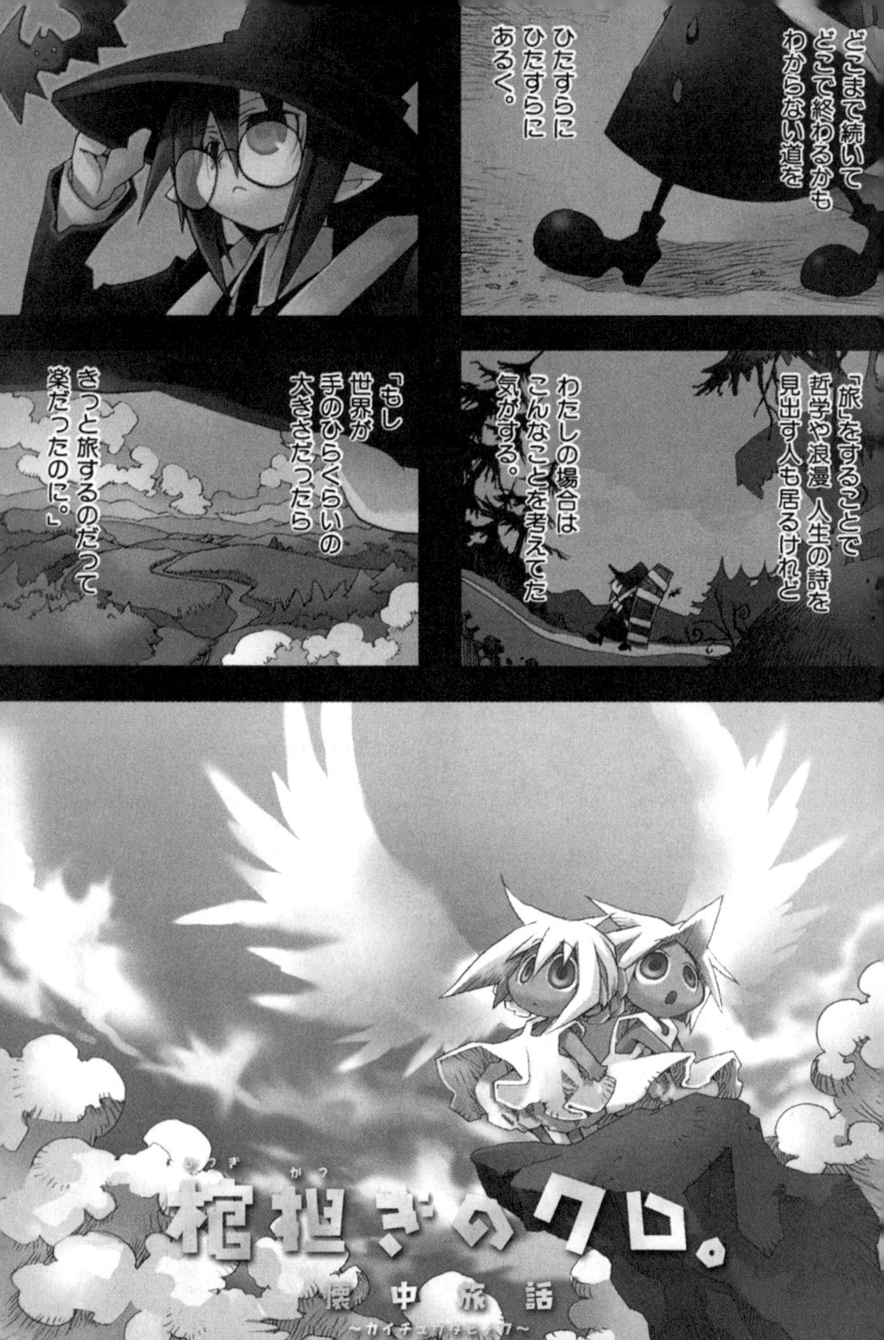
どこまで続いてどこで終わるかもわからない道を
ひたすらにひたすらにあるく。
「旅」をすることで哲学や浪漫 人生の詩を見出す人も居るけれど
わたしの場合はこんなことを考えてた気がする。
「もし世界が手のひらくらいの大きさだったら
きっと旅するのだって楽だったのに。」
棺担ぎのクロ。
懐中旅話

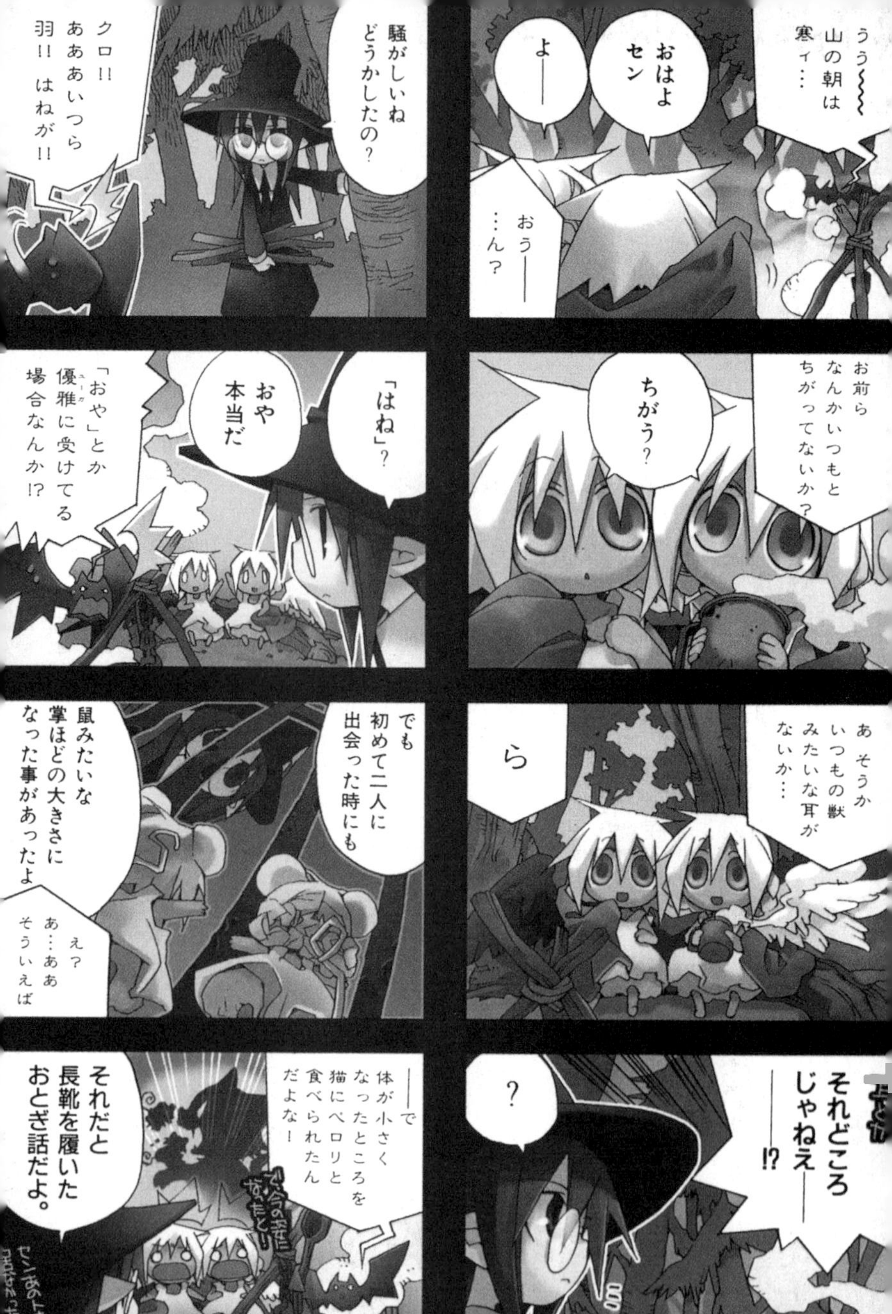
うう〜〜 山の朝は寒ィ…
おはよ セン
よ――
おう―― …ん？
お前ら なんかいつもと ちがってないか？
ちがう？
あ そうか いつもの獣 みたいな耳が ないか…
ら
それどころ じゃねえ―― !?
？
騒がしいね どうかしたの？
クロ!! あああいつら 羽!! はねが!!
「はね」？
おや 本当だ
「おや」とか 優雅に受けてる 場合なんか!?
でも 初めて二人に 出会った時にも
鼠みたいな 掌ほどの大きさに なった事があったよ
え？
あ…ああ そういえば
――で 体が小さく なったところを 猫にペロリと 食べられたんだよな！
で今の姿に なったと！
それだと 長靴を履いた おとぎ話だよ。

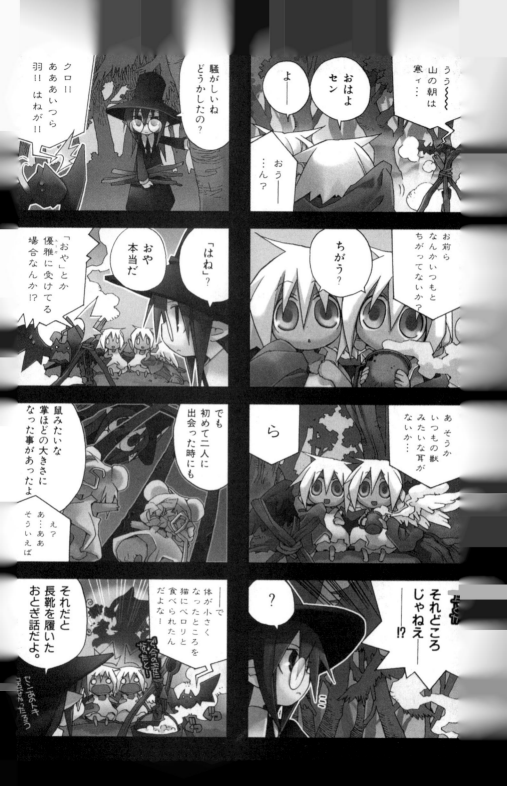

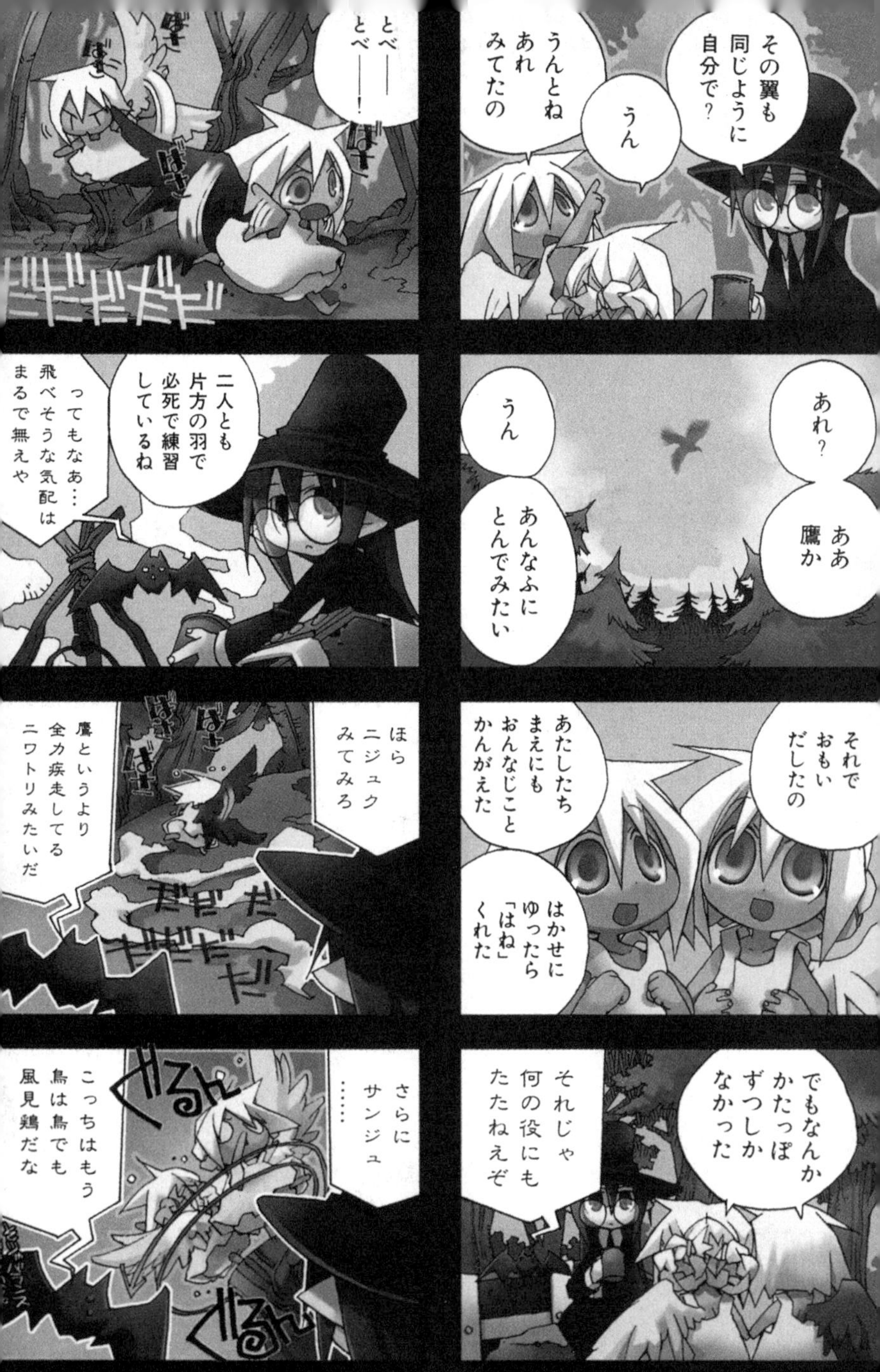
その翼も同じように自分で？
うん
うんとねあれみてたの
あれ？
ああ鷹か
うん
あんなふにとんでみたい
それでおもいだしたの
あたしたちまえにもおんなじことかんがえた
はかせにゆったら「はね」くれた
でもなんかかたっぽずつしかなかった
それじゃ何の役にもたたねえぞ
とべーとべー！
二人とも片方の羽で必死で練習しているね
ってもなあ…飛べそうな気配はまるで無えや
ほらニジュクみてみろ
鷹というより全力疾走してるニワトリみたいだ
さらにサンジュ
……
こっちはもう鳥は鳥でも風見鶏だな
ぐるん
ぐるん

Kuro's journey continues in SHOULDER-A-COFFIN KURO, Vol. 2!

SHOULDER-A-COFFIN KURO ①

SATOKO KIYUDUKI

Translation: Satsuki Yamashita   Lettering: Alexis Eckerman

HITSUGI KATSUGI NO KURO ~KAICHU TABINOWA~ Vol. 1 © 2006
Satoko Kiyuduki. All rights reserved. First published in Japan in 2006 by
HOUBUNSHA CO., LTD, Tokyo. English translation rights in the United
States, Canada, and the United Kingdom arranged with HOUBUNSHA CO.,
LTD. through Tuttle-Mori Agency, Inc., Tokyo.

Translation © 2008 by Hachette Book Group USA, Inc.

Yen Press
Hachette Book Group USA
237 Park Avenue, New York, NY 10017

Visit our Web sites at www.HachetteBookGroupUSA.com and
www.YenPress.com.

Yen Press is an imprint of Hachette Book Group USA, Inc. The Yen Press
name and logo are trademarks of Hachette Book Group USA, Inc.

First Yen Press Edition: May 2008

ISBN-10: 0-7595-2897-7
ISBN-13: 978-0-7595-2897-0

10 9 8 7 6 5 4 3 2 1

WOR

Printed in the United States of America